MIGRATION
and
SOCIAL WELFARE

Report of the Research Institute on the Social Welfare
Consequences of Migration and Residential Movement, 1969:
San Juan, Puerto Rico, November 2–5, 1969,
Alvin L. Schorr, conference chairman.

Joseph W. Eaton, Editor

*Professor of Sociology in Public Health and Social Work Research,
School of Public Health, University of Pittsburgh,
Pittsburgh, Pennsylvania*

NATIONAL ASSOCIATION OF SOCIAL WORKERS, INC.
2 Park Avenue, New York, New York 10016

To Marjorie Herzig

For her ten years of creative service
to the National Association of Social Workers
and its Council on Social Work Research

The reports included in this book were commissioned for an invitational Research Institute on the Social Welfare Consequences of Migration and Residential Movement. The institute on "Social Welfare Consequences of Migration and Residential Movement," for which the articles in this book were commissioned, was supported by funds from grant IR 13 MH 15866-01 of the National Institute of Mental Health. Points of view or opinions expressed in this book do not necessarily represent official policy of the sponsoring agencies or of the editor. Each of the authors was free to express his professional judgment and, subject to editorial suggestion, organize his presentation to conform to his preferences.

3

Contents

Part III. Toward a National Migration Policy

Preface

Large-scale residential movement, both within and between regions, makes it increasingly less likely that citizens will live and die in the place of their birth. As they migrate, rich and poor alike confront a mixture of opportunity and stress. Yet planning with respect to internal migration is a frontier of social work practice that has been but partly explored. The benefits for migrants, for the communities they leave, and for the areas into which they move could be maximized if more comprehensive planning took place that would keep disruption at a minimum.

A national migration policy may be in the wings. To help bring it about, the Council on Social Work Research of the National Association of Social Workers convened an institute on the theme "Social Welfare Consequences of Migration and Residential Movement." Invitations were extended to ten researchers to prepare papers on designated topics. Five of these were social workers; the remainder specialized in related social sciences: there were three sociologists, an economist, and a social anthropologist. Papers written by these ten were distributed in advance to an invited panel of thirty persons from diverse fields, among them eighteen social workers—ten university professors and eight practitioners—five sociologists, one psychiatrist, one economist, two psychologists, two anthropologists, and one political sci-

entist. (All participants are listed in the appendix.)

The idea of calling a research conference on migration had been conceived more than seven years prior to the institute. The Executive Committee of the Research Council of the National Association of Social Workers addressed itself to the question: "What are the areas of knowledge that deserve priority because of their present significance for social policy and social action?" The Research Council had just begun an institute on race relations.[1] Migration was selected as the next subject on its agenda, and a planning committee consisting of Alfred H. Katz, Maurice Hamovitch, and the editor was assigned to plan a program and prepare a grant request for the necessary funds.

At that time (1964) migration was not the focus of social work education, nor were many social workers doing research in this field. The profession and the country as a whole were preoccupied with the struggles for peace and against poverty and for justice for disadvantaged ethnic minorities—all critical social problem

---

[1] The Institute on Research Toward Improving Race Relations was held at Airlie House, Warrenton, Virginia, August 13–16, 1967. The report of that institute was published as Roger R. Miller, ed., *Race, Research, and Reason: Social Work Perspectives* (New York: National Association of Social Workers, 1969).

areas. But there is room for optimism that solutions to these problems can be found if mankind can survive the self-incurred physical threats of environmental pollution, nuclear holocaust, and overpopulation.

Why such optimism? It is justified by the fact that there is widespread agreement as to the existence of these social problems. Means to deal with poverty and racial injustice are known. What remains is to close the gap between what we know and what we—as a society and as individuals—are willing to do.

But even when poverty is abolished and racial inequity becomes a topic of history, social workers are not likely to be technologically unemployed. What seems more likely is a shift of priorities to other issues. Many of these will not be new. They have existed for a long time, but have been considered relatively unimportant. Migration may be one of these overlooked challenges.

San Juan, Puerto Rico, where the workshop was held from November 2 to 5, 1969, exemplifies some of the complex factors in America's migration patterns. Planes come to San Juan bringing tourists attracted by the sumptuous vacation facilities that few islanders can afford to frequent. Planes return to the United States carrying Puerto Ricans, at home on this lovely island and deeply rooted in their own culture, but voluntarily migrating to live in the slums of New York and other cities. Poverty at home drives them to seek a better living in an area where they are a despised minority group, in a foreign and often harsh environment.

Inherent in this population exchange is a paradox that symbolizes the complexity of migration patterns. As division of labor increases—and it must in all modernizing societies—more and more persons will shift their place of residence in search of new opportunities for economic, social, and recreational benefits.

In order to permit more intensive coverage of an already complex area of social policy, the conference was limited to domestic migration. But the participants were aware that what happens in the United States could be affected by the fact that, for example, about 25 percent of the Latin American labor force was unemployed or underemployed in 1960.[2] Such unused human resources do not simply represent a waste. With a rapid population increase a population seemingly condemned to abject poverty represents a migration time bomb that is likely to have an effect not only on the parent country, but on the world beyond as well.

Part I of this book is concerned primarily with a conceptual reassessment of the migration phenomenon as a focus for social welfare policy-making. Part II provides data for a case study of black migration. Its inclusion had not been planned specifically, but among those invited to participate were several who were studying black Americans, a previously neglected migrant population. Reports more generally concerned with migration policy requirements are presented in Part III.

The discussion sections include abstracts of major ideas that were discussed. It was impractical to print transcripts of the spirited interaction that occurred at times during the three days of discussions. What is printed are selected ideas, abstracted from the total conference because of their direct relevance to the papers that are presented. Left out were the many tangents, which were often interesting, but which have meaning only if they can be viewed in their total context. The discussion ideas are a selected sample of the total exchange.

JOSEPH W. EATON

Pittsburgh, Pennsylvania
January 1971

---

[2] Secretary General Gale Plaza, "Address at the Inaugural Session of the Organization of American States," October 10, 1969, Washington, D.C. Mimeographed.

Acknowledgments

The production of this volume and the institute that preceded it were based on careful planning. Mrs. Marjorie Herzig of the National Association of Social Workers served as the gracious and stimulating coordinator of the project. She did more than supervise the physical arrangements. In this as in prior conferences of the Council on Social Work Research she provided significant intellectual inputs and helped locate many of the experts who were invited to participate. The fact that a relatively small section of NASW—its research council—has become an influential segment of the organization is in no small part due to her organizational and catalytic capacities. A good deal of the day-to-day efficiency was ensured by Mrs. Herzig's secretary, Mrs. Nancy Larsen.

The editor was also helped by the efficient services of NASW's Publications Department, especially Mrs. Patricia Ann Lynch, editorial adviser, who was responsible for the technical editing; Mrs. Wendy Almeleh, senior editor; and Mrs. Beatrice Saunders, director of the department.

Alvin L. Schorr served as chairman and discussion leader—a "Speaker of the House"—who subtly kept the conference discussions on the topic and on ideas that were academically relevant. He wrote the Postscript to this volume.

Introduction

In the minds of many the term migration will conjure up a picture of homeless refugees, clutching their meager belongings, or of poverty-stricken migratory workers with nothing to show for their toil but a bit more wear. Many such migrants exist, but they are probably not a majority. Migration is an inherent condition of modernization, specialization, and planned social change.

Migration Reconsidered

Migration built this nation. Franklin D. Roosevelt once shocked an audience of the Daughters of the American Revolution by addressing them as "my fellow immigrants." Few people would be so shocked today. Senior points to "our 44 million immigrant ancestors and the millions who have moved within this nation's boundaries" who sought a new environment, largely to enhance their opportunity structure.[1]

Few Americans today can expect to live and die in the place where they were born.

As the contributors to this volume document, the vast majority of migrants are on the move voluntarily, in search of environments that will offer them advantages that were lacking in the areas they left. More and more of these migrants travel by jet and have their moving expenses paid by their employers. They treasure the options of being able to choose their job, their associates, and the environment in which they live.

Both the poverty-stricken and refugee migrant and his more affluent counterpart have problems, some of which are directly traceable to the impact of geographic mobility and could be greatly cushioned by more relevant welfare planning. But migration is not only a problem situation. Migrants have built new countries, regions, cities, and institutions. Migration is a force that sustains democracy, helping to break down inequitable class distinctions.

Unlike war, poverty, and illness, migration is not an essentially negative symptom. It is a necessary by-product of man's capacity to control his environment. When people feel their environment is unsatisfactory, they need not adjust to it—they can leave. We cannot change our skin if

---

[1] Clarence Senior, "Movers, Migrants, and the National Interest," this volume, p. 23.

we are dissatisfied with it. But we *can* change our territory. This is why dictators block migration with walls, machine guns, and regimes of terror among those who remain behind.

Freedom to move is a cherished human right withheld in many parts of the world. Men have risked and given their lives in Eastern Europe for wishing to leave their countries. Movement within countries can also be subject to restrictions. Until the recent United States Supreme Court decision declaring residence requirements for public assistance unconstitutional, poor people in the United States lacked full equality in their right to migrate.[2]

Migration can help anyone in his search to improve his life condition. It is an experience common to the rich as well as the poor. They move for similar reasons, but with quite different social supports. When the mover is poor, his lack of financial reserves exacerbates the problems inherent in mobility. But other problems that often arise, such as poor medical services, inadequate schooling, and slum housing, are not simply situational. "The capacity of our society to mangle people is virtually limitless," as one survey of migration problems put it.[3] The consequences of poverty are difficult to escape for both movers and those who remain.

Local residential movement is not the same as migration over long distances. A change in address within the same area may mean locating a new cleaner and supermarket, but chances are these will have the same policies and offer the same services as the old ones. People will view the same television programs and can read the same newspaper as they did previously. But such similarities of life-style must not be allowed to mask the fact that even short-distance moves often reflect new social

roles, a different social status, and new social relationships.

Territorial Therapy

In dealing with clients' problems social workers can weigh the relative costs and benefits of three major supportive strategies: microsocial system intervention, macrosocial system programming, and territorial therapy. In past decades the social work profession has concentrated on microsocial system techniques. Help was offered to people and families in enhancing their capacity to adjust, with the environment being more or less taken as given. Unemployed men, for example, were offered training, casework, group work, hobbies, and relief, but not much was done about their joblessness. Such intervention clearly has many limitations.

A slum environment produces stresses for many of the people within it. Through macrosocial interventive techniques such as community organization there has been an increasing tendency in social work to advocate solutions to problems that involve modification of laws, creation of new employment opportunities and housing facilities, and other patterned alterations of the environment.

Problems also exist that are not readily resolvable in the existing environment, which may be too stable or too hostile. Nothing short of movement to a new location is likely to be of help. The concept of territorial therapy describes this strategy of planful movement of an individual or a group into a new social system with differently patterned interactions and opportunities and where their present condition will no longer be defined as a problem.[4]

---

2 *Shapiro* vs. *Thompson*, 394 U.S. 618, 1969.
3 Senator Walter F. Mondale, as quoted by William Robbins, "Doctors Decry Health Conditions of Migrant Workers," *New York Times*, July 21, 1970, p. 23.

4 The writer first elaborated the concept of territorial therapy in Joseph W. Eaton, in collaboration with Michael Chen, *Influencing the Youth Culture: A Study of Youth Organizations in Israel* (Beverly Hills, Calif.: Sage Publications, 1970), pp. 62–63, 195.

In premodern societies migration occurred mostly in the face of calamity—to escape famine, war, or persecution. The baby born in today's world must be prepared to move a number of times in his life. He may want to go to a college away from home, obtain work experience overseas, and later accept repeated job transfers while rising on the occupational ladder. Territorial change, as Part II of this book documents in detail, has been and is an attribute of modern life, an essential by-product of the division of labor and specialization to which modern nations have resorted in order to maximize their socio-economic development.

The decision to migrate is often related to a desire to try out new roles. Men who accept a promotion to express their drive for status are not necessarily unhappy with the job and the people they chose to leave behind, even when they give up considerable power and accept the loss of their previous network of sustaining social relationships. Movement within a locality of migration over a distance often create new opportunities for the mover, even if accompanied by initial painful experiences owing to dislocation and alienation. *Landsmannschaften*—clubs of persons hailing from the same locality—are sometimes formed for mutual aid and social recognition on the basis of "who *was* who" in the hometown. The opposite pattern also occurs, especially when an in-migrating group of persons who have improved their lives feel threatened by being followed by "too many" of their low-status former associates. Senior reported being asked by Jamaican immigrants in Liverpool, England, for advice on how other Jamaicans could be prevented from coming.[5]

A technological society rewards the "cosmopolitan" person who is ready to move and apply his skills where they might be most needed and where the material pay-off is high. By this means technical personnel who may be scarce in one area can be made less scarce through immigration from another area. In terms of Rohrlich's economic model, such personnel pursue optimum economic gain by moving their labor power to an area where it is in demand.[6] But in an unfamiliar environment these economic benefits may accrue without the human associations that would make them meaningful.

Not all territorial therapy is elective. Refugees are forced to escape from grave danger, psychic or physical. More often the territorial solution is resorted to for less compelling, but nevertheless essentially negative reasons—the desire to move away from some fixed aspect of the environment, as when a young married couple wishes to put distance between themselves and their in-laws.

All these situations have a common therapeutic potential. Through migration many tensions and dangers previously experienced will largely disappear, even though the process of moving is not without pain and sacrifice. There is suffering when people leave familiar surroundings, but one can only speculate about how much greater pain is thereby avoided.

Perhaps much of the suffering incurred by persons involved in massive population movements—as between India and Pakistan following World War II, out of Hungary and Cuba, and by blacks out of the South—could have been reduced by more planful movements of these populations. But few of these migrants would wish to restore their prior circumstances.

Migration as a planful approach to problem resolution inspired many of the European masses who left their ancestral homes to help settle the United States, Canada, Australia, and the other immigrant-receiving countries. Theodor Herzl advocated territorial therapy as a major ideological component of his prescription

---

[5] Personal communication from Clarence C. Senior.

[6] George F. Rohrlich, "Economic Cost-Benefit Approaches to Migration," this volume, pp. 55–70.

for ending the persecuted and pariah status of Jews, although he never used this particular concept. He lived and worked in the same Viennese milieu as did Sigmund Freud. Both of these men, founders of worldwide social movements, were concerned with the reduction of human conflict. Freud explored the psychodynamics of hatred, while Herzl addressed himself to sociological variables and their political consequences. While not mutually exclusive, their theories called for different strategies to reduce the acting out of man's destructive impulses.

Freud showed that persons who want to overcome pathological emotions could be helped by individual psychotherapy, a permissive relationship between a gifted human healer and a person suffering from fear and anger. Herzl focused on the limitations of this approach for intergroup relations, in which conflicts are rooted in culturally supported myths about ethnic incompatibilities and are reinforced by many institutional arrangements.

It is not without theoretical significance that the seminal founder of psychotherapy had himself to resort to the territorial solution. But for this solution the 82-year-old Sigmund Freud might have been among six million fellow Jews murdered in German concentration camps. He was among the privileged few for whom a program of territorial therapy was fashioned with the help of diplomats of Western nations at a time when the Nazis were still willing to accept this approach before they adopted what they euphemistically called the "final solution."

In the United States black citizens have always relied on the territorial solution ever since the abolitionist movement organized the Underground Railroad. They had to leave the slave states to find freedom and paid employment and later to find better-paying jobs or to bring up children where there was less prejudice. Even now there is such planned movement, although macrosystem intervention is being used

more and more actively to expand the black opportunity structure through civil rights legislation and more effective enforcement of existing legislation. Part II of this volume deals with this phenomenon in detail on the basis of considerable original field study data.

Migration remains a significant strategy for the management of many individual and group problems. It allows people to try to reorganize their lives on a planful basis, free from the constraints with which they found it difficult to cope in their prior social system. Territorial therapy, as illustrated by sending children unwilling to conform to parental control to college or by the orderly migration of anti-Castro Cubans to the United States through the cooperation of the two otherwise nonrelated governments, reduces problems that would be hard to solve "at home." [7] In turn the Cuban government has greatly reduced the need for police methods to keep dissidents in line by allowing those who are not imbued with the acceptable ideology to emigrate.

Social Cost Account of Migration

Migration is more than the act of moving from one location to another. As Reul points out, it is a process involving many stages.[8] It begins when conditions exist in communities that encourage or discourage population movement. Individuals and groups react to these conditions by weighing the pros and cons of moving. The social, political, psychological, economic, and legal variables that influence individuals or groups to consider migration or to decide against it are part of the

---

[7] Office of the White House Press Secretary, *Memorandum of Understanding Concerning the Movement of Cubans Wishing to Live in the United States* (Washington, D.C.: U.S. Department of State, November 6, 1955).

[8] Myrtle R. Reul, "Migration: The Confrontation of Opportunity and Trauma," this volume, pp. 3–22.

process. Anyone concerned with a better understanding of the social welfare impact of these phenomena needs to look at the decision-making process and the environmental opportunities that exist whenever people think about moving.

Many labels are used, reflecting the balance of positively and negatively perceived forces that usually exist in the minds of the individual, the community he leaves, and the area into which he moves:

> promotion *vs.* leaving familiar associations
>
> vacation *vs.* being away from home
>
> retiring to a healthier climate *vs.* missing the old home and old friends
>
> a new home *vs.* an abandoned old one

Decisions about migration are based on the way these variables are assessed by persons and by political systems. As Rohrlich points out, a modern economy favors a great deal of movement as a way of optimizing the cost-benefit structure of employing skilled labor where they can be paid the most.[9]

In-migrants generally are at a disadvantage when competing with residents for local jobs. Newcomers usually lack the informal network of social supports that provide "connections" and "pull." These play a part whenever scarce privileges and opportunities must be allocated among competing candidates. Yet in spite of these disadvantages there is more and more job-related migration. Poor people move to take up entry-level jobs, the posts that few of an area's settled residents want to take. This is how each wave of ethnic immigrants, including blacks, moved into the ghettos of the large northern cities. They began as peddlers, street cleaners, handymen, domestic servants, and low-level civil servants, moving slowly up the occu-

pational ladder. Higher level migrants are also used to fill more skilled positions, primarily when there are no local candidates. This is the basis for the regional and international brain drain.[10]

There is an increasing number of perpetual movers, having only nominal roots anywhere. Catherine Hiatt dubbed these people as showing the "Eisenhower syndrome." Like the late President, they were born in a hometown in which they never live after early childhood. They grow up in many places, going wherever the opportunity lies. Theater people, traveling salesmen, career armed services personnel, state department officials, and an increasing proportion of business executives must live such a nomadic life in order to "get ahead." For these people migration is economically rational. But there are also drifters who feel threatened by permanence and stability and are therefore always on the move. Such flight migration is probably most common among those with distressed family backgrounds.

Social workers have in the past primarily focused on the negative social-psychological symptoms. They are hired to counteract unemployment, deal with the consequences of divorce, and try to prevent delinquency. Migration is a different kind of symptom. It is not inherently "deviant." There are always problems for the mover, often even more for members of his family, the community he leaves, and the area that receives him. But migration is also an opportunity, more often a choice than an imposition. Social workers need to concentrate on maximizing the benefits of migration along with clinical understanding that migration represents a period of uncertainty during which latent social and psychological tendencies in people are likely to surface.

---

[9] Op. cit.

[10] Committee on the International Migration of Talent, *Modernization and the Migration of Talent* (New York: Education and World Affairs, 1970).

FIGURE 1. PARADIGM OF SOCIAL WELFARE ASPECTS OF MIGRATION AND RESIDENTIAL MOVEMENT

Territorial Stance	Therapeutic Consequences	Stressful Consequences
Migrating	Freedom from ascribed low status. Opportunity to achieve a new status. Optimum economic use of one's labor. Freedom to follow new avenues of endeavor.	High risk of loneliness and anomie. Need to adjust to a strange environment. Help may be unavailable in an emergency or must be purchased commercially.
Remaining	Continuity of ascribed status with support from a familiar environment. Good knowledge of local conditions. Continuity of primary group relationships and friendship ties with parents, relatives, and neighbors of long standing.	Limited opportunities to achieve new status. Limited economic use of one's labor. Low rate of upward mobility. High degree of social control in primary groups with strong ties—parents, relatives, and neighbors of long standing.

The influx of migrants has often stimulated the overt expression of prejudices among the settled population. One or two blacks in a school are a novelty. They document by their presence a dedication to the American dream. But if blacks multiply to constitute a much larger proportion of the population, they begin to be perceived by some as a threat.

When people move they must consciously make choices between alternate policies. Communities can adopt priorities such as, for example, whether to use local funds to set up a program to help migrants adjust or to use the money for their own people. In Washington, D.C., a black neighborhood council turned down funds for a Travelers Aid program to migrants, even though most of the migrants were blacks moving from the South.[11]

Those who study migrants or try to help them professionally will quickly recognize that a large proportion of people respond positively to territorial therapy. They seek opportunities that would not have been available if they had not been prepared

---

[11] Personal communication from Mrs. Catherine Hiatt.

to change their environment. Others will be overcome by the separation from family, friends, and other sources of social support. Migration tests people's capacity for autonomy, their dependency needs, and their overall ability to cope with problems of living.

Migration and residential movement is a two-sided phenomenon that fits the Chinese word for crisis, *wei-chei*, which is written as a combination of two characters: those for danger and opportunity. The relationship of these two alternatives—the therapeutic and stressful consequences of migrating or staying—are schematically contrasted in Figure 1.

National Policy Issues

In the course of living, men can solve the bulk of their personal and environmental problems on their own. But no one can solve them unaided all the time. Some people require chronic and intensive support in order to live decently. Mutual aid, without which no social system can survive, is provided largely by family and kinship systems in premodern countries.

FIGURE 2. WELFARE POLICY ALTERNATIVES WITH RESPECT TO MIGRATION

Policy Alternatives	Economic Measures	Welfare Service Measures	Legal Measures	Social Acceptance Measures
Supportive Welfare Policy	Travel cost payments. Settlement subsidies and loans. Tax exemptions.	Emergency counseling. Special support programs.	Honoring acquired tenure rights. Moratorium on violations of rules not yet known to newcomers.	Making arrangements to help people make new social contacts. Open-door policy for newcomers by clubs, churches, and other social programs.
Neutral Welfare Policy	Absence of special measures or of concern for the problems of migrants in the area of destination; absence of efforts to interfere with migration or to limit the rights of movers in the area of destination.			
Hostile Welfare Policy	Higher charges for services. Lower wages for newcomers. Exclusion from fringe benefits and many public services.	Residence restrictions on welfare eligibility. Arrest or harassment of people in need of help. Deportation from area of destination if help is needed. Second-class services in clinics and schools used by newcomers.	Failure to give work permits; residence requirements. Legal restrictions on voting, public services, and other rights. Discriminatory treatment by police and courts. Harassment by arrest for vagrancy. Shooting persons crossing borders.	Social exclusion of newcomers. Viewing migrants only as labor, not as people and neighbors. Closed-door policies in clubs and other social facilities. Restrictive covenants in residential areas.

When people are on the move, these primary group supports are insufficient or may be completely absent. If they are to develop they must be planned for by the government. The welfare state theory postulates that no man should die or bear unusual suffering that can be avoided by the application of knowledge.

In Part III of this volume many of these issues of national migration policy are discussed. Policy always involves normative choices on the basis of priorities that are held by those in power to give direction to the way public resources will be expanded. They can be planfully supportive, neutral, or hostile, as Figure 2 indicates by illustrations applicable to different subsystems.

The institute participants were in favor of more supportive measures. They advocated cushioning the stressful impact of migration, both on the migrants and their families and on the sending and receiving communities. They analyzed, but held no brief, for past policies, which were largely neutral or hostile to the idea of supportive welfare measures. Part II of this volume documents this in detail with respect to black migration.

There are minimum health and safety standards for livestock being moved across state lines. Those for people are more erratic. The rationale for this is the fact that many persons, unlike livestock, can make plans on their own. But nearly all can utilize some public support. American policy has varied in the past from the highly planned and supportive reception of Cuban and Hungarian refugees to a do-nothing—or close to nothing—policy for domestic migrant poor. There are beginnings, such as interstate claims on unemployment insurance or the abolition of residence requirements as a condition for local public assistance eligibility. Public policies, however, do not as yet reflect the fact that migration is a normal condition of living during which vulnerability to stress and crisis can be expected to be heightened. Supportive services beyond those now in existence need to be fashioned as a matter of public policy rather than charity.

Migration planning is a task that can be separated in part from reform proposals affecting the total population. But there are inherent relationships between migration and poverty: many of the poor are on the move. Nevertheless a national migration policy needs to involve more than a remedial program for people in trouble. It requires the development of procedures to help all persons find an optimum location for what they wish to do. Conversely, migration planning, like special aid for schools in areas with many newcomers, can bring new resources into an area so that the people already in residence can remain without suffering from a reduction of their own opportunities and services.

In a democratic system, planning involves an increase in the variety of choices of which citizens can avail themselves to get what they want. Migration is one of these alternatives. Its efficient use requires far more systematic attention from the helping professions than has been customary. This was the theme of the institute reported here. Those who participated found much confirmation for this admittedly normative point of view in the reports that were presented.

Part I

Territorial Therapy or Social Deviance

Migration: The Confrontation of Opportunity and Trauma

MYRTLE R. REUL

This paper is based on the fact that the migration episode has become a widespread, normal experience of all people in all walks of life in most parts of the world.[1] The term migrant still calls to mind the troubled or troublesome, the hopeless and the helpless. To most people, including social workers, the migrant is a destitute farmer moving to the city, a poor unskilled black man moving his family to the North, an illiterate fruit picker following the crops. Seldom does one think of the wealthy and highly educated Cuban immigrant, the upper middle-class branch manager, or the active retired couple in search of a more comfortable climate.

Although there is a considerable body of information available on the generalized causes and effects of population mobility, little seems to be known about the ways in which migration directly affects individual family members. Early studies on the effects of mobility tended to stress the pathological aspects. It was pointed out almost unanimously that the mobile individual or family was unstable, a high employment risk, or a disorganizing factor in the community.[2]

These theories and conclusions came about mainly because the researchers studied highly mobile population groups in cities—groups that had a high incidence of unemployment, family breakdown, illegitimacy, delinquency, venereal disease, mental illness, suicide, and crime.[3] Since mobility semed to be the one consistent variable in all these groups, it was identi-

---

[1] The term "migration episode" was suggested by Dr. Paul Deutschberger. The author expresses deep appreciation to the families who were willing to share their experiences for use in this report.

[2] See, for example, Nels Anderson, *The Hobo* (Chicago: University of Chicago Press, 1923); Robert S. Wilson, "Transit Families," *Family*, Vol. 11, No. 8 (December 1930), pp. 243–251; Nels Anderson, *Men on the Move* (Chicago: University of Chicago Press, 1940).

[3] See Thomas Minehan, *Boy and Girl Tramps in America* (New York: Farrar & Rinehart, 1934).

fied as the primary disorganizing factor. Today the situation is quite different, although there is still a tendency to speak mainly of the disruptive factors of migration.[4]

This paper is written in the belief that many of the common setbacks or problems encountered by migrants are temporary and that even these may have ego-enhancing aspects. More often than not the migration process results in positive psychological gains for the migrant and his family, not to mention the benefits to the community. Much of this paper is based on observations made by the author while traveling as a migrant farm worker, staying in trailer courts in all parts of the country, and moving twenty-one times in three geographic areas of the United States, as well as from experiences shared with the author by families representing different socioeconomic classes and having varied reasons for migration.

Moving As a Fact of Life

In the 1920s and '30s migration was seen as a rare, unusual episode that seemed mainly to affect the disadvantaged segments of the population—and only a small percentage among these. We know today that the vast majority of the population of the United States has experienced at least one migration episode; large numbers have experienced several. One out of four U.S. families makes a major move each year. Only 5 percent of all Americans die in the community in which they were born.[5] It is unusual for an adult still to be living in the house in which he was born or even in the same neighborhood where he started

school. Abroad, uprootedness is no longer a problem involving refugees alone, although the refugees of the world can be counted in the millions. Families are moving by choice, by design, and because of changes over which they have no control. Whole populations have experienced forced migration as a result of construction. The building of the Aswan Dam in the Sudan resulted in the movement of six thousand families.[6] In the United States both urban renewal and highway construction are common reasons for family relocation.[7] It is estimated that at the present pace of operation, urban renewal and federally financed highway programs will dispossess more than one million families by 1972.[8]

The world and regional U.S. picture also shows widespread voluntary migration of rural residents into cities, as well as a post-World War II phenomenon known as "brain drain." [9] This is a situation in which persons with a high degree of education migrate to an area that can offer them greater opportunities for professional development or economic advancement.

While this voluntary and unorganized world movement of workers and their families is going on, training courses are being developed to prepare workers for employment in certain undeveloped countries. The result is a two-way traffic of highly qualified migrants—those leaving poor coun-

---

[4] *See*, for example, R. Bar-Josef, "Social Absorption of Immigrants in Israel," in Henry P. David, ed., *Migration, Mental Health and Community Services* (Geneva, Switzerland: American Joint Distribution Committee, 1966), p. 56.

[5] Bernard J. Frieden and Robert Morris, eds., *Urban Planning and Social Policy* (New York: Basic Books, 1969), p. 28.

[6] Maria Ammende-Pfister, "Migration and Mental Health Services," in David, ed., op. cit., pp. 46–54.

[7] H. Eldredge Wentworth, ed., *Taming Megalopolis* (New York: Doubleday & Co., 1967); *Relocation—Unequal Treatment of People and Businesses Displaced by Governments* (Washington, D.C.: Advisory Commission on Intergovernmental Relations, January 1965), p. 12.

[8] Cited in an address by Representative Clifford Davis, Chairman, House Select Subcommittee on Real Property Acquisition, reprinted in *Congressional Record*, 88th Cong., 2nd Sess., Vol. 110, No. 11 (1964), A2998.

[9] Enrique Oteiza, "A Differential Push-Pull Approach," in Walter Adams, ed., *The Brain Drain* (New York: Macmillan Co., 1968), pp. 120–134.

tries for better opportunities (usually in the United States [10]) and highly trained technical experts being sent to those same poor countries under the auspices of the United Nations, UNESCO, or specialized agencies.[11]

Historically there were many factors that influenced 50 million Europeans to migrate overseas in the nineteenth century, but economic crisis seems to have been the most dominant.[12] Today personal freedom and the opportunity for personality development are equally as important as improving economic circumstances—or even more so—in world migration.[13]

Whether workers move from Mozambique to the mines of South Africa, or migratory farm workers in the United States move from one harvest to another, or Bolivian *braceros* move to Argentina's sugar plantations, or North Africans to the coal mines of France and Belgium, or Italian, Greek, and Spanish domestics to Australia and Canada, they all have in common not only a desire to share more equally in the affluent society but to do something to better their situation in other ways.[14]

Social workers and other professionals concerned with migration have not sufficiently recognized that the migration episode can be a positive experience. It not only provides a chance for a family to better its economic situation, it can at the same time provide an opportunity for personal and family integration, as well as a degree of individual self-evaluation and insight. Inherent in the process of moving is a self-searching experience that can open up further opportunities for the individual and that has implications for the professional.

Whether migration is examined by the application of decision theory, role-strain theory, or theories of cognitive dissonance, balance, exchange, bargaining, or conflict, the basic questions are the same: How do interacting personalities define, assess, interpret, and act on the necessity to move? How do the processes of selection operate in the struggle for social-cultural structure?

A Broader View

The purpose of this paper and this approach is to make available to the social worker a new, broader view of the migration process in order to foster a better understanding of the universal, normal elements of the migrant's adjustment process. From the point of view of treatment, this paper should provide the social worker with some guidelines for evaluating an individual migrant's problems in the context of the broad outlines of the migration episode. An understanding of those processes and feelings that are common to all migrants—whether they are executives transferred to branch offices or fruit pickers following the harvest—should enable the social worker to help his client to size up his situation, his reaction to it, and its eventual outcome.

In addition it is hoped that this paper will promote research into many aspects of the increasingly common phenomenon of migration, especially those areas that are singled out as especially in need of study. Finally, implications for community orga-

[10] Brinley, in a paper for an international conference on the "brain drain" held in Switzerland in 1968, pointed out: "The United States is by far the largest in the preferred destination of professional migrants. . . . in 1965, 16,000 professional immigrants were admitted from outside the Western Hemisphere." Thomas Brinley, "Modern Migration," in Adams, ed., op. cit., pp. 29–49.

[11] "The Role of International Migration and the Development of Modern Society," *Migration*, Vol. 2, Nos. 3 and 4 (July and December 1962), pp. 19–28.

[12] H. A. Citreen, *European Immigration Overseas, Past and Future* (The Hague, Netherlands: Martinus Nijhoff, 1951), pp. 4–5.

[13] "Migration Between Countries at Different Stages of Development," *Migration*, Vol. 2, Nos. 3 and 4 (July and December 1962), pp. 17–57.

[14] *See* Baldwin Ch. Sjollema, "World Council of Churches," *Migration News*, No. 4 (July–August 1967), pp. 19–21; *Migration, Facts and Figures*, No. 66 (January 1969), p. 4; "Report of the Intergovernmental Committee for European Migration for the Year, 1961," *Migration*, Vol. 2, No. 1 (January–March 1962), pp. 35–36.

nization and social welfare policy have been outlined at the conclusion in the hope that awareness of the increase in migration will become a factor in planning at all levels.

No longer is the migrant in the minority —the majority of the population is on the move. We have reached a point in time when migration, which was such a disquieting element prior to World War II, is in this space age an expected and accepted way of life.

The author suspects that the volume of migration will grow rather than decrease. There will be more interregional, national, and international migration, and the distance between moves will increase. There is even the possibility of future colonization of the other planets. In view of these facts it would seem logical for a profession such as social work to deal with migration as a normal stage in the life cycle of man, much like birth and death, health and illness.

The Migration Episode

It is assumed that the migration process —regardless of the mover's class, culture, or reason for moving—comprises four stages, each involving specific psychological reactions: (1) making a decision, (2) breaking with the past, (3) the transitional period, and (4) the adjustment period. Each of these four stages will be discussed in detail in the pages that follow.

The Decision-Making Process

The first stage of any migration episode is the actual decision-making process that precedes a move. Shibutani describes this process generally in the following way:

Decision-making is recognized as a process of selecting from available alternatives . . . . Each alternative is evaluated in terms of the expected consequences and the probability of their occurrence. Restrictions are set by previous commitments, the limits of permissibility, and the available time, resources, and information. Goals are stated, and

choices are made in terms of the relative desirability of various solutions.[15]

The decision to migrate is usually a family decision. This is true even in those cases in which only one member is directly involved in the move. The family member with whom the idea originates may or may not be the decision-maker for the family. Therefore, until the actual decision-maker hears the suggestion and accepts the plan, migration cannot take place. The identity of the decision-maker in a family is determined by culture, by class and caste, and by family structure (whether authoritarian or democratic). As Bell and Vogel point out:

Even if decision-making is conscious, it is not a simple matter of obtaining the desired number of votes before action can be taken. Because of the long period of intimate relationships between the family members, various subtle considerations enter into the process. . . . Although one family member may receive formal deference from others, this does not necessarily mean that he has the power to ensure that his opinions are carried out by others. Often the person who exercises the greatest actual leadership is one who "works behind the scenes." Even if the one receiving the most deference formally makes the decisions, the critical issues in the decision may, in fact, have been settled by other members of the family.[16]

Any migration, regardless of cause or destination, entails a set of values that are more middle class than they are typically lower class. These values include the aspiration to get ahead—to be successful—and a willingness to take responsibility for personal change.

Migration is an attempt to control one's own destiny—to achieve something one

[15] Tamotsu Shibutani, "A Cybernetic Approach to Motivation," in Walter Buckley, ed., *Modern Systems Research for the Behavioral Scientist* (Chicago: Aldine Publishing Co., 1968), p. 335.
[16] Norman W. Bell and Ezra F. Vogel, "Toward a Framework for Functional Analysis of Family Behavior," in Bell and Vogel, eds., *A Modern Introduction to the Family* (New York: Free Press, 1968), pp. 23–24.

does not have at some point in time or in a certain place. It may be a need for a better job, more security, money, prestige, recognition, or freedom; or a different way of life for oneself or one's family. It may be the need for personal gratification or the need to be near relatives.

But regardless of the individual's reasons for moving, he must conquer the tendency to adhere to the familiar. In order to migrate, the inertia of maintaining the status quo must be overcome. Bad as it is, the local situation is known and familiar. Good as it sounds, the new destination is untried, unknown.

In order for this inertia to be overcome, the drive to better the situation must be great enough to warrant the risk that change entails. Early research pointed out that the decision to migrate always involves these two factors, either directly or by implication: (1) the personal or financial disadvantages of the place of origin, the push force, and (2) the advantages of the place of destination, the pull force.[17] The inadequacies of the place of origin and the advantages of the place of destination are not absolutes—they are relative to each other.

From observations of migrants on the move, the author believes that given the existence of a family decision-maker who has a sufficient amount of dissatisfaction with the status quo and a sufficient amount of drive to initiate a change, any individual will usually go through the following steps to arrive at a decision to move:

1. He thinks about it—mulls it over silently, weighing the pros and cons. He experiences conflict.

2. He discusses it with some significant other—a family member, a friend—someone he trusts or who has had a similar experience. His discussion at this point will be more lengthy and more in depth

than it will be after he makes his decision.

3. He decides to move.

4. He says he will accept the new position.

5. He begins to have doubts. He questions the wisdom of his decision. He experiences conflict again and has ambivalent feelings. He wants to be asked to stay and at the same time to be encouraged to go, or even to be given permission to leave.

6. At this point he again discusses his decision with a significant other or others, asking for reassurance. His conflict will be increased if he is not assured that he has made the best choice. On the other hand, if there is too much exploration of feelings at this time, it increases his ambivalence and he may withdraw from any discussion.

Of course there are variations of this general pattern. Migrant farm workers, for example, often move impulsively. They may make the decision to go to a new area without much discussion, although they will talk it over with fellow migrants. They will usually ask questions about the crops, the amount of money they can make, the weather, or the crew leader.

On the other hand, those who are part of folk cultures—Appalachian Highlanders, American Indians, and Spanish-speaking persons—usually do not make a decision to move without extensive consultation with relatives beyond the immediate family. Permission to move may even need to be granted by the family patriarch, a grandmother or an aged uncle.

The process of making the decision to move can in some families be a strengthening experience that helps to clarify roles and gives the family a unifying goal toward which to work. The same process in another family may be a devastating experience. It may bring out dependency needs, separation anxiety, scapegoating, destructive coalitions, and various neurotic interactions that could require professional help.

An examination of the decision-making process as it pertains to migration can

---

[17] John N. Webb and Malcolm Brown, *Migrant Families* (Washington, D.C.: U.S. Government Printing Office, 1938).

give the professional worker an insight into the allocation of family roles, family coalition patterns, and task performance. Who in the family initiated the idea of the move? Who made the actual decision to move? Who implemented the process of moving?

A more concerted study of cognitive processes—especially under conditions of uncertainty and conflict—is needed for a better understanding of the migrant in this first stage of migration, which could in turn have a direct bearing on treatment techniques. We need to ask how structure affects, determines, and channels actions and interactions. We should ask how structure is created, maintained, and changed. Buckley says that when this happens

we can move from structure to social interrelations and from social relations to social actions and interaction processes—to a matrix of "dynamic assessments" and inter-communication of meanings, to evaluating, emoting, deciding, and choosing.[18]

This brings a decision-making plan into focus.

Reasons for moving. Theories used in the analysis of findings include general systems theory as discussed by Ludwig von Bertalanffy; the dissonance theory as researched by Elliot Aronson, J. W. Brehm, and Leon Festinger; the cognitive consistency theory as seen in the writings of Herbert Kelman and Reuben Baron; and social identity as viewed by Erik Erikson.[19]

_____

[18] Walter Buckley, "Society as a Complex Adaptive System," in Buckley, ed., op. cit., p. 499.

[19] According to Bertalanffy, general system theory "in the narrower sense tries to derive from a general definition of system as a complex of interacting components, concepts characteristic of organized wholes such as interaction, sum, mechanization, centralization, competition, finality, . . . and to apply them to concrete phenomena." *See* Ludwig von Bertalanffy, "General System Theory —A Critical Review," in Buckley, ed., op. cit., p. 13. *See also* Von Bertalanffy, *General Systems Theory* (New York: George Braziller, 1968); Elliot Aronson, "Dissonance Theory: Progress and Problems," pp. 5–27; Herbert C. Kelman and Reuben H. Baron, "Inconsistency as a Psychological Signal," pp. 333–336, and Kelman and Baron,

The network of factors that make up the migrant's life in his place of residence could be identified as the macrosystem. Within that system are the many subsystems that make up his existence. His physical and psychological selves are perhaps the two most basic subsystems. To these must be added all those subsystems or outside factors that impinge on his physical and psychological selves. These might include such diverse items as climate and topography, cost of living and life style, government policies and business conditions, and health and recreational facilities in the community. Another large and important group of subsystems is made up of the roles performed by family members in the community. These would include his children's school, his wife's job, and his father's Golden Age Club.

The migrant's decision to move or to stay must be related to a thorough knowledge of all the subsystems involved, as well as a realistic evaluation of the importance of each in relation to the others. While for some purposes each subsystem must be viewed individually, there is utility also in seeing them as parts of a larger system.[20]

_____

"Determinants of Modes of Resolving Inconsistency Dilemmas: A Functional Analysis," pp. 670–683, in Robert Abelson et al., eds., *Theories of Cognitive Consistency: A Sourcebook* (Chicago: Rand McNally & Co., 1968); J. W. Brehm, "Dissonance Analysis of Attitude-Discrepant Behavior," in M. G. Rosenberg et al., eds., *Attitude, Organization and Change: An Analysis of Consistency* (New Haven: Yale University Press, 1960), pp. 198–232; Leon Festinger, *Conflict, Decision and Dissonance* (Stanford, Calif.: Stanford University Press, 1964); Festinger, *Theory of Cognitive Dissonance* (Evanston, Ill.: Row Peterson, 1957); Erik H. Erikson, *Childhood and Society* (2d. ed.; New York: W. W. Norton & Co., 1963); and Erikson, *Identity, Youth and Crisis* (New York: W. W. Norton & Co., 1968).

[20] Dechert has defined a system as "an organized collection of interrelated elements characterized by a boundary and functional unity." Charles R. Dechert, ed., *The Social Impact of Cybernetics* (New York: Simon & Schuster, 1966), pp. 23–29. Buckley sees a system as "a complex of elements or components directly or indirectly related in a causal network, such that

Every move entails gains as well as losses, and each gain and loss in turn is related to the individual's network of subsystems. Migration affects family relationships, children's education, and welfare. In every decision there are certain trade-offs that have to be reckoned with. In order to earn money, a migrant agricultural worker must follow the harvest. This means giving up living near aging relatives or having his children attend school regularly, although his cultural values might include both education for his children and family care for the aged.

However, regardless of the complexity of factors involved, there is usually one main reason behind the migrant's decision to move on to another place. While a desire for a better salary was mentioned most frequently as the main reason for their move by those interviewed for this paper, further exploration disclosed what the authors of *The Motivation To Work* have called "job attitude factors." [21] These cause the worker to move because he thinks he will enhance his work experience through having more of the following:

1. Recognition from superiors or peers.
2. Possibility for personal growth with opportunities for additional education or a chance to work with a recognized authority in a certain field.
3. Enhanced interpersonal relations with superiors, subordinates, and/or peers.
4. Advancement through a change in status, rank, or position.
5. Delegated responsibility.
6. Variety in work assignments (more creative or less difficult work).
7. Job security as represented by tenure or company stability.

8. A position with higher status (a private secretary, private office, or a company car).

Herzberg and his colleagues state the following:

One of the tragedies of modern industries is that many workers do not have the sense of making a genuine contribution. . . . many jobs have been broken down into small parts. . . . the result is that many people have little idea of what they are doing from the standpoint of real relation to the finished product, or to the social order as a whole.[22]

Migration in this case may be a fight against being controlled by a job. Moving can give an individual the feeling that he *does* have self-determination, that he has some authority to direct his own affairs. Even migrant agricultural workers may at times use migration as a means of escaping from a situation that is intolerable to them.

Breaking with the Past

In the second stage of the migration episode, the migrant breaks with the past to plan for the future. As he cancels his newspaper delivery service, says goodbye to friends and family, resigns from his job, or packs his belongings, these physical actions are accompanied by the realization that he will be losing many familiar situations and relationships. Since all the familiar things around him—even the unpleasant ones—are part of his sense of identity, this sense of loss creates conflict for the migrant that may be seen in some form of separation anxiety.

These losses are traded against anticipation of the future, both in terms of expectations and physical arrangements. The migrant chooses a destination (if this was not part of the initial decision), makes inquiries and arrangements for living and working there, and begins to form a mental picture of what life will be like in his new home.

His reaction to this and subsequent stages of the migration episode depends

---

at least some of the components are related to some others in a more or less stable way at any one time." Walter Buckley, "Society as a Complex Adaptive System," in Buckley, ed., op. cit., p. 493.

[21] Frederick Herzberg et al., *The Motivation to Work* (New York: John Wiley & Sons, 1959), pp. 44-54.

[22] Ibid., p. 27.

on how successfully he can break with the past and prepare realistically for the future. This in turn depends on many circumstances surrounding his move, both in and out of his control. Is migration forced or voluntary, abrupt or planned, undertaken with fear or confidence, wholeheartedly or reluctantly, and planned with or without sufficient information about the destination?

Attempting to break away from the familiar and make the plunge into the unknown can be an anxiety-producing process. Under any circumstances it is a busy time for the migrant—a time when he must make physical arrangements to leave and must investigate as well as plan for his arrival in his new home.

Although the excess energy requirement of handling all these details is often blamed for the migrant's psychic distress at this stage (as is the actual experience of moving in the transitional stage), these complications are not necessarily the core of conflict. They may serve as a plausible scapegoat for the migrant's anxieties about leaving the familiar past and moving to an uncertain future.

Most migrant farm workers fall into the category of movers for whom the process is accepted as a part of life, as expected and necessary. During the Depression the mobility of some southern farm tenants (especially sharecroppers) was amazing. Statistics gathered by the Cotton Section of the Agricultural Adjustment Administration show that a considerable percentage of tenants had moved six or seven times since they started farming, and a few had lived on as many as fifteen different farms.[23] The average tenure of black sharecroppers in two counties in Georgia was 2.8 years, and among whites only 2.4 years.[24] An extensive study by the Agri-

cultural Adjustment Administration of 13,575 tenant families on relief revealed that 41 percent made some type of move in 1934.[25] The moving occurs, but need it be as disorganizing as it so often is for the people involved?

The Transitional Stage

During this third stage of the migration process, the migrant is traveling to his new destination and, having arrived, is registering his first reactions to his new environment. At this stage he still gives much thought to what he has left behind and what is familiar. He has not yet become a part of the new situation. He is between systems.

In his new home he usually experiences cultural shock in finding a different standard and style of living, different norms and values, or perhaps a landscape or climate to which he is not accustomed. Some or all of the local cultural trappings may be new to him: food, regional accent, architecture, traffic regulations, the rhythm and pace of life.

Besides being temporarily rootless in a strange environment, the migrant is forced to come to terms with his hopes and expectations when he gets to his new home. Although it will take some time and experience for him to make a final appraisal of its advantages and disadvantages, during this stage the migrant makes some tentative evaluations and sometimes unconsciously compares his findings to his prior expectations.

During the following stage—the adjustment stage—the migrant will expend a great deal of psychic energy trying to bridge (or ignore) two uncomfortable gaps: the gap between what he is used to and what the new culture and environment present to him, and that between what he expected and what he in fact found to be the reality of his new situation.

During the transitional stage, however,

---

[23] Agricultural Adjustment Administration, Cotton Section, *Arkansas Plantation Study*, NA, RG 145.

[24] Arthur F. Raper, *Preface to Peasantry* (Chapel Hill: University of North Carolina Press, 1936), p. 61.

[25] "Agricultural Adjustment Administration—Federal Emergency Relief Administration Survey," File 119, NA, RG 145.

he is not yet at the point of being able to act. At this stage he is reacting more than acting. He is still occupied with observing and evaluating the new situation. He is busy trying to absorb and understand the things about him and to figure out how he —with his own values, experiences, and plans—can fit into the picture.

While the adjustment stage is far from effortless for many migrants, the transitional stage is probably the more disconcerting. Not yet ready actively to take one course or the other, the migrant is in a kind of no-man's-land of impressions, anxieties, and unknowns. He is trying to sort out his own values at the same time that he is probing the new world around him.

Dissonance: the most common problem. Dissonance was found to be the problem most common among migrants during the transitional stage. Dissonance results from situations that produce cognitive inconsistency, just as static on a radio results from a mixing of radio signals. Dissonance is, in the author's opinion, the most appropriate term because it goes beyond cognitive inconsistency. It includes the feelings, reactions, and drives of a person who has experienced cognitive inconsistency, and is therefore the more inclusive term for the purposes of this paper.[26] Dissonance is used here to describe the state of being that arises from the many discrepancies and inconsistencies the migrant perceives. According to Aronson's definition, dissonance is "a negative drive state which occurs whenever an individual simultaneously holds two cognitions (ideas, beliefs, opinions) which are psy-

chologically inconsistent." [27] In the case of the migrant, cognitive inconsistency arises out of the gap between what is and what was or the gap between what is and what was hoped for. In regard to the latter, Wright states:

It is part of the nature of man to search for explanations and connections so that his experience in the world about him becomes comprehensible. So it is in the case of expectation discrepancy. It is disturbing to the subject when his expectations do not match the presenting facts, and he feels a need to reconcile the two. This may be accomplished by such cognitive changes as expectation revision altering the apparent reality and anormalizing the person. . . .[28]

Aronson and Festinger point out that individuals always experience dissonance after making a difficult choice.[29] To reduce their dissonance, people tend to emphasize the positive aspects and deemphasize the negative aspects of the chosen object. Conversely, they emphasize the negative and deemphasize the positive aspects of the unchosen object. Brehm reached the same conclusions in some of his early experiments.[30]

Combating dissonance. Persons who experience dissonance in any situation all have one thing in common—the desire to put an end to it. As Feldman says:

The person tends to behave in ways that minimize the internal inconsistency among his interpersonal relations, among his intrapersonal cognitions, or among his beliefs, feelings, and actions.[31]

This holds true, of course, for migration too. It will therefore be useful for social

---

26 Cognitive inconsistency has been studied under a number of other names, as Biddle and Thomas point out: "Two behavioral partitions are defined as cognitively inconsistent if one of them implies an event that is denied by the other. Inconsistency has been studied as 'cognitive imbalance,' 'ambivalence,' and 'conflict,' depending partly upon the behaviors that are inconsistent." Bruce J. Biddle and Edwin J. Thomas, eds., *Role Theory: Concepts and Research* (New York: John Wiley & Sons, 1966), pp. 35–36.

27 Op. cit., p. 5.
28 Beatrice A. Wright, "Disability and Discrepancy of Expectations," in Biddle and Thomas, eds., op. cit., p. 161.
29 Aronson, op. cit., p. 6; Festinger, op. cit.
30 J. W. Brehm, "Dissonance Analysis of Attitude—Discrepant Behavior," in M. G. Rosenberg et al., eds., *Attitude, Organization, and Change: An Analysis of Consistency* (New Haven: Yale University Press, 1960), pp. 198–232.
31 Shel Feldman, *Cognitive Consistency* (New York: Academic Press, 1966), p. 1.

workers to explore what types of migration episodes produce the most dissonance and to look at the different ways in which migrants in varying circumstances attempt to minimize dissonance or avoid dissonance-producing situations. They tend to emphasize the positive aspects of their new home and to minimize its negative aspects. The migrant may feel he has escaped from the unbearable and dares not return, or that he has made a thoughtful choice and dares not look foolish.

In either case, many try to see everything about the new environment in a positive way with almost unrealistic enchantment. In fact many might not be able for some time (if ever) to recognize the negative aspects of their job or living conditions. To do so would increase dissonance, and dissonance is hard to bear.

The strangeness of a new situation produces many kinds of cognitive inconsistency. These serve as a signal to the individual that "his coping mechanisms may not be functioning" effectively.[32] For this reason those who have moved recently will often express thoughts such as these: "I am so glad we came here to Georgia instead of going to Utah. They are having such a bad winter out there." The migrant agricultural worker may say: "We can make more money here. The crop is better. It is easier to pick cherries than to thin sugar beets." But regardless of how it is phrased, this is an attempt to decrease dissonance.

If the newcomer is confronted with a sharp discrepancy between actual events and his expectations of these events, he may become concerned with his own reality-testing, or he may sense an opportunity to gain insight into his new environment. If the new migrant is confronted with a discrepancy between his opinions and those of significant others, he may worry about status and acceptance in the new group, he may revise his opinions, or he may

change his group membership. Discrepancy between what is found and what was expected can be the motivating force for quitting a new job or moving.

Dissonance is also caused by the process of moving from one social system to another. All migrations involve a crossing of social system boundaries, whether these systems are defined as national entities, regional subcultures, classes or castes, family kinship networks, work associations, or friendships.

As Brody explains, all migrants leave behind the supports and stresses

of the donor system from which they depart including the push factors which contributed to their decision to move. These families also lose the support of social and geographical familiarity, of long-term relationships and values which were built into them while growing up. At the same time, they are freed of some of the constraints and some of the threats inherent in the donor system. . . .[33]

The dissonance migrants experience is brought about by the changes in role patterns or, more correctly identified, role expectations. The migrant is not certain of his role because he does not know the rules of the game—the expectations of the new environment. The change in role expectations tends to throw the individual back on himself—an anxiety-producing experience that in turn forces him to examine his behavior or attitude. He feels that his very self-identity is threatened. He becomes aware of his cognitive inconsistency, and this leads to self-evaluation.

Aronson and Mills found that individuals experience dissonance whenever they have gone to a good deal of trouble to gain admission to a group that turns out to be dull and uninteresting: "The cognition that they worked hard to become members of the group is dissonant with cognitions concerning the negative aspects of the group.

[32] Herbert C. Kelman and Reuben H. Baron, "Inconsistency as a Psychological Signal," in Abelson et al., eds., op. cit., p. 335.

[33] Elaine B. Brody, "Migration and Adaptation: General and Conceptual Aspects (Migration: A Process of Social Change)." Paper presented at the annual meeting of the American Psychiatric Association, Miami Beach, Florida, May 1969.

One does not work hard for nothing." [34] The authors claim that in order to reduce dissonance in this situation the individual will distort his perception of the group in a positive direction.

In the case of a migrant who moves to a community that proves to be dull and uninteresting, it would seem safe to assume that there will be less dissonance on the part of individuals who feel they had no control over the decision with respect to their location. These would include employees of a large corporation who are moved because of company policy or migrant farm workers whose destination is determined by the current crop and their selection of a crew leader. Likewise it would be safe to assume that those who make their own selection of a place in which to live and work will experience more dissonance than those with little or no choice.

But migration requires a heavy financial as well as emotional investment. It is not unusual for a family to spend a good deal of money on the move as well as on the new house and furnishings. Unless the employer assumes the expense of the move, this expense will have to be absorbed by the family. Consequently if they have reasons to feel their new investment is not worth the purchase price, they will experience dissonance.

In order to avoid admitting they were foolish, they tend at first to minimize or even deny obvious faults. Noticing a clogged drain or a needed repair in the house they have purchased will arouse dissonance. Yet it must be noticed in order to be repaired.

Dissonance and utility are often in conflict immediately after a move when, according to Aronson and Ross, "individuals tend to manifest dissonance-reducing behavior in spite of the fact that the future consequences of their behavior tend to be unpleasant." [35] For the present they are more comfortable ignoring the clogged drain than acknowledging its existence as a flaw in their environment.

Still another potential cause of dissonance is faulty anticipation of the new environment. When a person makes a decision on the basis of limited information, he runs the risk of finding out later that his decision has negative consequences. In the case of the migration episode, the decision to move could have been made on promises or premises that never materialized.

These unfulfilled expectations often pertain to work. In the case of the migrant farm worker, there may be no work when he arrives at a distant destination. In the case of a college professor, the employment conditions may prove to be disappointing.

Discovering faulty anticipation of the new environment will arouse dissonance, according to Carlsmith and Freedman, only when the person knows, or thinks he *should* have known, about the negative consequences before he made his decision to move: "The critical factor determining whether or not dissonance is aroused in these situations is, therefore, the extent to which a person could reasonably have foreseen the negative consequences." [36]

The degree of dissonance will also be affected by whether the individual has a choice in the decision to move. If he is being evicted, he has no choice. He may have faulty information about the house into which he is moving and he may find negative consequences, but the urgency of the need to move lessens or even removes entirely any dissonance he might experience.

Need to prove oneself. While emphasis thus far has been on exaggeration of the positive as a way of avoiding dissonance, this is by no means the only means

---

[34] Elliot Aronson and Judson Mills, "The Effect of Severity of Initiation on Liking for a Group," *Journal of Abnormal and Social Psychology*, Vol. 59, No. 2 (September 1959), p. 177.

[35] Aronson, op. cit., p. 26.
[36] J. Merril Carlsmith and Jonathan L. Freedman, "Bad Decisions and Dissonance: Nobody's Perfect," in Abelson et al., eds., op. cit., p. 486.

of coping with it. During the transitional stage, before the migrant has had time to work out a more permanent adjustment to his new environment, his impromptu reactions to the many dissonance-producing situations tend to be polarized. This may be seen as the "I-love-everything-about-this-place" attitude toward his necessarily less-than-perfect new home. He needs to take this attitude in order to fend off disquieting thoughts about such things as these:

1. His feeling that he is not accustomed to or accepted in the environment.
2. His second thoughts, which most people experience, about the advisability of moving in the first place.
3. His hopes and expectations, which probably were not completely fulfilled (reality, in most cases, is better, worse, or different from what was imagined to be the case).
4. The possibility that the new environment will prove inhospitable or inadequate for his needs.

All these doubts and anxieties about the adequacy of the new environment tend to be somewhat alleviated if migrants can convince themselves that the situation is, in fact, tolerable. However, there is another large category of doubts and anxieties—namely, self-doubts and anxieties about personal adequacy—that cannot be alleviated by a romanticized view of the environment. They can only be lessened by a romanticized view of self.

The migrant may react to this frustration simply by working as hard as he can (or being as nice as he can) to prove himself. Or, at the other extreme, he may vent his frustrations in overtly hostile acts toward some innocent target, trying to prove he is in some way superior.

In any case, many migrants experience this period of frustration in one way or another. The migrant may suddenly feel disillusioned with his choice of a new location. He may feel betrayed by those who encouraged him, brought him, or forced him to come. At the same time, he often experiences a feeling of self-anger for having made the choice—a sense of emptiness as if he had suffered a bereavement or a loss of identity.

This type of dissonance is usually expressed and relieved by negative thoughts, words, or actions directed at the new community or job ("Nothing is right—why did I come?"). It may be directed toward some other group and may take the form of prejudiced or bigoted behavior ("If it were not for those filthy, dirty Polacks . . . .").

Instead of having consciously negative thoughts about a scapegoat or his new home, he may view his former location in an unrealistically glamorous way ("Nothing here can quite compare . . . ."). The migrant may have come to appreciate realistically what he had and lost, but more than likely he is only struggling to become a significant part of the new experience.

As action replaces reaction in the next stage of the migration episode, the migrant is more likely to adopt more constructive ways of gaining acceptance and self-esteem. This frustration syndrome or dissonance-reducing behavior is a normal part of every migration episode. Frustration is often vented on the mechanics of the move. The migrant may find it easy and convenient to get unduly upset about damaged or delayed furniture, lost or unpacked items, or utilities that have not been connected.

Agricultural workers who migrate the most do not experience as much of this type of frustration. Constant moving is an experience farm migrants come to accept as a normal part of the life they live. Therefore they seem to be less emotionally involved in the actual move itself than those who migrate less frequently.

They learned through seasons of moving to relax and to rest while the trucks rolled toward the harvest of tomorrow. . . . They knew they eventually would reach the sugar beets of the midwest, the strawberries of the Santa Maria Valley, the asparagus of New Jersey or the potatoes of Alabama. The roads they took to these places or the direction they traveled, that was the concern of the driver. It was not the concern of the riders. . . .[37]

The transitional stage is a rootless, anxious stage of the migration episode during which the migrant tends to react impulsively to its many frustrations. He usually experiences dissonance in his new environment, mainly because of the gaps between what was and what is and between what is and what he had hoped would be.

The migrant often reacts to these discrepancies by being overly enthusiastic about his new situation or overly romantic about the advantages of the place he left. Added to his need to like the destination he has chosen is his need to prove himself. The migrant often attempts to buoy up his confidence by putting forth his best efforts or by downgrading other people and things in his new environment.

The nature and intensity of the migrant's reactions during the transitional stage depend on many factors: how and why he decided to leave his former residence, how and why he chose his new destination, the extent to which he obtained information about his destination, the nature and intensity of his hopes for life in the new community, the extent of the cultural differences between his former home and his new one, and the whole gamut of circumstances and people he finds in his new location.

The Adjustment Period

There is, of course, no clear line between the transitional period and the adjustment period in the migration episode. Adjustment occurs when the migrant begins to recover from the initial shock of being in a new environment and proceeds with the long, hard, and purposeful task of becoming part of a new social system and its subsystems.

Interviews with migrants often disclosed reactions to the migration experience at this state that were conscious, controlled, and constructive toward the status quo. Instead of merely responding, often emotionally, to his new situation as he did in the transitional stage, he begins to follow a plan of action in order to change either himself or his environment to suit his needs.

Some attitudes in both stages will remain essentially the same, although feelings will decrease—for example, from hate to dislike or from enthusiasm to appreciation. In other cases the initial impressions and reactions of migrants change during the adjustment period. After spending enough time in the new environment to learn more about it and understand it better, the migrant alters his original opinion. In place of an originally negative response, the migrant becomes accustomed to his destination's disadvantages or resignedly accepts the inevitable. He gains a stronger sense of identity and acceptance of the new situation.

Expectations and acceptance. Any move, even one within the same neighborhood, requires changes in identity. The old expression "a new place, a new face" applies to the move across the street as well as the move across the nation or world. Most of the dissonance and maladjustment in the migration episode is brought about by differences in role expectations. Often these differences are between the migrant's role patterns and the role the community expects him to play in terms of his behavior. At other times the conflict is between the migrant's expected role and his real one.

A report on a twelve-year study of immigrant assimilation in Western Australia shows that the amount of satisfaction expressed by the migrant family with their new place of residence depends "on the degree to which current rewards, or expected future rewards, match their level of aspiration."[38]

---

[37] Myrtle R. Reul, *Where Hannibal Led Us* (New York: Vantage Press, 1967), p. 217.

[38] Robert Taft, *From Stranger to Citizen* (Nedland, Australia: University of Western Australia Press, 1965), p. 65.

Soskis studied the adjustment of two hundred Hungarian refugee families eleven years after they arrived in New York City. He asked them: "Have your expectations in the United States been fulfilled?" From their answers he reported that since their greatest aspiration in coming to this country had been for

freedom, advancement for their children, and a reasonable standard of living, it is not surprising that 147 families said their hopes had been fully realized. Twenty-five felt they were still working on their goals. Only 17 of the 200 answered this question negatively. They were in older and lower income groups.[39]

The Australian researchers also found that "social acceptance and respect for the vocational and cultural aspiration of immigrants are the keys to assimilation."[40] This opinion is shared by others. Shannon and Krass, in their Wisconsin study, found:

The degree to which immigrants are accepted in the urban community is related to their success or failure in assimilating the dominant values of urban society and in modifying their behavior accordingly.[41]

Speaking at a symposium on mental health and migration held in Geneva, Switzerland, Dr. Maria Pfister of that country stressed that the adaption of refugees and international migrants "depends a great deal on the social attitude of the population in the receptive country. . . ."[42]

One of the critical problems for the migrant is that he is usually expected to give up or modify his value system to meet the expectations of the new environment.

Cultural pluralism, while much avowed in theory, is in most communities accepted only to a limited degree. The migrant is expected to do most of the adjusting, although any abrupt change in his value system has a direct effect on his ego functioning and tends to strip away his sense of self-identity. Sister Frances Jerome comments that values are

as a rule, changed only slowly and reluctantly. Any attack on them, especially in the nature of ridicule, is deeply resented. Others are expected to respect them, if not to accept them. In fact, one's values are usually regarded as desirable for other persons. . . .[43]

American Indians who leave the reservation often experience a traumatic change in values and role expectations. The movement from a reservation where Indians are virtually the total society to a city where they are a tiny minority is a major step toward assimilation into white society. It also is a continuous series of dissonance-producing situations. Price, writing about Indian migration, points out that there is constant moving once the Indian reaches the city. The address directory at the Los Angeles Indian Center changes by about 10 percent every month, with a complete changeover of addresses among the entire membership each year.[44]

The Appalachian Highlander living in Chicago who still considers himself a visitor in a city where he has worked ten years has managed to maintain a sense of stability by acceptance of inconsistency through the use of denial, distortion, or rationalization of change.[45] He maintains ties

to his relatives in the mountains of Kentucky or Tennessee. He may also have a strong psychological tie to the mountains. These

[39] Philip Soskis, "Adjustment of 200 Hungarian Refugee Families in New York City," *Migration News*, No. 1 (January–February 1969), p. 12.

[40] Taft, op. cit., p. 74.

[41] Lyle W. Shannon and Elaine M. Krass, *The Economic Absorption and Cultural Integration of Immigrant Mexican-American and Negro Workers* (Iowa City: State University of Iowa Press, 1964), p. 5.

[42] Maria Ammende-Pfister, "Community Mental Health Work for Migrants," in "Symposium on Mental Health and Migration," *Migration News*, No. 2 (March–April 1967), p. 25.

[43] Sister Frances Jerome Woods, *Cultural Values of American Ethnic Groups* (New York: Harper & Bros., 1956), p. 8.

[44] John A. Price, "Migration and Adoption of American Indians into Los Angeles," *Human Organization*, No. 27 (Summer 1968), pp. 170–174.

[45] Herbert C. Kelman and Reuben H. Baron, "Determinants of Modes of Resolving Inconsistency Dilemmas: A Functional Analysis," in Abelson et al., eds., op. cit., pp. 670–683.

bonds may cause him to quit a job and go "home" to attend a wedding or funeral of a fourth or fifth cousin to whom he may not have spoken in ten years.[46]

When he returns to his mountain neighborhood for a visit, he falls into old patterns of speech and actions. He reverts to a life-style that is inconsistent with that required by his new environment in Chicago, but that is part of his own culture. Under these circumstances it is both easy and functional for him to compartmentalize the two situations: life in Chicago and life in Appalachia.

Kelman and Baron also discuss the individual who maintains inconsistency by stressing its positive motivational implications.[47] The negative consequences of an experience are made acceptable because they are overshadowed by positive ones. Such behavior is seen in the migrant who uses his larger income or better house as a means of proving to himself that life in the new community is better, thus bolstering his own conviction that he made a good decision.

Should the recent migrant be confronted with his discrepancies, he will be forced to examine himself to determine whether his own inconsistencies indicate a threat to the achievement of his goals in this new place, or whether there is a possibility of a more effective utilization of his resources for the achievement of these goals.

This self-search behavior provides an opportunity for self-understanding. If he is going to accept or reject the values he finds in his new location, the migrant will need a firm awareness of his cognitive map. Only in this way can he gain consistency through cognitive reorganization. He must be clear on what he stands for and what he wants to become in the community.

Major gains from migration. While turmoil and trauma are often symptoms of

the migration episode, on balance the net result has been shown frequently to be positive and constructive for the individual migrant and the receiving community. All of the families interviewed for this paper were asked to indicate what they considered to be the major gains from their migration episode. Their answers were varied, but they generally stressed the benefits accruing to themselves, rarely those accruing to the community into which they had moved.

Generally migrants claimed personal benefits that fell into two broad categories —work and nonwork gains. Those who were employed in semiskilled and unskilled positions, or who were classified as hourly employees, tended to focus on salary increases and improved working conditions. Those who were salaried employees—professionals and executives—spoke mostly of gains in terms of job satisfaction, increased responsibility, opportunities to be creative, or personal growth.

While several families mentioned being near relatives as a major gain, some wives said that being away from in-laws was the real gain in their move. The common belief that geographic separation destroys family interaction has not held true in the migration episodes of these families. Those with strong kinship ties are able to migrate and still maintain a relationship to the extended family through letters, long-distance telephone calls, tape recordings, and/or frequent visits.

Those families in which the decision-making process is invested beyond the sphere of the nuclear family unit (parents and children) continue to operate with the same decision-making process. For instance, the matriarch clan head continues to give her opinion or permission via letter or telephone, and the person empowered to carry out her decisions does so. This maintenance of family ties across geographic distances as expressed by these families agrees with the findings of a study of extended family relations made of middle-class migrants located in the Cape Kennedy region of east-central Florida.

[46] Myrtle R. Reul, "Isolation of Farm Workers," *Michigan State Economic Record*, Vol. 9, No. 6 (June 1967), p. 6.

[47] Kelman and Baron, "Inconsistency as a Psychological Signal."

That study found that family relationships were maintained over great geographic distances because of modern advancements in means of communication.[48]

The majority of farm-reared migrant families also report that their economic position has improved in many ways as the result of moving.

These ways included having a better job with more regular hours, higher pay or better working conditions, having more friends, having a better social life, having better schools for their children and feeling more settled. Many reported having better living conditions or nicer homes.[49]

Benefits to the community. Emphasis of many past analysts has been on diagnosing and discussing the disruptive influences of migrants and migration on the community. The writer's data confirmed their existence, but there was even more impressionistic evidence of benefits to the community. The migrant often brings skills or an educational level that enriches and contributes to the economy and cultural life of the new area. An example of this is the educational level of the Cuban refugees. Thirty-six percent are reported to have at least a high school education and 12.5 percent have four or more years of college.[50]

Another way in which communities benefit from the influx of migrants is that migrants tend to spark changes—most of

them constructive and progressive—in accepted but outmoded ways of doing things. Quite often the newcomer, with his different experiences and greater objectivity, can see more clearly what needs improving in a community and can suggest new ways of approaching old problems. Frequently the lifelong resident of a community has either gotten used to its shortcomings or become weary of trying to change them.

In those instances when local leaders have not, in fact, been doing their best to make improvements, the influx of newcomers can help to overcome stagnant ideas and stagnant leadership. Newcomers may not tolerate the kind of conservatism they find in education, government, and local administration in the new community.

Besides gaining new skills, new talents, and a new perspective on themselves, communities also gain in affluence and sophistication as a result of in-migration. According to Dynes et al.: "Geographical mobility is an integral factor in the development and maintenance of the entire industrial system."[51] Today the nation's entire economy is dependent on the ability of workers and managers to function efficiently wherever they may be moved by the changing pressures of industrial decline or expansion.

In intangible ways every community benefits from this national industrial wealth and expansion. In addition, of course, specific communities receive tangible, specific benefits when a new industry or branch office comes to town.

Each community can count its gains in terms of additional dollars that the new industry's payroll adds to the economy. But the community will also benefit in terms of the quality as well as the quantity of goods sold to newcomers. The demand for food, clothing, housing, and recreational facilities that reflect the tastes of other sections of the country will usually

[48] F. M. Berard, "Kinship Interaction and Communication Among Space-Age Migrants," *Journal of Marriage and the Family*, Vol. 29, No. 3 (August 1967), pp. 541–554.

[49] Ward W. Bauder and Lee G. Burchinal, "Adjustments to the New Institutional Environment," *Family Mobility in our Dynamic Society* (Ames, Iowa: Iowa State University Press, 1965), p. 214. *See also* Lyle W. Shannon, "Occupational and Residential Adjustment of Rural Migrants," *Labor Mobility and Population in Agriculture* (Ames, Iowa: Iowa State University Press, 1961), pp. 122–123.

[50] Richard R. Fagen, Richard A. Brody, and Thomas J. O'Leiry, *Cubans in Exile* (Stanford, Calif.: Stanford University Press, 1968), p. 19.

[51] Russell R. Dynes et al., *Social Problems, Dissensus, and Deviation in an Industrial Society* (New York: Oxford University Press, 1964), p. 22.

be met by merchants, making these new products increasingly available. The net result is bound to be greater variety, more choice, and less provincialism in the community.

Conclusion

As pointed out earlier, migration is experienced by a significant percentage of this country's population and the number is likely to increase further. It is an event that occurs in the lives of people in all socioeconomic groups, ethnic groups, and age groups. It is a significant episode in the life of the laborer, the executive, and the professional.

Like any other normal risk of living, migration has certain potentialities for enhancing ego function and solidifying families which should be taken into account in community planning, preventive mental health programs, as well as treatment techniques.

The migration episode represents a conceptual vehicle for integrating various theories of behavior such as cognitive consistency, ego psychology, group psychology, role theory, social psychology, group dynamics, and community planning. As has been shown, the experience of moving has its trials, its challenges, and its compensations. What is lacking in the picture is recognition of the benefits of migration and constructive intervention in its frustrations and discomforts. Much of this must and should come from the social work profession, in terms of exploration, action, or leadership.

One of the families interviewed stated the problem well. They said they feel that "communities should recognize the contributions that are made by migrant workers. They are the temporary residents without whose assistance—physical and intellectual—the receiving community would be badly handicapped."

Without migrant farm workers the crops could not be harvested. Without transient construction workers tunnels and bridges could not be built. Without the visiting professor, the consulting executive, or the so-called troubleshooter, it would be difficult or impossible to upgrade education, business management, government, or services.

Implications for Research and Practice

In a paper prepared for the 1960 White House Conference on Children and Youth, Cowgill stated:

It is difficult to generalize about the effects of mobility, because the term encompasses so many experiences, so many varieties of people with many different reasons for moving, and living under widely varying circumstances.[52]

The frequency of moving, the distance moved, the reasons for the move, whether the move is voluntary or forced, whether it is permanent or temporary, the effect the move has on personal status, and whether the family maintains a psychological, physical, or legal home base somewhere else are all factors in the migration episode.

While it is as difficult to generalize about migration as it is to generalize about people, there *is* a thread of common factors running through the migration episode. As the previous sections of this paper point out, migrants go through the stages of decision-making, breaking with the past, transition, and finally adjustment, and they tend to have certain common problems, reactions, benefits, and disappointments in each stage, which vary by such variables as age, occupation, race, sex, culture, lifestyle, social class, family size, and the time in space of the family life cycle.

To be of help to the migrant in these four stages, the social worker must be equipped with understanding based on knowledge of what the stages entail. While fairly extensive demographic information exists about migration, our knowledge

[52] Donald O. Cowgill, "The Effect of Mobility," *Children and Youth in the 1960's* (Washington, D.C.: White House Conference on Children and Youth, 1960), p. 33.

about the migration episode as it affects individuals is more limited. More effective treatment will have to go hand in hand with a sharp increase in research.

Research required in the decision-making stage. In the area of decision-making, for example, agencies can combine treatment and research by investigating the ability of husbands and wives to recognize their roles in the decision-making process. Bales's system of interaction process analysis could furnish an objective account of the decision-making session and would serve as a theoretical rationale for analyzing behavior in groups involving family members.[53] Kenkel's study at Iowa State University would provide some useful background material.[54]

There is also need for more concerted study of the cognitive processes, especially under the conditions of uncertainty and conflict that are part of the decision-making process. Finally, we must study the decision-making process more closely as it relates specifically to migration. Not only will we then be better able to cope with migrants' problems at this stage, but we will gain wider insights into family roles.

Aspects of breaking with the past. Research is also needed on different aspects of the second stage—the attempt to break with the past. We must find out about what couples anticipate to be the probable consequences of moving. Their preconceptions—valid or not—will have implications for helping other migrants and will also shed light on other facets of their lives. The information could be used to assess the couple's reality-testing as well as the kind and amount of agreement that exists between them.

Other studies that would be useful in

regard to the second stage would be an investigation of the roles of members of extended families in the communication network when one of them migrates. A better understanding is also needed of the factors and feelings involved when people leave a place in which they have firm roots and when they leave a place where they have no roots. In the former case it is difficult to say goodbye to close friends. In the latter, it is difficult to leave without any goodbyes. Since many migrants operate under the assumption that it will be less painful to leave a place if they do not become tied to it emotionally, it would be useful to test this assumption in the light of facts. Related to this is the ritual of the farewell party, the significance of which has not been fully explored.

Unknowns in transition and adjustment. With regard to stages three and four—transition and adjustment—a great deal more must be known about the part geographic location plays in feelings of self-identity. People do not feel tied to a city or region simply because it has more advantages, quantitatively speaking, than some other location. Yet emotional ties do exist and sometimes persist even when an individual has lived for years in another community. The age of the migrant, the culture of the community, and the degree of acceptance may have something to do with attraction to one place or another. Or perhaps other factors are involved more significantly. In any case split loyalties or undying loyalty to one specific place are common enough among migrants to warrant further investigation.

In order to help the migrant when he is called on to modify or give up his value system in a new location, we must know more about this phenomenon. Why and when does it occur? Can it be ameliorated by increasing community acceptance of people with different value systems? Are there ways of helping a migrant to avoid such a change or to make the change less damaging to his sense of self?

[53] Robert F. Bales, *Interaction Process Analysis* (Cambridge, Mass.: Addison-Wesley Press, 1950).

[54] William F. Kenkel, "Observational Studies of Husband-Wife Interaction in Family Decision-Making," in Marvin B. Sussman, *Sourcebook on Marriage and the Family* (Boston: Houghton Mifflin Co., 1963), pp. 144–156.

Faulty perception of reality factors in the new environment is still another common problem of transition and adjustment. We should know more about what kinds of information a migrant needs about his destination and how he can go about getting this. Furthermore, we must know more about how people choose and interpret the information they seek and how they can be helped when their hopes and plans are not fulfilled.

Courses in family life education would benefit from research correlating migration with stages in the family life cycle. Can moves in this mobile society be predicted, anticipated, and planned for in advance? We know that upwardly mobile families usually move two or three times—even if they remain in the same community—as their family size and income increase.[55] We know too that different career lines call for certain moves at certain intervals. A more thorough investigation of the area of social mobility would permit social workers and educators to help potential migrants— a category that includes most people today —to make more realistic plans for the future.

General areas in research. Geographic mobility is another general area where much needs to be learned. A new approach to this topic is needed, one that differentiates between the environmental system, the personal system, and the behavioral system. In the past these important distinctions have been lost in a sea of statistics that fail to give insights into the effects of migration on individual human beings.

Well-designed longitudinal research in the social sciences is needed to answer questions about process and development in the migration episode. Mobility should be included, at least as a variable, in all such studies. Mobility as a subject of such research would provide a wider base for

[55] August B. Hollingshead, "Class Differences in Family Stability," in Sussman, ed., op. cit., p. 259.

investigation. Most social science research to date has placed heavy emphasis on the school-age child. But because all segments of the American population migrate, studies on migration would give an accurate picture of the effect of change on all age groups.

Further research is needed to find out more about the constructive, strengthening results of migration in terms of its effects on both individuals and communities. The migration episode offers an opportunity for personal and family integration and for heightened self-insight. The potential advantages to communities and migrants were discussed at length in the preceding section. Further research could corroborate these and would uncover other benefits that have largely been ignored (or outweighed) by more pessimistic views of the effects of migration.

Other studies that have direct implications for treatment might ask such questions as these: How is moving related to separation anxiety and/or bereavement? How should the experience of moving be used in crisis intervention? And, leading into the next topic, what are the implications of the migration episode for social welfare policy?

Implications for Social Welfare Policy

The most significant issue facing policymakers in the mobile seventies is the tremendous gap between the existence and excessively local distribution of services and the demand or need for these services by persons irrespective of place of residence. The implication of this fact is clear: the services available must be examined in light of migration trends and patterns, both numerical and geographic.

This must be done in order to find out the following: Who are our actual and potential clients? Where are they? What do they need and when? What can the community do? What can agencies do? How useful are the services now being rendered and how can they be improved? How can they be organized or reorganized? How can they be staffed and distributed? How can policies and services aimed at migrants be used to reach other problems? How much effort should be spent on prevention and how much on therapy?

Industry is far ahead of social welfare in its recognition of the importance and benefits of planned intervention to minimize the adjustment problems of migrants. All too many of the policies of health, welfare, education, and governmental agencies are still geared to the existence of some mythical nonmobile population.

As a result many migrants are victimized by conflicting policies as they move from one place to another. They fail to meet local residence requirements for voting or are shortchanged when they try to make transfers of school or medical records, insurance or other benefits. To meet this inequity head on, ways must be found of unifying laws and services so that the migrant is not penalized for pursuing a course that is both necessary and desirable in today's world.

In addition a reappraisal of the purpose and functions of all agencies would have to be based on a recognition of the relationship between urban and rural areas and of the arbitrary nature of boundary lines. In many cases this will result in the realization that services need to be expanded in addition to being updated and strengthened.

It has already been proved that preparation of the migrant and the receiving community pays high dividends in terms of the adjustment of both. In fact the whole area of preparation for migration deserves a great deal of attention from policy-makers in social welfare, education, mental health, and community planning. A coordinated effort must be made to help the migrant and the community plan for migration and to improve services for orienting newcomers when they arrive.

Education for family living has tended to overlook migration as an accepted and expected episode in a family's life cycle. In the past, courses in marriage and the family have been taught with the unspoken but nevertheless real assumption that the student would spend all his married life in one house or one town. The result has been a rather widespread ignorance of the need for and inevitability of migration.

Young people need to be armed with facts about the effects of mobility on marital and family relationships. They also need to learn the skills they will need to plan moves, to cope with problems at all stages of migration, and to maintain communication with their families.

A full understanding of the migration episode will require its being seen as a personal experience involving the psychic apparatus, the cognitive map, the concept of self, and object relationships of the individual. It must be viewed as an experience in which the individual interacts with his family as well as other groups—one in which the group influences the individual and the individual influences the group, which in turn influences the community.

Movers, Migrants, and the National Interest

CLARENCE SENIOR

The epic Apollo journeys to the moon were in pursuit of goals comparable to those of the early Americans who first came to these shores. But the moon trips are also different. They are incredibly more highly organized, more minutely planned, fabulously financed—and provide for what has so far been correctly hoped would be safe return.

Our 44 million immigrant ancestors and the millions who have moved within this nation's boundaries were also seeking to discover something important to them. Ambition, hope, and courage were—and are—almost always present. Differential economic opportunities also have been and are involved overwhelmingly.

This massive movement of people will be reviewed in this paper in four ways. Major trends as shown by demographic data will be discussed in the first part of this paper. In the second part the socio-economic question of "why people move" will be explored. Problems faced by migrants will be covered next. And finally,

ways in which these problems arising from mobility can be ameliorated will be discussed.

The major source of data on population movement within the United States is, of course, the decennial censuses conducted by the U.S. Bureau of the Census. The ten-year time lag between censuses is, as will be seen, a distinct disadvantage in a nation such as the United States that has so fast moving an economy.

The demand for annual data during the hectic days of World War II led to the establishment of the Current Population Survey, which since 1948 has taken place each spring, on a sample basis. Year after year, with only minor variations, around 20 percent of the nation's population over 1 year of age has been found to have changed residence since the previous spring. Most of them (12–14 percent of the national total) are called "movers"—those who change their residence within one of the nation's some three thousand counties.

23

"Migrant" is the term reserved by the census bureau since 1940 for those who move their homes across county lines. Mobility is used to describe both types of address-changing, migration as well as moving. These conceptual distinctions are followed in this paper.

Major Demographic Trends

The ebb and flow of immigration to the United States has been recorded fairly accurately since 1820 (see Table 1). It is estimated that some quarter of a million immigrants arrived in the preceding century. Once they arrived, large numbers of these immigrants began a steady movement westward; the continuing influx kept full the population reservoir that fed one of this nation's major internal movements.

Mainstreams of Internal Migration

Migration statistics of the United States since 1820 portray a massive westward population movement. Much of this movement was spurred economically by the availability of free or cheap land, discoveries of gold and silver, and more recently by both increased industrial job opportunities and retirement possibilities. Individuals and families braved the risks of moving in the hope that their personal welfare would be enhanced at their destination. The growth and dispersion of the national population from the initial 210 settlers on the Atlantic shore in 1610 to almost a million times that many throughout the country today provide themes for much of the nation's folklore and many songs, plays, movies, and television programs.

This movement may be illustrated by plotting the shifting center of population as fur-trader, miner, cattle- and sheep-raiser, farmer, and others migrated westward. The 1790 census placed the center of population in eastern Maryland; by 1800 it was a few miles west of Baltimore, and by 1810 in the northern tip of Virginia.

TABLE 1. IMMIGRANTS TO THE UNITED STATES, 1820–1970

Period	Immigrant Aliens (thousands)
1820–30	152
1831–40	599
1841–50	1,713
1851–60	2,598
1861–70	2,315
1871–80	2,812
1881–90	5,247
1891–1900	3,688
1901–10	8,795
1911–20	5,736
1921–30	4,107
1931–40	528
1941–50	1,035
1951–60	2,515
1961	271
1962	284
1963	306
1964	292
1965	297
1966	323
1967	362
1968	454
1969	359
1970	373

Source: *Annual Report of the Immigration and Naturalization Service* (Washington, D.C.: U. S. Department of Justice, 1970), Table 1.

It crossed West Virginia by stages for the next four decades and during 1860–80 moved across Ohio. For sixty years it moved somewhat more slowly across Indiana, crossing into Illinois with the 1950 census and remaining in that state in 1960.[1]

Further statistical evidence is found in the figures available by census years since 1890 for persons born east of the Mississippi River but enumerated by the census-takers as residing west of it. At least as interesting is the number born west of the Mississippi who were found living east of that river. (See Table 2.) The net popu-

---

[1] U.S. Bureau of the Census, *United States Census of Population, 1960*, "United States Summary: Number of Inhabitants," P.C. (1) 1A (Washington, D.C.: U.S. Government Printing Office, 1963), pp. XII–XIII.

lation gain of the West, however, far out-weighs the loss to the East. It is widely agreed that in general the westward move-ment contributed greatly to the growth of the democratic spirit and to the establish-ment of democratic institutions.

A second major stream of internal mi-gration has been from South to North. The data for 1890–1960 show the same two-way flow as does the East-West migra-tion. (See Table 3.) This characteristic of large-scale migrations was listed by Ravenstein, a British statistician, as one of his "Laws of Migration" in articles pub-lished in 1885 and 1889.[2] His first paper was based on the 1881 British census; the second, on experience in some twenty coun-ties. This two-way flow of population came close to being the most definitely established trend in a field marked by thou-sands of empirical studies but few water-proof generalizations.

There is a tremendous amount of litera-ture on the movement from the South, which has also been overwhelmingly a rural-urban migration.[3] Although a num-ber of factors were involved in the spurt of northward migration in the 1910–20

[2] E. G. Ravenstein, *Journal of the Royal Sta-tistical Society*, June 1885 and June 1889. Avail-able in the Bobbs-Merrill Series in the Social Sciences, Reprint Numbers S-482 and S-483.

[3] Possibly the most important single recent arti-cle on the subject is C. Horace Hamilton, "The Negro Leaves the South," *Demography*, Vol. 1, No. 1 (1964), pp. 273–295. Even more recent data are found in the census bureau's *Current Population Reports*. *See* especially "Social and Economic Conditions of Negroes in the United States," Series P-23, No. 24, and "Negro Popula-tion: March 1968," Series P-20, No. 175 (Wash-ington, D.C.: U.S. Government Printing Office, October 1967 and October 23, 1968, respectively). It should be noted in passing that census reports sometimes deal with Negroes specifically and at other times with "nonwhites." Although nation-wide the latter term consists 92 percent of Negroes, it also includes American Indians, Japanese, Chinese, Filipinos, Asian Indians, Koreans, Poly-nesians, Indonesians, Hawaiians, Aleuts, Eskimos, and others.

TABLE 2. NATIVE POPULATION BORN EAST OF THE MISSISSIPPI RIVER AND LIVING WEST OF IT OR VICE VERSA, 1890–1960

Year	Born East, Living West	Born West, Living East	Net Gain of West
1890	4,360,516	282,359	4,078,157
1900	4,512,097	518,543	3,993,554
1910	5,276,879	684,773	4,592,106
1920	5,227,850	1,038,905	4,188,945
1930	5,145,922	1,648,832	3,497,090
1940	4,651,399	1,910,482	2,740,917
1950	5,822,865	2,698,815	3,124,040
1960	7,416,453	3,571,970	3,844,483

Source: U.S. Bureau of the Census, *United States Census of Population, 1960*, "State of Birth," P.C. (2) 2A (Washington, D.C.: U.S. Government Printing Office, 1963), Table 2.

TABLE 3. NATIVE POPULATION BORN IN THE SOUTH AND LIVING IN THE NORTH OR VICE VERSA, 1890–1960

Year	Born South, Living North	Born North, Living South	Net Gain to North
1890	1,135,620	635,594	500,026
1900	1,295,853	1,021,450	274,403
1910	1,527,107	1,449,229	77,878
1920	2,151,549	1,721,349	430,200
1930	3,297,329	1,878,192	1,419,137
1940	3,456,979	2,065,624	1,391,355
1950	5,009,675	3,101,280	1,908,395
1960	6,569,567	4,546,921	2,022,646

Source: U.S. Bureau of the Census, *United States Census of Population, 1960*, "State of Birth," P.C. (2) 2A (Washington, D.C.: U.S. Government Printing Office, 1963), Table 3.

decade, the most important was the need of northern industries and services for manpower following war-caused interrup-tion of foreign immigration. Not only did overall immigration drop by one-third, but the flows from Canada and Mexico in-creased substantially; the latter more than doubled its previous year's total, undoubt-edly owing at least in part to the 1910–21 revolutionary struggle.

The restrictive immigration legislation of the 1920s cut European immigration further. Those northern employers experiencing labor shortages continued recruiting in the South for both Negro and white workers. Although the Depression of the 1930s reduced the number of northern job vacancies, World War II labor shortages resulted in increased out-migration of both Negro and other workers from the South to northern industrial cities.

Another set of figures helps document internal migration: the percentage of the native population enumerated as living in a state different from their state of birth. These figures, by census years since 1850, are as follows:

Year	Per- centage	Year	Per- centage
1850	24.0	1910	21.6
1860	24.7	1920	22.1
1870	23.2	1930	23.4
1880	22.1	1940	22.4
1890	20.8	1950	25.2
1900	20.6	1960	26.2

But these figures *underestimate* migration: persons moving back to their state of birth, moving to a foreign country, or dying during the census period are not counted as migrating at all. Further, those who might have moved to several states within the decade are counted for only one move. As mentioned earlier, the ten-year time lag between censuses is clearly a disadvantage in a fast-moving economy. Despite their admitted deficiencies, the state-of-birth statistics arranged to show gains and losses for the nine census divisions are informative. (See Table 4 for the 1960 figures.)

An economic and social history of the United States would be necessary to explain adequately the social costs and benefits portrayed by these statistics. Clues to where the frontiers are become more precise when further breakdowns are given by states and by the more recently developed concept of state economic areas. Here we can give only a suggestion of how

rankings vary when the perecntage of a state's total population born in other states is used as the criterion, bearing in mind that the United States average of persons born in a state different from the one in which they are counted by the census is 24.9 percent. The top ten gainers were as follows:

State	Percentage
Nevada	66.1
Alaska	61.5
Arizona	55.6
Florida	54.2
Wyoming	52.9
District of Columbia	51.5
Oregon	48.0
California	47.8
Colorado	46.7
New Mexico	45.1

The ten states lowest in "attractiveness" as measured by the percentage of their 1960 population born in other states were these:

State	Percentage
Pennsylvania	11.5
Mississippi	12.3
New York	13.2
Kentucky	13.3
Alabama	13.3
North Carolina	13.8
Massachusetts	13.9
Maine	14.0
West Virginia	14.8
Wisconsin	14.9

Possibly even more indicative of a state's economic and social "health" are data on net loss through interstate movement. The 1960 census found net loss in thirty-three states; twenty-four had shown net losses in all four census periods between 1930 and 1960. Six states started showing such losses in 1870 and lost consistently each decade up to and including 1950–60: North Carolina, Georgia, Kentucky, Tennessee,

TABLE 4. NATIVE POPULATION BY DIVISION OF BIRTH AND DIVISION OF RESIDENCE, WITH NET GAIN OR LOSS THROUGH INTERDIVISIONAL MOVEMENT, 1960

Division	Born in Specified Division, Living in Another (percentage)	Living in Specified Division, Born in Another (percentage)	Net Change
New England	16.1	12.1	−438,648
Middle Atlantic	14.6	10.9	−1,266,420
East North Central	15.9	18.5	+1,023,161
West North Central	30.4	14.1	−3,422,737
South Atlantic	16.6	17.6	+285,447
East South Central	31.0	10.3	−3,534,030
West South Central	22.3	14.7	−1,580,145
Mountain	30.4	40.5	+935,961
Pacific	9.7	48.0	+7,997,411

Source: U.S. Bureau of the Census, *United States Census of Population, 1960*, "State of Birth," P.C. (2) 2A (Washington, D.C.: U.S. Government Printing Office, 1963), p. 3.

Alabama, and Mississippi. Seven states show a gain in population through in-migration during the entire 1870–1960 period: California, Connecticut, Florida, Michigan, New York, Oregon, and Washington. Massachusetts, one of the earliest industrial states, started losing through net out-migration only in the 1930s.[4]

Similar analyses show substantial losses for various counties. Almost half of all counties throughout the nation sustained losses through out-migration between 1940 and 1950 and slightly over half lost during 1950–60.

A special study of data on internal migration during 1955–60 gives a detailed picture of losses and gains in the 509 groupings called state economic areas into which the census has divided the country since 1950. Data on migrants 5 years of age or over are given by sex, color, age, type of

migration, education, marital status, employment, occupation, income, and so on.[5] These statistical tabulations, it will be seen later, reflect the individual decisions of millions of persons seeking to fulfill their conception of the "good life."

Chief Types of Migration

Migration between noncontiguous states accounted for around 4 million persons annually during the 1960s. Nine categories of such migration have been identified by Shryock and ranked in descending order of numerical importance: urban to urban, rural nonfarm to urban, rural farm to urban, rural farm to rural nonfarm, urban to rural nonfarm, rural nonfarm to rural nonfarm, urban to rural farm, rural nonfarm to rural farm, rural farm to rural farm.[6] A fascinating pattern of these types of moves by distance shows farm-to-farm migrants tending to move the shortest distances; urban-to-urban, the greatest. Of course, intracounty and intrastate moves

---

[4] U.S. Bureau of the Census, *Historical Statistics of the United States, Colonial Times to 1957* (Washington, D.C.: U.S. Government Printing Office, 1960), pp. 44–45; Current Population Reports, *Population Estimates, 1950–60* (Washington, D.C.: U.S. Government Printing Office, April 8, 1965), p. 18. For background and analysis *see* Hope T. Eldridge and Dorothy Swaine Thomas, *Population Redistribution and Economic Growth, United States, 1870–1950*, Vol. II (Philadelphia: American Philosophical Society, 1964).

[5] U.S. Bureau of the Census, *United States Census of Population, 1960*, "Mobility for States and Economic Areas," P.C. (2) 2B (Washington, D.C.: U.S. Government Printing Office, 1963).

[6] Henry S. Shryock, Jr., *Population Mobility Within the United States* (Chicago: Community & Family Study Center, 1964), pp. 322–324.

are by definition eliminated from these generalizations.

Rural-urban migration, another major directional dimension of internal migration, has transformed this nation from a predominantly rural one to an urban one. The urban sector of the national population in 1960 was 618 times as large as it was when the first census was taken in 1790: 125 million as compared with 202,000.[7]

Proportionately, urbanites grew from 5.1 percent in the first census to 70 percent in the most recent, while rural-dwellers dropped from 94.9 to 30 percent. Recent years have seen an increase in the speed of urban growth. Urban areas not only grew rapidly, they became increasingly differentiated into central city and urban fringe; they reached out and annexed surrounding territory, including towns and smaller cities.

The most important point to note for present purposes is that cities are built primarily by in-migration. No known rate of natural increase could have produced what has become known as the "exploding metropolis." Metropolitan areas of the United States as a whole received a net in-migration of 8,143,000 persons in 1950–60, almost a million more than their 1940–50 increase through migration of 7,218,000. Nonmetropolitan areas, on the other hand, lost 5,483,000 persons, somewhat less than their loss in the previous decade of 5,923,000.[8]

Movement within metropolitan areas

TABLE 5. COUNTIES WITH NET OUT-MIGRATION OF 100,000 OR MORE, 1950–60

County and State	Net Out-migration
Kings, New York (Brooklyn)	383,000
New York, New York (Manhattan)	364,000
Philadelphia, Pennsylvania	285,000
Wayne, Michigan (Detroit)	218,000
St. Louis City, Missouri	213,000
Suffolk, Massachusetts (Boston)	182,000
District of Columbia	158,000
Bronx, New York	156,000
Baltimore City, Maryland	138,000

Source: U.S. Bureau of the Census, *Current Population Reports*, "Components of Population Change, 1950 to 1960, for Counties, Standard Metropolitan Statistical Areas, State Economic Areas, and Economic Subregions," Series P-23, No. 7 (Washington, D.C.: U.S. Government Printing Office, November 1962).

(some of it technically migration, some of it "moving," since the persons involved do not cross county lines) is obviously of concern to social workers. Newcomers, especially if they differ from the resident population in some visible way (in color, class, speech, clothing, manners, or the like) and if they compete with the "old-timers" for community facilities, will be defined either as *causing* social problems or as *being* social problems. The Los Angeles–Long Beach Standard Metropolitan Statistical Area illustrates the difference a political definition can make: it gained 1,583,000 migrants in the 1950s (as compared with 1,088,000 in the 1940s), but Los Angeles County gained only 1,171,000. Los Angeles county headed the list of twenty-nine counties that gained 100,000 or more persons in the 1950s. Nassau County, New York, with a 463,000-person net inflow, was in second place. Nine counties that are also central cities each lost at least 100,000 persons in the 1950–60 decade (see Table 5). The influence exerted on metropolitan change is shown in Table 6 for the period 1960–65, compared with projections for 1965–70 and 1970–75.

The United States has become not simply

[7] U.S. Bureau of the Census, *Statistical Abstract of the United States: 1966* (Washington, D.C.: U.S. Government Printing Office, 1966); and "Urban and Rural Population of the United States, by States, 1960 and 1950," P.C. (51)4 (Washington, D.C.: U.S. Government Printing Office, June 9, 1961).

[8] U.S. Bureau of the Census, *Current Population Reports*, "Components of Population Change, 1950 to 1960, for Counties, Standard Metropolitan Statistical Areas, State Economic Areas, and Economic Subregions," Series P-23, No. 7 (Washington, D.C.: U.S. Government Printing Office, November 1962).

TABLE 6. WHITE AND NONWHITE POPULATION OF METROPOLITAN AND NONMETROPOLITAN AREAS, 1960–75

| Area of Residence | Number (thousands) | | | | Percentage Increase[a] | | |
	1960 April 1	1965 July 1	1970 July 1	1975 July 1	1960–65	1965–70	1970–75
Total	179,323	193,795	205,290	218,620	8.1	5.9	6.5
Metropolitan[b]	112,885	124,670	135,040	147,330	10.4	8.3	9.1
In central cities	58,004	59,620	60,280	61,330	2.8	1.1	1.7
Outside central cities	54,881	65,050	74,760	86,030	18.5	14.9	15.1
Nonmetropolitan	66,438	69,125	70,250	71,290	4.0	1.6	1.5
White	158,832	170,725	180,020	190,790	7.5	5.4	6.0
Metropolitan[b]	99,688	109,000	117,100	126,750	9.3	7.4	8.2
In central cities	47,655	47,080	45,660	44,230	−1.2	−3.0	−3.1
Outside central cities	52,033	61,920	71,440	82,520	19.0	15.4	15.5
Nonmetropolitan	59,144	61,725	62,920	64,040	4.4	1.9	1.8
Nonwhite	20,491	23,070	25,270	27,830	12.6	9.5	10.1
Metropolitan[b]	13,197	15,670	17,940	20,580	18.7	14.5	14.7
In central cities	10,349	12,540	14,620	17,070	21.2	16.6	16.8
Outside central cities	2,848	3,130	3,320	3,510	9.9	6.1	5.7
Nonmetropolitan	7,294	7,400	7,330	7,250	1.5	−.9	−1.1

[a] A minus sign denotes a decrease.

[b] Data relate to the 212 standard metropolitan statistical areas in the United States as constituted in April 1960. An SMSA comprises at least one central city of at least 50,000 persons, together with the county or counties that are economically and otherwise oriented to the central city.

Source: 1960 census; and estimates for 1965 and projections by the Statistical Bureau of the Metropolitan Life Insurance Company, *Statistical Bulletin* (June 1967), p. 2.

an urbanized nation; it is overwhelmingly metropolitanized—some say "megalopolized." Negroes have participated in this process more rapidly than have whites. The 1960 census found that during the previous two decades the Negro population in metropolitan areas had more than doubled, from 5,840,000 to 12,941,000. Having started later, Negroes overtook and surpassed whites in proportion in both urban areas in general and metropolitan areas specifically (see Table 7).

This trend toward urbanization of Negroes follows one that has been noted for sixty years: the ratio of the Negro population in central cities to that outside the city tripled between 1900 and 1960, whereas for whites it decreased by nearly half.[9] The

[9] *The Negroes in the United States: Their Economic and Social Situation*, Bulletin No. 1511 (Washington, D.C.: U.S. Department of Labor, June 1966).

proportions that will be living in metropolitan areas by July 1, 1975, will be, according to projections in Table 6: Negro 73.9 percent, white 66.4 percent.

For a general picture of nationwide population movement, the 1968–69 national experience of all types of mobility, both moving and migration, is fairly typical of each year since 1947–48. (See Table 8.)

Urban Mosaics

At least as important as rapidity of growth is another result of in-migration—heterogeneity. This characteristic of urban areas has for centuries been looked on by many essayists as making them more stimulating and thereby more attractive. If "variety is the spice of life," cities have long supplied that condiment.

This country's original cities were quite heterogeneous; it is reported that nineteen languages were spoken in New Amsterdam. Foreign-born whites accounted for the following proportions of urban increase beginning with 1870–80, the first decade for which data are available:

Decade	Percentage
1870–80	16.5
1880–90	23.5
1890–1900	14.6
1900–1910	23.7

The following two decades showed a sizable drop, to 6.8 and 5.1 percent respectively.[10] Presumably immigrants moved to farms rather than to cities during those decades and the native-born migration from farms to cities accounted for most of the urban increase. In any case almost all large cities, especially in the North and West, were for many decades quite cosmopolitan. New York City even today has radio broadcasts in seventeen languages and publishes sixty-nine periodicals (daily and weekly) in twenty-four languages other than English. The 1960 census enumerated 1,558,690 foreign-born and 3,785,451 persons of foreign stock in a population of about 8 million. Given the almost universal presence of ethnocentrism, the variety that makes the city attractive to some increases the problems of those who believe in democracy.

Intergroup relations and interpersonal relations influenced by ingroup values are exacerbated by high urban population densities (e.g., Chicago, 15,836 persons per square mile; Jersey City, 21,238; New York City, 24,697; St. Louis, 12,296; San Francisco, 16,599). Add to this the deteriorated physical plant of so many cities (housing, school, medical, hospital, and recreational facilities and so on), plus the

---

[10] Eldridge and Thomas, op. cit., p. 216.

TABLE 7. PROPORTIONS OF WHITES AND NEGROES LIVING IN URBAN AND METROPOLITAN AREAS, 1910–60

Census Year	Urban		Metropolitan	
	Negro	White	Negro	White
1910	27	49	29	48
1920	35	53	34	51
1930	44	58	42	56
1940	49	59	45	56
1950	62	64	57	60
1960	73	70	65	63

Source: *The Negroes in the United States: Their Economic and Social Situation*, Bulletin No. 1511 (Washington, D.C.: U.S. Department of Labor, June 1966), Tables IA-6 and IA-7.

TABLE 8. MOBILITY STATUS OF U.S. POPULATION 1 YEAR OLD AND OVER, APRIL 1968–MARCH 1969

Status	Number (thousands)	Percentage
Movers, total	35,933	18.3
Same county	22,993	11.7
Migrants	12,940	6.6
Within state	6,316	3.2
Between states	6,625	3.4
Contiguous	2,170	1.1
Noncontiguous	4,454	2.3
Abroad the previous March	1,399	0.7

Source: U.S. Bureau of the Census, *Current Population Reports*, "Mobility of the Population of the United States, April 1967 to March 1968," Series P-20, No. 193 (Washington, D.C.: U.S. Government Printing Office, December 26, 1969).

environmental poisoning that is becoming a major hazard to survival. Add also the widespread tendency to exploit the weak and the ignorant that has been documented throughout history.[11] The result makes one

---

[11] For a revealing treatment of immigrants coming to the United States, *see* Robert Ernst, *Immigrant Life in New York City, 1825–1863* (New York: King's Crown Press, 1949). A recent study deals with two New York City slum areas: David Caplowitz, *The Poor Pay More* (New York: Free Press of Glencoe, 1963).

wonder not why there have been riots in city slums and violence in intergroup relations, but why there have not been more such manifestations of frustrated ambitions and hopes.

Migration not only adds to the cultural variety of city life by bringing in new and sometimes conflicting ethnic elements, but it adds to the difficulty of coping with urban problems by the rapidity with which change takes place. Natural increase is inherently a slower process than is in-migration; usually even decrease through biological factors is slower than that sometimes occurring through out-migration. And social change at a slow rate can sometimes be weathered without the disruptions occasioned by rapid changes.

One trouble in the building of cities in Europe and the United States has been that time has been needed to allow various factors to mesh—and time has often been lacking. Reports of the early days of "new" cities echo and reecho with similar tales of land speculation, shoddy housing, pigs used as a means of garbage disposal, open sewers, unpaved streets, insufficient schools, "paucity of public space," lack of civic spirit, lack of fire and police protection, antagonism between the more affluent outlying neighborhoods and the central city, and so on.[12] The vulnerability of cities to national economic depressions is well known. For example, Pittsburgh was economically crippled during the ten-year period 1815–24, losing "two market houses and its watch and was unable to cope with mounting relief requests."[13]

Negro Migration

Cincinnati is a good point from which to start an examination of another part of the urban mobility mosaic, an aspect of city growth that has always been complicated by a fundamental weakness of many cultures, including American democracy—color discrimination. Escaped and freed slaves gravitated to cities along the northern edge of slave territory. Cincinnati's Negro population made up 10 percent of its total by the late 1820s. While escaped slaves were aided by many liberal whites, more powerful majority elements engaged in discrimination of various kinds including segregation, armed raids into Negro neighborhoods, threats of deportation, and plans for Negro "colonization" in either Africa or Canada. At least eleven hundred Negroes left the city within a few months during one outbreak, including "many of the most industrious, stable, and prosperous members of the Negro community. They had the financial resources and social energy needed for movement, while the less successful and weaker stayed behind."[14] Many resettled in Canada.

The Civil War gave all Negroes for the first time the legal right to migrate from the South to other parts of the country. Economic and social conditions were not favorable, but there was a steady movement North and West. The number and percentage of the total Negro population enumerated in nonsouthern regions rose slowly. The South's share of the Negro population dropped from slightly over 90 percent in 1870 to just 89 percent in 1910, 60 percent in 1960, and 55 percent in 1966.

It is instructive to go beyond regional population gains and losses of both whites and nonwhites. Data are found in Table 9 for figures by region and state for the years since the 1960 census. Forty states and the District of Columbia lost population from some segments through out-migra-

---

[12] Reports containing such experiences range geographically from the Ruhr Valley to Manchester and the western frontier of the United States in the early 1800s (at that time the cities of Cincinnati, Lexington, Louisville, Pittsburgh, and St. Louis). Among numerous others, *see* Bert F. Hoselitz, "The City, the Factory, and Economic Growth," *American Economic Review*, Vol. 45 (May 1955), pp. 166–184; and Richard C. Wade, *The Urban Frontier, the Rise of Western Cities, 1790–1830* (Cambridge, Mass.: Harvard University Press, 1959).

[13] Wade, op. cit., pp. 274–275.

[14] Ibid., pp. 224–229.

TABLE 9. RECENT POPULATION CHANGES BY RACE [a]

Geographic Area	Population, July 1, 1967 (thousands) White	Nonwhite	Change in Population (percentage) April 1, 1960—July 1, 1967 White	Nonwhite	Net Total Migration [b] (thousands) White	Nonwhite	Nonwhite Population (percentage) April 1, 1950	April 1, 1960	July 1, 1967
United States									
Including armed forces overseas	175,055	24,063	9.8	17.2	2,584	288	10.7	11.4	12.1
Excluding armed forces overseas	173,921	23,942	9.5	16.8	2,089	184	10.7	11.4	12.1
New England	10,964	380	7.0	42.3	−30	56	1.6	2.5	3.3
Maine	975	7	1.2	17.2	−63	−1	.3	.6	.7
New Hampshire	687	4	13.7	54.6	36	0	.2	.4	.6
Vermont	417	3	7.2	280.2	−3	2	.1	.2	.7
Massachusetts	5,267	166	4.9	32.3	−105	17	1.7	2.4	3.1
Rhode Island	874	27	4.2	30.0	−22	2	1.9	2.4	3.0
Connecticut	2,744	173	13.2	55.3	127	36	2.7	4.4	6.0
Middle Atlantic	32,869	3,807	5.1	31.8	−291	443	6.4	8.5	10.4
New York	15,977	2,046	4.5	36.8	−228	284	6.5	8.9	11.4
New Jersey	6,244	737	12.7	39.6	323	111	6.7	8.7	10.6
Pennsylvania	10,648	1,024	1.9	18.3	−386	48	6.1	7.6	8.8
East North Central	35,380	3,809	6.4	28.2	−652	361	6.1	8.2	9.7
Ohio	9,545	943	7.1	18.4	−92	41	6.5	8.2	9.0
Indiana	4,695	317	7.0	15.7	−76	0	4.4	5.9	6.3
Illinois	9,529	1,358	5.8	26.8	−126	89	7.6	10.6	12.5
Michigan	7,553	1,055	6.6	43.1	−211	211	7.1	9.4	12.3
Wisconsin	4,058	136	5.2	46.4	−147	20	1.2	2.4	3.2
West North Central	15,266	742	3.5	15.1	−613	−9	3.4	4.2	4.6
Minnesota	3,562	63	5.6	49.1	−131	12	1.0	1.2	1.7
Iowa	2,741	31	.5	7.5	−185	−3	.8	1.0	1.1
Missouri	4,136	451	5.4	13.6	−17	−4	7.6	9.2	9.8
North Dakota	616	16	−.6	24.0	−66	−1	1.8	2.0	2.5
South Dakota	638	30	−2.3	9.4	−73	−5	3.7	4.0	4.5
Nebraska	1,403	40	2.1	9.4	−83	−5	1.8	2.6	2.8
Kansas	2,170	111	4.4	11.1	−58	−3	4.0	4.6	4.9

South Atlantic	23,197	15.7	7.8	1,404	−421	24.3	22.8	21.6
Delaware	448	16.6	22.6	25	3	13.9	13.9	14.5
Maryland	3,069	19.2	16.0	240	3	16.6	17.0	16.6
District of Columbia	265	−23.2	29.7	−85	55	35.4	54.8	67.2
Virginia	3,639	15.8	9.4	180	−26	22.2	20.8	19.9
West Virginia	1,724	−2.6	−8.1	−165	−11	5.7	4.9	4.6
North Carolina	3,863	13.6	3.4	146	−122	26.6	25.4	23.6
South Carolina	1,804	16.3	.3	99	−123	38.9	34.9	31.6
Georgia	3,326	18.1	3.4	227	−135	30.9	28.6	25.9
Florida	5,059	24.5	10.1	737	−65	21.8	17.9	16.2
East South Central	10,345	10.8	−1.6	223	−405	23.6	22.5	20.5
Kentucky	2,981	5.7	.9	−85	−17	6.9	7.2	6.9
Tennessee	3,333	11.9	2.3	115	−61	16.1	16.5	15.3
Alabama	2,572	12.6	−2.3	91	−149	32.1	30.1	27.2
Mississippi	1,459	16.0	−3.9	102	−178	45.4	42.3	37.8
West South Central	15,848	12.5	10.5	343	−145	17.2	16.9	16.6
Arkansas	1,598	14.5	−4.2	100	−82	22.4	21.9	19.0
Louisiana	2,512	13.6	10.1	66	−58	33.0	32.1	31.4
Oklahoma	2,288	8.5	3.5	42	−26	9.0	9.5	9.1
Texas	9,450	12.8	16.9	135	21	12.8	12.6	13.0
Mountain	7,382	13.3	30.9	103	5	4.5	5.0	5.7
Montana	670	3.0	20.7	−38	−2	3.2	3.6	4.1
Idaho	691	5.1	2.0	−32	−2	1.2	1.5	1.4
Wyoming	311	−3.7	12.0	−44	−1	2.2	2.2	2.5
Colorado	1,931	13.5	52.1	59	18	2.1	3.0	4.0
New Mexico	903	3.1	31.5	−102	−1	7.5	7.9	9.9
Arizona	1,474	26.0	22.9	161	−13	12.7	10.2	10.0
Utah	1,003	14.8	13.1	0	−2	1.7	1.9	1.9
Nevada	399	51.5	69.5	99	8	6.4	7.7	8.5
Pacific	22,670	17.4	35.0	1,602	299	7.8	8.9	10.1
Washington	3,076	11.8	30.0	112	10	2.6	3.6	4.1
Oregon	1,941	12.1	9.1	90	−4	1.6	2.1	2.0
California	17,240	19.3	38.8	1,423	240	6.3	8.0	9.2
Alaska	205	17.4	27.9	0	−1	27.9	22.8	24.4
Hawaii	208	2.9	28.2	−23	54	77.0	68.0	72.6

a A minus sign denotes a population loss.

b Comprises net in-migrants from abroad, net interstate migration, and movement of persons in the armed forces.

Source: 1967 population and migration, for geographic areas, computed by the Statistical Bureau of the Metropolitan Life Insurance Company from data of the U.S. Bureau of the Census and the National Center for Health Statistics, *Statistical Bulletin* (May 1969), p. 8.

tion: thirteen lost white population only; fifteen, nonwhite only; and thirteen lost both white and nonwhite. Ten states gained in both categories.

The District of Columbia reported that 67.2 percent of its population was nonwhite in July 1967, up 24.4 percent in seven years. Other nonwhite gains, less dramatic with respect to percentage, are still impressive in absolute numbers, as for instance New York's increase of 284,000 nonwhites, California's 240,000, and Michigan's 211,000.

Negro increase in urban residence in this century has been most dramatic. Southern cities with a population of over 10,000 in 1890 contained a total of 700,000 Negroes, or almost 43 percent of the southern Negro population, but increasing dissatisfaction with prevailing discriminatory practices seems to have led some of these persons to migrate northward.[15] The new southern industrial centers such as Atlanta, Birmingham, and Memphis had Negro populations of 33–40 percent. Border cities such as Baltimore, Louisville, and Washington were between 15 and 28 percent Negro.

By 1930, 44 percent of America's Negro population was living in cities, but the rate of urban increase fell between 1930 and 1940 because of the Depression. In the latter year, 48.6 percent of Negroes were living in cities, but "war prosperity" accelerated migration and increased the proportion to 62.4 percent in 1950. By 1960 there had been a further increase to 73 percent. Even in the South, where 74.2 percent of Negroes had been living in rural areas in 1900, only 25 percent were so listed in the 1960 census. An insignificant number leaving the South had gone to

farms in either the North or the West. As a matter of fact, the proportion of Negroes on farms in the North was reduced from 3 percent in 1900 to 1.5 percent in 1960.

Almost one-third of all the Negroes in the nation (6,330,273) were living in the twenty-five largest cities by 1960. Their proportion in the total population of these cities varied from 3.2 percent in Minneapolis to a majority—54.8 percent—in the nation's capital (see Table 10). New York City's nonwhite percentage was almost 15 percent; it ranked ninth among the nation's twenty-five largest cities.

Why People Migrate

Why do so many people pull up roots so often? Reasons are found in both statistical analyses and in personal testimony. First one must differentiate between what the Columbia University study of Puerto Rican migration to New York City called "deciders" and "followers."[16] Fifty-four percent of those interviewed said they had made "their own" decision. It often turned out to be the decision of the family and it also influenced the decision of relatives and friends. This *caveat* should help us understand the following summary of a tremendous amount of material on the causes of migration.

Immigration and Business Cycles

Studies of the ebb and flow of immigration to the United States all come broadly to the same conclusion as that reached by the first major effort to analyze the subject objectively: that the movement from Europe to this country was "on the whole

---

[15] Blake McKelvey, *The Urbanization of America 1860–1915* (New Brunswick, N.J.: Rutgers University Press, 1963), p. 69; Florence M. Cromien, *Negroes in the City of New York 1790–1960* (New York: City Commission on Intergroup Relations, 1962), pp. 8–9.

[16] C. Wright Mills, Clarence Senior, and Rose K. Goldsen, *The Puerto Rican Journey: New York's Newest Migrants* (New York: Harper & Bros., 1950), pp. 45–56. Shryock, op. cit., pp. 404–408, later used "primary" and "secondary" to make the same distinction.

TABLE 10. NONWHITE POPULATION OF NATION'S TWENTY-FIVE LARGEST CITIES, 1950–60,
BY NUMBER, PERCENTAGE OF TOTAL POPULATION, AND PERCENTAGE INCREASE

City	Total Nonwhite Population, 1960	Percentage of Total Population, 1960	Percentage Increase, 1950–60
New York	1,141,322	14.7	47.2
Chicago	837,656	23.6	64.4
Los Angeles	417,207	16.8	97.2
Philadelphia	535,033	26.7	41.2
Detroit	487,174	29.2	60.4
Baltimore	328,416	35.0	45.3
Houston	217,672	23.2	73.2
Cleveland	253,108	28.9	69.3
Washington, D.C.	418,693	54.8	47.3
St. Louis	216,022	28.8	39.9
San Francisco	135,913	18.4	66.8
Milwaukee	65,752	8.9	189.1
Boston	68,493	9.8	60.2
Dallas	131,211	19.3	125.6
New Orleans	234,931	37.4	28.6
Pittsburgh	101,739	16.8	22.6
San Antonio	43,221	7.4	47.3
San Diego	44,712	7.8	143.5
Seattle	46,528	8.4	73.9
Buffalo	73,388	13.8	94.7
Cincinnati	109,682	21.8	39.4
Memphis	184,725	37.1	25.7
Denver	35,261	7.1	92.9
Atlanta	186,820	38.3	54.0
Minneapolis	15,594	3.2	84.2

Source: U.S. Bureau of the Census, *United States Census of Population, 1960* (Washington, D.C.: U.S. Government Printing Office, 1963).

dominated by conditions in the United States. The 'pull' is stronger than the 'push.' " [17]

Thomas, studying Swedish emigration, concluded after an exhaustive examination of business cycles in both Sweden and the United States and their interrelationships that "industrial 'pull' to America . . . played an overwhelmingly important role in respect to the annual fluctuation from the seventies to the end of the emigration era just before the war." [18] A British scholar approached the problem by analyzing the cyclical economic relationships between Great Britain and the United States. Essentially his explanation puts less emphasis on cyclical pull as such than on (1) components of business cycles (railroad and canal building, availability of land, fluctuations in foreign trade, and investment) and (2) on balances between push and pull factors.[19] The result is a more complicated statement of how important economic growth is to understanding migration. Several econometrists have analyzed United States internal migration and pinpointed the availability of jobs as

[17] Harry Jerome, *Migration and Business Cycles* (New York: National Bureau of Economic Research, 1926) chaps. 4–8.

[18] Dorothy Swaine Thomas, *Social and Economic Aspects of Swedish Population Movements, 1750–1933* (New York: Macmillan Co., 1941), pp. 166–169.

[19] Thomas Brinley, *Migration and Economic Growth* (New York: Cambridge University Press, 1954).

the single most important factor in why people move.

Inadequacy of the Push-Pull Dichotomy

A major objection to the use of the concept of push and pull is that it falls into an error common to reasoning by analogy —it oversimplifies the process through which the migrant must go in reaching a decision to migrate. Even worse, it treats the migrant as if he really does not have a part in the decision at all. However, it is in the nature of man to make choices. Few of the many empirical studies of areas of out-migration give any support to the idea that the person who migrates could not have chosen to remain in his own area. There are obvious exceptions: political or racial persecution, war, floods, and various natural catastrophes may literally drive people from their homes and make it impossible for them to return. The number of such cases is fortunately relatively small.

Usually we are dealing with decisions that must be made between remaining in one's original locality at a given level of living or migrating to a new locality in the expectation that that level can be raised. The close direct relationship between the economic cycle and migration, which will be discussed later, indicates the validity of this statement.

In order to illustrate this subject, let us look at a movement that technically is internal migration but that resembles immigration in that it involves (1) air or water transportation to the United States and (2) the migration of persons who, while legally citizens, are often different enough culturally to be treated as "foreigners."

Migration was taking place from Puerto Rico to the United States long before the island was taken over in 1898 as part of Theodore Roosevelt's plan to protect the Isthmus of Panama. Records of the annual population flow have been kept since 1908–09, and they are revealing whether

stated as annual numbers or as yearly averages for the following significant periods: 1909–30, 1,986; 1931–40, 904; 1941–50, 18,794; 1951–60, 41,212; 1961–66, 9,522.

The slump in the 1930s is plain; a ragged pattern by years in the 1940s would reflect lack of transportation in the earlier years and a spurt to fill waiting jobs as airplanes began to meet the travel demand. Annual data show that in fourteen of the 57 years between 1909 and 1966 (1909 is when records were first kept), there has been a net migration back to Puerto Rico. There have been other times when the flow dropped but did not reverse in response to changes in employment opportunities in the states; the most brusque brought a 69 percent reduction, from 69,124 in 1953 to 21,531 in 1954, in response to what was called a "rolling readjustment." Two recent years of net return migration were 1961 and 1963.[20]

One has only to compare data on levels of living on the island for the periods 1909–30 and 1951–60 to see that the pull of employment opportunities on the mainland is far more decisive than the so-called push factor. Conditions on the island were worse when migration was lowest. The death rate, for example, was around 22–24 per 1,000 in the earlier period, compared with 7–10 per 1,000 in 1951–60. Such rates are quite sensitive to economic conditions and are at least as meaningful as the much higher per capita income in the latter period. An analysis of the motivations of the Puerto Rican migrant made in 1948 found that the subjective feelings of the migrants conform to what would be expected by reasoning from the economic data and the comparison of levels of living

---

[20] Figures are from the San Juan office of the Immigration and Naturalization Service and have been published by the Commonwealth of Puerto Rico Planning Board and in recent years by the Migration Division of the Puerto Rico Department of Labor.

as these might influence the flow of migration.

Two of the classic studies of Negro migration northward make the same point. In fact, St. Helena Island, South Carolina, was chosen for a 1928 study specifically because "problems of racial friction and lawlessness, often mentioned as important causes of general Negro migration, were absent." [21]

The key to the decision to migrate that must be made by each individual (even most of those labeled "followers" by the Columbia University study) was well stated by Lively and Taeuber in 1936:

People do not move primarily because the level of living in the area where they are is low but rather because they have become aware of a different level of living which appears more attractive.[22]

They cite the fact that often large-scale migration has taken place from farming areas such as the Corn Belt that are far above average in wealth and amenities. However, these areas lie within the zone of influence of metropolitan areas that, through mass media, present a picture of another way of life.

This helps us shift our pattern of thinking from the idea of migration as a mechanical reaction to a combination of poor conditions at home and employment opportunities elsewhere to a more adequate social framework.[23]

California in the 1930s is sometimes cited as an example of push preeminence. But net migration into California fell off in that decade and shot up again in the 1940s.[24]

Gordon and Thompson have both studied the relation between in-migration and business conditions. They and Stanbery all agree that, in Gordon's words: "Marked fluctuations in population growth and in net immigration have been associated with pronounced variations in the rate of employment expansion." Gordon sums up the study by writing that "decisions as to timing of migration appear to depend very largely on what is happening to job opportunities." [25]

A study of in-migration to Los Angeles, 1891–1953, found a moderately high, significant coefficient of correlation between local business conditions in and migration to the city. For the entire 63 years, it was .56; for 1925–53, it was a much higher .79.[26]

Evidence from a somewhat different angle is found in a study of how the new industrial labor force was built up in the early stages of Puerto Rican industrialization. Reynolds and Gregory found that most male factory workers had transferred from other sectors of the economy: 43 percent from agriculture and 35 percent from service and other industries.

The men recruited from agriculture were virtually all wage workers rather than proprietors, and so were used to being in a wage system. They were not, however, from the lowest levels of the rural proletariat. Most

---

[21] Clyde V. Kiser, *Sea Island to City* (New York: Columbia University Press, 1932), p. 10. *See also* Louise V. Kennedy, *The Negro Peasant Turns Cityward* (New York: Columbia University Press, 1930).

[22] Charles Elson Lively and Conrad Taeuber, *Rural Migration in the United States*, 1936, p. 79.

[23] Suggestions for such a framework are found in Stephen L. McDonald, "Farm Outmigration as an Integrative Adjustment to Economic Growth," *Social Forces* Vol. 33, No. 2 (December 1955), pp. 119–128.

[24] Henry Van Beuren Stanbery, *Some New Techniques for Area Population Projections* (Los Angeles: Haynes Foundation, 1960).

[25] Margaret S. Gordon, "Immigration and Its Effect on Labor Force Characteristics," *Monthly Labor Review*, Vol. 82, No. 5 (May 1959), pp. 495, 500. *See also* Gordon, *Employment Expansion and Population Growth: The California Experience* (Berkeley: University of California Press, 1954); and Warren S. Thompson, *Population* (Los Angeles: Haynes Foundation, 1955).

[26] Robert M. Williams, "Fluctuations in Urban Growth," *Papers and Proceedings*, Vol. 1 (Philadelphia: Regional Science Association, 1955), pp. E-1–14.

of them held year-round jobs, which are the best farm jobs in Puerto Rico, and few were unemployed. They were somewhat superior in education to the island population in general. They were also quite young, typically under 30 and often under 20, at the time of entering industry. The picture is that of a superior group drawn into industry by its inherent attractiveness rather than the dregs of the countryside forced into the factory as an escape from misery.[27]

Economic Growth and Internal Migration

There is a wealth of material on the direct relation between the general level of economic opportunity in the United States and the response of persons residing in the coterminous area. Only one major source will be cited here: a monumental study of movements (of both immigrants and migrants) between 1870 and 1950 undertaken by the Population Studies Center of the University of Pennsylvania. Among its major conclusions are these:

Over a span of seven decades, net migration to and within the United States responded positively and significantly to decadal swings in economic activity, increasing in periods of prosperity and falling off during depressions. All the major identifiable nativity-race-color classes of the population responded to these temporal variations in economic activity: the response of native whites was strong during the whole period considered; that of foreign-born whites was equally strong until immigration restrictions stemmed their influx; that of Negroes was more noticeable after opportunities in the industrial North were opened in the early decades of the century and firmly established during World War I.[28]

Who Migrates?

More light is cast on the socioeconomic factors of migration by asking the question: What kinds of persons migrate? In seeking an answer, still another question must be considered: Which migration do you mean?

Migration can be highly selective with respect to a given characteristic in one area, and be selective to only a mild degree, or not at all, in another area. If the selectivity of migration can vary in both pattern and intensity between different places, it is equally plausible that it can vary between different periods of time. Hence, it is fruitless to seek permanent flexible differentials in migration that will not vary, to some degree at least, in pattern or intensity with time and place.[29]

However, a mass of data and a flood of studies may be summarized for major migrations, especially when attention is concentrated on the "deciders": late adolescents and young adults make up the largest category. An increasingly important stream must be noted—older persons migrating because of retirement. There is, of course, a natural age differential between original and return migrations, which is accentuated by the retirement factor.[30]

When sex is added to age as an analytic variable, inferences become more difficult. The movement from farms to cities (a decreasingly important migrant stream) seems generally to be selective of females if shorter distances are involved; males, if distances are greater. Overall it seems Bogue's generalization comes close to the consensus of students of migration: "Males are slightly more migratory than females between the ages of 20 and 64. At ages older and younger than this, females were as migratory as males, or more so." [31]

---

[27] Reynolds and Gregory, op. cit., p. 297.

[28] Hope T. Eldridge and Dorothy Swaine Thomas, *Population Redistribution and Economic Growth, United States, 1870–1950*, Vol. VIII, "Demographic Analyses and Interrelationships" (Philadelphia: American Philosophical Society, 1964), p. 368.

[29] Donald J. Bogue and Margaret J. Hagood, *Differential Migration in the Corn and Cotton Belts* (Oxford, Ohio: Scripps Foundation, 1953), p. 125.

[30] Hope T. Eldridge, "Primary, Secondary, and Return Migration in the United States, 1955–1960," *Demography*, Vol. 2 (1965), pp. 444–455.

[31] Donald J. Bogue, *The Population of the United States* (Glencoe, Ill.: Free Press, 1959), p. 377.

Negroes on the whole are less likely to migrate than whites, but when they do migrate their decision seems to be closely related to economic opportunity. Generally they migrate shorter distances than do whites, but two peaks of longer distance shifts, World War I and the later stages of World War II, indicate how economic pull alters the situation.[32]

Age also is a differentiating factor in Negro migration, as Bogue points out:

Although the white population was more migratory than the non-white at every age, the greatest disparity in rate between the two groups was found at ages 20 to 24 years. At these ages young white persons were more or less freely wandering in search of their fortunes, but many non-white youths were being forced to accept whatever opportunities were available in their local communities. However, when they had attained the age of about 30, non-white persons tended to become only slightly less migratory than white persons of the same age.[33]

Usually migrants are better educated than the population from which they move. Dozens of studies have documented this "brain drain," which is detrimental to the economy of the sending area. The most recent nationwide data are analyses of the 1960 census and the 1968 Current Population Survey, in which years of school completed are shown by division of birth and of residence, by age, sex, and color.[34] It must be noted that this usually does not mean that the newcomer's education is above that of those in the receiving community. Higher educational levels are generally found in areas with higher incomes.

Personal Reasons for Migration

We have been dealing with migration streams somewhat as if they had a life of their own. Obviously millions of people are involved, and some studies have asked these people "why?" Occupational selectivity was quite general in all United States internal migration, including the Puerto Rican stream.[35] Shryock summarizes what has been found in census surveys:

A majority of adult males move to take a job or to look for work whereas the mobility of most women and children is derivative, i.e., contingent upon the mobility of the husband or father. Even among adult males, reasons not directly connected with employment, such as a change in marital status, a housing problem, or a health problem, account for many moves. These noneconomic reasons are more prominent in the shorter than in the longer types of moves. Mobility differentials by age and sex are closely tied in with the family cycle as broadly defined.[36]

The Columbia University study found that 89 percent of the Puerto Rican deciders were primarily job oriented. Even they had complementary reasons, however. In many cases relatives or friends had already made the move; in addition to having located jobs for those still in Puerto Rico, they represented old ties of family or friendship. Better schools for the children, richer cultural environment, and so on were also cited frequently.[37]

The stated motives of Negroes migrating to several cities, mainly New York, from an island off the South Carolina coast were studied from 1928 to 1930 by Kiser. He

---

[32] Shryock, op. cit., pp. 404, 422–424.

[33] Bogue, op. cit., p. 415.

[34] U.S. Bureau of the Census, *United States Census of Population, 1960*, "Lifetime and Recent Migration," P.C. (2) 2D, Table 8; and *Current Population Reports*, "Educational Attainment," Series P-20, No. 182 (Washington, D.C.: U.S. Government Printing Office, 1963, and April 28, 1969; respectively).

[35] Bogue, op. cit., pp. 384–386, 416; and Mills et al., op. cit., pp. 30, 33–36, 184.

[36] Shryock, op. cit., p. 424.

[37] Mills et al., op. cit., pp. 45–46, Table 18. A more recent study of a national cross-section of the mobile population of the United States by survey research methods comes to the same general conclusions; see John B. Lansing and Eva Mueller, *The Geographic Mobility of Labor* (Ann Arbor: University of Michigan Institute for Social Research, 1967).

sums up his findings in the following two sentences:

Racial, religious, and political problems have played little part. Farmer boys and girls of St. Helena, as elsewhere, are imbued with the idea that they must go to the cities in order to find "good jobs" and a more stimulating environment.[38]

If most migrants have job-related reasons for moving, then what about "movers," that is, those who move within county lines? They are by far the largest category of those reported each year to be living in a house different from the one occupied the year before. One of the Current Population Surveys has reported on motivation of both migrants and movers.[39] Job-related reasons were given by 65 percent of the male migrants aged 18–64, but this dropped to 12.4 percent among the movers. Among these housing held first place, being given as a reason by 61.9 percent of all movers in this age group. Change in family status impelled 18.2 percent to move, but that figure almost doubles in the age group 18–24, rising to 36.1 percent.

The family life cycle was found highly relevant by one of the most thorough studies of reasons for moving. Rossi, in his study in four Philadelphia neighborhoods, concluded: "Mobility is the mechanism by which a family's housing is brought into adjustment with its housing needs."[40] The early years may not bring a move until children come. Unless the family grows unexpectedly large, the child-rearing period may well be spent in the same house. When children leave home for school, military or civilian public service, or to marry,

family housing needs shift again. It is at this stage that the much-heralded "return to the central city" is most popular. Thus far there does not seem to be a dependable study of the extent to which this movement exists and how much consists only of verbal reports.

Return Migration

As Ravenstein noted almost a century ago, migration is not a one-way stream.[41] Many of those who migrate eventually return to their original place of residence. A number of studies of worker mobility cite "work gave out" as a reason for "going home." Other widely given reasons are illness of the respondent or illness or the death of a family member. An early study of Puerto Ricans who returned from jobs on the mainland showed family reasons in first place. Forty-five percent of all who returned to Puerto Rico after a term of work for which they had been recruited by the War Manpower Commission gave "death (or illness) in the family," or simply "I wanted to see my family" as their reason. Second, with 23 percent, was "contract expired"; illness, with only 7 percent, ran a poor third.[42]

Almost half of the 3,000 men recruited (47 percent) had *not* returned to Puerto Rico, however, and most of the returnees (81 percent) said that they would go back to the states if they were offered a permanent job. Forty-five percent said they would go back if offered another temporary job.

Two years later the Columbia University study of Puerto Ricans in New York City found that about 8 percent of the sample of migrants interviewed who had been adults when they left Puerto Rico had been "trial migrants," that is, they

[38] Op. cit., p. 144.
[39] U.S. Bureau of the Census, *Current Population Reports*, "Reasons for Moving: March 1962 to March 1963," Series P-20, No. 154 (Washington, D.C.: U.S. Government Printing Office, August 22, 1966).
[40] Peter H. Rossi, *Why Families Move* (New York: Free Press, 1955), pp. 7–8, 42, 121–122.

[41] Op. cit.
[42] Clarence Senior, *Puerto Rican Emigration* (Rio Piedras, Puerto Rico: Social Science Research Center, University of Puerto Rico, 1947), p. 32.

had previously lived and worked in the states, had returned to the island, and then came back to stay. The return migration most often was for "family reasons." [43]

A study in 1962–64 of some 34,000 migrants who returned to Puerto Rico divided them into successful (12 percent), moderately successful (63 percent), and unsuccessful (25 percent). The last means that the individuals involved had received in the previous year an income that was average or lower-than-average by Puerto Rican standards. Many case studies are cited to show the components of the decision to return.[44]

Benefits from Migration

Would people migrate if they did not feel they could benefit thereby? Would migration be encouraged—even permitted—if there were not also benefits to the national economy, the receiving area, and even perhaps to the sending area? Let us examine ways in which each of these might profit from mobility.

To the worker. The tremendous amount of internal migration indicates that millions of persons at least *believe* that pulling up roots and preparing to sink them elsewhere will benefit them and their families. Many studies indicate that generally they are correct, especially if they migrate from depressed areas. Studies of workers migrating from Harrison County, West Virginia, Mt. Vernon, Illinois, and Puerto Rico give details for specific migrations. A national study based on records of the Bureau of Old Age and Survivors Insurance for 1939–47 shows that the multistate worker is almost always above the national average in wages.[45] A more

directly relevant study of OASI data for Michigan and Ohio found the following:

The exchange of workers with other States and among areas within the two States resulted in an absolute decrease of workers in the lowest income categories, and a disproportionately large increase in male workers with average or just below average incomes.[46]

Usually increased income arises from upward occupational mobility. This may well be even more important to a worker's sense of well-being than the increased wage. Social status is a crucially decisive factor in human behavior. Opportunity to rise from floor sweeper to machine-wiper, then to mechanic's helper, and from there to mechanic is an integral and invaluable part of this country's economic and social system. Freedman and Hawley tested and proved the hypothesis that migration resulted in occupational mobility, even during the Depression of the 1930s.[47] The occupational mobility of a group of migrants was compared with the mobility of control groups of nonmigrants of similar characteristics at either end of the migration route. The researchers analyzed the work histories from 1930 to 1935 of all white male migrants to Flint or Grand Rapids from other places in Michigan who

---

[43] Mills et al., op. cit., p. 57.

[44] José Hernandez Alvarez, *Return Migration to Puerto Rico*, Population Monograph Series, No. 1 (Berkeley: University of California Press, 1967).

[45] Vincent F. Gegan and Samuel H. Thompson, "Worker Mobility in a Labor Surplus Area,"

Monthly Labor Review, Vol. 80, No. 12 (December 1957), pp. 1451–1456; Richard C. Wilcock, "Employment Effects of a Plant Shutdown in a Depressed Area," *Monthly Labor Review*, Vol. 80, No. 9 (September 1957), pp. 1047–1052. *See also* Mills et al., op. cit.; W. S. Woytinsky, *Employment and Wages in the United States* (New York: Twentieth Century Fund, 1953), p. 388; Lloyd G. Reynolds and Peter Gregory, *Wages, Productivity, and Industrialization in Puerto Rico* (Homewood, Ill.: Richard D. Irwin, 1965), chaps. 8 and 10.

[46] Donald J. Bogue, *A Methodological Study of Migration and Labor Mobility in Michigan and Ohio in 1947* (Oxford, Ohio: Scripps Foundation Studies in Population Distribution, June 1952), p. 60.

[47] Ronald Freedman and Amos H. Hawley, "Migration and Occupational Mobility in the Depression," *American Journal of Sociology*, Vol. 55, No. 5 (September 1945), pp. 170–177.

were at least 25 years old at the time of their migration.

The study indicated, for this wide sample, that after migration the migrants were more frequently occupationally mobile than the control nonmigrants at either the source or the destination of the migration. Although the migrant-nonmigrant comparisons were made in several ways with somewhat different results, in no case was the occupational mobility of the migrants less than 2.7 times as great as that of the nonmigrant controls.

As a rule the migrant improves his occupational status and his income. Exceptions to the rule undoubtedly occur, and it must also be noted that often only one person in a family—the breadwinner—is in the labor force. It may well be, especially in the case of families from underdeveloped areas, that the immediate impact of migration is not a happy one for the remainder of the family. Many families foresee this; the breadwinner precedes and "gets settled" before sending for the other members.

The social selectivity that has been seen to operate in all voluntary migrations is likely to skew the age, sex, skill, and other characteristics of migrants as a group in the direction of categories in which higher-than-average income levels are found. Color interferes and helps hold down economic gains among migrants, however. Age also interferes with increasing incomes beyond a certain point and even entrance into many occupations. However, even with these qualifications, generally workers can depend fairly well on increasing their incomes from new jobs obtained through migration.[48]

To the national economy. The "national economy" is an abstraction that sometimes seems difficult to relate to everyday life and work. However, a moment's thought will remind us that full employment at adequate incomes and fairly stable price levels are helpful for the vast majority. The evidence from general economists, business groups such as the Committee for Economic Development, and many others is well stated by Palmer in an epilogue to a series of studies on labor mobility:

One element in the rising level of national productivity over past decades that is frequently overlooked is the willingness of American workers to move from less productive to more productive types of economic activity. Such changes sometimes necessitate geographic shifts and sometimes not, but the combinations and permutations of occupational, industrial, and geographic mobility that are characteristics of the American labor market have been an important factor in maintaining and raising levels of productivity in the nation and in reducing extreme localization of unemployment, when major changes occurred in the structure of local employment. These social values are important to conserve.[49]

It must be obvious that internal migration is far more than the means by which an individual worker improves his income, the satisfaction he receives from his job, and the greater amenities and "life chances" in a new locality for himself and his family. It is also an indispensable method by which the complex, highly productive economic

---

[48] For factors interfering with a worker's ability to obtain new employment in specific cases of plant shutdowns, *see* Felician F. Foltman, *White-and Blue-Collars in a Mill Shutdown* (Ithaca: New York State School of Industrial and Labor Relations, 1968). The chief handicaps were found to be age, blue-collar status with what that implies in lower educational levels, and lower skill levels even within blue-collar ranks. Re-

sistance to moving was found to be quite deleterious to obtaining a new job, especially for the older, lower skill level, blue-collar worker.

[49] Gladys L. Palmer in E. Wight Bakke, ed., *Labor Mobility and Economic Opportunity* (Cambridge, Mass.: MIT Press, 1954), pp. 113–114. *See also* Paul H. Douglas, *Real Wages in the United States, 1890–1926* (Boston: Houghton-Mifflin, 1930), p. 395; Lloyd G. Reynolds, "Structural Determinants of Cost Inflation and Remedial Measures," *Monthly Labor Review*, Vol. 82 (August 1959), pp. 872–875; and *How to Raise Real Wages* (New York: Committee for Economic Development, 1950), p. 7.

mechanism of this country can keep itself adjusted to the stresses and strains produced by differential growth in various industries and services and differential population growth by various occupational and geographic sectors of the nation.[50]

Stagnation is part of the price of inflexibility. Today this truism is usually accepted in our economic life, except by those who have a vested interest in inflexibility! If they command key positions, they may add to the nation's difficulties in adjusting to constantly changing conditions. The need for flexibility and change in our social structure is not so widely accepted. Old ideas and habits, suitable for the simple life of the horse-and-buggy era, must constantly be examined, reassessed, and many of them changed to meet the demands of the present day. Just as our acceptance in the past of 44 million immigrants from many cultures helped us to keep from becoming provincial and inflexible in our social thinking, the tremendous internal migration of the present helps us remain flexible and willing to adjust to life's new requirements.

The nation, then, benefits economically and socially from migration, though not without friction. There is social and economic cost to individuals, families, and areas. It must also be pointed out that migration, while indispensable to economic and social growth, is not sufficient. Also necessary are adequate investment in both human resources and productive technology, coupled with fiscal and social policies to promote better health and housing and to reduce widespread pockets of poverty, hunger, and misery.[51] There is some interesting and indicative experience in the promotion of mobility by public agencies to relieve unemployment.[52]

To the receiving area. The receiving area benefits. If it is a city with an expanding industrial base, it needs workers, since urban areas seldom produce their own labor force. Migration will bring in "made-to-order" workers with the cost of their production met somewhere else. The experience of the billions of dollars donated to the United States by the rest of the world in the persons of some 44 million immigrants is being repeated in our prosperous cities today.

The stream of migration—except when it is composed of refugees who leave their homes under duress—not only brings workers if and when they are needed, but by and large brings the kinds of workers who are needed. And not only do the migrants bring help needed in the basic industries; they also bring consumers for and participants in local industries and services, as the California experience indicates (to say nothing of the entire history of the United States!).[53]

A stagnant industrial base will result in less in-migration. However, it will not do to assume that even in that case none is needed. The usual attrition in a labor force leaves jobs vacant every day. Workers die, retire, or leave the labor force for other reasons and, especially if the future

---

[50] For an analysis of rural-urban migration in this framework, *see* Stephen L. McDonald, "The Process of Integration and Agricultural Problems," *Journal of Farm Economics* (August 1953), and McDonald, "Farm Outmigration as an Integrative Adjustment to Economic Growth," *Social Forces*, Vol. 33, No. 2 (December 1955), pp. 119–128.

[51] *A Balanced National Program Attacks the* *Conditions of Poverty in America,* Planning Pamphlet No. 128 (Washington, D.C.: National Planning Association, 1970) deals with many of the elements of the sort of program that is required.

[52] A brief review is found in Audrey Freedman, "Labor Mobility Projects for the Unemployed," *Monthly Labor Review*, Vol. 91, No. 6 (June 1968), pp. 56–62.

[53] *See,* for example, California's experience analyzed by Warren S. Thompson, *Growth & Changes in California's Population* (Los Angeles: Haynes Foundation, 1955), chaps. 14 and 16; and Margaret S. Gordon, "Immigration and Its Effect on Labor Force Characteristics," *Monthly Labor Review*, Vol. 82, No. 5 (May 1959), pp. 492–501.

does not look promising, families will move elsewhere. Given occupations may be left with openings because of the ethnic history of the labor force in that occupation. The educated sons and daughters of European immigrants are usually reluctant to enter the trades followed by their fathers and mothers.

The local population must not only re-produce itself biologically in sufficient numbers to replace the labor force without in-migration; it must in addition time its reproduction so that children are at labor force age when they are needed! [54] It must also produce those kinds of workers who will carry on in the occupations left with shortages by attrition and by changes in local standards of what constitutes accept-able jobs.

To the sending area. Usually the sending area is characterized by labor sur-pluses in relation to developed resources. These surplus workers become the target of recruitment by receiving areas because it is often less expensive to import trained adults to occupy existing jobs than it is to invest in plant, equipment, and manage-ment in a new location and to educate and train a labor force *de novo*.

Some sections of the country are "over-populated" because they have for decades deliberately refused to allow certain seg-ments of their population to participate in the more desirable sectors of the economy. Negroes, Mexican-Americans, and Ameri-can Indians are the major groups involved in this discrimination. Manufacturers in parts of the South are now being forced to utilize workers from groups hitherto for-bidden to them by regional custom. A combination of labor shortages and pres-sure from the federal government has fairly widely broken the discriminatory pattern of southern textile mill employment.[55]

Overpopulated areas in which the chief problem is a high birthrate may well bestir themselves and help their population con-trol the size of families; out-migration often reduces the rate of natural increase in any case, since it is so highly selective of young adults in the reproductive ages.

If the reason for the area's overpopula-tion lies in a stagnating economy, it is pos-sible that social action, including govern-mental action, may result from knowledge of the disuse of valuable human resources. It may well be that the best possible use of land and resources would not support the local population at adequate levels of living. Then two overlapping courses would seem indicated: (1) to help some of the existing population to relocate or (2) to help support the existing population by outside remittances. Both courses are found in current unplanned situations.[56]

Out-migration can and does help in both courses: the younger persons establish homes and contacts in new areas and often send for relatives and friends; remittances from abroad have helped Greece, Italy, and many other countries for many decades. Remittances by emigrants from Arkansas, Puerto Rico, or other areas within the na-

---

[54] One of the gains from in-migration, especially to areas with a long history of settlement, is that the age structure of the population may need to be supplemented. A study of the population of New York State, for example, has a section headed "The State continues to benefit from the influx of persons in the productive ages." Wilfred A. Anderson, *The Characteristics of New York State Population* (Ithaca: New York State College of Agriculture, 1957), p. 34.

[55] Roy Reed, "Industry in South Woos Negro Labor," *New York Times*, May 19, 1959, pp. 1, 42.

[56] That more attention must be paid to "stranded" populations is indicated by British experience over the past few decades and recent efforts by the U.S. Department of Agriculture, by state and local "development commissions," and so on. Two groups of U.S. counties studied re-cently indicate something of the dimensions of the problem: (1) a growing number (2 in 1950 but more than 200 by 1960) were experiencing natural decrease, i.e., more deaths than births, and (2) 185 counties lost 20 percent or more of their population during the 1950–60 decade. *See* abstracts of papers in *Population Index*, Vol. 34, No. 3 (July–September 1968), pp. 292–294.

tional economy now serve the same purpose
here. The migrant's former home may well
serve as a "recession" refuge and itself be
aided by performing that function.

Scattered reports from both the Southern
Appalachians and the Ozarks indicate that
retirement housing and recreation are becoming important factors in the economy
of some of the smaller towns in those areas.
An Arkansas case that made the headlines
in July 1961 probably could be duplicated
many times. The four-county area that
received the first assistance under the new
Area Redevelopment Act includes one
county which reports that it had received
"some 600 retired couples in the last
decade," in spite of which "the average
family income is under $2,000." The re-
corder of the city of Gassville, in the area,
said: "The retired people and the unemployment checks for the boys laid off from
construction up north was what kept this
county last winter." [57]

Detailed cross-tabulations would be required to indicate to exactly which areas
workers migrate during periods of unemployment, but numbers of interstate claims
and amounts paid substantiate what has
been widely observed and reported. For
example, during slowdowns in the automobile industry one constantly sees Michigan
license plates throughout the Southern
Appalachians; in states directly south of
the Chicago metropolitan area, recessions
in steel are reflected in the numbers of
Chicago area plates.

Quantitative evidence on the importance
of moves "home for unemployment" is
found in the 874,528 interstate claims
handled under state unemployment compensation programs in the final quarter of
1968, for example. The top six states paying claims to persons located in other states
during that quarter and the amounts paid
as benefits were as follows: [58]

State	Claims (number)	Amount Paid
California	21,088	$3,549,704
New York	19,798	3,795,980
Illinois	11,253	2,026,101
New Jersey	7,367	1,635,922
Michigan	6,371	685,972
Ohio	6,325	739,884

OASDI benefits were being paid on June
30, 1964, to 150,641 persons living abroad,
at the monthly rate of $9,644,000.[59] Pre-
sumably most of those receiving benefits
are returned immigrants or their survivors.

Problems of Mobility

One of the results of the various population flows has been the movement of hundreds of thousands of persons into new
cultural environments. New patterns of
living are required of these migrants, but
often unclear or conflicting models are
available to the newcomers. This, plus
inadequate or nonexistent physical facilities, has exacerbated personal and group
conflict.[60]

In particular, movement of Negroes into
urban areas has led to an increasing concentration of this group in central cities.
During the period 1960–68 the Negro population of central cities grew in all four
regions, from 52 to 54 percent.[61] Con-

[57] "Ozarks First To Get Depressed Area Aid," *New York Times*, July 24, 1961.

[58] U.S. Department of Labor, *Unemployment Insurance Statistics* (Washington, D.C.: U.S. Government Printing Office, April 1969), Table 21.

[59] U.S. Bureau of the Census, *Statistical Abstract of the United States, 1965* (Washington, D.C.: U.S. Government Printing Office, 1966), p. 293.

[60] For an example of problems typical of areas experiencing "war-boom" in-migration, *see* the discussion of Willow Run, Mich., this article, pp. 47–49.

[61] U.S. Bureau of the Census, *Current Population Reports*, "Trends in Social and Economic Conditions in Metropolitan Areas," Series P-23, No. 27 (Washington, D.C.: U.S. Government Printing Office, February 7, 1969).

versely, the white population dropped from 30 to 26 percent; only in the West was there a slight increase. In spite of the fact that in general education, income, and employment have been rising, median family incomes increased more rapidly in the 1960–68 period in the suburbs than in central cities—the incidence of central city poverty was twice that among suburban residents.

Much more important than the proportion of Negroes in central cities is the difference in age distribution: 40 percent of the inner-city Negro population is under the age of 16, whereas only 27 percent of the whites are that young. So high a proportion of under-16 youths would be a burden for any group, but the Negro central-city population suffers especially, because one-third of its teen-agers were unemployed in 1967, compared with about one-eighth of white teen-agers.

However, in spite of this, Table 10, p. 35, indicates that emphasis on Negroes as the chief problem in present-day social conflict can be misleading. Mexican-Americans, for example, have been the chief victims of discrimination and the chief sufferers from poverty in at least four or five of the cities listed. The proportion of Negroes among that group is miniscule, and they are not included in the table. American Indians, who *are* included, have been major sufferers in several cities.

Over the years each of the nonwhite groups that have migrated to urban areas have suffered from the same kinds of problems now so widely recognized in the case of Negroes. In fact, the Southern Appalachian mountaineers, possibly the most "Aryan" of this country's ethnic groups, have widely met the same response in northern cities as have their black southern neighbors. The overwhelmingly white Puerto Ricans have undergone the same experiences and, in their turn, Italians, Poles, Jews, and other earlier immigrants found similar receptions.

The U.S. Riot Commission felt that it must deal with this tendency to emphasize the problems of Negroes to the detriment of other groups.

We wish to make it clear that in focusing on the Negro we do not mean to imply any priority of need. It will not do to fight misery in the black ghetto and leave untouched the reality of injustice and deprivation elsewhere in our society. The first priority is order and justice for all Americans.[62]

The writer, being from the Ozarks, knows firsthand how sterile and unproductive an isolated rural mountain life can be. Movement to an urban area can be a vitalizing experience and can open untold new vistas. New friends, new neighbors, new possibilities in economic, social, and political life, including a wider selection of marriage mates, are only a few items on the new menu for living.

Given widespread ethnocentrism, however, these possibilities cannot be fully utilized. The new arrival may be welcomed or the greetings he receives may be hostile in tone. "The city is the people," as Aristotle said, but "the people" seldom act unanimously. The key question is: Which people? Reactions depend on many factors other than those usually dramatized by attacks on the personal characteristics of the newcomers. Even angels would have difficulties—and be viewed as causing difficulties—in the circumstances under which much urban migration occurs.

Even the highly lauded Anglo-Saxons who came in this nation's early years were not free from criticism. The early English immigrants were considered "the worst type of workers" by many factory managers, despite the fact that their skill levels were higher than those of workers of other nationalities. The trouble was that this made them more "independent," more willing to shift to more promising jobs, and

---

[62] *Report of the National Advisory Commission on Civil Disorders* (New York: E. P. Dutton & Co., 1968), p. 33.

more interested in union organization! [63]

Furthermore, habits, by which we live most of the time, do not change easily with change of habitat. Newcomers may be ridiculed or even attacked because they "do not do things the correct way"—meaning, of course, that they "do not do things *our* way." Intermarriage is usually frowned upon by closely knit ethnic groups and may well lead to ostracism by the social networks of both bride and groom. Migrants can end as marginal men, estranged from both the receiving and sending areas.

Two students of family life and the strains it is undergoing sum up the relation between migration and personal competence and enrichment: "Migration thus might be termed strong medicine, good for those who can take it and bad for those who cannot." [64]

Movers—those who move only within county lines—probably do not experience an increase in personal problems, as do so many migrants, especially those who go to the central city from underdeveloped areas. This does not mean that white suburban families are not forced to go on relief during emergencies, however. Public welfare officials in New York's Nassau, Suffolk, and Westchester counties recently reported respectively that 65, 70, and 52 percent of their relief rolls were white. Many of these seem to be movers or migrants from New York's central city who overreached themselves in buying a home. In many cases the husband works at two jobs in an attempt to carry heavy payments on home mortgage, "suburban" furniture and carpeting, and the like, and then deserts his family when the load becomes too great. Many of these suburban welfare recipients are ostracized and harassed by neighbors who believe, as they themselves probably did once, that the welfare system is responsible for high taxes.[65]

Housing and the Newcomer

Housing has of course been one of the most serious of big city problems for at least a century, both in the United States and abroad. It is important to note here another cycle to add to the family life and poverty cycles already mentioned—the neighborhood life cycle. Buildings and neighborhoods have a natural history that has been traced by dozen of ecologists, sociologists, economists, and planners. Unless there is an extraordinary group of neighbors or an alert and vigorous planning body that takes timely action, buildings deteriorate, the families for whom the housing was originally built move to the suburbs, and families of the same socioeconomic status no longer are attracted to the neighborhood. Vernon, in a study of the New York metropolitan region, defines five stages in the natural history of a neighborhood, and notes:

It is in stage 3 that the old structures in the aging neighborhoods begin to be offered to the newest in-migrants in the Region—today to Puerto Ricans and Negroes, yesterday to the Italians or Jews, before that to the Germans and Irish. Ignorant of the housing market, strapped by lack of income, anxious to be part of a large labor pool, these groups take what they can get in the crowded central areas of the Region; and what they can get is usually the structures just giving up the ghost as middle-income habitation.[66]

Disorganization at Willow Run

World War II gave rise to tremendous internal migration: "war-boom" in-migra-

[63] Charlotte Erikson, *American Industry and the European Immigrant: 1860–1885* (Cambridge, Mass.: Harvard University Press, 1957); Barbara Miller Solomon, *Ancestors and Immigrants* (Cambridge, Mass.: Harvard University Press, 1956).

[64] Nelson N. Foote and Leonard S. Cottrell, Jr., *Identity and Interpersonal Competence* (Chicago: University of Chicago Press, 1955), p. 24.

[65] Agis Salpukas, "Majority on Relief Are White on L.I. and in Westchester," *New York Times*, August 17, 1969, pp. 1, 68.

[66] Raymond Vernon, *Metropolis 1985* (Cambridge, Mass.: Harvard University Press, 1960), pp. 140–241.

tion took place in hundreds of localities, some of which were studied intensively. One of the most penetrating studies was that of the Ford-built bomber plant at Willow Run, Michigan, near Detroit.[67] Some 42,000 men and women were concentrated six days a week in the middle of a former soybean field three miles from an overcrowded town of 12,000 inhabitants and twenty-seven miles from the nearest shopping center. Among other problems, the 42,000 workers had to drive 2 million miles a day.

A microcosm of present-day urban problems was created almost overnight. Inadequacies and shortages of physical facilities, police, fire, housing, manpower, retail stores, medical care, venereal and other disease control, child care, education, recreation, food, fuel, and transportation were experienced daily. These inadequacies were directly reflected in absenteeism, employee turnover, antagonistic attitudes of workers in the plants toward foremen and other supervisors, adjustment difficulties between old-timers and newcomers, children's difficulties in school and at play, and all of the familiar lists of adjustment problems. One result was that competition sharpened:

Competition for a place to live, for seats on the bus, for a place in line at the chain store, for seats at the movie, for seats in a school room, for medical attention, for all the facilities and services whose orderly procurement constitutes such a large part of the ordinary citizen's way of life. All that, the bomber invasion disrupted and threw into confusion. Strange faces thronged the streets. Traffic lanes formerly quiet and orderly suddenly became turbulent with traffic jams. It was a rare old-timer who could remark philosophically as some war worker nearly took off his fender that it was all for the best, the victory over the Axis! For John Q. Public as for the business community, the Axis was a long

way off; the crazy drivers and the noisy crowds were right here now.[68]

The employer had shown that he needed the workers—desperately—but he took no responsibility for their housing and other needs. The middle class "welcomed the outsiders as customers but rejected them as neighbors."

Middle class and wage workers alike regarded the hillbillies as of definitely lower status than any local whites. Hence the intrusion of a hillbilly family into a working-class neighborhood jeopardized the self-confidence of local residents in their own standing. There were always exceptions, and even the most rabid local patriot might occasionally admit that there "may be some good ones," but the prevalent attitude was grudging acceptance at best. Not infrequently it was one of actual fear and suspicion. In a little town where neighborhoods still meant acquaintanceships, social distance came in with the newcomers.

All this was too general in the Willow Run area to be attributed to the peculiarities of individuals. It was clearly a consequence of the lurking sense of insecurity on the part of the old-timers and of the failure of mass communication to break down the psychology of sectionalism. Sure, they were all Americans, but. . . .[69]

There was much talk about why this happened, which the authors label the "Devil Theory"; another explanation they dub the "Theory of Individual Incompetence." It is in the demolition of such oversimplifications, so popular in almost any social crisis, that their outstanding contribution lies. Their conclusion is that

the industrial culture still has not come to terms with its own dynamism. The social fiasco at Willow Run happened the way it did, then, because Americans haven't yet given thought to making such things happen in any other way; because in a disturbed situation we still prefer to rely on the political power struggle rather than to subordinate our own interests and prejudices to the technological

---

[67] Lowell J. Carr and James E. Stermer, *Willow Run: A Study of Industrialization and Cultural Inadequacy* (New York: Harper & Bros., 1952).

[68] Ibid.
[69] Ibid.

needs of a common objective, and because we have not yet learned how to live with social change.[70]

Problems of Philadelphia's Newcomers

Boom communities had many enlightening experiences that should be helpful in preparing civic forces for future action. Closer to current problems are recent developments in older cities. Philadelphia's experience is relevant.

The nation's fourth largest city has always been a sizable consumer of persons born outside the city. Recent years have seen a pattern there common to many other big cities: in-migration of Negroes and others from depressed areas and net out-migration of whites.

Philadelphia's total population fell from 2,072,000 in 1950 to 2,003,000 in 1960, and the white population dropped from 1,693,000 to 1,468,000. In the same period the nonwhite population increased from 379,000 to 535,000, or an increase of 156,000 compared with a decrease in the white population of 225,000. The number of those of Puerto Rican birth or parentage was 14,424 in 1960 compared with 1,910 in 1950. Four percent of the Puerto Ricans were classified as nonwhite by the census. The average annual net in-migration to Philadelphia from Puerto Rico during the 1950–60 decade was 900. There was a scattering of European immigrants.

Most of the newcomers, at least the "visible" ones, moved into the inner city. A 1962 study labeled the majority of them underprivileged and classified their problems as follows: [71]

1. Problems arising from migration per se.

a. Lack of information on Philadelphia's community facilities, services, and laws.

b. Disorganizing effects of migration.

2. Problems arising from the in-migrants'

a. Unfamiliarity with sanitation, housekeeping, diet, and food preparation practices required in northern urban communities.

b. Lack of the type of work habits required for urban employment.

c. Language problems.

d. School adjustment difficulties.

e. Adjustment to a new social milieu in which the letter (if not the spirit) of equal rights is the law of the community.

3. Problems common to both in-migrants and natives in the underprivileged class.

a. Obtaining and retaining a job. ·

b. Obtaining decent housing.

c. Maintaining health.

d. School problems—absenteeism, lack of motivation.

e. Protecting children from criminal influences.

The report points out, in short, that the most serious problems that confront underprivileged in-migrants—employment, housing, health, and crime—are those problems that are common to other persons with similar social and economic status.

Community facilities and services in eight fields about which the underprivileged newcomer needs to be informed are listed by the report:

1. *Employment.* Availability of employment and of agencies that can assist in finding employment.

2. *Housing.* Where to obtain adequate housing at a price he can afford.

3. *Transportation.* What are the routes and fares of the various means of public transportation?

4. *Emergency health and welfare care.*

---

[70] Ibid., pp. 351–352.
[71] "Special Assimilation Problems of Underprivileged In-Migrants to Philadelphia" (Philadelphia: Pennsylvania Economy League, Eastern Division, July 1962). (Mimeographed.)

Where to obtain emergency medical and welfare care.

5. *Legal aid.* If arrested, what are the procedures for obtaining release prior to the hearing, and where can he obtain a lawyer?

6. *Schools.* What kinds of schools are available for both normal and exceptional children?

7. *Recreational and cultural facilities.* Where are recreational and cultural facilities for children located?

8. *Day care facilities.* Where can day care for children of working mothers be obtained?

These and other aspects of the strange environment that can cause problems for many newcomers are set forth in Alvin L. Schorr's valuable book, *Slums and Social Insecurity*.[72] Relations with the police are not listed as one of the newcomer's major problems, but many other reports indicate that in general it should be included.[73]

Aiding the Newcomers

Plans to aid the newcomer, the resident poor, and the disadvantaged of varied types are being formulated by a number of organizations.[74] No attempt will be made

[72] Washington, D.C.: U.S. Government Printing Office, 1963.

[73] Among many other reports are "Social Services in Detroit's Central City (Detroit: United Community Services of Metropolitan Detroit, 1960), (mimeographed); Mayor's Study Committee on Social Problems in the Inner Core Area of the City, Final Report to the Honorable Frank P. Zeidler, Mayor, Milwaukee, April 15, 1960; *Report of the National Advisory Commission on Civil Disorders*; various reports of the United States Commission on Civil Rights; and Alfred McClung Lee and N. D. Humphrey, *Race Riot* (New York: Dryden Press, 1943).

[74] A well-rounded treatment, although focused primarily on Negro-white problems, is found in Part III of the *Report of the National Advisory Commission on Civil Disorders*; this is indispensable for every concerned citizen.

here to duplicate such efforts. Instead, an attempt will be made to suggest approaches and frames of reference for the helping professions and the concerned citizen. The inadequacy of social services has been the burden of innumerable reports for generations. Another criticism found in the Detroit survey already mentioned is this:

A considerable amount of public and voluntary money is being spent in the central city, but it seems to be directed at maintaining the status quo rather than seeking change on the part of individuals and families that would benefit them and the community at large.[75]

Increasingly, organized groups of welfare clients are drawing parallels between a decaying international colonialism and "welfare colonialism." Minority group criticisms of big city school systems are placing great stress on criticisms of middle-class values, which they contend hamper teachers in their relations with working-class and culturally different pupils.[76]

Attitudes of those in authority, whether teachers, doctors, social workers, police, or public officials, make a great difference to those with whom they deal. Recent years have seen a series of studies of the conduct of such professionals as physicians, nurses, psychiatric social workers, and so on in relation to ethnic and class differences between patients and clients. It is of critical importance that such authority figures be aware not only of their own feelings but of the manner in which they express themselves.

[75] "Social Services in Detroit's Central City," p. 10.

[76] That class differences are important is proved by many scholars. *See*, for example, Martin Deutsch, Irwin Katz, and Arthur R. Jensen, *Social Class, Race and Psychological Development* (New York: Holt, Rinehart & Winston, 1968). For ways in which ethnic differences contribute to group conflict, *see* Andrew M. Greeley, *Why Can't They Be Like Us?* (New York: Institute of Human Relations Press, 1969).

Commonly Held Stereotypes

Certain common verbal habits can be deleterious to relations between residents and newcomers. Such terms as "the Puerto Rican problem," "the Negro problem," and "the hillbilly problem" are examples of the heedless use of words that hurt, that damage self-esteem. Many of these usages are analyzed and attacked in Gordon W. Allport's *The Nature of Prejudice*.[77]

Stereotypes and "loaded" words are widely recognized as psychically harmful, of course. What is not so widely recognized is that sometimes a stereotype can block action that may be necessary to protect the health or even the lives of minority group members. The *New York Times* reported, for example, that Puerto Rican sewing machine operators in a Manhattan loft factory began to act hysterically one morning.[78] Some screamed, some fainted, some cried, some started running for the fire escape. A physician who was summoned stated that "Puerto Ricans are a very high tensioned people," and advised that nothing needed to be done. Fortunately someone else called the fire department, which discovered that the workshop air contained "a very high, deadly concentration of carbon monoxide." Continued exposure might well have meant many deaths among the workers.

There are more subtle ways of expressing rejection. The use of loaded words when writing of those already struggling against great odds to find their place in the world is especially unfortunate. Some years ago three New York settlement houses published a report on migration that referred to "thousands upon thousands of Southern Negroes *swarming* to the Northern industrial cities." Puerto Rico, it also said, "has become the most prolific *spawning* ground for the American migrant."[79] [Italics added.] Note the use of terms usually applied only to animals.

Most harmful of all, perhaps, has been the use of the term "the culture of poverty" and all this implies. We are told that such-and-such a group (or individual) will not (or cannot) do something "for his own good" because he suffers from "the culture of poverty." Teachers explain that some (or all) of their pupils are so "culturally deprived" that "they can't learn."

Oscar Lewis, whose writings about Mexican and Puerto Rican slum families popularized the expression, was trying to find common denominators in what might be labeled the lower-lower lower class.[80] Even he later began to qualify some of his earlier statements, but "the children of Lewis" are scattered widely about the country, speaking and writing articles.[81]

There has been wide interference with family planning programs; statements such as "The poor won't use such facilities anyway" sound almost identical to the arguments met by Margaret Sanger in Brooklyn in 1912. Her autobiography relates the story of physicians who assured her that "the people you are worrying about wouldn't use contraception if they had it; they breed like rabbits." She was working at that time among Jewish immigrants— who flocked to her meetings in the Jewish Workmen's Circle Hall in Brownsville and adopted contraception as soon as it became available to them. It was so successful, in fact, that the Brooklyn district attorney who

---

[77] Garden City, N.Y.: Doubleday & Co., Anchor Books, 1958.

[78] *New York Times*, April 22, 1958.

[79] Dora Tannenbaum, Sara McCaulley, and H. Daniel Carpenter, *The Puerto Rican Migration* (New York: Hudson Guild, Colony House, and the Grand Street Settlement, 1955).

[80] Oscar Lewis, *The Children of Sanchez* (New York: Random House, 1961), p. xxvi.

[81] Oscar Lewis, "The Culture of Poverty," *Trans-action*, Vol. 1, No. 1 (November 1963), pp. 17–19.

prosecuted her for opening the Brownsville clinic told the jury that "the clinic was intended to do away with the Jews." [82]

Loose use of Lewis's slogan is harmful to those working with the poor. Hylan Lewis and his colleagues, in their five-year investigation of "Child Rearing Practices Among Low Income Families in the District of Columbia," have demonstrated the great variety found in such families. Lewis examined the concept of a culture of poverty and found it lacking in precision, "too all-encompassing." He points out also how it affects unfavorably "the perceptions of the poor by the non-poor; and they affect the self-image, the self-awareness, and the expectations, as well as the demands, of the poor." [83]

"If the concept is to be useful at all," Herzog concluded after examining its various aspects, "it must be explicitly recognized as a subculture rather than a culture; but under any name, poverty lacks the essential elements of a culture." The term offers "a pat phrase . . . is a substitute for thought and action." [84]

"Adjustment" Is Inadequate

"You must learn to adjust," the newcomer is often told. Teachers and social workers often say with respect to a recently arrived migrant that he is having trouble "adjusting." When asked if they really want the newcomers to adjust to living in an expensive, overcrowded slum-dwelling infested with vermin and rats, they

---

[82] Margaret Sanger, *Autobiography* (New York: W. W. Norton, 1938), pp. 93, 226.

[83] Hylan Lewis, *Syndromes of Contemporary Urban Poverty*, Psychiatric Research Report 21 (April 1967), pp. 1–11. *See also* Camille Jeffers, *Living Poor* (Ann Arbor, Mich.: Ann Arbor Publishers, 1967) ; and Elliot Liebow, *Tally's Corner* (Boston: Little, Brown & Co., 1967).

[84] Elizabeth Herzog, "Facts and Fictions About the Poor," *Monthly Labor Review*, Vol. 92, No. 2 (February 1969), Reprint No. 2604, pp. 42–49.

have difficulty in answering. Foote and Cottrell contend that the concept of adjustment "masks a conservative ethic" in defense of "some given status quo." If the answer is that a person's "good" is being sought, their answer is:

One man's happiness is another man's gloom. We reject such a formulation because (a) while we no doubt share the middle-class norms which are idealized, they too often imply a sort of subcultural ethnocentrism that neither can nor should be forced upon other segments of society, (b) it treats conflict as evil in itself, and conceives it unrealistically as unnatural and expungeable, and (c) by setting up a stable state of affairs as the end of action by family agencies, it dooms such action to inevitable futility, while closing the door to the exploration and the discovery of new experience and forms in family life. Joint involvement in constructive activity is much more than absence of disagreement.[85]

What of the Future?

An examination of historical trends and present realities suggests the following as premises for future social action:

1. Internal migration will continue and probably increase if the present speed of economic development is maintained or improved.

2. It is essential to the health of the entire national economy that migration continue and even increase, in the interests of efficient allocation of human and other natural resources.

3. Migration at present is often wasteful of time, money, and energy. It penalizes many of those who pull up their stakes to travel in search of a job—or a better job—or better life chances for their children. Often tiny life savings are gambled on the move. It may well turn out to be relatively successful economically; often it is harmful to family life and to the personal development of the individuals involved.

4. Migration also often helps contribute to the further complication of life in large

---

[85] Op. cit., p. 49.

urban areas. Probably most city-dwellers do not understand the dynamics of urban change; that the flight to the suburbs has a natural history of many decades is not widely realized. The entry of conspicuously different ethnic groups into areas that have been declining steadily for years dramatizes the deterioration, may well cause further flight, and may lead to deterioration in human relations. The stranger becomes both the symbol of the end of an era and the "cause" of urban blight.

5. Successful urban living often involves a variety of patterns of learned behavior.

a. The newcomer must learn, and learn rapidly, how to cope with new and strange problems. Habits learned in different, and usually simpler, surroundings do not make for satisfactory results in the new environment. Customary ways of making a living, keeping house, raising children, visiting friends and neighbors, playing, and worshipping may all—and all at one time—be called into question. Matters treated casually in the old environment may in the new suddenly become invested with high emotional content. Added to all these puzzling changes is often the reduction in self-esteem that comes from being labeled as a problem, from being treated as a member of a conspicuous minority instead of as a person with a meaningful place in society.

b. The "host" people must also learn to cope with new situations, to understand what is happening and how they can help speed up the integration process. Neighborhood and city transitions can be brought about peaceably and without major personal, social, economic, and political disruption. However, citizens must be aware of the factors involved and organize to guide the process.[86]

A Framework for Understanding Newcomers

"The stranger" has been a problem for settled societies for many centuries, as witness Biblical injunctions on the subject of fair treatment for him. Usually he has been expected to submit himself to all the rules, regulations, and even foibles of the receiving society. Democratic traditions built up during the pioneering stages of this country and as a result of the integration of some 44 million immigrants have begun to teach us to value cultural democracy, or at least cultural pluralism.[87]

Kluckhohn some years ago criticized social work practitioners for neglecting what inclusion in our system meant for strangers (Mexicans in her discussion): "a lack of mobility and a general lower-class status." She wrote that we neglected "the enduring quality of cultural orientations [of the newcomers]." Since great stress has been placed on this factor in recent years, that will not be emphasized. However, she pointed out that "those doing the educating or giving the guidance were insufficiently aware of the nature of their own cultural orientations." [88] In summary, understanding the newcomer involves the following:

1. Knowledge of the background of the migrant.

a. His culture.

b. The social structure in his community of origin.

c. His place in that structure.

---

[86] Adapted from "Migration and Urbanization," a background and premises statement drafted by the author in connection with a study in which he has been engaged for the American Society of Planning Officials.

[87] Clarence Senior and William S. Bernard, eds., *Toward Cultural Democracy* (New York: Associated Educational Services Corporation, 1968).

[88] Florence R. Kluckhohn, "Cultural Factors in Social Work Practice and Education," *Social Service Review*, Vol. 25 (March 1951), pp. 38–47.

2. Knowledge of one's own community.
   a. The culture.
   b. The social structure.
   c. One's place in that structure.
   d. The newcomer's place in that structure.
3. Perspective on both 1 and 2 and their interrelations.

It is too often assumed that all we need to know is the culture of the newcomer—that is what Kluckhohn criticized. Even knowing the differences between the two cultures is not sufficient. The "gatekeepers" of the receiving communities often are promoters of conflict without realizing it; part of their work is to help bring about cultural change without personal and family disorganization. The report of a settlement houseworker on "cultural conflict" in a family of recently arrived Kentucky hillbillies illustrates how pervasive cultural change can be:

We were trying to learn how to do a quick job of dishwashing. The girls were very proud of themselves. One girl expressed herself. "Well, I want to tell you what my mother said. She won't let me wash dishes this way because it is just a lot of nonsense. But you know what I do? My mother likes to go to the movies. Every time she goes it's my job to wash the dishes. I say, you just go on, and wait until she is gone and then wash the dishes our way." [89]

The Role of Roles

The framework just noted should be used in applying what social scientists know of the importance of the roles each person

has been taught to play in the groups to which he belongs. Role conflicts take place during the most peaceful social change; even in fairly isolated areas there will be misunderstandings between males and females, young and old, as their roles develop throughout life.

Role conflict is even more probable when a family is transported into a new social setting. It is likely to be even more productive of friction if persons who were the majority in their original home are forced to assume roles considered appropriate for minorities in their new locality.

The probability of acute troubles rises precipitously if the newly created minority must play the role of scapegoat, which has been the case throughout so much of human history. Perhaps the most basic research orientation that could be adopted would be one in which we undertook to understand why it is we so often try to solve the problem of scapegoats by eliminating them, instead of the conditions that seem to make them necessary.

Maybe we should attempt to examine all our attitudes and our programs with Bernard Shaw's approach in mind. He wrote that he

loathes almsgiving, not only sentimentally because it fills the paupers with humiliation, the patrons with evil pride, and both with hatred, but because in a country justly and providently managed there could be neither excuse for it on the pauper's part nor occasion for it on the patron's. Those who like playing the good Samaritan should remember that you cannot have good Samaritans without thieves. Saviors and rescuers may be splendid figures in biography and romance; but as they could not exist without sinners and victims they are bad symptoms.[90]

[89] *Report of a Workshop on the Southern Mountaineer in Cincinnati* (Cincinnati: Mayor's Friendly Relations Committee and Social Service Association of Greater Cincinnati, 1954). *See also* the warning about leadership in the assimilation process in Greeley, op. cit., pp. 31–37.

[90] George Bernard Shaw, *The Intelligent Woman's Guide to Socialism and Capitalism* (Garden City, N.Y.: Garden City Publishing Co., 1928), p. 96.

Economic Cost-Benefit Approaches to Migration

GEORGE F. ROHRLICH

The core concern of economics is the optimum allocation of scarce resources. To the extent that this problem is ubiquitous and all pervasive, everyone, whatever his calling, shares this concern. In this sense everyone is an economist, if only with regard to the optimum allocation of his own resources. The very choice of how a person spends his time and energy—as between various gainful or otherwise rewarding pursuits (including leisure-time activities, rest, and whatever else is required for self-renewal)—is essentially an economic decision. In making this choice a person determines not only what he is going to do, but also what doing it will cost: that which he is precluded from doing because of what he actually does do constitutes the "price tag" of this choice. Economists call this

the "Principle of Alternative or Opportunity Cost," whereby the cost of anything can be expressed in terms of the alternative or opportunity that must be forgone. As some wit put it: "Everything has its price; nothing is free—even death costs us our life."

Classical economists, like their liberal counterparts among the political philosophers, had an abiding faith that such individual decision-making would work for the best, not only of each person, but of society, in that the myriad individual choices would combine, as Adam Smith said, "as if guided by an invisible hand" toward maximizing the common good.[1]

Factor Mobility

Insofar as classical economics could be said to have a macro-policy component at all, its essence was to enable individuals (and nations) to pursue their self-interest as freely as possible, thereby furthering the commonweal most effectively, even if indi-

NOTE: Acknowledgment is made of the research help given the author in preparation of this paper by two graduate student assistants, Mrs. Mary Sharp of Temple University and Warren Greenberg of Bryn Mawr College, and to the U.S. Department of Labor, whose Manpower Research Institutional Grant to Temple University made this possible.

[1] Adam Smith, *The Wealth of Nations* (New York: Random House, 1937), p. 43.

rectly and not in any calculated or pre-meditated manner. Division of labor, development of specialized skills, and above all freedom of movement were regarded as principal avenues toward increasing a person's efficiency, hence his productive worth and, concomitantly, his financial rewards (these being his share of the greater returns for a larger output or a more valuable product). Next to the free flow of people, the free movement of goods was deemed the best way of bringing about individual and national economic gain.

Ricardo showed that this held equally true in the realm of international economic relationships (where the movement of persons is fraught with higher costs and other complications) by demonstrating convincingly (in what came to be called the "Theorem of Comparative Advantage") the all-around gain to be derived by all countries from concentrating on their greatest natural strength and then trading their products for those of other nations doing the same.[2] The later development of theories of industrial or plant location could be viewed as a more sophisticated synthesis involving both inputs and outputs of production processes.

In any case, "factor mobility"—whether as the sole or as a principal vector of this self-leveling adjustment process—was recognized quite early to be of the essence. Its premise is the unhampered capacity of each of the productive factors—land, labor, and capital—to respond promptly to changing conditions, especially newly emerging opportunities. For labor and capital the mobility concept comprises not only geographic displacement but also change of occupation, industry, and so on—that is, changes in the use made of any given factor, even though no change of location is involved. With regard to land, of course, shifts of the latter type—different land uses —constitute the only variety of the mobility concept that is applicable. The ultimate outcome of these simultaneous processes is

what economists call a state of equilibrium, one that constitutes the best possible allocation of known and available resources and that could last as long as conditions remain substantially unchanged, notably pending any progress in the state of the industrial arts.

The advent of the mixed and the command economies, that is, forms of national economic organization in which the freely flowing movement or spontaneous change in the use of the factors of production has been replaced in varying degrees by government intervention and planning, has changed only the conditions under which the aforesaid process takes place. The core concern of economics—the optimum allocation of scarce resources—continues unchanged, as does the economist's reliance on factor mobility as the principal vector for achieving the desired goal.[3] However, no longer is the initiative left entirely or, as the case may be, to any significant extent to individual spontaneity; nor is the same reliance placed on Smith's "invisible hand" to act as the quasi-miraculous harmonizer of individual and collective interests. Instead the allocation process has become the end product of a complicated maze of analyses involving national income statistics, production functions, input-output data, and the like, and comprehensive projections based thereon of the volumes and types of inputs required to achieve certain overall economic goals such as a certain growth rate and concrete targets, for example, the rehabilitation of certain depressed areas.

There is an important concomitant to this transformation from an out-and-out free-enterprise economy toward some degree of government intervention. It is the actual or potential admixture of broader objectives, some political and cultural as well as economic, to those that result from

---

[2] David Ricardo, *The Principles of Political Economy and Taxation* (New York: E. P. Dutton & Co., 1911), pp. 77 ff.

[3] A recent "Special to the *New York Times*" from Moscow by Bernard Gwertzman, "Surplus Russian Workers Face Job Loss," *New York Times*, October 10, 1969, p. 3, points to the timeliness and importance of this problem in the planned economy of the Soviet Union.

the mere accumulation of the myriad independent and uncoordinated demands of the economic marketplace. Two conclusions follow, both of signal importance to a proper understanding of the way a once popular but rather slanted slogan, "the End of Economic Man," [4] may come to take on a new meaning. Not now or in any foreseeable future will there be an end to the ever present necessity to select, in the husbanding of resources, from a large and probably growing number of mutually exclusive choices the pursuit of some gratifications and attainments at the expense of forgoing others. In this sense "economic man"—the economist-economizer—is bound to live on. The area in which he may—or at least could—succeed himself in a new and different posture is that of social accounting. Here he *may* transcend the conventional, rather myopic, profit-and-loss calculus, and even the newer macro-economic but too narrowly market-oriented national accounts system that has been developed in the last several decades. Here lies the present challenge and the new frontier: to devise a more comprehensive approach that would reflect as well as test our budding insights into some of the long neglected social ramifications of economic decision-making and that would take account of the chain reactions and feedbacks of what might be called "social ecology."

In the following an attempt is made to illustrate the conventional approach and to sketch some of the elements that a socially more perceptive stock-taking might add to it on the example of a cost-benefit analysis of domestic migration.[5]

The Conventional Model

Human migration being viewed in purely economic terms as one aspect of factor mobility, that is, of the factor "labor," the economic analysis of migration to date has been confined largely to studying its impact on members of the labor force, that is, those employed gainfully or seeking gainful employment (including self-employment). Any effects on the migrant's family, while not altogether ignored (especially when the family contained actual or potential secondary workers), have played a subordinate role and have received relatively little attention. Prior to the mass migrations, especially of southern blacks and of Puerto Ricans, to the urban centers of the North and West that took place during and after World War II, the interest of economists centered less on geographic than on interoccupational and interindustry shifts in the American labor force, notably the dramatic exodus of millions of workers from farming and to a lesser extent from coal-mining into manufacturing, commerce, and service industries. The fact that in many cases this involved a shift from a rural to an urban setting was more or less regarded as incidental.

Likewise, until recently—actually the early 1960s—there was hardly a basis for concern with any but the spontaneous and self-induced kind of domestic migration, what with the absence of any significant programs of subsidized relocation, government-sponsored or otherwise, with or without retraining. On the other hand, in many of the more recent economic studies bearing on migration there appears to be greater interest in exploring the profitability of the newly established worker retraining programs—with or without relocation—than in migration per se.

Within this general frame of reference, and subject to the conceptual and methodological limitations referred to, economists who have studied worker migration proper, with a view to evaluating it as a tool for optimizing resource allocation, have set up working models that include the following suppositions: By comparing wages before and after migration and adding in the costs of the move, the loss of earnings owing to

---

[4] Peter F. Drucker, *The End of Economic Man* (New York: Van Rees Press, 1939), chap. 6.

[5] The term migration will be used throughout to cover residential mobility within the United States, especially rural-to-urban, regardless of whether it involves the crossing of lesser political boundaries.

the move, and in some instances "psychic costs"—insofar as these are quantifiable—it should be possible to assess whether (1) there were net financial rewards and (2) these were large enough to justify the move —especially when comparing earnings levels of movers and nonmovers over a period of years following the move. Not only with respect to the migrant, but also in assessing the consequences of his move for the economy at large, the measure applied is that of the marketplace—the comparative dollar returns of gainful employment before and after migration. These are taken to reflect accurately the worker's contribution to the national product (and indeed they enter into our national accounts as such). Consequently, from the economist's point of view a move is judged efficient in terms of better resource allocation if earnings can be shown to have increased. In the alternative event, the move must be judged to have been inefficient or misdirected, which gives rise to the expectation that it may be reversed. (In fact the substantial volume of remigration is frequently explained in that manner, at least a priori.)

From what has been said it will be evident that the traditional bias of the economist relative to migration is a positive one. He is generally in favor of factor mobility, hence he is bound to think well of a worker's preparedness to move in pursuit of better opportunities. He favors individual initiative as the mainspring of economic advancement. Hence he approves of the worker who puts his avowed readiness to move to the actual test. He sees gains, both to the individual and to society, as deriving from factor reallocation that puts a worker in a job vacancy (or, for that matter, that meets a need for capital or for land) yielding higher returns to the worker (or to the capitalist or the landowner respectively) than he enjoyed before, owing to the fact that in the new location, occupation, industry, or context his contribution (in terms of the economic results) is deemed more valuable.

Within the economist's own reference

terms, the chances that worker migration will fulfill such expectations are generally favorable, provided the migrant is tolerably well informed about employment opportunities and earnings in the receiving community and is reasonably successful in landing a job there. The chances that a move will turn out to be efficient are all the better the less favorable the conditions of employment and wages are in the community the worker left, the lower the costs of and connected with the move, and the better the job market and wage levels in the receiving community. The leveling influence of the move (in terms of labor allocation and wage levels) is seen as accruing not only to the migrants, but also to the workers remaining in the community from which the out-migration occurred.

To be sure there is recognition of several possible offsets to these gains: inasmuch as the most enterprising and more vigorous (younger) individuals may be those who choose to leave in pursuit of better opportunities, their exodus, if massive, may constitute something of an adverse selection with respect to those remaining. Also, the beneficial results of the out-migration may be lost, at least in part, to the extent that a high birthrate among those remaining replaces the migrating population. However, with reference to the latter point it can be argued that the oversupply of labor in a certain area or industry would be even greater and the position of its workers worse had out-migration not taken place. (This is a commonly accepted position with regard to the manpower situation in farming; that is, while the number of people trying to make their living from the land is still considered to be too large even after years of substantial out-migration, it is estimated that it would be even larger except for this continued drain.)

On balance, however, and considering the principal variables taken into account, migration of workers in the right direction is viewed as efficient and therefore is generally regarded with favor by economists. For the migrant such efficient moves bring their own reward in meeting their presumed expectations, as is expressed, for example, in the following summary of findings in a recent study of geographic mobility in Appalachia:

In summary, those who migrate increase their wages faster than those who do not migrate; those who migrate long distances increase their wages faster than those who migrate short distances. Long-distance Appalachian migrants increased their wages faster than short-distance migrants; the latter in turn increased their wages faster than those who have remained in Appalachia. Those who remained in Appalachia had higher initial wages than those who migrated from Appalachia. Among migrants, short-distance movers earned lower wages than long-distance movers.[6]

The Model Applied: Selected Findings and Problems

A much-cited study on "The Costs and Returns of Human Migration" by Larry A. Sjaastad sets out to test what its author calls the "two broad and distinct questions [that migration poses] for the economist": (1) ". . . the direction and magnitude of the response of migrants to labor earnings differentials over space" and (2) ". . . how effective is migration in equalizing interregional earnings levels of comparable labor?"[7]

Response to Earnings Differentials

In answer to the first question, the author cites the general consensus of earlier findings attesting to a relationship in the expected direction, albeit a weak one and subject to many qualifications. He then offers his own findings, based on a study of interstate migration between 1940 and 1950, showing that "an increase in per capita labor earnings of $100 (1947–49 dollars)

induces net in-migration or retards net out-migration by only 4 or at most 5 per cent of the population aged 15 to 24 years at the end of the decade."[8] The percentage was even lower for other age groups.

Of course, net migration tells only part of the story and may be misleading. For while low-wage and declining industries may be disgorging unskilled workers or workers with obsolete skills that are no longer marketable, higher skill and higher wage employment opportunities may be opening up in the very same locations or near them, where establishments need and might be hiring workers. However, if those displaced are not qualified or are otherwise not acceptable for the higher paid, higher skilled jobs, then in-migration will occur at the same time as out-migration. This blurs the picture somewhat deceptively and reduces the net out-migration figures. To a considerable extent this is precisely what has happened in the South: low-skilled and unskilled black workers have been displaced, especially from agriculture, and many have migrated into the large metropolitan cities, while white in-migrants have helped to man the developing manufacturing industries. (In terms of industrial growth, the South has been the fastest growing region of the postwar United States.)

If a closer look is taken at the out-migrants alone, especially blacks as a group, the job-and-earnings hypothesis appears to be next-to-no help in explaining the flow of their migration. For in the big cities the number of jobs that can be filled by unskilled or low-skilled workers is shrinking, and employment opportunities for such workers are therefore less favorable than in the smaller urban areas. Their trek to the American metropolis (seemingly in preference to an intensified job search in the smaller communities and towns either closer to home or with suitable job openings) appears even more puzzling in purely economic terms in those instances when the

[6] David A. Hirschberg, "The Impact of Geographic Mobility on the Appalachian Region 1957–63," unpublished master's thesis, New York University, 1968, p. 31. (Processed.)

[7] *Journal of Political Economy*, Supplement (October 1962), pp. 80–93.

[8] Ibid., p. 82.

migrants' former source of livelihood has been wiped out (as in the case of the mechanization of cotton picking) and when it must be presumed, therefore, that the need to find paid employment is even greater and more pressing. In part this contradiction might be explained by lack of information or by the not implausible, even though not necessarily correct, belief that the larger the city, the more numerous the job opportunities.

A far-more-telling explanation—not of a type that one would readily think of if one searched for reasons that conform to the traditional model's assumptions about migrants' motivations—has been advanced by another student of the problem, Lowell E. Galloway. In a study on "Geographic Labor Mobility in the United States 1957 to 1960," based entirely on data collected by the Social Security Administration as part of the information it accumulates on covered workers' employment and earnings taxed and credited toward entitlement to benefits under the social security program, Galloway reports among other things the following: [9] In general the geographic mobility patterns of the male workers studied appear to bear out the hypothesis that "earnings differentials are a significant factor in influencing the allocation of labor within the United States." [10] An even more potent variable appeared to be the distance (i.e., the attraction of close as against remote opportunities for improved earnings). [11] In contrast to this "pull" relationship of better earnings prospects (even those just a little better if they were close by), the push toward out-migration exerted "by a lack of economic opportunity in one's present location" (long thought to be a principal determinant of labor movement) appeared of lesser significance. [12]

Black Mobility Patterns

The mobility patterns of black males, however, appeared to deviate from or even run counter to this general pattern. For one thing, they showed a lower propensity toward out-migration, even though they were concentrated in low-wage (southern) regions known to have more pronounced discriminatory practices. Galloway concludes that "Negro men tend to stay in those areas where there are more Negroes and these happen to be areas where the relative income of Negro men is low." [13] Even more important, and directly relevant to the question raised earlier, was the further discovery that insofar as black males did move, the rationale for their movement again did not seem to conform to any clearcut orientation toward economic improvement. Galloway's regression analysis strongly suggested that, rather than being governed by higher earnings expectations, "Negro men tend to move wherever other Negroes are numerous." [14] Moreover, the element of push in the form of lack of opportunity at the place of origin, which seemed of lesser significance for male migrants as a whole, appeared to be a pronounced component in the black mobility pattern:

Geographic mobility on the part of Negro men is characterized by involuntary movements brought about by job displacements rather than by movements that represent a voluntary decision to change the region of major job. [15]

Given the observed lower propensity to move among blacks than among whites, it would seem that blacks are less given to migrating unless they have to, and when they do move many of them tend to go where blacks have already settled in large numbers. This interpretation of black mobility behavior would go a long way in explaining analogously the substantial black migration into the South—probably in large part re-

---

[9] Research Report No. 28 (Washington, D.C.: U.S. Department of Health, Education, and Welfare, Social Security Administration, Office of Research Statistics, 1969).

[10] Ibid., p. 20.

[11] Ibid., p. 35.

[12] Ibid., p. 20.

[13] Ibid., p. 43.

[14] Ibid., p. 47.

[15] Ibid., p. 48.

migration—as individual moves gravitating toward areas with black population concentrations. In the case of remigrations a purely and narrowly economic motivation may be present in a negative sense (i.e., failure to land or to hold a job, notably during periods of recession), but may not be the only or major one. Apart from this it appears to play an even lesser role.

Effect of Mobility on Income Differentials

We may now turn to the second of Sjaastad's two "broad and distinct questions [that migration poses] for the economist": its effectiveness in reducing interregional earnings differentials for comparable work. Given the vast population movements of the last several decades, it has been something of a puzzle to economists that income differentials among states should have continued virtually unchanged. Assuming that it was all efficient, should not a greater degree of equalization be in evidence? And if, on balance, it was not significantly efficient (that is, either moves were in the right direction but did not go far enough or else efficient and inefficient moves canceled each other out), where does this leave the traditional economic theory of migration?

Frequently when broadly inclusive global figures defy meaningful interpretation, Sjaastad rightly observes, a better understanding of the situation to which they refer may be gained by the process of disaggregation—by breaking conglomerates down into their component parts. It is therefore important to take account of the occupational and age factors and perhaps other circumstances that are relevant to migration.

Insofar as occupational distributions vary among the labor forces of different states, principally because of the states' different industrial composition and because different occupations do command different levels of remuneration, earnings differentials can exist without misallocation of resources. Certain extremes, such as Mis-

sissippi's personal income per capita in 1967 of $1,896, compared with Connecticut's $3,969 and New York's $3,759, can thus in part be reconciled. Interoccupational "migration" may take a generation or more and is in any event slower to come about than are geographic and/or interindustry migrations, either by themselves or in combination with each other. Moreover, technological changes may occur in such rapid succession as to outpace any efforts (especially if unorganized and uninformed) among members of the labor force to adjust to them.

Age retards mobility not only when it constitutes a physical handicap, but when it deters workers from migrating (with or without being retrained) because their expected work-life span is deemed too short for this to pay off. Thus it is evident from all available data that the propensity to migrate is heavily conditioned by age, especially among certain population groups, notably those engaged in farming.

Realistically, the magnitude of the obstacle to successful migration posed either by a skill gap or by age may be overestimated by those affected. It would seem more likely that so-called psychic costs are overlaid and intertwined with the age factor conditioning a worker's decision-making about migration to a greater extent than are the strictly economic considerations. Thus roots in a community, children's schooling, home-ownership, and a general feeling of belonging may be crucial deterrents. But this category of costs to individuals has so far defied inclusion in the conventional model—either because they are deemed to "involve no resources for the economy" [16] or because, although they are viewed as important, "they are not readily amenable to economic interpretation." [17]

The specific answer, however, to the question under discussion—whether in fact

---

[16] Sjaastad, op. cit., p. 85.

[17] James G. Maddox, "Private and Social Costs of the Movement of People out of Agriculture," *American Economic Review*, Vol. 50, No. 2 (May 1960), p. 396.

migration has reduced earnings differentials for two critical groups, farm workers and blacks—is to be answered in the negative. Two students of the field pass the verdict and point to important causes of this negative result. Johnson writes:

During the decade now ending, the net migration from farm to nonfarm areas has totalled almost 10 million persons out of a farm population of slightly more than 25 million in 1950. Despite so high a rate of out-migration, the return to farm labor has not risen relative to labor earnings in the rest of the economy. The natural increase of the farm population offset about two-fifths of the net migration. The resulting net reduction of the farm population has simply not been great enough to offset the combined effects of a rapidly increasing physical product per worker, low and declining income elasticity of demand for farm products, and the low price elasticities of demand for farm output.[18]

And Galloway concludes:

The process of geographic labor mobility makes very little contribution to improving the relative economic status of the Negro male. In fact, it may even lead to a worsening of that status. . . .

. . . . .

. . . This pattern of movement [into geographic regions where there are substantial numbers of other Negroes] would tend to produce a lowering of the earnings levels of Negroes due to the fact that earnings levels of Negroes [especially relative earnings] are negatively related to the number of Negroes in a region.[19]

As if to bear out this causal connection, a recent report of the successful (planned) migration of black families from the South to the Midwest emphasizes that painstaking scrutiny and selection along with severe numerical limitation must be regarded as essential parts of the positive results.[20]

---

[18] D. Gale Johnson, "Policies to Improve the Labor Transfer Process," *American Economic Review*, Vol. 50, No. 2 (May 1960), p. 403.

[19] Op. cit., pp. 49 and 107.

[20] Edward B. Jakubauskus and Neil A. Palomba, "Relocation of Farm Workers from Mississippi to Iowa," *Proceedings of the 1969 Annual Spring Meeting of the Industrial Relations Research Association* (Madison, Wis.: Industrial Relations Research Association, August 1969), pp. 479–496.

Social Costs and Benefits of Migration

Other economic studies than Sjaastad's, both earlier and later, have sought to explore in greater depth the effects of migration on communities and on society. Maddox, whose study was referred to earlier, attempted to conceptualize and quantify the losses caused to farm communities by the out-migration of farm workers and their families. He did this by representing the out-migrant contingent as "human capital from which they [the farm families remaining behind] receive few financial returns." [21]

Depending on whether out-migration of the younger element is so massive as to cause virtual abandonment of farming in the area of origin, there may be additional capital losses. Thus the loss to the community of origin consists, in any case, of the costs "of rearing and educating children who move away from their farm homes about the time they reach a productive age" plus, in some cases, a decline in total income, in capital values of fixed assets accompanied or followed by a rise in per capita costs of public services, and in business failures and disappearances.[22] Maddox cites other economists' earlier estimates and makes estimates himself on the basis of which the child investment drain alone would have cost the farming sector around $2 billion during the 1950s. No numerical estimate is given by Maddox of the additional losses: "Where farm abandonment is heavy, capital and entrepreneurship, as well as labor, are drained away with the result that large areas stagnate and remain dormant." [23]

At the receiving end also Maddox finds several categories of significant costs accruing to the affected communities, provided the inflow of migrants is rapid and large. Their expenditures on schools, police protection, and other governmental

---

[21] Op. cit., p. 397.
[22] Ibid.
[23] Ibid., p. 399.

services, he reasons, are likely to expand more rapidly than tax revenues. Consequently the quality of these services will decline; as further consequences, educational and cultural levels will fall and so may property values. Reinforcing (even though not being the initial cause of) migration to the suburbs on the part of former inner-city residents, these developments bring about a deterioration of the inner city while causing uneconomical capital needs and concentration for new housing and ancillary facilities in the suburbs, thus keeping the cost of borrowing high and entailing unnecessary waste of time and money on commuting. A further cost item or category of costs not developed in this enumeration may turn out to be crucial. It pertains to induced results that transcend the traditional economic cost or benefit concepts and that fall squarely within the realm of psychosocial dysfunctions and disutilities:

One of the heavy costs of the present pattern of off-farm migration is the continued concentration of low-income, farm-reared people in the congested slums of large cities. The resulting psychic costs to the individuals involved must be extremely high. It is a way of life which is completely foreign to their past experiences, and commonly results in high rates of crime, juvenile delinquency, and absenteeism from jobs. These, in turn, result in heavy public expenditures for police protection and welfare activities. The waste of human resources arising from slum conditions of living is a social loss of imponderable magnitude. This country is much too rich and powerful to allow these blights of the city to continue.[24]

Subsidized Migration

While Maddox does not analyze countervailing social benefits of farm-to-urban migration, he summarily dismisses these as likely to be of comparatively "minor offsetting significance."[25] On balance, therefore, he pronounces himself in favor of a movement in reverse—not of labor but of the complementary factor, capital (in the

form of industrial and commercial enterprises)—into areas of heavy rural unemployment. He also recommends "appropriate public action [involving] capital and income transfers into such areas which will enhance both the abilities of the people and the productiveness of the organizational units by which the natural resources are utilized."[26]

While this recommendation and its evaluation fall outside the purview of this paper, Maddox's reference to government programs designed to foster factor movement (of whatever sort) logically leads us to consider the approach to cost-benefit analysis taken in connection with labor mobility programs under government auspices and involving subsidized migration. In the assessment of these relatively new (in the United States) programs there may be in the offing a conceptual expansion of the social cost and benefit categories that might be developed in formulating future cost-benefit migration models.

Experimental and demonstration projects to test the practicality of guided and subsidized migration for unemployed and underemployed workers, notably in certain disadvantaged categories, were authorized under the Manpower Development and Training Act of 1962, as amended. Pursuant to this authorization, about one-third of the states undertook pilot projects to that effect. Reports on several of these became available during the early part of 1969.[27]

The applied research or demonstration model in all instances consisted of a total

[24] Ibid., p. 401.
[25] Ibid., p. 401.
[26] Ibid., p. 402.
[27] Among these are the following: *Final Report of the Labor Mobility Demonstration Project* (Atlanta: Georgia State Employment Service, March 31, 1969); "Relocation in Illinois. A Final Report" (Chicago: Illinois State Employment Service, January 20, 1969) (processed); "Final Report, Texas Labor Mobility Experimental and Demonstration Project" (Texas Employment Commission, April 1969) (processed); "West Virginia Labor Mobility Demonstration Project. Final Report" (Charleston: West Virginia Department of Employment Security, March 1969), and an earlier report dated October 10, 1967 (both processed).

population of workers (mostly unemployed and underemployed) in the local labor market that had to be screened first, with a view to determining their eligibility under the terms of relocation aid and second, to sift out those with special problems likely to make them unfit for referral (e.g., drinking, family instability, and the like). Before relocation assistance allowances and other benefits could be given, a bona fide job offer had to be available in a line of work in which the applicant was qualified. On these premises the relocation program tested was judged beneficial when successful relocation with job placement was achieved for a substantial proportion of those willing to move, when the number of unsuccessful relocations was small relative to the successful ones, and when benefits and administrative costs appeared reasonable. These conditions appear to have been met to a sufficient degree, in the judgment of the agencies conducting the experiments, to recommend adoption of a full-scale program of this type.[28]

Cost-Benefit Models

Given the facts that the great bulk of workers were out of work for six weeks or more before relocation and that there was no ready prospect of their local reemployment, this somewhat truncated assessment of program effectiveness may be a sufficiently telling one at the operational level, despite its limitations. For analytical purposes a model developed in connection with occupational mobility programs (i.e., for the purpose of evaluating U.S. government programs to retrain unemployed and other disadvantaged workers) could be applied—

with the necessary changes having been made—to geographic migration as well.

An original study of this type was made by Borus.[29] He included among the cost items accruing to the government those of selection, referral, and processing of candidates, as well as overall administrative costs, educational costs (i.e., instructor's and ancillary costs), and retraining allowances. (Considering government at all levels as one, presumably any savings in unemployment or welfare benefits would have to be deducted from these.) Going beyond the costs accruing to the government to those that accrue to the economy at large, Borus argued that, given less than full employment, retraining of the unemployed and the underemployed or even of unskilled employed workers will not cause any significant costs to arise from production lost as a result of retraining. Even in training the hard-core unemployed, both the government and the economy are sustaining putative costs only in the sense that the same retraining efforts, had they been applied to more capable workers, would yield presumably greater gains.[30]

Borus also elaborated the benefit side of his model in a threefold way, taking account of gains (and partial offsets to these) that accrue to the individual worker who is retrained, to the government, and to the economy—all applicable (with changes) to government-sponsored relocation programs as well. Aside from increased net-wage income to the individual (which Borus establishes not only by reference to the worker's earnings before retraining but also by comparison with the earnings of comparably situated unretrained workers who were

---

[28] Typically all or nearly all workers found eligible for relocation assistance were also found willing to move. Roughly between one-third and one-half of these were physically relocated. From one-eighth to one-fifth of these relocations proved unsuccessful. Average cost per case of relocation allowance ranged from below $400 to above $700 (covering transportation costs, subsistence for the worker and his family, and moving or storage expenses); administrative cost per case averaged from well below $200 to nearly double that figure.

[29] Michael E. Borus, "The Economic Effectiveness of Retraining the Unemployed," unpublished doctoral dissertation, Yale University, June 1964. (Processed.)

[30] Ibid., pp. 45, 65 ff., 77, and 83. The last-named point is a purely theoretical one, because as Borus himself adds: "Based on the experience of the workers in the sample, by retraining workers, the government's revenues will be increased much more than its costs, almost regardless of the characteristics of the workers who are retrained." (P. 83.)

members of a control group) and con-comitantly higher tax yields for government and a greater national product for the economy at large, there is reduced unemployment, entailing lowered expenditures for government and, again, an increase in national product. The gains are viewed as cumulative over the years following retraining insofar as workers do not leave occupations related to their retraining. (The rough analogy to this in relocation, presumably, would be remigration.) In a full-employment situation the ensuing gains for the economy could be offset in part if retrained persons displaced other workers or if workers not in the retraining program entered the occupations for which workers were being retrained. Under less-than-full-employment conditions the collective gains owing to fuller employment, multiplier effect, and so on are apt to be larger for the economy as a whole than for the individual.[31]

Aggregating and comparing benefits with costs incurred over time (i.e., by discounting future benefits to the present and including them in the count), Borus arrives at substantial margins of gain varying for individuals, government, and the economy (depending on a number of stated conditions with respect to each) but reaching the highest values for the collective excesses of benefits over costs.[32] Leaving aside any reference to the specific values in Borus's calculations, but using some of the information on successful relocation derived from the labor mobility studies cited, there are good reasons to expect that a model with similar concepts and calculations applied to government relocation programs may yield comparable ratios in support of the economic efficiency of these programs. As Mangum has put it: "The mobility projects, by requiring firm job offers, have increased the economic rationality of the moves."[33]

However, just as the economic rationality, although clearly emerging from the high ratios of successful relocation, becomes self-explanatory by virtue of the "firm job offer" premise of the move, so the dysfunctional outcomes that are apparent from the unsuccessful relocation figures gain concrete meaning only in light of the observations made by the would-be relocatees and by the administrators of the pilot programs. Both groups point to lack of suitable housing as the primary obstacle to successful relocation. In the accounts of the returnees this is followed by various adjustment difficulties (conditions of living and work), while the administrators appear to refer to the same phenomenon, albeit in a roundabout way, by singling out the lack or dearth of supportive services (especially, but not exclusively, postmigration) as the most critical gap.[34] Clearly not all essential information is conveyed in terms of the model.

The most comprehensive and potentially informative mobility cost-benefit model to date has been advanced in this connection by Jenness, a staff member of the Canadian Department of Manpower and Migration, in a highly technical analysis of the benefit-cost position of Canada's well-developed Federal Manpower Mobility Program.[35] The approach centers on the family rather than on the individual worker; secondary or indirect effects, as well as the impact of psychic factors, form part of the inventory both on the benefit and cost sides.

---

[31] Ibid., pp. 15–47.

[32] Ibid., pp. 80–85.

[33] Garth L. Mangum, "Moving Workers to Jobs," *New Generation*, Vol. 50, No. 3 (Summer 1968), p. 14.

[34] *See*, for example, the two West Virginia studies op. cit., p. 12 of the 1969 report and p. C4 of the 1967 report.

[35] R. A. Jenness, "Manpower Mobility Programs. A Benefit-Cost Approach." Paper presented at the North-American Conference on Cost-Benefit Analysis and Manpower Policies, Madison, Wis., May 1969. (Processed.) This Canadian program is among the most advanced of its kind. It comprises resettlement grants up to $1,000 or higher (depending on family size), full travel and household removal expenses, and a housing allowance of $1,500. Unemployed or underemployed workers with job offers in another community are eligible for these benefits without a means or need test.

(See the Manpower Mobility Program table.[36])

In presenting his table, however, the author informs his readers that while the numerical data for the primary or direct benefits and costs (except the last-named items on either side) are available as a by-product of the Manpower Mobility Program's operational statistics or can be derived from the model equations or attributed on the basis of other labor market information, the benefit and cost components named on the last line in the first benefit and cost category as well as the component parts of the second and third categories had to be omitted from consideration in making the benefit-cost comparison for lack of actual or estimated data.

Toward a Concept of Social Ecology

Modern economists have long acknowledged that certain economic activities had spillover or fallout effects for persons other than the parties involved in a given economic transaction. These have been called external effects or "externalities." For example, the case of a company that trains a novice who on completion of his training leaves that firm to take a job in the same industry, where he puts his newly acquired knowledge to good use (as far as he and that industry are concerned, but hardly for the benefit of the firm that provided the training), has given rise to the term "external economies." Conversely, the producer of a good whose manufacturing operation gives rise to harmful wastes or noxious by-products (which the producer neither prevents nor removes, but leaves to the community to worry about) causes an "external diseconomy." In neither case does the effect—beneficial or harmful—enter into the profit-and-loss calculus of the individual firm unless ultimately, at least in the latter instance, remedial legislation,

a court order, or a city ordinance pinpoints the responsibility for preventing, removing, or compensating for the damage.

For the longest time such externalities were simply ignored, both by the actors on the economic scene and by public policymakers. When external diseconomies reached the point of becoming a public nuisance, the redress of insufferable conditions was laid as a rule on the doorstep of government, and the costs were put on the shoulders of the general taxpayer.[37] Since the phenomenon was (and is) not considered important enough in its incidence or order of magnitude to affect the public interest, the subject has received relatively little attention.[38]

An important methodological breakthrough occurred as recently as June 1969, with the publication of an article by two researchers associated with the Quality of Environment Program, Resources for the Future, Inc.: Robert U. Ayres and Allen V. Kneese.[39] The authors point out that rather than being few and exceptional,

at least one class of externalities—those associated with the disposal of residuals resulting from the consumption and production process

---

[36] This table is taken from ibid., following p. 15.

[37] Even recent instances are readily at hand, e.g., the congressional compromise whereby the cost of extending workmen's compensation benefits to disabled miners who had become victims of black lung disease (pneumoconiosis) is to be financed not by the mining industry but from general revenues. See "Foes of Compensation to Miners Stall Senate Vote on Safety Bill," *New York Times*, October 1, 1969, p. 20. For text of legislation, see Federal Coal Mine Health and Safety Act of 1969, P.L. 91–173, December 30, 1969, Title IV.

[38] To be sure, a score or more theoretical treatments of the subject have appeared in print over the past several years. (*See* bibliography.) In the main they single out for analysis special situations of limited social significance. Among the important exceptions is the paper by Ayres and Kneese, to which further reference will be made later. *See* Robert U. Ayres and Allen V. Kneese, "Production, Consumption, and Externalities," *American Economic Review*, Vol. 59, No. 3 (June 1969), pp. 282–297.

[39] Ibid.

MANPOWER MOBILITY PROGRAM

Primary or Direct Benefits	*Primary or Direct Costs*
Real Output attributable to workers moved into the new job in the destination area.	Travel and Removal Expenditures.
	Administrative Costs of Mobility Program.
Real Output attributable to workers in subsequent jobs in the destination labour market.	Real Output attributable to the workers in their old job.
Real Output attributable to their (i) wives, (ii) children in immediate or potential employment in destination market.	Real Output attributable to workers in subsequent occupations in the old area.
	Real Output attributable to their (i) wives (ii) children in immediate or potential employment in the old labour market.
Additional real output attributable to the owners of capital employing the (i) workers (ii) wives (iii) children who moved.	Additional Real Output attributable to the owners of capital employing the (i) workers (ii) wives (iii) children who moved.
Secondary or Indirect Benefits	*Secondary or Indirect Costs*
"Multiplier Effect" stimuli to destination areas.	Negative "Multiplier Effect" in leaving areas.
Economies of scale in destination areas.	Reduced economies of scale in leaving areas.
Unemployed in leaving areas can fill the jobs vacated.	Reduced job vacancies for unemployed in destination areas.
Reduction in the demand for social overhead capital in leaving areas.	Increased demand for social overhead capital facilities in destination areas.
Less pressure on price increases due to faster filling of vacancies.	Possible interference with normal free market forces and individual incentives.
Better productivity, international competitiveness and foreign exchange earnings.	
Psychic or Social Benefits	*Psychic or Social Costs*
Greater overall sense of family security.	Greater family uncertainty.
Job satisfaction and permanent employment.	Job dissatisfaction and heightened likelihood of additional unemployment.
Positive encouragement to new investment.	Negative impact on employers' investment plans.
Social dynamism due to interchange of ideas, and productive methods.	Social tension due to increased congestion, pollution, and urban over-crowding.

—. . . are a normal, indeed, inevitable part of these processes. Their economic significance tends to increase as economic development proceeds. . . .[40]

The authors ascribe the common failure to appreciate this fact to the prevailing view of production and consumption processes "in a manner that is somewhat at variance with the fundamental law of conservation of mass."[41] They draw attention to the overriding importance of a natural environment capable of absorbing and assimilating such waste products and call such an environment "an important natural resource of increasing value."[42]

A considerable further broadening of the concept of externalities and of its application is highly indicated. It is an essential premise for any truly adequate conceptual system of accounting for social costs and benefits. Comparable to the law of conservation of mass, if only in a loose manner, and perhaps by way of a somewhat closer parallelism to the ecological principle in nature (i.e., the delicate balance between life-and-death-dealing forces and the myriad transformations that lend relative stability and permanence to the natural world),

---

[40] Ibid., p. 282.
[41] Ibid., p. 283.

[42] Ibid., p. 282.

there can be said to exist in human society a cause-and-effect relationship whose far-flung reverberations and interconnections have not yet been fully uncovered. Even to the extent to which they are known, they have been largely ignored in the analytical work of the various scientific disciplines simply because they cannot readily be confined to any one discipline. Instead they transcend each and cut across several, if not all.

Characteristically, however, the interrelationship is of a zigzag kind; that is, after leaving, for example, the realm of economics, a later feedback of certain economically generated noneconomic consequences reverberates or boomerangs back into the realm of economics during subsequent phases. For instance, those diseconomies that at the time and in the place where they are generated may be external to the individual firms or consuming units in their market transactions—such as obsolescent skills, human redundancy, and deterioration of the environment—if left to take their course may turn into acute threats to the smooth operation and ultimately to the very existence of the market economy once they attain certain proportions and degrees of intensity. In at least a loose sense, therefore, we can discern a social ecology engendering a circular flow of inputs and outputs somewhat comparable to that found in the ecology of nature and its circular flow of materials.

Galbraith, probably the most imaginative among present-day economists, has astutely added to the three essentials of life usually cited by economists—food, shelter, and housing—a fourth: "an orderly environment in which the first three might be provided." [43] Similarly it can be said, with equal justification, that the premises for the effective exercise of private initiative and the operation of the (basically) free market—both cornerstones of our economic system—include not only the individual

drive and ability of the buyers and sellers, but also an exacting web of smoothly functioning institutional arrangements appropriate to the state of the industrial arts. To put it differently, a nation's economy is part and parcel of the larger social fabric of society, and the quality of its functioning cannot be abstracted from the functioning of the rest of society. Any dysfunctional aspects of a society are bound to make their impact on its economy, no matter how "private" (i.e., removed from government intervention) the latter may be.

Inferences for Model-Building

Some inferences for model-building emerge from the foregoing:

1. It behooves the economic analyst—with the help of specialists from other disciplines—to trace the consequences of economic activities in all their fullness. For example, he will have to follow through in evaluating a restructuring of regional production patterns that entails the displacement of workers and their out-migration and—seen from the other end—its impact on urban life and growth, beyond the point at which these induced events temporarily leave the economist's accustomed frame of reference. Moreover he will have to recognize when a more remote consequence reenters the economic framework, albeit in different garb at a later stage, and he will have to be able properly to diagnose it as a member in the same unbroken chain of cause and effect. With specific reference to the subject matter of migration, those secondary and tertiary benefits and costs that Jenness identified in his model but failed to include in his calculations (and probably many others as well) must be included in this social profit-and-loss roundup.

2. The argument centering around the real or alleged elusiveness of psychic effects and certain other concomitants of migration reveals itself as spurious. For what needs to be ascertained and measured is not really these phenomena themselves, but

---

[43] John Kenneth Galbraith, *The Affluent Society* (Boston: Houghton Mifflin Co., 1969) p. 129.

rather their subsequent feedback in economic coin. Once one proceeds on the assumption that some effects are bound to ensue, the task becomes one of sifting the multiple impacts on the economy and quantifying them, or else finding some other form in which their quality as a benefit or cost can be assessed in terms that are comparable or at least susceptible to being reduced to a common denominator. Thus it is the social opportunity cost of the psychic effect that counts, rather than that effect itself. For example, if the psychic cost of uprooting a family, notably the children in it, selling the family's house (and writing off all the family labor invested therein), and so on is judged to be insufficient to dissuade the family from a move, the economic consequences of its possible ill-effects owing to precisely these causes (that is, its unstabilizing results), will have to be assessed against the ill-effects of staying (the perpetuation of suboptimal conditions and possibly social decay).

3. It appears that in a socioecological perspective, economic phenomena take on the character of "social implicators." [44] Seen in this light, not only a transsocietal but a transgenerational appraisal of their consequences is of the essence. Again, a practical example may serve to clarify the point: Family migration has a multiple long-range impact on educational facilities and services, housing, health, recreation, transportation, and other administrative services—to name only some of the public sector areas that are implicated. The implication is both in terms of substantial capital outlays—a one-time expenditure—and long-term increases in staffing and other operational costs, all continuing encumbrances.

Once these implicated areas are identified and acknowledged, the cost side of the benefit-cost appraisal must not be in terms of actual expenditures that have been incurred in the receiving communities, but in terms of the estimated necessary costs of the expansions called for in each of these several categories of public expenditures. One need only cite one or two instances from actual experience to highlight the immense difference such a change in concepts and procedures would make:

Out of seven metropolitan cities that absorbed some of the largest in-migration during the decade 1950–60, several experienced an actual decline in public housing in that period (New York, Philadelphia, St. Louis, and Newark), while only one (Cleveland) experienced a substantial increase in public housing. [45] Nor did the private housing sector move in any consistent fashion, except perhaps in Cleveland. In New York and Chicago private building permits increased dramatically; in Detroit and St. Louis there was a drastic decline. [46] Obviously the costs of in-migration computed in terms of actual housing expenditures in the receiving cities would constitute a vast understatement. To be sure some costs not shown under housing might enter the cost-benefit table—either currently or in subsequent periods—under different headings. They might appear in the form of a heightened incidence of communicable diseases (compare the recent reports of steep increases in new tuberculosis cases). Rises in crime rates, police costs, and other such things may absorb some of the hidden costs.

Expenditures for pre- and postmigration counseling and supportive services might have constituted an initial increase in costs only to be more than offset—in light of the testimony of the labor mobility counselors cited earlier—by a substantial decline in unsuccessful migration, notably remigration, and might thus reduce the true economic cost of migration.

Welfare expenditures may in part depend

---

[44] The writer is indebted for this apt expression to Warren Greenberg, who coined and used it in one of his preparatory notes for this paper.

[45] In terms of awards of construction contracts for new public housing units. Computed from U.S. Department of the Census, *Housing Construction Statistics 1889–1964* (Washington, D.C.: U.S. Government Printing Office, 1966), Table B-7.

[46] Ibid., Table B-5.

on both of the foregoing categories of expenditure. We seem to be far from knowing all the interconnections. Some unexpected findings resulted from an examination of nonwhite migration during the 1950s into seven cities having the largest nonwhite populations (in 1960). Those experiencing the largest in-migration showed a decline in per capita welfare costs based on the city's total population (for example, Chicago, Cleveland, and Newark), whereas those with low in-migration rates (Philadelphia and Detroit) had the opposite experience. On the other hand, some of the cities with the highest rates of net in-migration of persons aged 20–34 incurred the highest increase in police expenditures during the decade 1950–60.[47] Could it be that to some extent increased welfare expenditures and increased police expenditures are representative of different modes of a community's adjustment to an influx of migrants?

Not only would a socioecological approach drastically change the economic cost-benefit model of migration, it would also clarify public policy needs and alternative courses. For society, even more than for a family or an individual, discounted earnings possibilities of the migrant in the new as compared with the old location can serve at best as a first approximation toward evaluating a move in cost-benefit terms. The aggregate benefit-cost picture may reveal a balance that not only differs in magnitude but that might even bear in front of it the opposite sign from the result of this preliminary reckoning.

---

[47] Compare *Net Migration of the Population 1950–60 by Age, Sex and Color* (Stillwater: Oklahoma State University Research Foundation and U.S. Department of Commerce Area Redevelopment Administration, 1965); and *Compendium of City Government Finances* (Washington, D.C.: U.S. Department of Commerce, Bureau of the Census, 1950 and 1960).

Choices of Policy

The policy choices are several. One is to pursue a continued "hands-off" policy with respect to migration, except for substantial improvements in job and labor market information, such as have been proposed by the present administration in the form of computerized nationwide job-banks underpinned by stepped-up retraining programs, as envisioned in the current manpower proposals.

Another is to convert the pilot labor mobility programs into full-blown operating programs following the Canadian or Swedish examples but concentrating efforts, at least initially, on areas and population groups that are in greatest jeopardy. (The financial incentive provisions could be applied to entice not only the would-be migrants but conceivably also would-be employers.)

A third is a much more broadly conceived social and population policy encompassing both incentive and regulatory provisions toward planned area development pursuant to regional and national socioeconomic development plans. This far-reaching policy would necessitate an element of planning not heretofore engaged in at the federal level except in wartime. It would probably necessitate the establishment of a long-term capital outlay budget for socioeconomic development and the earmarking to that end of a large part of the nation's anticipated annual economic growth. Substantial increases in the allocation of economic resources to such domestic development would no doubt be required. However, not inconsiderable savings should be possible from a searching review of the multiplicity of currently existing programs with the object of eliminating conflicting and overlapping efforts as well as reassigning priorities in terms of the overall goal of social betterment.

Discussion

CATHERINE C. HIATT: The presumption in much of what has been said is that we are talking about planned relocation, that is, pulling up roots in one community and then putting them down in another. But some people never grow roots anywhere; some people's parents never had any roots. Some of the rootless ones have a nominal base to which they return; some may have no base at all. Yet among these are persons who are part of the active labor force and are functioning members of society. They may stay in one community on one job for two, four, or five years and then go to another community for another span of time.

A number of jobs that are germane to our economy involve being on the move— the entertainment professions, traveling salesmen, some construction jobs. What we need to examine and develop plans for is just these lines of employment that are rooted in mobility, since they have emotional and social dynamics for the persons concerned.

I would like also to draw a distinction within the migrant population between those relocating planfully and those Travelers Aid identifies as being "in flight." Persons of all races, classes, and socioeconomic levels can appear in either category.

As we view the mobility phenomenon we see that persons can readily start out in one category and end up in another. People who begin with planned relocation, for example, may be thwarted by lack of jobs, rejection by new neighbors, and so on. They may then move on, with the same result, leading to further moves. After a while they can easily slide over into the faceless, stateless group of perpetual movers. We also know that people who start out running away from discomfort with themselves or their life situation can, with help, end up as successful relocatees. I don't think we have looked at this aspect of mobility.

Sometimes when a Travelers Aid worker has made contact with a person on the move, it is difficult to determine which dynamic is at work. If, however, his original purpose in pulling up roots was planned relocation and if comprehensive job market information and orientation to a possible community destination are made available in advance so that he can choose knowledgeably—where to go, what to expect, and how to prepare—there is certainly a much greater likelihood of successful outcome.

It may be a truism that the better the preparation given to people about to move and the greater the readiness of the receiving community to accept, buttress, and absorb them, the less need there may be for formally organized and separate post-migration supportive social services. I would add one thing: to date all pilot labor relocation programs for poor people have been built around starting with the people in their home communities before they begin to move.

I have long dreamed that a way could be found to give persons who start out on their own in a new city the option of taking a job and receiving any needed social supports to stay there or being placed in a financially assisted relocation program—that is, to be helped financially to move to a third community where a job may be assured and community considerations found. I suspect that what we must reach for is some kind of mix of the several types of programming within a comprehensive federal policy of internal migration, based on existing research and allowing for urgently needed research yet to be done.

Repeat Migration

HYLAN G. LEWIS: For most rooted persons, the first migration is the most difficult. It is then that they must break familiar ties and give up an assured status. Once one move is made, other moves come more easily. People do not reestablish roots in the new area equal to those in the place of origin. This is true of professionals and the poor alike, black as well as white. There is now a good deal of black movement between former areas of reception of black migrants from the South like New York and Chicago to cities where in the past there were few blacks—Milwaukee, San Diego, Los Angeles, and Buffalo. The rates of increase of the black population in these new reception centers have been high.

The Straddler Effect

MARC FRIED: How long does a person remain a migrant? Our study [in Boston] distinguishes among recent migrants, persons who have been in the city for five years or longer, and those who were born there. At what point does a person cease to be considered a migrant?

Many migrants are really straddlers. They live in one place but often visit "back home"; they may even go back for a while. Sometimes—especially now that transportation is so easily available—people maintain two residences. Often they are buried in the place from which they came. The real break comes when family members are not brought home to be buried or no longer return there to attend the funerals of old friends.

An Economist's View

GEORGE F. ROHRLICH: In my paper I stressed the fact that the bias of the economist is in favor of migration, because presumably there is an economic gain at both ends. This is where cost-benefit reckoning comes in. A set of problems soon discovered suggested the need for several modifications of this somewhat simplistic model. Among the problems was the discovery that some migrants appeared to be motivated differently than economists had presumed them to be, and as a result in a number of cases the moves were inefficient in the economist's sense. The most sophisticated cost-benefit model uses the concept of the family of the migrant and "negative multipliers" or social overhead have to be added to the cost of migration. Social overhead includes housing, education, and other such facilities and services, as well as the psychic or social effects of migration, ranging up to and including social upsets and alienation.

This approach is sound but rarely used because of the difficulties of coming to grips with the technical problems of conceptualizing and measuring these social phenomena. But we ought to develop gradually the necessary know-how whereby we can identify them. No longer would we compare, for example, the comparative costs of having and not having a program to rehabilitate wayward youths. Rather than just taking into account actual program costs, we would, with the help of our newly gained insights, assess the necessary costs against those of either not permitting the event to happen or steering the event in the desired directions.

As an example I make reference in my paper to the "investment" aspect of counseling programs in making labor mobility more planful and more successful. Among the pilot studies sponsored by the U.S. Department of Labor—and there are about eighteen of those now—study after study shows that with better guidance, both before and after migrations under the experimental labor mobility programs, a significant proportion of so-called inefficient migration—that is, migration that leads to maladjustment and frequently to remigration and that is therefore an economic loss—could have been prevented.

Economists generally favor migration as a way of rationalizing the power of labor but they are becoming more and more aware of indirect costs or externalities. These can be losses or gains that accrue to people who are not involved in a transaction between a buyer and seller. For example, river pollution resulting from the economic activity of paper-making hurts the public, who are not involved in the process.

In migration there are often externalities —waste production. In cost accounting it is important to differentiate between the cost of a social program in money, the cost of human externalities, and the cost of not offering the social program at all.

ROBERT MORRIS: We are often engaged these days in reorganizing social services and their structure. Much of the time this is talked of in economic and efficiency terms: "It is going to be more reasonable; it is going to be more coordinated; it is

going to be simpler. It is not going to be so expensive." Less often one hears the question: "What are the social purposes of the reorganization?" If the social purpose of a regional development plan is to spread economic well-being in the farmlands, is it to reduce the mobility? Is it to stabilize society? If that is the social purpose, then what kind of a price does one pay for the benefits one gets?

RAUL A. MUÑOZ: When people leave an area, some think this has positive results. In Puerto Rico, for instance, young people who leave thus reduce overpopulation and the number of unemployed. However, the national impact of this migration is more negative. Young people leave who might object to the status quo; some of the more talented young people leave. Farms are being abandoned and there is a shortage of labor. Interestingly enough, Puerto Rico has absorbed 80,000 Cuban immigrants into its population as skilled workers. There is now talk of importing workers from the Dominican Republic as farm laborers.

Migration As System-Crossing

EUGENE BRODY: One footnote about the matter of migration of upper middle-class professionals: Fred Sysanin, who studied the movement of migrants into Santiago de Chile, said that the person who migrates encounters new places, new faces, and new norms, and therefore it follows that the essential characteristic of the migrant is that he is a crosser of social systems. By and large, migrating men don't always cross social systems. They may simply be doing their work in a different place, conforming to the same norms. But a considerable number of wives of migrating professionals are forced to shift roots in a manner much different from their husbands. They are the system-crossers and they have a harder time because of this.

Part II

Black Migration:
A Test Case of Welfare Policy

Black Migration and the Struggle for Equity: A Hundred-Year Survey

DEMITRI B. SHIMKIN

[Statistical tables referred to in this article appear in consecutive order beginning on p. 106.—ED.]

This paper examines two complementary pairs of questions: How has migration influenced the life conditions and thus the cultures of black people in the United States? Conversely, how have cultural values and dynamics affected the patterns and consequences of migration of black people in the United States? What are the salient implications of these tentative findings for research and social action? How are future developments likely to affect these findings?

Migrations and Black Cultures

In brief, this paper will explore the nature of the two interacting phenomena, migration and the cultures of black Americans, beginning with an outline of the stages and cultural associations of nationwide black migration since 1866. This will provide the context for a more detailed examination of the interactions of culture and migration originating in the sample black community of Holmes County, Mississippi.[1] The conclusions and projections will be derived from these data and comparison of findings with those of selected other groups.

Underlying this paper are materials from continuing research on Mexican-American migrants in Illinois, the Polish-American

---

[1] Undertaken by the Milton Olive III Memorial Corporation of Lexington, Miss. (Mr. Samuel Friar, President), in cooperation with the University of Illinois under Grant H-00438-01, National Center for Health Services Research and Development. (Principal investigator, Mrs. Bernice Montgomery; program director, Mr. E. W. Logan.)

Research on this paper was completed in August 1969. Since then, the census of the Holmes County black community (winter 1969-70) has established the January 1, 1970, population to be about 18,100. Out-migration for 1960-69 is now estimated to have been about 4,900 and at a rate only slightly lower than in 1950-59. At the same time, the proportion of in-migrants in the Holmes County population was determined to be 13 percent, rather than 25 percent as originally thought.

77

community of Hamtramck, Michigan, and a considerable body of published reports.[2]

The preliminary and qualitative nature of this essay must be emphasized. For example, a careful census that will generate much information on migration to and from Holmes County has recently been completed.[3] Many needed measurements —for example, on the comparative growth and development of closely related children in Holmes County and Chicago—are matters for the future. And of course comparable data have yet to be gathered for other representative black migrant populations.

Migrations

Migrations are the spatial displacements of populations or parts thereof either to new areas or within a defined circuit.[4] They

are basic elements of animal behavior and of the dispersion, selection, and evolution of species. Migrations have increased in scale, distance, and demographic and other effects with the rise of centralized and stratified states, occupational specialization, the mechanization of transportation and agriculture, and the growth of cities. The sources of migratory impulses are multiple and include individual economic, intellectual, and family-forming drives, especially in young adults; economic, political, and other pressures in the area of origin; and perceived attractions of the destination.

The development and maintenance of a migratory stream depends on the capacity of migrants to reach their destination, survive there and maintain their identities, and send back information to the area of origin. On this basis, the maintenance of a gradient of attraction to the destination and a continuing demographic capacity in the area of origin, colonization develops. Colonization involves viable relations with the receiving population, sociocultural modifications to preserve both viability and internal cohesion, and appropriate recruitment. Initial migration, feedbacks from returning migrants and through remittances of whatever nature, and new recruitment modify the area of origin, including the relation of the source population to others.[5] Accompanying these social dynamics are

---

The demographic impacts of out-migration have been especially severe among younger men, the numbers of those now aged 20–29 falling by 80 percent over the decade. This has intensified problems of economic viability and social control. The effects on fertility have been minimal. Sociopolitically, the boycott against Lexington's white merchants in 1969 led to divisions in the black community that have healed only slowly. Nevertheless, the farmers' cooperative has grown to over three hundred families since 1969 and is becoming a significant economic asset. Another new development is the Kennedy Civic Improvement Association, which promises to be an important factor in the community's efforts at capital formation.

[2] For research on Mexican-American migrants, *see* C. H. Gilkeson and G. M. LaMarsh, "Migrant Families and Their Use of Community Resources." Master's thesis, University of Illinois at Urbana, 1969.

[3] This covered past residences (for the preceding six and twelve months) of each black person residing in Holmes County in the critical period; identified temporary (eleven-month or shorter) and permanent departures within six and twelve months of the critical period; and described the age, sex, relation to head of household, educational status or attainment, occupation, and current activity of each. Reports on this census are now in preparation.

[4] This follows the analysis in M. Sorre, *Les migrations des peuples* (Paris, France: Flammarion, 1955), esp. pp. 7–8. Demographers usually exclude cyclical or continuous migrations;

compare E. S. Lee, "A Theory of Migration," *Demography*, Vol. 3 (1966), pp. 47–57. Conversely, animal ecologists include only cyclical mobility under migrations, using "dispersals" and "irruptions" for other types of movement. *See* S. C. Kendeigh, *Animal Ecology* (Englewood Cliffs, N.J.: Prentice-Hall, 1961), pp. 145–162, 234–244.

[5] This model is based in particular on studies of Chinese and Indian migrations. *See* D. T. C. Cheng, "Acculturation of the Chinese in the United States: A Philadelphia Story." Ph.D. dissertation, University of Pennsylvania, 1948; T. Chen, *Emigrant Communities in South China* (New York: Institute of Pacific Relations, 1940); and C. Jayawardena, "Migration and Social Change: A Survey of Indian Communities Overseas," *Geographical Review*, Vol. 58 (1968), pp. 426–449.

profound biological changes that in turn have social consequences. Such changes include the selection and selective survival of migrants, the modification of migrant physiology and behavior through new stresses and stimuli, and changes in mating and fertility rates and patterns.[6]

A general model of migrations has been developed.[7] Its utility has become apparent in the writer's research, but many aspects of migration mechanics and the effects of migration are still little understood. This paper seeks to broaden understanding by means of a case study placed in comparative context.

---

[6] That biological changes accompany migration is clear, but the mechanics thereof are still unknown. Significant studies include those on accelerated growth among immigrant Japanese, Polish children relocated to urban areas, and growth limitations among American children in the tropics. *See* H. L. Shapiro, assisted by F. S. Hulse, *Migration and Environment* (London, England: Oxford University Press, 1939); N. Wolanski, "Environmental Modification of Human Form and Function," *Annals of the New York Academy of Sciences*, Vol. 134 (New York: New York Academy of Sciences, 1966), pp. 820–840; and P. B. Eveleth, "The Effects of Climate on Growth," *Annals of the New York Academy of Sciences*, pp. 750–759. Among the literature on the stresses of migration, the best study—which indicates a heightened probability of mental illness during the first five years of residence—is Benjamin Malzberg and E. S. Lee, *Migration and Mental Disease. A Study of First Admissions to Hospitals for Mental Disease, New York, 1939–41* (New York: Social Science Research Council, 1956). A suggestive study on the long-term behavioral effects of urbanization is S. D. Singh, "Urban Monkeys," *Scientific American*, Vol. 221, No. 1 (January 1969), pp. 108–115.

[7] The best general analysis is Lee, op. cit., modifying Ravenstein. Recent studies on Chile, Japan, and the U.S.S.R. confirm this model. *See* B. H. Herrick, *Urban Migrants and Economic Development in Chile* (Cambridge, Mass.: MIT Press, 1965); S. Noziri, *Internal Migration of Rural Population in Japan*, "Studies on Population Problems in Japan, VI" (Tokyo: Japanese National Commission for UNESCO, 1964); V. I. Perevedentsev, *Migratsiya naseleniya i trudovyye problemy Sibiri (Migration and the Manpower Problems of Siberia)* (Novosibirsk: Izd. "Nauka," 1966).

Black Cultures

If we accept a culture as a set of characteristic behavioral codes, environmental modifications, and population compositions of a given interacting community, it appears to be inherently unstable. For instance the culture of a city can only be maintained and developed by constant instruction of the young and by innovation.[8] Cultures are also adaptive; behavioral codes appropriate in one environment may be disastrous in another.[9]

The black cultures of the United States have evolved from West African roots modified through slavery and prolonged repression by means of extensive innovation, borrowing, and selection. Although a single technically adequate ethnography of either a rural or an urban black community in the United States has yet to be made, it is clear from field studies that these black cultures exhibit a distinctiveness, complexity, and variability comparable to those of modern European peasant communities.[10] It must be stressed that many "contradictory" features—for example, Frazier's "matriarchate" and "black Puritans"—are in fact simply different adaptive facets of a bilateral extended family structure.[11] One assures physical survival under maximum stress; the other provides a capacity for sociocultural development. Moreover, many features of these cultures, such as the systems of customary law and adjudications, have not been studied.

In general present-day black cultures are believed to comprise a common tradition,

---

[8] Julian H. Steward and Demitri B. Shimkin, "Some Mechanisms of Sociocultural Evolution," *Daedalus*, Vol. 90, No. 3 (Summer 1961), pp. 477–497.

[9] Demitri B. Shimkin, "The Calculus of Survival," *Medical Opinion and Review*, Vol. 4, No. 10 (1968), pp. 47–67.

[10] *See*, for example, J. M. Halpern, *A Serbian Village* (New York: Columbia University Press, 1956).

[11] E. Franklin Frazier, *The Negro Family in the United States* (Chicago: University of Chicago Press, 1939), esp. pp. 125–145, 246–267.

composed largely of symbols of identity, features of social structure, and codes of interracial and class interaction. The special traditions include an Old Elite culture and a variety of rural and urban cultures.[12] These are changing rapidly, both as local adaptations and in response to stimuli from other groups. This paper will explore a number of these developments as they are affected by migration.

Patterns and Contexts of Black Migration, 1865–1966

In the century following the Civil War the black population of the United States quadrupled and was redistributed geographically (see Table 1). The proportion living outside the South rose from 8.6 percent in 1870 to 45 percent in 1966. Black people became urbanized more rapidly than whites in the North and West and in proportion to whites in the South. The largest urban concentrations of blacks shifted correspondingly (see Table 2). By 1960 New York City had more blacks than Georgia; Chicago had almost as many as Mississippi. These redistributions took place in five fairly distinct time phases: 1866–1915, 1916–30, 1931–41, 1942–60, and 1960 to the present.

Repression, 1866–1915

The earliest period was dominated by the success of southern whites in defeating the Reconstruction effort and reimposing bondage on blacks. This repression intensified after the "separate-but-equal" (*Plessy* versus *Ferguson*) decision of 1896; Booker T. Washington's ideology of accommodation sanctioned the civil inferiority, disenfranchisement, and educational disability of the black people, yet it failed to stop mobility.[13] In the Southeast the breakup of plantations opened up opportunities for independent farm operation, eagerly seized by the black population.[14] In the Upper Mississippi Delta, in Arkansas, and (to a degree) in the Midwest, new farmlands attracted black pioneers.[15] These movements, although relatively small, developed a social stratum—"black Puritans," in Frazier's words—characterized by family cohesion, thriftiness, and ambition.[16]

Others, especially young women, landless youths, and those endangered by lynch law, moved to cities. There was little to attract them. There were few and menial jobs, bad housing, disease, crime, and prostitution. In 1900 the median death rate for Negroes in the fourteen cities with the largest black populations was 31 per 1,000 persons; the median infant mortality rate was 393 per 1,000 births.[17] Small wonder that the black population in the North and West failed to reproduce itself for some thirty years (see Table 3).

Yet even in the cities some progress was realized. Between 1890 and 1910 the proportion of male nonagricultural workers

[12] For a discussion of the Old Elite culture *see* Arna Bontemps and Jack Conroy, *They Seek a City* (New York: Doubleday, Doran & Co., 1945), esp. pp. 28–36, 98–110; and E. Franklin Frazier, *Black Bourgeoisie* (New York: Free Press of Glencoe, 1957). Partial studies of merit include C. G. Woodson, *The Rural Negro* (Washington, D.C.: Association for the Study of Negro Life and History, 1930); C. S. Johnson, *The Shadow of the Plantation* (Chicago: University of Chicago Press, 1934); S. H. S. Lorenzi, ed., *Blacks and Black Communities* (Urbana: University of Illinois Press, 1969); W. E. B. Dubois, *The Philadelphia Negro*, "Series in Political Economy and Public Law," No. 14 (Philadelphia: University of Pennsylvania, 1899); and St. Clair Drake and Horace R. Cayton, *Black Metropolis* (2d ed., 2 vols.; New York: Harper & Row, 1962).

[13] W. E. B. Dubois, "The Souls of Black Folk," in *Three Negro Classics* (New York: Avon, 1968), esp. pp. 240–255; C. V. Woodward, *The Strange Career of Jim Crow* (New York: Oxford University Press, 1953), esp. pp. 49–65.
[14] T. J. Woofter, Jr., *Negro Migration* (New York: Gray, 1920), esp. pp. 105–121.
[15] C. G. Woodson, *A Century of Negro Migration* (Washington, D.C.: Association for the Study of Negro Life and History, 1918), pp. 126–146. For a case study *see* J. O. Wheeler and S. D. Brunn, "An Agricultural Ghetto: Negroes in Cass County, Michigan, 1845–1968," *Geographical Review*, Vol. 59 (1969), pp. 317–329.
[16] *The Negro Family in the United States.*
[17] U.S. Bureau of the Census, *Negro Population 1790–1915* (Washington, D.C.: U.S. Government Printing Office, 1918), pp. 331–335.

who were household laborers, servants, and other domestics fell from 54.6 to 34.0 percent, while that of those in manufacturing, construction, and mining rose from 21.6 to 36.0 percent; transportation workers, from 13.9 to 17.1 percent; and white-collar workers, from 4.9 to 6.0 percent.[18] Moreover, Dubois's 1896 study of Philadelphia's black population already reveals a weak yet exclusive elite; both large, highly structured congregations and tiny, itinerant centers of emotional worship; secret societies (Masons, Odd Fellows, and others), burial societies, Negro unions, and weak cooperative stores; community newspapers; political clubs; organized gambling, hustling, and prostitution—that is, the basic features of ghetto culture.[19] Dubois also noted that 55 percent of the Philadelphia Negroes were born in the South, especially around Chesapeake Bay, and furthermore, that denial of opportunity consonant with an individual's education forced extensive outmigration of the educated and the skilled to other areas in the North and even the South.[20]

The Great Migration, 1916–30

In 1916 sudden opportunities precipitated the Great Migration.[21] This was generated by wartime industrial demands and the cessation of white immigration from Europe, and was further stimulated by the destruction of the cotton crop by the boll-weevil in the South and the militant advocacy of the Chicago *Defender*. In a fifteen-year period well over a million blacks from southern towns, plantations, and farms resettled in northern cities (see Tables 3 and 4). This time their adaptation was more successful. By 1930 the median death rate for Negroes in the fourteen cities with the largest black populations had dropped to 19.5 per 1,000; the median infant mortality rate was 105 per 1,000 births.[22] By 1930 the proportion of domestics among non-agricultural male workers had fallen to 10.9 percent, while those in manufacturing, construction, and mining, transportation workers, and white-collar workers made up 46.7, 17.1, and 6.4 percent respectively of the total.[23]

In general the northern urban colonies were consolidated in the period 1916–30. Supporting this development was an aid program not available to earlier migrants, in which labor recruiters from northern industries, northern black churches, and, to some degree, civic organizations such as the Urban League were active.[24] The new migrants from the South came with firm social as well as economic goals: freedom from injustice and educational opportunities for their children.[25] In considerable measure they were conscious builders:

Of the Pittsburgh Negroes interviewed, 15 percent of 162 newly arrived families had savings, 82 percent of the 139 married ones with families in the South were sending money home, and nearly 100 (46 percent) of the 219 single Negroes interviewed were contributing to the support of parents or other children.[26]

Furthermore, the new migrants, in contrast to many of the old urban blacks, were determined to stand up for their rights. In 1917 white terrorism in East St. Louis had precipitated the flight of many blacks; by 1919 black resistance in the Chicago riots

---

[18] Ibid., pp. 526–527.

[19] *The Philadelphia Negro,* pp. 197–234, 368–384.

[20] Ibid., pp. 75, 352–355.

[21] *See* U.S. Department of Labor, *Negro Migration in 1916–17* (Washington, D.C.: U.S. Government Printing Office, 1919), esp. pp. 19–33; and Bontemps and Conroy, op. cit., pp. 131–146.

[22] U.S. Bureau of the Census, *Negroes in the United States 1920–1932* (Washington, D.C.: U.S. Government Printing Office, 1935), pp. 381–407, 453.

[23] Ibid., pp. 310–327. These data have been recalculated for comparability with the statistics of 1890 and 1910.

[24] U.S. Department of Labor, op. cit., pp. 118–122, 149–156.

[25] Ibid., esp. pp. 29–36, 58, 86–89, 101, 106–107; T. J. Woofter, Jr., *Negro Problems in Cities* (New York: Doubleday, Doran & Co., 1928), pp. 96–97.

[26] U.S. Department of Labor, op. cit., p. 150.

had forced white accommodations. During the 1920s bombings in the Hyde Park area of Chicago failed to deter an advance of black settlement.[27]

The growth and modest prosperity of these colonies permitted the development of black business areas, notably in New York and Chicago. New outlying middle-class districts emerged, with substantial proportions of homeownership and even with neighborhood improvement associations. Memphis and Chicago (especially Morgan Park) led in this regard.[28] In contrast to the self-abasement of the 1890s, racial pride became an explicit integrating theme. It expressed itself, especially in Chicago, in an attempt to build up black churches and businesses. More significantly, the Negro Renaissance in Harlem and elsewhere articulated in literature and music the nature and significance of the black experience. Extreme manifestations of this search for identity came through Marcus Garvey's short-lived back-to-Africa movement and through the founding of an explicitly antiwhite organization, the Black Muslims.[29]

Even during these years black urbanism exhibited weaknesses. White efforts to contain black settlement were varied. In the ghettos housing, sanitation, police protection, and educational facilities were shameful. High rentals forced one-third of the urban families in the North and one-sixth of those in the South to take in lodgers. This, with lowered infant mortality, increased both illegitimacy rates and the proportion of female-headed households. The high frequency of working mothers promoted juvenile delinquency, including the formation of delinquent gangs. These difficulties of adjustment were especially acute during the first five years of urban residence.[30]

---

[27] Bontemps and Conroy, op. cit., pp. 125–131; Drake and Cayton, op. cit., pp. 65–76, 178–180.
[28] Woofter, *Negro Problems in Cities*, pp. 100–104, 142–143, 162–164.
[29] Bontemps and Conroy, op. cit., pp. 162–186.

The Great Depression, 1931–41

The Great Depression began early for black people: by 1930 every black bank in Chicago had failed.[31] The full depth of misery suffered by blacks during the Depression remains obscure. In general it was a period of occupational retrogression, imposed by discrimination by employers and repression by white workers. In 1940 only 71.3 percent of the Negro male urban labor force was employed, the comparable figure for whites being 82.5 percent.[32] By 1940 the share of manufacturing, construction, and mining jobs in Negro male nonagricultural employment had fallen to 39.0 percent and that of transportation, communications, and utilities to 11.6 percent, although white-collar jobs had risen slightly, to 8.8 percent of the total.[33]

In 1936 a survey of 78,330 Negro male skilled workers in eighty-one cities showed that unemployment among them had risen to 17.7 percent, compared to 8.4 percent in 1930. Of those employed, only 74.5 percent were able to follow skilled pursuits.[34] In agriculture a 28 percent drop in the number of farm tenants kept forcing mi-

---

[30] Woofter, *Negro Problems in Cities*; Frazier, *The Negro Family in the United States*, pp. 347–357, 570–571. Extensive detail is given in E. Franklin Frazier, *The Negro Family in Chicago* (Chicago: University of Chicago Press, 1932). Malzberg and Lee, op. cit., pp. 119–124, found that psychoses developed within five years of migration to New York among nonwhites at rates three times higher than among permanent residents or longer resident migrants.
[31] Drake and Cayton, op. cit., p. 84.
[32] U.S. Bureau of the Census, *Sixteenth Census of the United States: 1940*, Vol. 2, Part 1 (Washington, D.C.: U.S. Government Printing Office, 1943), p. 47.
[33] Ibid. Figures have been recalculated for consistency with earlier data. A reconciliation of statistics on domestic and allied employment could not be made.
[34] U.S. Department of the Interior, Office of the Adviser on Negro Affairs, *The Urban Negro Worker in the United States, 1925–1936*, Vol. II, *Male Negro Skilled Workers in the United States, 1930–1936* (Washington, D.C.: U.S. Government Printing Office, 1939), p. 3.

grants into the cities throughout the decade 1930–40.[35]

The general effect of these troubles was an increase in mortality rates, which reduced the natural growth rate of the black population from the 1920–30 rate of 1.3 percent per year to 0.7 percent annually (see Table 1). These effects were apparently concentrated among the least fortunate, who suffered the hell of Claude Brown's *Manchild in the Promised Land*.[36] Among other groups, at least the essentials were retained, in large part via relief.[37] The percentage of married men, the proportion of male-headed families, and the rate of homeownership changed but slightly over the decade.[38]

Detailed studies of Chicago in 1934 underscore the marked differences between areas of genteel-to-serious poverty and those of disorganization. At two extremes were the black populations south of 55th Street and between 22nd and 31st Streets respectively. In the first, indexes of disorganization (insanity, male juvenile delinquency, illegitimate births) ranged from 100 to 194; infant mortality, from 44 to 89 per 1,000 births; the proportion of quasi-families from nil to 1.1 percent. In the second, indexes of disorganization ranged from 285 to 422; infant mortality, from 97 to 135 per 1,000 births; and quasi-families, from 7.8 to 17.7 percent. In part these differences reflected economic ones: the median grade completed in school was 8.3 years in the former area and 6.4 years in the latter; the median proportion of unheated houses, 30 percent in the one and 68 percent in the other. Yet such indexes as the incidence of families doubling up, the proportion of large families, and the burden of newcomers showed no differences.[39] Thus antecedent traditions, e.g., in Morgan Park, as well as current characteristics must have aided survival during the Depression.

The Depression discouraged black intellectual activity, but it also forced a dispersal of black writers and artists, which brought them in contact with men and ideas abroad.[40] Cosmopolitanism in turn was important in influencing American liberalism, with consequences such as the entry of New York State into equal opportunity and other civil rights legislation.[41] In the countryside a few interracial experiments such as Providence Cooperative Farm and the federal purchases of land for black farmers (both in Holmes County, Mississippi) were initiated. In the cities, notably Chicago and New York, black voters and politicians achieved a modest weight after 1936.[42] This limited an earlier swing to desperate direct action and to escapist cults such as that of Father Divine.

Urbanization, 1942–60

Between 1940 and 1954 the black population enjoyed better economic opportuni-

---

[35] U.S. Bureau of the Census, *Statistical Abstract of the United States, 1967* (Washington, D.C.: U.S. Government Printing Office, 1967), p. 613.

[36] New York: Signet Books, 1965.

[37] Drake and Cayton, op. cit., p. 88, state that half of all Chicago black families were on some type of relief by 1939.

[38] The relevant statistics are as follows for 1930 and 1940 respectively: percentage of males aged 15 and over and married, 59.8 and 60.0; percentage of male-headed families, 80.7 (including 74.7 urban, 86.1 rural) and 77.6 (including 71.0 urban, 84.8 rural); percentage of homeownership, 25.2 and 23.6. See U.S. Bureau of the Census, *Negroes in the United States 1920–1932*, pp. 147, 257; U.S. Bureau of the Census, *Sixteenth Census of the United States: 1940*, Vol. IV, Part 1, p. 17; U.S. Bureau of the Census, *Statistical Abstract of the United States: 1967*, p. 727.

[39] M. E. Ogden, directed by H. R. Cayton, *The Chicago Negro Community: A Statistical Description*, Works Project Administration Official Project 165–54–6999(3), Chicago, Ill. (Washington, D.C.: Works Project Administration, 1939).

[40] For a brilliant account *see* Langston Hughes, *I Wonder as I Wander* (New York: Hill & Wang, 1964).

[41] State of New York, *Second Report of the New York State Temporary Commission on the Condition of the Colored Urban Population*, Legislative Document (1939), No. 69 (Albany: Lyon, 1939).

[42] E. L. Tatum, *The Changed Political Thought of the Negro 1915–1940* (New York: Exposition Press, 1951).

ties and health than before. Throughout 1940–60 its numbers increased at a rate of almost 2 percent annually. This permitted both rapid out-migration and moderate population increases in the South, while in the North and West the number of blacks more than tripled. The regional shift was substantial, with the proportion of black persons in the North and West rising from 23 to 40 percent, but it was less marked than urbanization. The proportion of urban residents increased from 49 to 73 percent; the fourteen largest black urban concentrations alone comprised 30 percent of the nation's black population in 1960, compared to 17.5 percent in 1940. Then Philadelphia and St. Louis had been the sole major northern and western cities with more than 10 percent black inhabitants; in 1960 New York, Chicago, Detroit, Los Angeles, Cleveland, and Newark were also in this category. In the South, Washington became predominantly black, while Baltimore, New Orleans, Atlanta, and Dallas (but neither Birmingham nor Memphis) had increases in the proportions of black persons (see Tables 1–4). The salient mechanics and consequences of these profound changes may be summarized as follows.

On June 25, 1941, President Roosevelt, under pressure of a march on Washington to be led by A. Philip Randolph, issued Executive Order No. 8802, banning discrimination in the war industries. This act, reinforced by Executive Order No. 9346 (1943), permitted Negro employment in manufacturing to rise from 515,514 in 1940 to 1,256,000 (including 693,000 in munitions) in July 1944. Negro employment in government reached about 300,000, including 231,458 in the war agencies; the 1940 figure was 56,921. In general, while the new workers faced some acute conflicts —notably the Detroit riot of June 1943— and while they encountered serious housing problems, especially in Los Angeles, their overall treatment was fairly equitable. Negro union membership, which numbered

only 180,000 in 1935 and 600,000 in 1940, rose to 1,250,000 in 1944.[43]

In consequence the wartime migratory wave largely remained in the cities at the end of the conflict. In fact, it was reinforced both by relatives and by a considerable fraction of the 1,150,000 Negro veterans.[44] These men, although suffering from considerable discrimination, made use of their veterans' housing and educational benefits. Nonwhite homeownership rose from 23.6 percent in 1940 to 34.9 percent in 1950.[45] In 1947 veterans made up almost half of the male enrollment and 30 percent of the total Negro enrollment in institutions of higher education. These veterans broke both the long-standing educational predominance of black women in black colleges and the barriers to black education in the North. Overall black college enrollment in 1946–47 was 152,000, three times that of 1940 and only 37 percent less than that reached in 1965–66.[46]

A third major development, resulting from agricultural mechanization and arising from southern fears of black voting potentiality, was the out-migration of black rural people. Between 1940 and 1960 labor

---

[43] J. P. Guzman, ed., *Negro Year Book: A Review of Events Affecting Negro Life, 1941–1946* (Tuskegee Institute, Ala.: Tuskegee Institute, 1947), pp. 14, 136, 141–142, 146, 350.

[44] Ibid., pp. 381–382. *See also* F. Murray, ed., *The Negro Handbook 1949* (New York: Macmillan Co., 1949), pp. 280–287.

[45] U.S. Bureau of the Census, *Statistical Abstract of the United States, 1967*, p. 727. The 1960 proportion was 38.2 percent.

[46] Data for 1946–47 are from Murray, op. cit., pp. 120, 122–129; the total includes 91,000 men and 61,000 women; 91,208 students went to Negro schools, largely in the South, the remainder attending northern and western institutions. In 1940 Negro schools enrolled some 40,000 students, about half of them coming from the North; incomplete data show only 1,253 Negro students enrolled in northern schools (Guzman, op. cit., pp. 84, 95). The 1940 census showed that 57 percent of the Negro professionals were women; schoolteachers and nurses made up nearly this entire category (Guzman, op. cit., pp. 13, 142). For 1965–66 *see* U.S. Bureau of the Census, *Statistical Abstract of the United States, 1967*, p. 134.

productivity in cotton-growing rose 230 percent, but output was only 14 percent higher. Thus demand for labor fell by two-thirds; between 1940 and 1959 the number of Negro tenants and farm-owning families in the South fell from 680,266 to 265,621, or by 61 percent.[47] The rural migratory streams moved in large part to the marginal, chronically disorganized sections of northern ghettos and, in smaller part, to the urban South. Dr. Butts's studies of migration within Mississippi in 1950–60 show that centers of government and education exercised especially strong attractions.[48]

The economic effects of these changes were of two types. First, jobs in agriculture, forestry, and fishing declined from 41.8 percent of male employment in 1940 to 12.2 percent in 1960. Nonagricultural unemployment remained high among black men: 10.7 percent. Moreover, 9.8 percent of the employed listed no occupation. Of the remainder, 15.4 percent were white-collar workers, but only 33.0 percent were in manufacturing, mining, and construction; 11.1 percent were in transportation, communications, and utilities; and the remainder in a variety of service occupations and general labor.[49] Second, an important concomitant of structural underemployment and marginal employment, which was reinforced by the increasing possibility of survival via public aid and public housing, was the rise in female-headed families.[50]

In northern cities the emergence of an appreciable black middle class was accompanied by the growth of local political influence. Illustrative is the history of urban renewal in the prime area of Chicago's ghetto (Hyde Park). It resulted in stabilization as a lower-density middle-class interracial area; here blacks won acceptance by white university liberals, but lost effective contact with their own poor.[51] In the South national changes, notably the epochal *Brown* versus *Board of Education* decision of 1954, stimulated black political efforts despite intensifying white resistance. Mass actions, beginning with the Montgomery, Alabama, bus boycott of 1955–56, promoted voter registration. In the thirteen states of the former Confederacy, the median proportion of registered Negroes over 21 rose from 3 percent in 1940 to 23 percent in 1952 and 31 percent in 1960. In Mississippi Dr. Butts's study shows a close correlation for 1960 between the distribution of black voters and veterans and a significantly negative one between voting and rural farm residence.[52] In all, the phenomena leading to black migrations in 1940–60 had extensive related effects.

Imbalance and Tension: 1960 to the Present

The imbalances and tensions of 1960 intensified over the next six years. In 1966, a bad cotton year, the demand for agricultural labor was only half that in 1960.[53] In the cities the nonwhite male

---

[47] *Statistical Abstract of the United States, 1967*, pp. 613, 629.

[48] William A. Butts, "The Relationship of Economic and Social Variables to Population Change and Negro Voter Registration in Mississippi, 1940–1966." Ph.D. dissertation, Southern Illinois University at Carbondale, 1967, pp. 94–133.

[49] U.S. Bureau of the Census, *Statistical Abstract of the United States, 1967*, pp. 223, 232–234. Figures have been recalculated to accord with other data.

[50] Ibid., p. 283. The proportion of female-headed nonwhite families fell from 22.4 percent in 1940 (*see n.* 38) to 17.6 percent in 1950, then rose to 22.4 percent in 1960 and 23.7 percent in 1966. Corresponding proportions for the white

population have been as follows: 1940, 14.3 percent; 1950, 8.5 percent; 1960, 8.7 percent; and 1966, 8.9 percent. The difference in trends is in part that of family arrangements: white folks tend to leave grandma in her city apartment or to place her in an institution; black folks honor her as Big Mama. *Report of the National Advisory Commission on Civil Disorders* (New York: Bantam Books, 1968), p. 261.

[51] P. H. Rossi and R. A. Dentler, *The Politics of Urban Renewal: The Chicago Findings* (New York: Free Press of Glencoe, 1961).

[52] Butts, op. cit., pp. 142, 150–169.

[53] Calculated from U.S. Bureau of the Census, *Statistical Abstract of the United States, 1967*, pp. 628–629.

unemployment rates fell to 7.3 percent; however, special studies in nine large cities showed unemployment among 9.3 percent of the black men, with another 23.4 percent seriously underemployed.[54] As Bayard Rustin noted:

Negroes today [1966] are in worse economic shape, live in worse slums, and attend more highly segregated schools than in 1954. Thus . . . more Negroes are unemployed today than in 1954; the gap between the wages of the Negro worker and the white worker is wider; while the unemployment rate among Negro youths has increased to 32 percent (and among Negro girls the rise is even more startling). . . . To put all this in the simplest and most concrete terms: the day-to-day lot of the ghetto Negro has not been improved by the various judicial and legislative measures of the past decade. . . .[55]

At the same time, despite failures to improve life expectancies or infant mortality significantly, the high fertility of the black population maintained a natural increase rate of 2.2 percent annually (see Table 1).[56] The loss of the most fertile cohorts by migration reduced this rate to 1.8 percent in the South; correspondingly, the northern and western rate was 2.8 percent per year (see Tables 3 and 4). By 1966 the North and West, with 45 percent of the black population, were contributing about 56 percent of its natural increase. Sustained growth also increased the national proportion of black persons under 15 (31.6, 37.6, and 39.4 percent in 1950, 1960, and 1966 respectively).[57] In many localities those under 15 made up half the population. The difficulties of economic support, child care, discipline, and education under these circumstances were great. Small wonder that street-corner males became disorga-

nized.[58] These circumstances—and the insensitivity of traditional black leadership to them—abetted the growth of the Black Muslims and other bitterly alienated groups.[59] The stage was set among young, often-unemployed, men of local or migrant origin for the great riots of 1965–68.[60]

In the South the efforts begun in 1955–56 accelerated, despite killings and other types of repression. By 1966 the median proportion of Negroes registered to vote in the former Confederate states reached 49 percent of those over 21.[61] In 1967 even Mississippi had elected a black state legislator (the Honorable Robert Clark). But white economic counterpressures were intense; in Mississippi plantation workers daring to register were expelled. Everywhere work discrimination prevailed. As late as 1968 Negroes held only 22 percent of all reported jobs in the predominantly Negro counties of the Black Belt, and only 40 percent of the new Negro entrants into the labor force could expect jobs.[62] Yet industry systematically avoided new investments in the heavily black counties (certainly in North Carolina, Mississippi, and Georgia; probably elsewhere as well).[63] Nevertheless, southern blacks, with some federal aid and through intense new efforts

---

[54] *Report of the National Advisory Commission on Civil Disorders*, pp. 255–257.

[55] Quoted in Joanne Grant, *Black Protest: History, Documents and Analyses, 1619 to the Present* (New York: Fawcett, 1968), pp. 468–469.

[56] U.S. Bureau of the Census, *Statistical Abstract of the United States, 1967*, pp. 53, 56.

[57] Ibid., pp. 26–27.

[58] Street-corner males have been vividly described in a study of Washington, D.C.: Eliot Liebow, *Tally's Corner* (Boston: Little, Brown & Co., 1967).

[59] E. T. Clayton, *The Negro Politician: His Success and Failure* (Chicago: Johnson Publishing Co., 1964), pp. 169–187.

[60] *Report of the National Advisory Commission on Civil Disorders*, pp. 127–135. For Chicago, see W. Clements, "Profile of [a] Rioter," *Chicago Daily News*, April 27, 1963, pp. 1, 6.

[61] Butts, op. cit., p. 142.

[62] U.S. Senate Committee on Government Operations, 90th Cong., 2d Sess., *The Rural to Urban Population Shift: A National Problem* (Washington, D.C.: U.S. Government Printing Office, 1968), pp. 40, 57.

[63] R. E. Lonsdale, "Barriers to Rural Industrialization in the South," *Proceedings of the Association of American Geographers*, Vol. 1 (Washington, D.C.: Association of American Geographers, 1969), pp. 84–88.

—for example, agricultural cooperatives— have in large measure stood fast.[64]

Summary

To summarize the impact of a century's migration on black culture and of black culture on migration, the following appear plausible:

1. The periods of relatively free migration, 1916–30 and 1942–54, were those of rapid black socioeconomic progress. Conversely, the periods of inhibited migration before World War I and during the Depression were characterized by stagnation or even retrogression. Since 1955 differential opportunities for middle- and lower-class black people have intensified black class differences.

2. The establishment of viable black colonies in the North was long inhibited by extreme white repression and appalling health conditions. Since World War II these colonies have become the primary centers of both demographic expansion and black cultural innovation, but their fragile and dependent economies and their incomplete political activation are limiting further evolution.

3. The shift from highly rural to metropolitan environments has resulted in much cultural loss, especially in occupational skills, traditions, and social mechanisms, but has also led to borrowings (gangs), adaptations (welfare-oriented families), and innovations (Africanisms, black theater, new cults, and so on). Class differentiation has developed with both an Old Elite (with strongly exclusive groups centered around churches, clubs, and colleges), and a mobility-and-assimilation-oriented component set apart from the lower class. The differentiation of ghetto neighborhoods has correspondingly affected the economic and social opportunities of in-migrants.

Conversely, the stability of ghetto social stratification has been shaken by rapid population increases since World War II.

4. Limited opportunities for the black middle class in the North and West have persistently led to its return movement South. This in turn has transplanted new aspirations and large-scale religious organizations to southern cities. The latter, in turn, were basic vehicles of black political action in the South.

5. In general religion has remained an active element of black cultures, secularization even in politics being quite recent. Among lower-class blacks, fundamentalist Christian religion is basic in both the South and the North as an emotional vehicle and social focus. However, in the North and West black separatism and the reinforcement of new leaders have fostered new cults, such as the Black Muslims.[65]

6. Extended family structures have adapted to the urban scene, with patrifocal and matrifocal segments serving different functions. Even in areas of high disorganization, mutual support via kinship ties persists.

7. White cultures have affected black ones by aggressive inhibition and abasement, but also by loans and stimulation. In particular, white religious and political liberals, labor unions, and the armed forces have been important as both stimuli and threats to black mobility and cultural development.

Holmes County: A Case Study

Added understanding of the patterns, demographic and socioeconomic correlates, and behavioral consequences of the migration of black people within the United States can be gained from data on Holmes County, Mississippi, and its outposts. Only a start has been made in gathering and

---

[64] R. Beardwood, "The Southern Roots of the Urban Crisis," *Fortune* (August 1968), pp. 80–87, 151, 155–156, 158.

[65] Note also that readings from Eldridge Cleaver's *Soul on Ice* (New York: McGraw-Hill Book Co., 1968), are currently being used to sanctify Black Panther weddings. The *Black Panther*, August 23, 1969.

analyzing this material. Nevertheless, even the data available now yield a general statistical framework (see Tables 5–10) for delineating many of the forces and events intensifying or reducing pulses of migration and a preliminary model of the problems and alternatives faced by a community for which migration has become a way of life.

Migration History

From 1866 until the early 1900s Holmes County was apparently an area of moderate in-migration. It suffered in the late 1860s from the depredations of white terrorists—Heggie's Scouts—who boasted of killing 116 blacks and throwing their bodies into the Tallahatchie River.[66] But during the 1870s the county became Republican, electing a black sheriff (Sumner), and providing a haven after 1875 for black politicians and educators (including a member of the Clark family) who had fled for their lives from Hinds County, Mississippi.[67] Religious leadership also emanated from Hinds County, specifically the Jackson Baptist Association, with which almost all the black Baptist churches of Holmes County were affiliated.[68]

Economically, Holmes County was strengthened by railroad construction, land clearance and drainage in the Mississippi Delta, and the development of specialty agriculture. According to a 1907 source:

[Holmes County] . . . produces abundant crops of corn, cotton, oats, wheat, field peas, millet, sugar cane, sorghum, and grasses, and the Louisiana ribbon cane. Much attention is paid to the raising of fruits, such as peaches,

pears, early apples, figs, plums, and strawberries, which do well and are shipped north in considerable quantities. . . . The road system of the county is excellent and all roads are worked by contract. . . .[69]

Thus while black out-migration from Mississippi as a whole had begun in the 1800s, it is not surprising that Holmes County retained its black people until the beginning of the 1900s.[70] A probable factor in initiating out-migration from the county was the election in 1903 of Governor James K. Vardaman on an explicitly anti-Negro platform. For example: "His vote will either be cast aside or Sambo will vote as directed by white folks," and "There is no use multiplying words about it, the negro . . . will not be permitted to rise above the station which he now fills."[71] The development of out-migration from Holmes County can be clearly divided into two major epochs, 1900–39 and 1940–68.

Out-migration, 1900–39. In the first epoch, aggregate out-migration (see Table 5) was less than the natural growth of the population, so that the number of blacks in the county increased (with adjustment for boundary changes) from 1900 to 1940 by about 15 percent. The intensity and temporal pattern of out-migration, with a sharp peak in 1916–20, were quite similar to those manifest for the entire black population of Mississippi. However, the pattern

---

[66] V. L. Wharton, *The Negro in Mississippi: 1865–1890* (Chapel Hill: University of North Carolina Press, 1947), pp. 219–220.

[67] Ibid., p. 169; and personal communication from the Hon. Robert G. Clark, Jr. Jackson, Vicksburg, and Natchez were centers of black political leadership in the 1870s.

[68] Ibid., pp. 146–149, 259, 270–272. Church organization, the formation of secret societies and benevolent lodges, and black political leadership were closely intertwined.

[69] D. Rowland, *Encyclopedia of Mississippi History*, Vol. I (Madison, Wisc.: Selwyn A. Brant, 1907), p. 878.

[70] Foreman calculates a net out-migration of 34,581 black persons in 1880–90 and 25,452 in 1890–1900. The data prior to 1880 are insufficiently reliable for detailed migration estimates. P. B. Foreman, "Mississippi Population Trends." Ph.D. dissertation, Vanderbilt University, 1939, p. 83.

[71] A. D. Kirwan, *Revolt of the Rednecks. Mississippi Politics: 1876–1925* (Gloucester, Mass.: Peter Smith, 1964), pp. 145–146. (Quotations are from the Greenwood *Commonwealth*, June 30, 1899, and July 25, 1897, respectively.) Vardaman's administration was in fact much more constructive than his demagoguery suggests (ibid., pp. 162–177), but the justification he gave to white repression was calamitous for blacks.

of destinations appears from oral testimony to have been rather distinctive.

From 1900 to 1915 urbanization within the state, with movements to Jackson and Greenwood, appears to have predominated; little evidence has come to light of Holmes County participation in the large black migration to Arkansas.[72] During World War I migrants from Holmes County largely moved north along the Illinois Central Railroad, especially to Chicago, St. Louis, and Memphis. They also established a colony at Waterloo, Iowa, based primarily on employment at the John Deere tractor plant. All these settlements proved to be relatively successful, so that recruitment for factory work continued even during the Great Depression.

Gradually pressures intensifying out-migration developed within the county. Between 1910 and 1930 the socioeconomic position of its black residents became less favorable. While the population structure and the degree of dependence on agriculture changed little, average farm sizes and farmland per capita diminished significantly (see Tables 7 and 8). Cotton specialization replaced crop diversification and accelerated the destruction of the "black and sandy" upland soils.[73]

In comparison to the state average, the socioeconomic condition of black Holmes County residents had been quite favorable in 1910. Relevant figures for the county and state respectively were as follows: average value of black-operated farms, $1,054 and $936; percentage of farms owned, 12.9 and 12.8; proportion of illiterates at age 10 and over, 32.4 and 35.6 percent; school attendance among children aged 6–14, 74.3 and 63.7 percent.[74] By 1930 the relationships had changed, and Holmes County residents were less well off than the average black person statewide. Critical comparisons between the county and state respectively were as follows: average value of black-operated farms, $1,190 versus $1,362; percentage of farm ownership, 11.5 and 12.3; illiteracy, 28.3 and 23.2 percent. School attendance alone was more favorable—91.0 versus 87.6 percent of the 7–13-year-olds.[75]

The relative peacefulness of the county, which suffered a lynching rate half that of Mississippi as a whole, may have retarded out-migration, notwithstanding economic deterioration.[76] In the early 1930s, however, violence in Holmes County rose to major proportions, especially in the wake of land disputes between poor whites and the powerful Montgomery extended family. In fact, a general bloodbath was only narrowly averted in 1933. Data for 1930–31 show demographic disturbances—most likely a combination of a reduced birthrate because of the absences of males and underreporting of infant mortality, which also rose (see Table 9).

By the late 1930s black distress and awakening white liberalism led to two attempts to aid Holmes County. One was the establishment in 1939 of the Providence

[72] Foreman, op. cit., p. 121, shows an increase of 52,574 Mississippi-born black Arkansans between 1880 and 1920, with a drop of 7,522 by 1930. These data appear to represent a movement largely from river and Delta counties, which in turn was partly a stage in northbound movements. Holmes County ties with western Arkansas and Oklahoma are appreciable, but rest on kinship relations with members of the Choctaw Nation (including its later freedmen), maintained despite the westward movement after the 1830 Treaty of Dancing Rabbit Creek. Rowland, op. cit., Vol. II, pp. 799–803.

[73] C. S. Johnson et al., *Statistical Atlas of Southern Counties* (Chapel Hill: University of North Carolina Press, 1941), pp. 4–12, 165; Rowland, op. cit., Vol. I, p. 878.

[74] U.S. Bureau of the Census, *Negro Population 1790–1915* (Washington, D.C.: U.S. Government Printing Office, 1918), pp. 656, 728–730, 816.

[75] U.S. Bureau of the Census, *Negroes in the United States, 1920–1932* (Washington, D.C.: U.S. Government Printing Office, 1935), pp. 650, 756–757.

[76] Johnson, op. cit., pp. 161–174, 247–298. The absolute number of recorded lynchings, 1900–1931, is three, the rate per 100,000 total population in 1930 being 7.79, compared to the state average of 14.18. Twenty-four counties had no recorded lynchings, while the highest rate, in Issaquena County (Delta), was 87.20.

Cooperative Farm, which introduced a credit union, consumer cooperative, clinic, and instruction on "improved farming, community health, civic problems, and the Christian approach to social issues," via a biracial staff.[77] The other was the Farm Security Administration's purchase of white-owned land at Mileston and its resale to more than 120 black families in the Delta. Both efforts had profound results in providing a basis of new ideas and new economic strength, which culminated in the social changes of the 1960s; neither, however, appreciably offset the migratory forces generated by World War II.

Out-migration, 1940–68. Between 1940 and 1969 over 27,000 persons, on a net basis, migrated from the black community of Holmes County to other places, virtually all urban (see Tables 5 and 6). This migration was so great that, despite a vigorous rate of natural increase, the community's population decreased by 40 percent over this period. However, because the county's white population was also migrating out, albeit at a lower rate, and because its rate of natural increase was moderate and dropping, the ratio of black to white persons in the county changed only slightly.[78] This fact has been of considerable political and social importance.

Within the period 1940–68 the migration rates appear to have been highly variable (see Tables 9 and 10). Economic opportunities opened up by World War II precipitated rapid migration up to 1945. This was followed by a period of low migration and population increase evidently underlaid by the savings of and benefits gained by veterans and other returned migrants, which were to purchase farmland and agricultural equipment. Increasing agricultural labor surpluses and displacement of tenant

farmers initiated a second pulse of out-migration in 1949–50. This was followed by several years of relative stability and then a new wave of out-migration in 1954–57. At this time economic factors were probably less influential than the intense racial conflicts that followed the Supreme Court's desegregation decision. Since 1958 migration has again slowed down slightly notwithstanding severe economic and political pressures. New capacities for social action by the black community, federal legal actions and economic programs, and accommodations by and aid from significant elements of the county's white community have helped attract as well as retain older and less educated black residents. In contrast, the competitive position of young workers in urban markets has improved with the rise of average educational attainments to between ten and eleven years of schooling. Jobs for better educated black people are scarce in Holmes County. Thus strong new streams and counterstreams of migration are now in evidence.

The consequences of migration between 1940 and 1968 have been a redistribution of the county's black people nationally and profound structural and functional changes within the county. The early migrations along the Illinois Central Railroad were widened during World War II when Detroit, Los Angeles, and New York became important destinations. Military service, especially in airborne units of the regular army, further widened horizons from the Korean War onward. Such military service and higher education were fostered by the rapid expansion of black high school enrollments during the 1950s (see Table 10). The pursuit of higher education led in turn to ties with college towns in Mississippi (especially Jackson, Holly Springs, and Itta Bena, near Greenwood), and, to a lesser degree, Tennessee and the Midwest. Also, new opportunities for skilled, technical, and professional jobs led to moves to new communities: Milwaukee, Peoria, West Memphis (Ark.), and so on.

In general it is believed that by 1969

---

[77] *The Cooperative Farm Carries On* (Cruger, Miss.: Providence Cooperative Farm, 1947), p. 8.

[78] White natural increase rates in Holmes County were 8.0 per 1,000 persons in 1940, 12.4 per 1,000 in 1950, and 4.8 per 1,000 in 1960. For sources *see* Table 9.

only three out of eight black Holmes County natives still lived at home; a quarter or more were in Chicago and its suburbs and the rest were widely scattered (see Table 6). About one-sixth of the county's black population had been born elsewhere, almost entirely in neighboring Mississippi counties. This included many persons marrying into the county, since local customs frown on marriages with blood relatives, no matter how distant. And it includes many families evicted, since 1960 or so, from plantations in the Delta. The severely depressed slums of Tchula, with their high concentration of multiproblem families, are largely of this origin.

Migration Correlates for the County

Prolonged and extensive out-migration has greatly modified the composition of the county's black population. In particular the cohorts of prime working age, 21–44, have been severely depleted: by 1960 they comprised only 18 percent of the total population, compared to one-third in 1930 (see Table 7). Conversely, the number of aged persons has more than doubled, as a consequence of better survival and of return migration.[79]

These changes have had important effects on family composition. In 1930 the aggregate number of separated married women, divorcees, and widows had been only one-fourth as great as the number of married

men; by 1960 the proportion had risen to 44 percent. Reduced social controls in female-headed families have been associated with higher fertility rates. In 1940 51 children under age 5 were enumerated for every 100 black women aged 15–44 in the county; by 1950 the ratio had risen to 76/100 and by 1960, to 88/100.[80] Consequently the crude birthrate of the county's black people has changed little from an average of about 35 per 1,000 persons in 1940–45 to 32 per 1,000 persons in 1960–65 (see Table 9), the decrease in women of childbearing age notwithstanding.[81]

Health and mortality. It appears most likely that the rise of infant mortality among Holmes County blacks, from a level of about 45 per 1,000 births in 1940–45 to at least 65 per 1,000 births in the 1960s, has been a reflection of changes in family

---

[79] The 3,204 black persons aged 55 and over enumerated in the 1950 census would have had about 1,977 survivors at the 1950 age-specific death rates for Mississippi blacks. The number actually enumerated was 2,011. These data, with moderate allowances for out-migration at older ages, indicate substantial levels of return migration. *See* U.S. Bureau of the Census, *United States Census of Population, 1950* (Washington, D.C.: U.S. Government Printing Office, 1952), Vol. 2, Part 24, p. 64; U.S. Bureau of the Census, *United States Census of Population, 1960* (Washington, D.C.: U.S. Government Printing Office, 1963), Vol. I, Part 26, p. 27; M. B. King, H. A. Pederson, and J. N. Burrus, *Mississippi's People, 1950*, Sociological Study Series No. 5 (University: University of Mississippi, 1955), p. 31.

[80] *Sixteenth Census of the United States: 1940*, Vol. 2, p. 242; *United States Census of Population, 1950*, Vol. 2, Part 24, p. 64; *United States Census of Population, 1960*, Vol. 1, Part 26, p. 27.

[81] This is a graphical estimate from Table 9, eliminating suspect figures. The extreme decline in reported births in 1964–66 is an unequivocal artifact of underreporting, as it was in 1930–31. In 1966 birth control was known and practiced to a small degree by the county's black people, according to Helen Richardson, RN, and Patricia Weatherly, RN, who operated a clinic at Mileston in 1965–66 with the support of weekly visits from Alvin Poussaint, MD. Their unpublished report states: "Those who have a large family are questioned about their knowledge concerning contraceptives. Those who are interested are told about EMKO and given a supply, with specific instructions as to how it should be used. They are then invited to return to the family planning class which we have just begun." The writer's own inquiries of midwives in 1966–67 indicate that contraceptives, primarily condoms, were in limited use and that other practices such as coitus interruptus were not known. For 1969, 535 births (or a rate of 29.6 per 1,000, for a base of 18,081), 15 neonatal deaths, and 10 infant deaths (for an aggregate mortality of 46.7 per 1,000 births) have been reported by the State of Mississippi in unpublished data. The recent establishment of the University of Mississippi's County Health Improvement Program promises to reduce infant mortality in the near future.

composition.[82] These effects have been intensified by nutritional deterioration caused
by the abandonment of garden plots and
chicken and pig husbandry and subsequent
dependence on unbalanced purchased diets;
by high infection rates, numerous falls, and
fires in crowded and rotting houses; and
by child neglect among frequently alcoholic
mothers. But the battered-child syndrome,
homosexuality, and drug addiction appear
to be rare even in seriously deteriorated
families.[83]

Despite the problems mentioned, the
health of the black population generally
improved between 1940 and the mid-1950s.
The crude death rate changed little because
of the growing proportions of infants and
aged. However, if the age-specific mortalities of Mississippi's total black population in 1950 are applied to the age composition of the black people of Holmes County
in 1940, 1950, and 1960 respectively, the
trend of the observed as compared to the
standardized death rate was quite favorable.
The death rate decreased by 17.5 percent
between 1940 and 1950 and by another
9.2 percent between 1950 and 1960, but
rose appreciably thereafter.[84] In 1950 the

life expectancy of Holmes County blacks
was almost exactly the average for Mississippi nonwhites: 61.1 years at birth for
males and 62.9 years at birth for females.[85]
In that year 13 percent of the deaths were
to be expected to occur before age 1 and
another 41 percent at age 65 and over.

These relatively good health levels appear attributable to a diet suitable for hard
physical work outdoors—high in calories,
moderate in proteins, high in fat and salt,
with abundant minerals and vitamins—
largely from home-raised produce (corn,
turnips, watermelons, sugar cane, and the
like), chickens, and pigs, reinforced by
fish, small game, and purchased flour and
sugar. Other hygienic factors were dispersed settlement and the continuity of
care and psychological support for infants
and aged alike provided in well-structured
extended families. These conditions were
augmented after World War II by the eradi-
cation of malaria and the general control
of tuberculosis.

Holmes County also benefited from
rather vigorous programs of childhood
immunization promoted by the Mississippi
State Board of Health. Of particular importance were the freely available services
of a modern clinic at Providence Cooperative Farm, instituted in 1946 by David R.
Minter, MD, and Mrs. Lindsey Cox, RN,
and operated for a dozen years until it was
forced to close by pressure from the White
Citizens' Councils.[86] This closing and other
repressions forced the death rate up to a
level of at least 15 per 1,000 during the ter-

---

[82] Rises in nonwhite infant mortality have been
evident in both Mississippi and North Carolina
since World War II. *See Infant Mortality Trends.
United States and Each State, 1930–1964*, Publication No. 1000, Series 20, No. 1 (Washington,
D.C.: U.S. Public Health Service, 1965), pp. 2,
64, 67.

[83] Private communication from Alvin Poussaint,
MD, currently associate dean, Harvard University
Medical School. Dr. Poussaint, a psychiatrist,
conducted a weekly clinic at Mileston in 1965–66.
Holmes County residents are well aware of the
frequency of these problems, even among their
own people, in Chicago.

[84] Mortalities have been calculated by applying
1950 Mississippi nonwhite age-specific mortalities
to the age compositions of each period. For basic
data, *see n.* 79. Here again, county and national
trends have coincided. For example, the life
expectancy (at birth) of nonwhite males in the
U.S.A., which had risen by 15.9 years between
1920 and 1955, has since been declining, to a
level of 60.7 years in 1966 versus 61.2 years in
the peak year. U.S. Bureau of the Census, *Statistical Abstract of the United States 1968* (Wash-

ington, D.C.: U.S. Government Printing Office,
1968), p. 53. For a fuller analysis of these
data, *see* D. B. Shimkin, "Man, Ecology and
Health," *Archives of Environmental Health*, Vol.
20 (January 1970), pp. 111–127.

[85] M. B. King, J. N. Burrus, and H. A. Peder-
son, *Mississippi Life Tables 1950–51*, Sociological
Study Series No. 4 (University: University of
Mississippi, 1954), pp. 8–9.

[86] *The Cooperative Farm Carries On*, pp. 9–11.
For a discussion of the White Citizens' Councils
in Holmes County and the expulsion of the white
leadership at Providence, *see* Frank E. Smith, *Con-
gressman From Mississippi* (New York: Random
House, 1964), pp. 264–265.

rible years of 1965 and 1966, when open terrorism, mass expulsions from plantations, joblessness, and severe weather led to extensive illness and even deaths from hunger and exposure. The damage to many child survivors of this period may well prove to be permanent.

Employment. In general migration was forced on tenants and farm laborers under the control of white landowners. The number of these workers diminished from about 5,300 in 1940 to some 3,800 in 1950 and 1,600 in 1960. It is certainly less than a thousand today.[87]

The plantation workers were generally of two strata: the more skilled tractor drivers and other machine operators and the hand-laborers—choppers (weeders) and pickers of cotton. While the latter suffered especially from extreme poverty and ignorance, both strata were subject to intimate interference from and dependence on their white patrons. Whites made medical and other services available to plantation workers only on the planter's "chit."[88] All were expected to inform on each other constantly to the planter, a habit that persists among the older workers, according to—and to the

[87] Figures are derived from the total number of farmers and farm laborers other than unpaid family workers, less the estimated number of farmowners. Basic data are in the census reports for 1940 (Vol. 2, p. 264), 1950 (Vol. 2, Part 24, p. 91), and 1960 (Vol. 1, Part 26, p. 210). This reduction in local farm jobs has been partly counterbalanced by an increasing participation of black Holmes County residents, especially young men, in migratory farm labor, not only in Louisiana sugar harvesting and in North Carolina tobacco fields, but as far afield as Vermont (apples). Robert Stewart, a former migratory worker now attending the University of Illinois, estimates that the number of such workers from Holmes County is at least, and probably currently exceeds, five hundred people.

[88] For a basic analysis of contrasts between plantation and independent farm ways of life, *see* P. V. Rushing, "The Black Rural Migrant: Three Groups of Agricultural Workers from Holmes County, Mississippi," in Susan Lorenzi, ed., *Some Views on Blacks and Black Communities* (Champaign-Urbana: University of Illinois, 1969).

intense disapproval of—their prouder children. These social factors created disabilities and vulnerabilities that were intensified by expulsion for economic or political reasons (e.g., voter registration), joblessness in refugee areas, and their migration to cities without resources and with few contacts.[89]

The contrast in adaptive problems faced by these refugees and the purposeful migrants from independent farm and craftsman families has been fundamental. Differences in the destinations of the two streams, one to the poorest section and the other to lower middle-class sections of Chicago, have also been important. The diminution of contrasts between plantation and independent farm people, in life-style and self-image, achieved since 1967 by Holmes County's black people appears to be one of the finest fruits of their cultural rejuvenation and reintegration.

Black nonagricultural employment in Holmes County changed little from at least 1940 to 1960. On the average it numbered some 2,200 persons, about 12 percent of whom were white-collar workers (especially teachers) and another 8 percent, craftsmen (especially in the building trades). Among the others a structural change took place, with jobs as operatives and service workers in private and public establishments tending to replace work in private households and casual labor. In 1940 the former two categories comprised 21 percent of the nonagricultural total; in 1960, 32 percent.

Since this period nonagricultural employment for black Holmes County residents has grown by about 750 jobs. The development of some 450 jobs via federal programs (Head Start, migrant-farmer trainees, Health Research Program trainees and employees, and others), at least 200 jobs in local and state government employment (teaching, service work in schools, roadwork, trash collection, and the like),

[89] Other refugee areas in Mississippi in 1966 included "Strike City" and "Freedom City" near Greenville.

and about 200 jobs in the private sector (employment in the house trailer, Talon, and sportswear factories; private construction; small business), less the estimated loss of 100 domestic and casual labor positions, constitute the components of this change.[90] The sources of labor for this added employment have been partly the unemployed, including former plantation labor, and partly independent farmers and their wives.

To remain economically competitive and also to adjust to the loss of family labor associated with greatly expanded high school attendance and the out-migration of family members, farm mechanization has been essential; the mule is rare in Holmes County today. Few black farmers have been able to utilize their expensive mechanization on a full-time basis; their new-won leisure is used, in good part, in local or long-distance commutation to urban work.

In general economic changes since 1940 have not only underlain much migration, but they have also brought about major structural and qualitative shifts in the labor force. In 1940, out of 10,708 persons employed, 2,539 were unpaid family workers and another 1,327 were domestics and casual laborers; in other words, only 6,842 persons could be considered effective earners. By 1960, 3,535 out of 4,575 employed persons were such earners. Today the estimated number, inclusive of migratory farm workers, is 4,300 out of 4,900, and employment has become predominantly nonagricultural: excluding unpaid family workers, the proportion of farm to total workers has declined from about 70 percent in 1930–40 to 53 percent in 1960 and about 39 percent in 1969 (see Table 8).[91] These shifts have necessitated the gaining of skills that facilitate migration; concur-

rently, better quality jobs have strengthened identification with the local community.

Racism. The aggregate changes described—intensified dislocation and misery, succeeded by a new economy—reflect the course of political as well as economic events. White hostility toward blacks intensified soon after World War II, in part through fear of black veterans and in part through competition for jobs in a shrinking agricultural sector. In 1946 one of the nation's eight recorded lynchings took place in Lexington, Mississippi (the county seat of Holmes County), when Mr. Leon McTatie, accused of the theft of a saddle, was beaten and drowned by a white mob. Six men arrested for the crime were immediately acquitted in a Holmes County magistrate's court.[92] Conditions became critical after 1954 despite the courageous opposition of a few whites such as Mrs. Hazel Brannon Smith, the editor of the Lexington (Mississippi) *Advertiser.* Her description of the period when racism and concocted anti-Communism had driven Mr. A. E. Cox and Dr. David Minter from Providence Cooperative Farm is poignant:

Today we live in fear in Holmes County and in Mississippi. It hangs like a dark cloud over us, dominating every facet of public and private life. None speaks freely without being afraid of being misunderstood. Almost every man and woman is afraid to try to do anything, to promote good will and harmony between the races, afraid he or she will be taken as a mixer, as an integrationist or worse, if there is anything worse by Southern standards. . . .[93]

Nevertheless, Mrs. Smith stood firmly for justice, defying ostracism, boycotts, and bombings. So, increasingly, did the black community.

Community Organization Efforts

Black community efforts to create a better life at home were accelerated during

---

[90] Current employment data have been developed largely by Mrs. J. Matilda Burns of the Milton Olive III Memorial Corporation, formerly research assistant in human ecology, University of Illinois.

[91] For sources on employment in 1940, 1950, and 1960, *see* n. 80.

[92] Murray, op. cit., pp. 94–95.

[93] Smith, op. cit., pp. 268–269.

the 1950s by the consolidation of black schools and the imposition of new academic requirements for black schoolteachers. Between 1951 and 1955 alone the number of schools fell from 85 (with 181 teachers) to 62 (with 177 teachers).[94] (Ten Negro schools and an integrated high school were in operation in 1969.) The small schools had been the centers of community action, including fairs, baby shows, and civic meetings. Their progressive closing, concurrent with much depopulation, loosened the tight local cohesions of kin, church, graveyard, and school that previously had made up Holmes County life. The teachers, largely local residents, were forced to broaden their outlooks not only by new affiliations but also through college courses in Mississippi and, to a limited extent, in neighboring midwestern universities.

The county's isolation was decisively broken in 1963 when Mr. Robert Moses of the Student Nonviolent Coordinating Committee began organizational efforts in Leflore County, with the county seat of which —Greenwood—Holmes County residents had longstanding kinship and trade relationships. Moses's work inspired interest in Mileston (in Holmes County); he was invited to speak there, with the hope of engendering initial voter registration efforts. Neither these first efforts nor several subsequent attempts were successful, but white repression succeeded only in strengthening the determination of black farmers to acquire their deeply felt rights. At an early time they gained the courage to return armed attacks with fire.[95]

By early 1964 the nascent civil rights movement had won the support of the powerful Montgomery and Bailey families, who, with the Mileston community, provided a core of action and protection for civil rights workers. The Ku Klux Klan threatened the black activists and the many young whites who came to the county that summer, for example, by hanging three buzzards to celebrate the Philadelphia, Mississippi, murders. But it did not dare to destroy the community center built by white volunteers at Mileston. This center became the residence of a young couple, Henry and Susan Lorenzi, who stimulated further development by training leaders, instituting a kindergarten, and helping to set up a clinic.

By late in the summer of 1964 the black population of Holmes County had coalesced into a new entity built on preexisting community and kinship groups, reinforced by religious faith, moderated by deliberative forms learned in church and benevolent society meetings, and led by a mixture of traditional and emergent leaders of whom farmers and rural teachers formed the core.

The new organization soon developed a mass base, the central expression of which was a set of monthly deliberations of county programs and policies in every community center. Its central leadership became increasingly involved in state-level and national efforts; county people participated in the strong efforts of the new Mississippi Freedom Democratic Party to gain a hearing in Washington and representation at the Democratic National Convention.

Nevertheless the process of sociopolitical development had few unequivocal successes until the march of the summer of 1966 linked it physically with two strains of national black leadership: Dr. Martin Luther King, Jr.'s Southern Christian Leadership Conference and Stokely Carmichael's increasingly militant SNCC. The Holmes County community chose the more conservative course, placing its faith in political representation and federal economic support.

The year 1967 was a turning point. The first great victory was funding for the

[94] *Public Schools for Negro Children, 1950–51* and *Public Schools for Negro Children, 1954–55* (Jackson: State of Mississippi Department of Education, 1951 and 1955, respectively), pp. 22–24 and 18–19, respectively.

[95] An important analysis of the black community's political evolution in 1963–67 is given in Henry J. Lorenzi and Susan Lorenzi, "The Management of Fear by a Community: Holmes County, Mississippi—1963 through 1967," in Susan Lorenzi, ed., op. cit.

community-run Milton Olive III Memorial
Program for Children. This Head Start
effort was launched after the experience
of the Child Development Group of Mississippi showed the necessity for foolproof
administration with the alternative of destruction for alleged fraud or misdoing.
Henry Lorenzi, aided by Alexander Shimkin, developed simplified but careful bookkeeping and other procedures consonant
with the capabilities of poorly educated
people. Only a handful of teachers could
be recruited; others, both volunteers and
paid staff, had to rise to the need. This
required a shift from kinship to merit as
the governing concept; the selection com-
mittees proved capable of making this
shift, despite the discontent that was en-
gendered. At the same time a delicate
balance was achieved. On the one hand,
the executive director, Mrs. Bernice Montgomery, a former rural teacher, was empowered to exact demanding work, full
time on duty, and precise accounting from
the staff. On the other, the locations of
the Head Start centers reinforced community groupings, while local councils exercised much influence in their direction.

The Milton Olive effort and the less independent programs conducted by the Community Action Program of Central Mississippi, Inc.—a six-county agency of the
Office of Economic Opportunity, with head-
quarters at Winona in Montgomery County
—and by Saints Junior College—a small
denominational school and junior college
for blacks established in 1926 at Lexington,
Mississippi—have been basic community
development undertakings. They have required their staffs, ultimately numbering
over three hundred persons, to master skills
ranging from writing business letters, to
motor-fleet operations, to the care, feeding,
and socialization of a thousand children.
They rehabilitated children suffering from
malnutrition, umbilical hernias, parasites,
impetigo, and anemia—children often isolated from all but their immediate family,
in many instances ignorant of the uses of
tableware, beds, and toilets. They in-

volved the community in a new level of
concern for its own people. This fed back
into numerous other efforts, ranging from
the development of a small home for the
aged, to housing placement of refugee
families on the land of black farmers, to
the increasingly aggressive pursuit of medical services and welfare aid for problem-
afflicted families.

The second basic achievement of 1967
was a major election effort that culminated
in the victory of Robert G. Clark, Jr.—a
highly respected teacher and farmer, a one-
time cook with a master's degree from
Michigan State University—being elected
to the House of Representatives in the Mississippi State Legislature. This victory
ended the need for technical political aid
by the Lorenzi-Shimkin team. It also demonstrated the primacy of political resolution over violence. This was tested in three
ways. During the summer of 1967 the
planned kidnapping and murder of a
former plantation worker active in civil
rights, Mr. Edgar Love, was narrowly
averted at Tchula through the aid of a
friendly white storekeeper. Later the mis-
deeds of a black policeman—part of a
still-continuing pattern of harassment of
the black community—precipitated a long
boycott that led to removal of the offender.
Finally the threat of a large-scale shoot-out
stopped interference in the November election at Ebenezer.

Subsequent developments have built on
this foundation.[96] Only one striking event
needs to be mentioned here. In the summer of 1969 the rank-and-file workers at
Milton Olive pressed for and gained a
strong effort to achieve high school equiva-
lencies by night-time study and subsequent
testing. Through the summer over 160
persons averaging 45 years in age and
about six years in schooling sought to at-

---

[96] For information on community development
in Holmes County in 1967–69, *see* Henry J.
Lorenzi and Susan Lorenzi, "On Research and
Development Operations in Holmes County,
Mississippi, 1968–1969" (Champaign-Urbana: De-
partment of Anthropology, University of Illinois,
September 1969). (Mimeographed.)

tain a new level of competence, with the help of Holmes County students at the University of Illinois and the Milton Olive staff. Few greater contrasts with the despondent, self-hating people who so upset Dr. Alvin Poussaint in 1966 can be imagined.

A Model of Migrant Adaptation

The cumulative effect on the lives of black Holmes County residents of more than half a century's interaction between migration and culture can be expressed most generally as a model of migrant adaptation. This model comprises five groups of variables—common and variable population characteristics, values, sources of stress, mechanisms of social mediation, and levels of adaptation—each with complementary resident and migrant aspects. These groups of variables interlink to provide a system of relationships that, in principle and with the accumulation of enough reliable data, defines the ecology or life situation of each black Holmes County resident. The model proposed is only suggestive.

Population characteristics. The common characteristics of black people in Holmes County center in their keen awareness of black identity. ("Colored" is still a common self-designation among persons in their 30s and older. "Negro" and "black" are also heard, but never "Afro-American.") This social division—hazel-eyed, brown-haired, or even blond and fair "Negroes" are not uncommon—is absolute in defining expectations and much behavior. The contrast with white people—the "other race," to use a patriarch's words—is taught in infancy and repeatedly reinforced through conflict and insult. One hears whites discussing an accident: "No one was hurt—just a couple of niggers." Even those whites who would be polite rarely refrain from the using of people's first names, although in the black community itself, lifelong friends, especially women, still refer to and address each other as "Mrs."

The consciousness of racial tension is reinforced by conflicts arising in particular from police and court harassment of the community and by living memories of every lynching since the turn of the century.[97] Land lost to whites is remembered and mourned; its forced or willful sale is an offense beyond forgiveness—the only known recent suicide among black Holmes County residents resulted from remorse at such a sale, made in the wake of a family quarrel.

Yet not infrequently deep friendships and responsive acts cross racial boundaries. In one instance the black community could not raise money to provide decent clothing so that the children of a young widow who was killed in an accident could attend her funeral (a basic ceremonial obligation). This need brought about a request to a respected planter, who clothed the children at his own expense. Conversely there are several elderly, lonely, illiterate white farmers who depend utterly on their black neighbors for aid in coping with tax matters and other bewildering complexities. Beyond all this is general knowledge of common genealogies and, derivatively, obligations between black and white in dire emergency.

Black identity is part of a large body of values, beliefs, customary law, and etiquette that is known to all. The behavioral code governs other basic identifications, namely, kinship, church affiliation, and locality. (e.g., Mount Olive, Second Pilgrim's Rest, Balance Due, or one of many other "communities"). And it provides an inventory of symbols—for example, deferential behavior to appease whites ("tomming"), signs of respect to one's own, and threats at various levels—utilized by old and young alike.

Important variations must also be recognized within this population. By common consensus a family's degree of economic

---

[97] Blacks are automatically convicted in the local court on the basis of unsupported white testimony. Since 1967 these convictions have been as regularly appealed and ultimately reversed by federal courts.

and psychological dependence on or independence from white people basically determines its status. Plantation and domestic workers are at one extreme; the stronger independent farmers and craftsmen are at the other. Teachers, storekeepers, and, to a degree, preachers have an ambivalent status. A few free spirits of low status—gamblers, peddlers, and others—represent other options. These variations, as well as those between "Hill" and "Delta," are intensified by extensive stereotyping. One person, whose family had lost its land and been forced into tenancy, denied "real" plantation status: "My mother always kept us clean. We never went hungry. . . ." All feel that Hill people are stricter with their women, especially unmarried girls.

Cutting across these variants are those of sex, age, and personal status. In general sexual roles are well defined; modesty and ceremonial (albeit not economic) deference to men are expected from girls and women. The housewife is expected to provide a hot meal at a moment's notice for the men of the family; there is emphasis on hospitality and a lavish table. Sociological maturity—economic responsibility for a household ("Big Daddy" or "Big Mama"), deaconship (for males), a major role in funerals, and, most recently, political leadership—earns deference from those younger or dependent and imposes restrictions on conduct. For instance, a black candidate for office was defeated in favor of a white because of sexual excesses; "He's been courting one and keeping two," an annoyed community member remarked. Seniority within a powerful extended family, generosity, skill in adjudication, oratorical ability, courage in a crisis, expertise in farming, long service as a midwife, competence and devotion as a teacher—these are among the many paths toward personal status. At the same time only a few deviances justify ostracism. Although feuds are well remembered, aggression is directed largely toward whites and the violent man is

treated gingerly as "crazy." Crippled and mentally handicapped children and adults may have inadequate care, but they are neither mocked nor abused. Thus biological or social weaknesses may lead to a denial of status, but not of acceptance.[98]

The accepted behavioral codes, social distinctions, and status devices of black residents present adaptive difficulties following migration. From fragmentary data, all on Chicago, the outcomes have been of three general types: (1) behavioral conservation within small, highly endogamous colonies, especially of former independent farmers, teachers, and craftsmen, (2) behavioral instability leading to severe conflicts or rapid absorption into lower-class ghettos, especially among former plantation field laborers, and (3) selective modifications among returned migrants. The dashiki, "natural" hairdos, and public hand-holding are just becoming acceptable; bare arms for women are questionable. In contrast to city ghettos with their traditional "dozens"—a game of insults among black city youths centered on ritual obscenities about mothers—and neosophisticated public use of obscenity, speech taboos are many.

Values. The values of black Holmes County residents are, in part, widespread. Economic success in familiar occupations—farming and teaching especially—is highly prized. The attachments of kinship by descent, marriage, and adoption are intense. In migrant areas kinship forms a fundamental basis of social recognition and mutual aid. Black strangers, according to in-

---

[98] The most widespread genetically related problem among Holmes Countians is diabetes. Sickle-cell disease is well recognized and has perhaps a 1 percent frequency. A number of developmental failures and anomalies, for example, polydactyly, can also be observed. At the same time a substantial frequency of genetic "hyperfitness," exemplified by mothers with twenty or more living children, can be identified here as well as in the black populations of several Delta counties.

formants and the writer's own observations, seek progressively to identify ties by county affiliations, locality, and, finally, even remote kinship. Religion acts as a conscious source of assurance in the home (especially in the utterance of grace at meals), in public gatherings, in the relief of emotional stress at prayer meetings, and in the reinforcement of social bonds at funerals. Home, symbolized ultimately by burial in the family plot, is an intense sentiment attested to by a regular flow of coffins from Chicago to the county. Yet while most young people migrate only for jobs and dignity, perhaps a quarter see the county as a place to leave for good.

Important distinctions are found between people in the civil rights movement and others, especially the older migrants. For the former, an intense faith in social action, an identification with the county and black people generally, a commitment to education and to science are clearly evident. The midwives, who average well into the 60s in age and who have little formal education, are nonetheless of this type; their efforts at self-improvement in the face of immense obstacles have been remarkable. Yet traditional beliefs in witchcraft and magical cures are still strong, as is also dour skepticism about new social ways.

To date acute value conflicts between the middle aged and the young have not emerged. In part this is because traditional ways are still strong and because the common perils of political emancipation, in which even young boys and girls have shared, have overridden divisiveness. The increasing participation in social action of respected male teachers has been another unifying factor. Recently the Freedom Democratic Party has sought to expand its youth organizations.[99] By all these means the tragedies of the northern ghettos, with their isolation of the young in social

or fighting gangs, contemptuous of their elders, have thus far been averted.[100]

Sources of stress. In Holmes County the black community is aware of and deeply concerned with a group of generic problems. These are the incompleteness and continuing precariousness of its civil rights in relation to the local police, the exercise of voting rights, disputes about land, access to loans and other economic resources, educational opportunity, and health services. Black Holmes County residents expect and deeply resent denial, trickery, and condescension from the local white community. Another source of stress is their economic weakness, manifested by continuing serious unemployment and inadequate earnings from farms and jobs. Even in June 1969, after considerable recovery from the disasters of 1965–66, 7,209 persons in the county (perhaps 80 percent of them black) were depending on nutritional aid via food stamps from the U.S. Department of Agriculture.[101]

Worries about health, coupled with inadequate, unreliable, and costly health services, are paramount. An abundant factual basis exists for these worries: infant mortality, developmental failures, accidents, chronic illness among adults, and the sufferings of the elderly are evident from vital statistics, Head Start and Migrant Farmer physical examinations, informants' accounts, and personal observations. Federal mandates notwithstanding, doctors'

---

[100] The writer is indebted to Frederick Horne, University of Illinois, for this important distinction, which in the case of fighting gangs is also associated with rising population densities and dropping economic levels.

[101] Lexington (Mississippi) *Advertiser*, July 31, 1969, p. 7. The rate of participation in Holmes County was 60 percent over the statewide average. The analysis of problems is based on extensive interviews in 1968. The writer is especially indebted to Mr. H. T. Bailey, Mrs. F. Booker, Mr. W. Bruce, Mrs. J. M. Burns, Mr. R. G. Clark, Jr., Mr. S. Friar, Mrs. D. Lewis, Mr. E. Love, Mr. and Mrs. E. Montgomery, Mr. and Mrs. O. Moore, Sr., Mr. C. Wade, and Miss V. Williams.

---

[99] A description of the Holmes County Youth Association is given in the Lexington (Mississippi) *Advertiser*, August 14, 1969, p. 8.

offices are still segregated and delays—
often denials—of service are common, even
in grave emergencies. Hospitals demand
cash in advance or crippling financial commitments. All of these stresses are intensified when mature adults are ill or dying.
The loss of work capacity and the possibility
of secondary disasters through foreclosures
on a house or farm multiply the concerns of
both the sick and the able. Strong family
bonds inflict severe traumas on survivors
when death comes; elaborate funerals are
both social and emotional necessities in
this environment.

Two recent areas of concern in the
black community are with recreational facilities and organized homes for the aged.
The former arose in the wake of several
drownings and traffic fatalities among
young children and because of fears of
rising delinquency among the community's
adolescents. The second reflects the difficulty of handling an increasing number of
aged, including returned migrants, within
the extended family.

Despite extreme overcrowding, inadequacies in housing are still regarded rather
stoically. Yet crowding averages close to
two persons per small room, water often
comes from surface wells, and even privies
may be absent. In winter, when tempera-
tures may drop to 18° F and icy roads
impose isolation, people suffer. Their inadequate, overused gas heaters and wood-
burning stoves cause fatal fires every year.
Similarly the high rate of traffic accidents
associated with bad roads, poorly maintained vehicles and equipment, inade-
quately trained drivers, and an all-too-high
frequency of drinking is not yet seen to
be a health menace.

Determination of the intensification and
reduction of stress in a migratory setting
is still tentative. At their worst, health
conditions in the ghettos are even poorer
than those in Holmes County. Conversely,
job opportunities are certainly greater for
persons as industrious and undemanding
as the Holmes County residents; high
school graduates fare well.

At present only two generalized suggestions can be advanced: (1) that stability
and the level of aspirations of adolescent
boys are more difficult to maintain in the
city than in the rural South and (2) that
a fair number of migratory stresses have
a delayed rather than an early onset, in
contrast to the experience of the Depression years. A case history in this regard
is revealing:

Mr. F came to Chicago at age 26 and discovered that excellent jobs were available in
high-steel work, with the pay rising with each
story. He took the challenge and became
a crew chief; he attracted several brothers to
this work and placed his sisters in cafeteria
employment for the building trade. He enjoyed not only the high pay but the autonomy
of the work. "It's always nice and quiet up
there." But continued exposure to the weather
brought on neurological injuries to his hands,
and these were intensified by worry. At age
39 he faced a crisis: his daughters were starting high school, he was buying a house
("You'd never guess how nice it was inside
from where it is"), and he was rapidly becoming disabled for heavy work. He would
lose half his pay if he were to go to ground-
floor duty. The union physician felt that his
ailment was psychosomatic and placed him on
sick leave, urging him to go home and rest.
So he went South (to a Delta county) for
only the third time since arriving in Chicago.
(The other occasions had both been to attend
funerals.) Staying with an uncle, he tried
to hunt, but his arms shook too much; his
uncle's squirrel stew, normally a sovereign
remedy, did not agree with him; and the
countryside was much too quiet. After three
days he was on the train, returning to Chicago.

Mechanisms of social mediation.
The social mechanisms moderating stresses
and underlying the attainment of goals
have, as shown earlier, been considerably
modernized over the past decade. Black
Holmes County residents have at least limited alternatives: white institutions, traditional means, and new resources of status
and opportunity such as the civil rights
movement. In contrast the migrants appear to depend heavily on kinsmen and
friends. Their church affiliations are more
fluid, although preachers from the county
present strong attractions. A typical or-

ganization is the Saints Junior College Alumnae Club.[102]

Levels of adaptation. In general the levels of economic success attained by black Holmes County residents at home or in the city are, so far as known, modest. In Chicago a fair number are teachers, many are skilled workers, and one is a dentist. In other ways the relative costs of staying or moving are not yet clear. All too often in either case the outcome is early death or, at best, passive withdrawal to rocking chair and bottle. Nevertheless the development of broad choices of movement and lifestyle is clearcut. The combination of conservative values and pragmatically progressive action that has become a hallmark of today's black Holmes County resident is likely to continue, either in a rural-urban balance or as a prelude to a decisive shift. Such a shift could well be toward southern urbanization rather than total absorption into the North.

Significance of the Experience

This detailed examination of a single county's migratory history is still incomplete. However, it shows that national generalizations can be applied here only in part. Certainly the presence of extensive interactions between migration and culture is evident. But the migration rate in Holmes County was far more intense than for the black South as a whole, while the cultural transformations have thus far been pragmatic adaptations rather than an overthrowing of values.

However, Holmes County has been much more representative of a smaller yet significant universe in the eighteen U.S. counties that were 70 percent or more black as late as 1960.[103] In many respects, such as

poverty, rurality, educational level, and lynching rate, Holmes County has been close to modal within this group. And this group is of specific importance as a carrier and transmitter of the rural black cultural tradition to the cities.

In particular the evolution of Holmes County has been most like that of Lowndes County, Alabama, also the scene of great political change. However, even here important differences become evident on closer examination.[104] The Alabama Black Belt still retains substantial tenant farming, by man and mule. Teachers, rather than being rural residents, commute from cities such as Selma and are more representative of the black bourgeoisie than of movement activists. Migratory patterns are influenced by the pressure of local industry in Birmingham and, more recently, Huntsville. Thus different patterns of adaptation are likely. Deep and many-sided understanding of the migratory process among black people in the United States is obviously only beginning.

Comparisons: What Do the Data Mean?

The data that have been reviewed on black migration in the United States, and especially data associated with Holmes

---

[102] Information from Miss Lillie McGee, developed as part of a study of 107 Holmes County families in Chicago, made under the direction of Dr. Ozzie Edwards, Department of Sociology, University of Illinois at Congress Circle, Chicago, and the writer.

[103] These include Wilkinson, Jefferson, Claiborne, Madison, Holmes, Tunica, Marshall, and

Noxobee Counties in Mississippi; Sumter, Greene, Hale, Wilcox, Lowndes, Bullock, and Macon Counties in Alabama; Stewart and Hancock Counties in Georgia; and Charles City County in Virginia. Macon and Charles City are distinctive in that they alone have had rising rather than falling populations since World War II. The influence of Tuskegee Institute in the former and of unusually high black farm ownership in the latter appear to be responsible. For a general survey of the population of predominantly black counties (262 in 1910; 134 in 1960), *see* T. L. Smith, "The Redistribution of the Negro Population of the United States, 1910–1960," *Journal of Negro History*, Vol. 51, No. 3 (1966) pp. 155–173.

[104] The writer is indebted to Shirley Masher of the Southwest Alabama Farmers Cooperative Association and to Donald Jellinek, formerly of the Southern Rural Research Project (Selma, Alabama), for the basic data on Alabama.

County, Mississippi, throw new light on generalizations and other specific studies dealing with migration, its correlates, and its consequences. The Ravenstein-Lee formulations are largely supported.[105] In particular the data verify the attractive capacity of "great centers of commerce and industry" for long-distance migration, the channeling of migration largely in definite streams and counterstreams, the higher propensity of rural rather than urban people to migrate, the importance of technological changes in accelerating migration rates, and the dominance of economic motivations for migration.[106] Above all the inhibition and later rise of black migration in the United States certainly have been reflections of the country's "state of progress," not only economically, but especially in the implementation of Constitutional equality under the law.

For other generalizations the new data suggest reexaminations. The volume and rate of migration appear to be defined by more than economic factors; their acceleration in World Wars I and II reflect sociopolitical fluidities as well. Migration by stages should be conceived of as involving increasingly protracted visits to a destination and military service as much as it does stays at intermediate places.[107] The pre-

dominance of women in short-distance moves seems to be validated by the analysis of expulsions from plantations in Mississippi in the 1960s, but cannot yet be more widely generalized.

Migration propensities among black people generally and Holmes County residents specifically are highly age dependent and also involve both the most and the least capable. But in the county selection for migration is greatly reduced by landownership and intensified by personal instabilities; departure is an accepted way of resolving conflicts with the police and with neighbors. Purposeful migrants from the county tend to be superior in education and work habits to most urban black people and are slow to become absorbed within the larger black community. Thus the theory of "intermediate characteristics" for migrants seems inapplicable. Similarly, analysis of the "efficiency" or the high net displacement effect of Holmes County migrations is complicated by the prevalence of return visits and the considerable probability of eventual returns.

Perhaps the key theoretical contribution of the Holmes County evidence is the concept of a spatially dispersed migratory community. Kinship and friendship links maintain a unity in which differential opportunities on the one hand and social obligations on the other define circuits of travel and communication. Such migratory communities appear to be recurrent among other U.S. black populations, British West Indians, and, in part, African black people; formerly among Chinese-Americans from South China and pre-Revolution Russian peasants; and even, in small-scale mobility, among city-and-suburban British.[108]

[105] Lee, op. cit., esp. pp. 48, 54–57.

[106] For an attempt to delineate the "fields of attraction" of major U.S. cities *see* R. B. Adams, "U.S. Metropolitan Migration: Dimensions and Predictability," *Proceedings of the Association of American Geographers*, Vol. 1 (1969), pp. 1–6. Even in the Soviet Union since 1956, individual motivations have predominated over governmental migratory direction; compare Perevedentsev, op. cit. The net effects of earlier rigorous controls on movement are discussed in Demitri B. Shimkin, "Demographic Changes and Socio-economic Forces Within the Soviet Union, 1939–1959," in C. V. Kiser and F. G. Boudreau, eds., *Population Trends in Eastern Europe, the USSR and Mainland China* (New York: Milbank Memorial Fund, 1960), pp. 224–258.

[107] On other mechanisms of developing information prior to movement, *see* W. A. V. Clark, "Information Flows and Intra-urban Migration:

An Empirical Analysis," *Proceedings of the Association of American Geographers*, Vol. 1 (1969), pp. 38–42.

[108] Data from Douglas Midgett, University of Illinois, unpublished studies of St. Lucia, B.W.I.; P. Mayer, "Migrancy and the Study of Africans in Towns," *American Anthropologist*, Vol. 64 (1962), pp. 576–592; Chen, op. cit.; Cheng, op. cit.; Demitri B. Shimkin and Pedro San Juan,

The importance of circulatory movements in enhancing cultural identity and increasing the informational resources in a community has previously been indicated by Sopher.[109]

The current study also brings out the extreme importance of interactions between migratory streams. Black migrations were greatly inhibited by white immigration, and the difficulties suffered by black migrants were intensifications of those endured by the foreign-born.[110] At the same time comparisons of American with British and French race relations show that, while discrimination against minorities exists in each country, tolerance of violence against them has been shamefully distinctive of the United States.[111]

The studies to date also suggest the utility of a number of analytical approaches, especially for future intensive research. Differentiation of migrants into the categories of "colonists"—oriented to and reinforcing existing enclaves—and "frontiersmen"—facing the alternatives of absorption or establishment of a colony—may prove fruitful.[112] The significance of this differ-

ence among U.S. black people is likely to rise in the future, especially with growing secondary migrations out of and between cities.[113]

Models of stress tend to be unmanageably vague. The promise of the following for studies of migratory adaptation is suggested from the work to date: "postisolation shock" and its associated informational overload, "role loss," "situationally derived psychological depression," and the psychosomatic "automation syndrome." [114] For the mechanics of adaptation, Shannon's stress on the critical roles of mediating subculture is of fundamental value.[115] Older studies of Jewish immigrants in New York and Chinese in Philadelphia can be interpreted in these terms.[116] The phenomena are of great importance in black communities—rural and urban, North and South—but the exact mechanics of brokerage with white institutions and other mediating processes are still little known.

"Culture and World View: A Method of Analysis Applied to Rural Russia," *American Anthropologist*, Vol. 55 (1953), pp. 329–348; and H. E. Bracey, *Neighbors: Subdivision Life in England and the United States* (Baton Rouge: Louisiana State University Press, 1964).

[109] D. E. Sopher, "Pilgrim Circulation in Gujarat," *Geographical Review*, Vol. 58 (1968), pp. 392–425.

[110] G. Abbott, *The Immigrant and the Community* (New York: Century Co., 1921); I. A. Hourwich, *Immigration and Labor: The Economic Aspects of European Immigration to the United States* (New York: G. P. Putnam's Sons, 1912; reprinted, New York: Arno Press, 1969).

[111] J. A. G. Griffith et al., *Coloured Immigrants in Britain* (London, England: Oxford University Press, 1960); W. W. Daniel, *Racial Discrimination in England* (Baltimore: Penguin Books, 1968); J. R. McDonald, "Labor Immigration in France, 1946–1965," *Annals of the Association of American Geographers*, Vol. 59 (1969), pp. 116–134.

[112] J. W. Moore, "Social Class, Assimilation and Acculturation," *Proceedings of the 1968 Annual Spring Meeting*, American Ethnological

Society, pp. 19–33; Alex Simirenko, *Pilgrims, Colonists and Frontiersmen* (New York: Free Press of Glencoe, 1964).

[113] J. O. Wheeler and S. D. Brunn, "An Agricultural Ghetto: Negroes in Cass County, Michigan, 1945–1968," *Geographical Review*, Vol. 59 (1969), pp. 317–329; P. H. Vernon, "Distance Selectivity of U.S. Labor Force Migration, 1960–1963," *Proceedings of the Association of American Geographers*, Vol. 1 (1969), pp. 153–156.

[114] J. L. Fuller, "Experiential Deprivation and Later Behavior," *Science*, Vol. 158 (1967), pp. 1645–1652; D. S. Stevenson, *Problems of Eskimo Relocation for Industrial Employment* (Ottawa: Northern Science Research Group 68-1, Department of Indian Affairs and Northern Development, 1968); Kermit T. Wiltse, "Orthopsychiatric Programs for Socially Deprived Groups," *American Journal of Orthopsychiatry*, Vol. 33 (1963), pp. 806–813; and R. W. Anderson, "Emotional Health in Industry," *Archives of Environmental Health*, Vol. 15 (1967), pp. 308–311.

[115] L. W. Shannon et al., *The Economic Absorption and Cultural Integration of Immigrant Workers* (Iowa City: University of Iowa Press, 1966), esp. pp. 427–446. For similar mediation among Mexican-American migratory farm workers, *see* Gilkeson and LaMarsh, op. cit.

[116] Hutchins Hopgood, *The Spirit of the Ghetto* (rev. ed.; New York: Schocken Books, 1966); Cheng, op. cit.

For individual adaptation, the concepts of random searches, pathways, and life-stage programming used in the analyses of housing histories will undoubtedly be useful.[117] The first is likely to be characteristic of the forced migrant; the second, increasingly, of the purposeful black migrant. Herrick's studies in Chile raise the necessity of comparing migrants with native persons of similar status; the evidence on relative adaptive successes for the two groups among U.S. blacks is ambiguous.[118]

Finally, the relevance of prior and concurrent migrations by other peoples to those of blacks and of the latter to those of still other groups must be brought out. It is clear that each migratory group—and indeed, the many components of each group—has numerous unique features. But significant resemblances and transfers of experience do occur, for example, between Jewish and black migrants. And the lessons of black migrant adaptation need study to reduce needless damage to the Mexican-Americans, Indians, and Eskimos who are migrating to urban areas in their wake.[119]

Conclusions and Implications

This study has shown that one hundred years of post-Civil War migration and differential natural growth have served to redistribute the black population of the United States. Once virtually entirely southern and rural, it is now strongly urban and almost half northern and western. In fact the bulk of the natural increase of the black population now comes from the North and West.

Appalling conditions of life in the cities, which partly reflected labor surpluses and exploitation made possible by mass white immigration, kept black populations in the North and West at low levels until World War I. Economic opportunities in that war, and especially during World War II, underlaid the rise of large and viable black colonies in northern and western metropolitan areas.

Black cultural traditions have influenced the outcome of migration especially through extended kinship bonds and through common participation in an adaptive, expressive religious system. One consequence, manifest in the case of Holmes County, Mississippi, has been the creation of spatially dispersed communities. Black cultures have suffered major losses through the denial of opportunity to practice higher economic skills (especially during the Great Depression) and through low status and the suppression of oral traditions. But they have also borrowed and invented new social, literary, musical, and religious traits in urban areas. These features have been selectively accepted in the South, which has itself undergone considerable cultural evolution, initially in urban centers and later in rural areas with predominantly black populations.

Stratification within black society, white diversion of black leadership, cultural differences and, in part, marital isolation between resident and in-migrant urban populations, and limited black access to mass

[117] R. L. Morrill, "The Negro Ghetto: Problems and Alternatives," *Geographical Review*, Vol. 55 (1965), pp. 339–361; R. R. Boyce, "Residential Mobility and Its Implications for Urban Spatial Change," *Proceedings of the Association of American Geographers*, Vol. 1 (1969), pp. 22–25; J. W. Simmons, "Changing Residence in the City," *Geographical Review*, Vol. 58 (1968), 622–651.

[118] B. H. Herrick, *Urban Migration and Economic Development in Chile* (Cambridge, Mass.: M.I.T. Press, 1965). Compare Malzberg and Lee and the Kerner Commission: Malzberg and Lee, op. cit.; *Report of the National Advisory Commission on Civil Disorders*, pp. 255–257.

[119] *See* Shannon et al., op. cit.; L. W. Shannon, "The Study of Migrants as Members of Social Systems," *Proceedings of the 1968 Annual Spring Meeting*, American Ethnological Society, pp. 34–64; N. A. Chance et al., "Modernization, Value Identification, and Mental Health: A Cross-cultural Study," *Anthropologica*, Vol. 8 (1966), pp. 197–216; N. O. Christensen, "Certain Socioeconomic Conditions in Greenland," *Archives of Environmental Health*, Vol. 17 (1968), pp. 464–473.

communications have blocked the development of cohesive communities except in a few areas such as Holmes County. In consequence continuing political-economic frustrations and rising pride through increased education, military service, and charismatic leadership have made the national black community sensitive and rather unstable.

Since World War II agricultural mechanization and federal subsidies to keep land idle have virtually eliminated black tenant farmers, who have been forced to migrate under especially adverse conditions. Southern anger at the prospect of school desegregation in 1954 and southern fears of black voting strength after 1960 intensified these expulsive pressures. The dislocations so generated have led to family disorganization, both in the North and the South, nutritional deterioration, and stresses on adults. As a consequence infant mortality has been rising and the life expectancy of black men has been dropping since 1960 or earlier. Frustrations of migrants appear to have been a significant factor in the Chicago riots of 1968, but were clearly outweighed by local issues in Detroit, Newark, and other cities in 1967.

Analytically, the evidence from black migrations supports many aspects of the Ravenstein-Lee hypotheses, as well as Shannon's concept of subcultural mediation. The importance of spatially dispersed communities as a recurrent outcome of migration is indicated.

Over the next decade the youth of the black population will result in a high rate of increase in the number of blacks in the cities, even if migrations from rural areas and cohort fertilities continue to drop. This factor, increased educational differences, and fewer restrictions on jobs and housing are likely to intensify black suburbanization, movement to smaller cities, return flows to the South, and even migration to rural areas.

Future black migrants are likely to be better educated, more aggressive, and more skilled in sociopolitical action than those in the past. Demographic disproportions and weaknesses in male roles, promoting a high frequency of female-headed households, are likely to diminish. In general polar possibilities of severe conflict or accommodation will arise in relation to the white population.

If depressions and their succeeding social upheavals are avoided, the direct welfare needs of the black population are likely to center in (1) the education, employment, family-forming, and housing needs of young adults, (2) the repair of past physical and psychological injuries, especially among those born in the 1960s, and (3) the needs of an elderly population that are beyond the capacities of extended family systems to meet. Black communities will be increasingly capable of handling these problems, given reasonable technical and financial assistance.

Black communities are likely to be dominated by increasing group concerns, desires for autonomy, and emphasis on internal socioeconomic cooperation. Their stability will depend heavily on opportunities for self-government, home and other property ownership, jobs, and education. These factors, rather than minimum economic guaranties per se or even health services, are likely to determine whether future black migrations will be essentially population adjustments within a stabilized system of settlements participating effectively in national life or irregular perturbations gaining limited advantages at great human cost to all.

Finally, the pattern of black migrations will be heavily influenced by migrations of the white population and will in turn exercise both negative and positive influences on smaller minorities such as Mexican-Americans, Puerto Ricans, American Indians, and Eskimos.

TABLE 1. DISTRIBUTION OF THE BLACK POPULATION, UNITED STATES, 1870–1966[a]

Year	Nationwide Black Population		South[b]		North and West[c]		National Urban[d]		Southern Urban		Northern and Western Urban	
	Number (thousands)	Percentage	Number (thousands)	Percentage	Number (thousands)	Percentage	Number (thousands)	Percentage	Number (thousands)	Percentage	Number (thousands)	Percentage
1870	5,392[e]	13.5[e]	4,933[e]	36.4[e]	459	1.7	n.a.[f]	n.a.	n.a.	n.a.	n.a.	n.a.
1880	6,581	13.1	5,954	36.0	627	1.9	n.a.	n.a.	n.a.	n.a.	n.a.	n.a.
1890	7,489	11.9	6,761	33.8	728	1.7	1,418	6.5	1,033	31.7	385	2.0
1900	8,834	11.6	7,923	32.3	911	1.8	2,006	6.5	1,365	30.9	641	2.5
1910	9,828	10.6	8,749	29.8	1,079	1.7	2,689	6.3	1,854	28.0	835	2.4
1920	10,463	10.0	8,912	26.9	1,551	2.1	3,559	6.6	2,251	24.2	1,308	2.9
1930	11,891	9.7	9,362	24.7	2,529	2.9	5,194	7.5	2,966	23.0	2,228	3.9
1940	12,866	9.7	9,905	23.8	2,961	3.3	6,254	8.4	3,616	23.6	2,638	4.5
1950	15,042	10.0	10,225	21.7	4,817	4.7	9,371	9.7	4,880	21.3	4,491	6.1
1960	18,860	10.6	11,312	20.6	7,548	6.1	13,801	11.1	6,608	20.5	7,193	7.7
1966	21,500	11.0	11,825	19.5	9,675	7.2	n.a.	n.a.	n.a.	n.a.	n.a.	n.a.

[a] The term "black" used here is an unofficial usage corresponding to "Negro" in United States governmental statistics. Attention is called to the fact that, prior to 1930, "black," and "mulatto" were official subgroups of differing admixtures with whites within the "Negro" total. Percentages given are of the total corresponding populations of all races.

[b] Includes Delaware, Maryland, District of Columbia, West Virginia, Kentucky, and Oklahoma as well as the former Confederate states.

[c] Excludes Alaska and Hawaii prior to 1940.

[d] Places of 2,500 inhabitants or more; also, inhabitants of urbanized areas from 1950.

[e] These figures have been revised for underenumeration in the South.

[f] n.a.—data not available.

Sources: U.S. Senate Committee on Government Operations, 90th Cong., 2d Sess., *The Rural to Urban Population Shift: A National Problem* (Washington, D.C.: U.S. Government Printing Office, 1968), pp. 19, 21; U.S. Bureau of the Census, *Negro Population, 1790–1915* (Washington, D.C.: U.S. Government Printing Office, 1918), pp. 91–92; U.S. Bureau of the Census, *Statistical Abstract of the United States, 1967* (Washington, D.C.: U.S. Government Printing Office, 1967), p. 24.

TABLE 2. FOURTEEN LARGEST BLACK URBAN POPULATIONS, 1910, 1930, 1940, AND 1960[a]

City	1910 Rank	1910 Number	1910 Percentage	1930 Rank	1930 Number	1930 Percentage	1940 Rank	1940 Number	1940 Percentage	1960[b] Rank	1960[b] Number	1960[b] Percentage
Washington, D.C.	1	94,446	28.5	5	132,068	27.1	4	187,266	28.2	5	418,693	54.8
New York, N.Y.	2	91,709	1.9	1	327,706	4.7	1	458,444	6.1	1	1,141,322	14.7
New Orleans, La.	3	89,262	26.3	6	129,632	28.3	8	149,034	30.1	9	234,931	37.4
Baltimore, Md.	4	84,749	15.2	4	142,106	17.7	5	165,843	19.3	7	328,416	35.0
Philadelphia, Pa.	5	84,459	5.5	3	219,519	11.3	3	250,880	13.0	3	535,033	26.7
Memphis, Tenn.	6	52,441	40.0	9	96,550	38.1	7	121,498	41.5	13	184,725	37.1
Birmingham, Ala.	7	52,305	39.4	8	99,077	38.2	9	108,938	40.7			39.7
Atlanta, Ga.	8	51,902	33.5	11	90,075	33.3	11	104,553	34.6	12	186,820	38.3
Richmond, Va.	9	46,733	36.6									42.0
Chicago, Ill.	10	44,103	2.0	2	233,903	6.9	2	277,731	8.2	2	837,656	23.6
St. Louis, Mo.	11	43,960	6.4	10	93,580	11.4	10	108,765	13.3	11	216,022	28.8
Louisville, Ky.	12	40,522	18.1									18.0
Nashville, Tenn.	13	36,523	33.1									37.4
Savannah, Ga.	14	33,246	**51.1**									35.7
Detroit, Mich.				7	120,066	7.7	6	149,119	9.2	4	487,174	29.2
Cleveland, Ohio				12	71,899	8.0				8	253,108	28.9
Houston, Tex.				13	63,337	21.7				10	217,672	23.2
Pittsburgh, Pa.				14	54,983	8.2	13	62,216	9.3			16.8
Los Angeles, Calif.[c]							12	63,774	4.2	6	417,207	16.8[c]
Dallas, Tex.							14	50,407	17.1			19.3
Newark, N.J.										14	139,331	34.4

[a] Figures are given only for the fourteen leading cities; others are omitted. Percentages given are of the total city population.

[b] The 1960 census, unlike earlier ones, aggregated blacks and other nonwhites into a single category. For this reason, Honolulu and San Francisco have been omitted from this table because of their large Oriental populations. It should be noted, however, that persons with Spanish surnames (Mexican-Americans, Puerto Ricans, and others) are included in the category "white." This leads to understatements of minority populations in such cities as New York as well as to minimizing the socioeconomic differences between majority and minority groups in the United States.

[c] The figures for Los Angeles include a significant Oriental population.

Sources: U.S. Bureau of the Census, *Negro Population, 1790–1915* (Washington, D.C.: U.S. Government Printing Office, 1918), p. 93; U.S. Bureau of the Census, *Negroes in the United States, 1920–1932* (Washington, D.C.: U.S. Government Printing Office, 1935), p. 55; F. Murray, ed., *The Negro Handbook 1949* (New York: Macmillan Co., 1949), p. 8; U.S. Bureau of the Census, *Statistical Abstract of the United States, 1967* (Washington, D.C.: U.S. Government Printing Office, 1967), pp. 22–23.

TABLE 3. DYNAMICS OF THE BLACK POPULATION OF THE NORTH AND WEST, 1870–1966 [a]

Period	Number of Persons (thousands)				Annual Rates [b]		
	Initial population	Natural increase	Net in-migration	Net increase	Natural increase	Net in-migration	Net in-crease
1870–79	459	97	71	168	2.0	1.4	3.2
1880–89	627	18	83	101	0.3	1.2	1.5
1890–99	728	—12	195	183	—0.1	2.4	2.3
1900–09	911	—29	197	168	—0.3	2.0	1.7
1910–19	1,079	—50	522	472	—0.4	3.9	3.7
1920–29	1,551	106	872	978	0.7	4.5	5.0
1930–39	2,529	68	364	432	0.3	1.4	1.6
1940–49	2,961	363	1,493	1,856	1.2	4.2	5.0
1950–59	4,817	1,274	1,457	2,731	2.4	2.7	4.6
1960–66	7,548	1,373	754	2,127	2.8	1.4	4.2

[a] The unofficial term "black" corresponds to the official term "Negro."
[b] Related to the initial population of the relevant period.
Sources: U.S. Bureau of the Census, *Negro Population, 1790–1915* (Washington, D.C.: U.S. Government Printing Office, 1918), pp. 91–92; U.S. Bureau of the Census, *Statistical Abstract of the United States, 1967* (Washington, D.C.: U.S. Government Printing Office, 1967), p. 24; U.S. Senate Committee on Government Operations, 90th Cong., 2d Sess., *The Rural to Urban Population Shift: A National Problem* (Washington, D.C.: U.S. Government Printing Office, 1968), p. 22. All net nonwhite in-migration from the South was assumed to be black. Black immigrants and emigrants from and to foreign countries have been ignored. Statistics on this small group, important primarily in New York and New England, are subject to much error. This omission tends to understate slightly the losses of population among black people in the North and West between 1890 and 1920.

TABLE 4. DYNAMICS OF THE BLACK POPULATION OF THE SOUTH, 1870–1966 [a]

Period	Number of Persons (thousands)				Annual Rates [b]		
	Initial population	Natural increase	Net out-migration	Net increase	Natural increase	Net out-migration	Net in-crease
1870–79	4,933	1,098	— 71	1,021	2.0	—0.1	1.9
1880–89	5,954	890	— 83	807	1.4	—0.1	1.3
1890–99	6,671	1,357	— 195	1,162	1.9	—0.3	1.6
1900–09	7,923	1,023	— 197	826	1.2	—0.2	1.0
1910–19	8,749	685	— 522	163	0.8	—0.6	0.2
1920–29	8,912	1,322	— 872	450	1.4	—0.9	0.5
1930–39	9,362	907	— 364	543	0.9	—0.4	0.6
1940–49	9,905	1,813	—1,493	320	1.7	—1.4	0.3
1950–59	10,225	2,544	—1,457	1,087	2.3	—1.3	1.0
1960–66	11,312	1,267	— 754	513	1.8	—1.1	0.7

[a] The unofficial term "black" corresponds to the official term "Negro."
[b] Related to the initial population of the relevant period.
Sources: U.S. Bureau of the Census, *Negro Population, 1790–1915* (Washington, D.C.: U.S. Government Printing Office, 1918), pp. 91–92; U.S. Bureau of the Census, *Statistical Abstract of the United States, 1967* (Washington, D.C.: U.S. Government Printing Office, 1967), p. 24; U.S. Senate Committee on Government Operations, 90th Cong., 2d Sess., *The Rural to Urban Population Shift: A National Problem* (Washington, D.C.: U.S. Government Printing Office, 1968), p. 22. All net nonwhite out-migration was assumed to be black. The few black immigrants and emigrants from and to foreign countries have been ignored.

TABLE 5. PRELIMINARY ESTIMATES OF THE DYNAMICS OF THE BLACK POPULATION OF HOLMES COUNTY, MISSISSIPPI, 1880–1969

Period	Initial Black Population		Total Change in Number of Persons	Natural Increase[a]		Net Migration[a]		Estimated 1969 Survivors	
	Number	Percentage of total		Number	Annual rate	Number	Annual rate	Number	Percentage
1880–89	20,233	74.5	+3,650	(3,100)	(1.4)	+(550)	+(0.2)	b	b
1890–99	23,883	77.1	+4,824	(4,824)	(1.9)	b	b	b	b
1900–09	28,707	77.9	+2,490	(3,700)	(1.2)	(1,210)	−(0.3)	35	7
1910–19	31,197	79.8	−(1,249)[c]	(3,350)	(0.8)	−(4,599)	−(1.6)	1,000	22
1920–29	26,628	77.2	+2,771	(4,875)	(1.7)	−(2,104)	−(0.8)	900	43
1930–39	29,399	76.3	+1,078	(3,300)	(1.2)	−(2,222)	−(0.7)	1,500	67
1940–49	30,477	76.7	−5,998	(6,310)	(1.9)	−(12,308)	−(3.5)	10,500	85
1950–59	24,479	73.5	−4,998	5,360	1.6	−10,358	−(3.0)	9,700	94
1960–69	19,481	72.0	−(1,400)	(3,300)	(1.5)	−(4,700)	−(2.5)	4,650	99
Net totals, 1900–69	n.a.[e]	n.a.[e]	−(8,709)[d]	30,095	n.a.	(37,501)	n.a.	28,335	76

[a] Rates are based on the initial population of each period.

[b] Negligible.

[c] This figure has been adjusted for the transfer of 3,320 persons (10 percent of the 1910 land area) to form part of Humphreys County in 1918. The estimated black population transferred (3,320 persons) is calculated at the average black density per square mile for Humphreys County in 1918 of 38.8 persons. *See* U.S. Bureau of the Census, *Negro Population, 1790–1915,* p. 783; and *Fourteenth Census of the United States. State Compendium Mississippi,* pp. 11, 13 (Washington, D.C.: U.S. Government Printing Office, 1918 and 1929, respectively).

[d] Includes a correction for the 1918 boundary change.

[e] n.a.—not applicable.

Sources: Initial Population: U.S. Bureau of the Census, *Negro Population, 1790–1915,* p. 783; *Negroes in the United States, 1920–1932,* p. 757; *Sixteenth Census of the United States: 1940,* Vol. 2, Part 4, p. 242; *United States Census of Population, 1950,* Vol. 2, Part 24, pp. 9, 60; *County and City Data Book: 1962,* p. 202. (Washington, D.C.: U.S. Government Printing Office, 1918, 1935, 1943, 1952, and 1962, respectively.) Natural Increase: 1880–1920, Table 3; 1920–29 and 1950–59, residuals from total change less net migration; 1930–39, Mississippi nonwhite data, from J. C. Belcher and M. B. King, Jr., "Mississippi's People," Sociological Study Series No. 2 (University: University of Mississippi, 1950); 1940–49, based on county vital statistics for 1943–48, *Vital Statistics, Mississippi* (Jackson: State Board of Health, 1943–48); 1960–69, based on county vital statistics for 1960–66 and field estimates for 1967–69. Net Migration: residuals from natural increase less total change, except for 1920–29 and 1950–59; P. B. Foreman, "Mississippi Population Trends," Ph.D. dissertation, Vanderbilt University, 1939, p. 144; *County and City Data Book: 1962,* p. 203. Mortalities of migrants: Based on a median age of 20–24 and a sex ratio of 150, with all migration attributed to the middle of each decade. The life tables for 1905–1925 (1910 nonwhite registration-area data), U.S. Bureau of the Census: *Negro Population, 1790–1915* (Washington: U.S. Government Printing Office, 1918), pp. 323–326; for 1945–69 (1950 nonwhite Mississippi urban rates), M. B. King, Jr., J. N. Burrus, and H. A. Pederson, *Mississippi Life Tables, 1950–51,* Sociological Study Series No. 4 (University: University of Mississippi, 1954); for 1925–45, the estimated rates were intermediate between those in the 1910 and 1950 sources.

TABLE 6. PRELIMINARY ESTIMATES OF THE NUMBER AND DISTRIBUTION OF THE NATIVE AND IN-MIGRANT BLACK POPULATION OF HOLMES COUNTY, MISSISSIPPI, 1969

Item	Total	Native Black Holmes Countians								Black In-migrants [g]
		Nonmigrants and returned migrants	Out-migrants							
			Other Mississippi counties	Other southern states [a]	Chicago and suburbs [b]	Other midwestern cities [c]	Eastern cities [d]	Far western cities [e]	Other and unknown locations [f]	
Number of persons	44,100	15,750	1,500	2,250	12,100	2,700	800	1,500	7,500	2,350
Percentage distribution	100	36	3	5	27	6	2	4	17	n.a. [h]
Sample family distributions (number of persons)	6	4	0	0	1	1	0	0	0	n.a.
	20	9	1	0	5	1	2	2	0	n.a.
	10	1	0	5	2	2	0	0	0	n.a.
	10	3	0	0	7	0	0	0	0	n.a.
	7	2	0	0	4	0	0	1	0	n.a.

[a] Especially Tennessee (Memphis) and Arkansas.
[b] Especially Maywood, Chicago Heights, and Evanston.
[c] Especially St. Louis, Detroit, Waterloo (Iowa), and Peoria (Ill.).
[d] Especially New York.
[e] Especially Los Angeles.
[f] Includes persons in military service and overseas.
[g] Estimated at 13 percent of the black resident population from a 100-household sample from the 1969–70 census of the Holmes County black population, conducted by the Milton Olive III Memorial Corporation.
[h] n.a.—not applicable.
Sources: for the total number of net out-migrants, Table 5; for the percentage distribution of migrants, obituary data in the Lexington (Mississippi) *Advertiser*, 1969, family records, and estimates by informants.

TABLE 7. CHANGES IN STRUCTURE AND HOUSEHOLD COMPOSITION OF THE BLACK POPULATION OF HOLMES COUNTY, MISSISSIPPI, 1910, 1930, AND 1960

| | Absolute Values | | | | | | Index Numbers (1930=100) | | | |
| | 1910 | | 1930 | | 1960 | | 1910 | | 1960 | |
	Number	Percentage	Number	Percentage	Number	Percentage	Number	Percentage	Number	Percentage
Population										
Age 0– 9	8,863	28.5	7,747	26.3	5,761	29.0	114	108	73	100
10–20	(8,351) [a]	(26.8)	7,563	25.7	(5,016)	(25.7)	110	(104)	66	(100)
21–44	n.a. [b]	n.a.	9,640	32.8	3,571	18.3	n.a.	n.a.	37	56
45–64	n.a.	n.a.	3,587	12.2	3,232	16.6	n.a.	n.a.	90	136
65 plus	n.a.	n.a.	862	2.9	2,011	10.3	n.a.	n.a.	233	355
21 plus	(13,983)	(44.7)	14,089	47.9	(8,812)	(45.2)	99	(99)	62	(94)
Total	31,197	100.0	29,399	100.0	19,501 [c]	100.0	106		66	
Median age (years)	19		19		18		100		95	
Households										
Total number	6,873		7,060		4,432		97		63	
Average size (number persons)	4.5		4.2		4.4		107		105	
Married men [d]	n.a.		5,912		3,274		n.a.		55	
Married women	n.a.		5,897		3,604		n.a.		61	
Widows and divorcees [d]	n.a.		1,536		1,105		n.a.		72	
Ratios:										
Married men/total	n.a.		84		74		n.a.		88	
Married men/ married women	n.a.		100		91		n.a.		91	
Widows, divorcees/ married women	n.a.		26		31		n.a.		118	

[a] Parentheses indicate a partial estimate.
[b] n.a.—not applicable.
[c] Compare this with Table 5.
[d] Age 15 and over in 1930, 14 and over in 1960.

Sources: U.S. Bureau of the Census, *Negro Population, 1790–1915*, pp. 187, 816; *Negroes in the United States, 1920–1932*, p. 757; *United States Census of Population, 1960*, Vol. 1, Part 26, pp. 67, 83 (Washington, D.C.: U.S. Government Printing Office, 1918, 1935, and 1963, respectively).

TABLE 8. ECONOMIC AND EDUCATIONAL CHANGES AMONG THE BLACK POPULATION OF HOLMES COUNTY, MISSISSIPPI, 1910, 1930, AND 1960

Item	Absolute Values						Index Numbers (1930=100)			
	1910		1930		1960		1910		1960	
	Number	Percentage	Number	Percentage	Number	Percentage	Number	Percentage	Number	Percentage
Farm population	(25,000)[a]	(82)	24,484[d]	83	8,488	43	(102)	(99)	35	52
Farm workers[b]	n.a.[c]		(6,320)[d]		2,347		n.a.		37	
Farm operators	(5,437)		(5,660)[d]		936		96		(17)	
Paid labor	n.a.		(660)[d]		1,411		n.a.		(214)	
Ratio of farm workers to farm population		n.a.		25		28		n.a.		108
Farms, total	5,437		5,660		1,612		96		28	
Size, acres										
Total	232,091		196,793		89,875		118		46	
Average	45		35		56		129		160	
Owned[e]										
Total	770		650		742		118		114	
Total acreage	84,451		60,169		67,044		140		111	
Average acreage	109		93		90		117		97	
Rented[f]										
Total	4,664		5,006		870		93		17	
Total acreage	166,427		136,518		22,831		120		16	
Average acreage	36		27		26		133		99	
Farmland per capita (acres)										
Total population	7.4		6.7		4.6		110		69	
Farm population	(9.3)		8.0		10.6		(116)		132	
Nonfarm workers										
Total	n.a.		(2,280)[d]	(29)	2,079	47	n.a.		(91)	(162)
White-collar workers	n.a.		(140)[d]		263		n.a.		(180)	
Craftsmen	n.a.		(170)[d]		207		n.a.		(122)	
Domestics	n.a.		(1,095)[d]		603		n.a.		(55)	
Others[g]	n.a.		(975)[d]		959		n.a.		(98)	
Ratio: white-collar and craftsmen to domestics and others		n.a.		(15)[d]		30		n.a.		(200)
School enrollment										
Total	5,780		6,895		6,753		82		98	
Elementary[h]	5,780		(6,770)[i]		5,570		85		85	
Illiteracy (percentage of population)		32[j]		28[j]		6[k]		114		21

TABLE 8—*Continued*

ᵃ Numbers in parentheses are estimates. This specific figure (25,000) is derived from the number of farm homes for that year (5,560) times the average household size (*see* Table 7). U.S. Bureau of the Census, *Negro Population, 1790–1915* (Washington, D.C.: U.S. Government Printing Office, 1918), p. 487.

ᵇ Unpaid family workers are not included.

ᶜ n.a.—not applicable.

ᵈ These estimates are from the 1940 labor force data adjusted to the number of farms in 1930. U.S. Bureau of the Census, *Sixteenth Census of the United States: 1940*, Vol. 2, Part 4 (Washington, D.C.: U.S. Government Printing Office, 1943), p. 264.

ᵉ Includes those fully owned, owned in part, and not mortgaged.

ᶠ Includes cash tenants, sharecroppers, share-cash tenants, renters with unspecified tenure, and managers.

ᵍ Includes operatives, service workers, other laborers, and occupations not reported.

ʰ Kindergarten and grades 1–8.

ⁱ In 1930–31 only 1.8 percent of the average daily attendance of black schoolchildren in Mississippi was in grades 9–12; 63.6 percent were in grades 1–3. *Public Education in Mississippi*, Bulletin 67 (Jackson: Mississippi State Board of Education, Division of Information and Statistics, 1931), p. 134.

ʲ Percentage of those persons over 9 years of age.

ᵏ Persons over age 24 reporting no schooling.

Sources: Those given in footnotes to the table; *also* U.S. Bureau of the Census, *Negro Population, 1790–1915*, pp. 656, 730, 816; *Negroes in the United States, 1920–1932*, pp. 650–651, 757; *United States Census of Population, 1960*, Vol. 1, Part 26, pp. 203, 210; *1964 Census of Agriculture. Statistics for the State and Counties. Mississippi*, p. 262. (Washington, D.C.: U.S. Government Printing Office, 1918, 1935, 1963, and 1967, respectively).

TABLE 9. VITAL STATISTICS, REPORTED OR ESTIMATED POPULATIONS, AND CRUDE VITAL RATES FOR THE BLACK POPULATION OF HOLMES COUNTY, MISSISSIPPI, 1930–31 AND 1940–66

Calendar Year	Number of Births	Number of Deaths		Reported or Estimated Midyear Population[b]			Reported or Estimated Crude Vital Rates Base: Series C		
		Total	Infant deaths[a]	A	B	C	Births per 1,000 persons	Deaths per 1,000 persons	Infant deaths per 1,000 births
1930	972	403	78	n.a.[d]	n.a.	29,400	33.1	13.7	80.2
1931	814[c]	379[c]	57[c]	n.a.	n.a.	(29,700)[e]	27.4[e]	12.8[e]	70.2[e]
1940	894[c]	338	44	n.a.	n.a.	30,501	29.3[e]	11.1	49.2
1941	903[c]	355	n.a.	n.a.	n.a.	(29,070)	31.1	12.2	n.a.
1942	851[c]	310	33[c]	n.a.	n.a.	(27,650)	30.8	11.2	38.8[e]
1943	941	299	34[c]	(26,848)	(25,623)	(26,235)	35.9	11.4	36.1[e]
1944	873	285	39	n.a.	(24,961)	(24,900)	35.1	11.4	45.0
1945	920	300	37	n.a.	n.a.	(25,350)	36.3	11.8	40.2
1946	907	257[c]	n.a.	n.a.	n.a.	(25,800)	35.2	10.0[e]	n.a.
1947	897	292	41	n.a.	n.a.	(26,250)	34.2	11.1	45.7
1948	960	278	n.a.	n.a.	n.a.	(26,700)	36.0	10.4	n.a.
1949	911	291	51	n.a.	(27,821)	(27,180)	33.5	10.7	56.0
1950	968	276	25[c]	(25,176)	n.a.	24,479[e]	39.5[f]	11.3[f]	25.8[e]
1951	924	260	36	(26,199)	(23,164)	(25,680)	36.0	10.1	39.0
1952	848	299	48	n.a.	(22,678)	(25,130)	33.7	11.9	56.6
1953	804	252	35	(25,011)	(23,056)	(24,580)	32.7	10.3	43.5
1954	876	253	35	(23,643)	(23,021)	(24,015)	36.5	10.5	40.0
1955	749	240	31	(22,432)	(23,106)	(23,375)	32.0	10.3	41.4
1956	798	246	36	(22,496)	(23,199)	(22,815)	35.0	10.8	45.1
1957	676	244	44	n.a.	(20,275)	(21,385)	31.6	11.4	65.0
1958	682	247	42	n.a.	(20,707)	(20,755)	32.9	11.9	61.6
1959	657	239	36	n.a.	(21,142)	(20,125)	32.6	11.9	54.8
1960	639	234	32	n.a.	n.a.	19,481	32.8	12.0	50.1
1961	639	268	41	n.a.	n.a.	(19,385)	33.0	13.8	64.2
1962	591	238	31	n.a.	n.a.	(19,290)	30.6	12.3	52.4
1963	643	234	25[c]	n.a.	n.a.	(19,200)	33.6	12.2	38.9[e]
1964	653	258	31[c]	n.a.	n.a.	(19,105)	34.2	13.5	47.5[e]
1965	507[c]	277[c]	34[c]	n.a.	n.a.	(19,010)	26.7[e]	14.6[e]	67.1[e]
1966	487[c]	259[c]	22[c]	n.a.	n.a.	(18,915)	25.7[e]	13.7[e]	45.2[e]

TABLE 9—*Continued*

a Deaths at less than 1 year of age.
b Census data (as of April) have not been adjusted to July 1 estimates.
c Datum believed to be significantly too low through underreporting.
d n.a.—not available.
e Parentheses indicate estimated figures.
f Datum believed to be significantly too high because of an undercounted base.

Sources: Numbers of births and deaths: 1930–31, U.S. Bureau of the Census, *Negroes in the United States, 1920–1932* (Washington, D.C.: U.S. Government Printing Office, 1935), pp. 408–409; 1940, F. E. Linder and R. D. Grove, *Vital Statistics Rates in the United States, 1900–1940* (Washington, D.C.: U.S. Government Printing Office, 1943), p. 745; 1941 and 1942, U.S. Bureau of the Census, *Vital Statistics of the United States*, Vol. 2 (Washington, D.C.: U.S. Government Printing Office) for corresponding years; 1943–48 and 1959–66, Mississippi State Board of Health, *Vital Statistics, Mississippi* (Jackson) for corresponding years; 1949–58, National Office of Vital Statistics, *Vital Statistics of the United States*, Vol. 1 (Washington, D.C.: U.S. Government Printing Office) for corresponding years. Population, Series A, for 1943, U.S. Bureau of the Census estimate for November 1, 1943, based on ration books, reported in *Vital Statistics, Mississippi, 1944*; for 1950–51 and 1954–57, Table 10. Series B. Assuming that calculated migration rates for those aged 0–9 are indicative of the entire population, the births reported for 1950–59 were averaged to 1960 and the estimated numbers of survivors were compared with the reported numbers by each year of age in the 1960 census. The pattern of differences provides the model for distributing migration year by year. The initial 1950 population, plus reported births and less reported deaths and less estimated net migration, yielded successive estimates for each year. The estimates for the 1940s are quite approximate because of the clearcut underreporting of births in 1940–42 and the limitation of early-age data in the 1950 census to "under 1, 1 and 2, 3 and 4, 5, 6, and 7 to 9." Nevertheless, the sharp difference between estimated and reported survivors aged 0 in 1950 (13.0 percent, or almost the same as for those aged 1 and 2) is indicative of major out-migration during 1950. The source for mortality coefficients used (1950 nonwhite rates) was M. B. King, Jr., H. A. Pederson, and J. N. Burrus, *Mississippi's People, 1950*, Sociological Studies No. 5 (University: University of Mississippi, 1955), p. 31. Series C. Census data for 1930, 1940, 1950, and 1960, Table 5; for 1943 and 1954–57, the averages of A and B estimates; for 1965, an aggregate 1960–65 out-migration estimate of 2,404 has been made from the 1959–64 reported reduction of the county's Negro farm operators (1,612 to 1,148) and the average size of nonwhite rural households in 1960 (5.18). *See* U.S. Bureau of the Census, *1964 Census of Agriculture, Statistics for the State and Counties, Mississippi* (Washington: U.S. Government Printing Office, 1967), p. 269; and U.S. Bureau of the Census, *United States Census of Population, 1960*, Vol. 1, Part 26 (Washington: U.S. Government Printing Office, 1963), p. 224. This out-migration estimate has been subtracted from the 1960–64 excess of births over deaths (1,933) to yield the population figure. The remaining figures are linear interpolations or extrapolations of Series C.

TABLE 10. SCHOOL ATTENDANCE AND ENROLLMENT AND ESTIMATED POPULATION CHANGES FOR THE BLACK POPULATION OF HOLMES COUNTY, MISSISSIPPI, 1949–60

| School Year | Average Daily Attendance at Negro Schools | | | | | Estimated Enrollment in Elementary Grades | | Estimated Total Black Population [a] |
| | Total Number | High School | | Elementary Grades | | | | |
		Number	Percentage	Number	Percentage	Multiplier	Number	
1949–50	5,933	(368) [b]	(6.2)	(5,565)	(93.8)	1.289	(7,173)	(25,176)
1950–51	6,144	459	7.4	5,685	92.6	(1.313)	(7,464)	(26,199)
1953–54	5,684	553	9.7	5,131	90.3	(1.387)	(7,117)	(25,011)
1954–55	5,387	613	11.4	4,774	88.6	1.411	6,736	(23,643)
1955–56	5,157	688	13.3	4,469	86.7	(1.430)	(6,391)	(22,432)
1956–57	5,185	762	14.7	4,423	85.3	1.449	6,409	(22,496)
1959–60	4,926	(872)	(17.7)	(4,054)	(82.3)	1.370	5,548	19,481

[a] Approximately midyear. Note that the calculated figure for 1950 is 2.8 percent higher than the census figure for April 1950 (Table 5). This discrepancy gives an approximation of the degree of reliability of the estimating procedure used. *See also* Table 9.

[b] Parentheses indicate estimated figures.

Sources: For total average daily attendance, 1949–50 and 1959–60, Legislative Education Study Committee, Reports of Advisory Study Group, *Public Education in Mississippi* (Jackson: State Department of Education, 1961), p. 216. For other years, the sources on corresponding school year issues of the State of Mississippi Department of Education, *Public Schools for Negro Children* (Section on Holmes County). These report data separately for high school and elementary grades. The division between the two was estimated for 1949–50 by linear extrapolation of the percentage trend. For 1959–60 the estimate was based on the enrollment proportions reported in the 1960 census (12.0 percent in high school). U.S. Bureau of the Census, *United States Census of Population, 1960*, Vol. 1, Part 26 (Washington, D.C.: U.S. Government Printing Office, 1963), p. 203, adjusted by the relative attendance multipliers for Negro schools at each level reported for the state in 1959–60. *See Public Education in Mississippi*, pp. 32 and 35. Enrollment multipliers were calculated in two stages. For 1959–60 this represents the ratio between elementary grade enrollment (5,548 persons) reported in the census and the estimated average daily attendance. This coefficient was adjusted for years other than 1950–51 and 1953–54 by changes in statewide levels in Negro elementary grades for the corresponding years. *Public Education in Mississippi*, pp. 32 and 35. The remaining adjustments were interpolated. Conversion to total population: a constant multiplier of 3.51, in view of the stable ratio of the 5–14 age group to total population in 1950 and 1960, and the high enrollment levels of elementary grade children. *Public Education in Mississippi*, p. 57.

Patterns of Migration and Adjustment Among the Black Population of Boston

MARC FRIED, PEGGY GLEICHER,
LORNA FERGUSON, AND JOHN HAVENS

Although the descriptive literature on migration is vast, systematic studies of the determinants, processes, problems, or consequences of migration are rare. Much of current knowledge concerns demographic and economic factors and is based on large-scale population data and ecological indexes. There remains a serious paucity of theoretical or methodological material clarifying the role of migration in modernization and social change or the fate of the individual in the process of transition. Empirical studies of migrating populations are thus beset by many ambiguities for which existing data provide only partial enlightenment.

The services reported herein were performed pursuant to a contract (B89–4279) with the Office of Economic Opportunity, Executive Office of the President, Washington, D.C. The opinions expressed herein are those of the authors and should not be construed as representing the opinions or policy of any agency of the United States government.

Problems in Migration Research

While there is little point in simply cataloging the dilemmas of investigation, a few points are worth noting. It is entirely unclear how different kinds of geographic movement can best be categorized and a consistent criterion for defining migration be established. What should be taken as the most meaningful basis for classification: mileage or movement between communities or across cultural or political boundaries? To what extent shall other interrelated phenomena—like the characteristics of the place of origin—be considered part of a migration typology? Or should the issue of different kinds of migration be left open?

In studies of migration from one country to another, distinctions among the different types of migration and to some extent, therefore, among the different types of migrants are obscured by the overriding visibility of cultural transition and of foreign

117

status in the host society. But the shift from one level of urbanization or modernization to another or a movement from a preindustrial community to a highly industrialized society can hardly be neglected as a factor of major importance in internal or international migration. This differentiation by origin serves to raise additional and unresolved difficulties. How can a rural-urban continuum (if continuum it be) best be measured: by population size, population density, metropolitanization, farmland acreage, extent of electrification, number of paved highways, or number of telephones? And how measure premodern-modern characteristics: by economic variables such as value added by manufacturing or size of business enterprises, or by noneconomic variables such as mean education or proportion of the population completing high school, the relative degree of voting participation, or by some measure of the facilities or resources available in the region? As further questions are raised, the methodological and conceptual problems rise to meet and challenge any hope of easy clarification.

One consequence of the conceptual and empirical gaps in the analysis of migration is that each investigation must make many technical decisions de novo leading, not only to a more massive undertaking than is desirable, but to results that are not entirely comparable with those of other studies. Several issues of the utmost importance have hardly been touched on by existing studies. Thus there is reason to believe that the reception accorded newcomers by the host society—as a characteristic of an economic and social system in that society—is of fundamental importance in understanding migration and its effects.[1]

It is readily recognized that the transition of rural southern blacks to the urban industrial North is beset with major threats and impediments owing to changes in cultural orientations and social roles and relationships. At the same time we are all too familiar with the toll taken by discrimination and inequality of opportunity. But the special effect discrimination may have in producing high-level difficulties for migrants is more generally neglected.

The effect of inequality may be spread uniformly among all categories of blacks, but it may well be that rural background, low education, and anxiety about the impersonality of an urban area, with all their sequelae, may cumulate to produce untoward results with special potency under conditions of discrimination. There is suggestive evidence, for example, that conditions in the host society and widespread acceptance or intolerance toward migrants are of central importance in differential rates of mental illness.[2] However, we would be hard pressed to do justice to a measure that seeks to isolate discriminatory differences in the opportunity structure, let alone one that adequately designates subtler differences in generalized prejudices toward people of lower occupational status, different ethnic groups, or newcomers.

The Boston Study

Although these conditions suggest the need for far greater investment in migration research than has yet been made, it is possible to begin dealing with a limited number of these issues in the hope that this will generate a dialectic of inquiry. The major stimulus for this effort to deal with problems of migration and adaptation comes from a study of the impact of rural-to-urban movement on black occupational achievement in a sample of the black

---

[1] For a significant discussion of this problem, *see* Lyle Shannon, "Economic Absorption and Cultural Integration of Immigrant Workers," in Eugene B. Brody, ed., *Behavior in New Environments: Adaptation of Migration Populations* (Berkeley, Calif.: Sage Publications, 1970).

[2] H. B. M. Murphy, "Migration and the Major Mental Disorders," in Mildred B. Kantor, ed., *Mobility and Mental Health* (Springfield, Ill.: Charles C Thomas, 1965).

population of Boston. This study, along with other published and unpublished materials, will also provide some preliminary data for answering several questions about the patterns and processes of migration. Data can be reported from only part of the total sample ($n=502$) since the rest are not yet available for analysis.[3] The data must also be viewed as preliminary since they have not yet been subjected to full-scale analysis.

A few words about the study may help to place it in context. In the fall of 1967 a model was formulated for a study comparing black migrants and nonmigrants in the greater Boston metropolitan area. An earlier study of a working-class slum had revealed the enormous and deleterious effect of rural background on occupational status and unemployment during the mild recession of 1961. This led to the hypothesis that the effect of rural-to-urban migration would be ameliorated by acceptance by and social cohesiveness in the receiving community. While a solidary and supportive community might not entirely overcome debilities in the migrants' backgrounds and the results of hostility in the

larger society, it could facilitate adaptation under conditions that might otherwise be intolerable, or at least permit the children of migrants to overcome the worst stigmata of a low-status migrant background.

Although the problem of measuring either community cohesiveness or opportunity structures and discrimination in the larger system remains only partially clarified, we have been able to solve a few otherwise knotty problems. We shall turn first to a descriptive presentation of the data on black migration to Boston, comparing migrants and nonmigrants living in the same neighborhood and examining more closely some of the conditions met by in-migrants on their arrival, and then turn to provisional analyses of the impact of migration. Finally, some of the tentative substantive as well as methodological conclusions from the study will be presented.

Demographic Characteristics

Black migration within the United States undoubtedly represents one of the largest internal population redistributions in history. Even before the Emancipation Proclamation a steady trickle of slaves escaped to the North or Midwest. After 1865 the movement of blacks out of the Deep South grew larger. One direction of movement was toward the Southwest; the other was northward and, increasingly, toward the Midwest and the West Coast. By 1900 black out-migration had become an exodus of major proportions. Between 1910 and 1960 approximately 6 million blacks left the South for other parts of the country. In that period cities outside the South absorbed almost as large a population as they did during the European migration prior to 1920.

And this was indeed a movement to more urbanized areas as well as toward the more industrialized areas outside the South. In 1910 approximately 78 percent of the blacks in the North and West lived in urban

---

[3] The total sample was 800. The distribution includes 600 interviews in the ghetto with males and females between the ages of 25 and 45 and 200 interviews, using the same criteria, proportionately distributed in the city and suburbs outside the core ghetto according to the ratio of each area's black population and the total nonghetto black population. Households were randomly sampled from listings drawn from either the *City of Boston Directory*, Suffolk County (Boston, Mass.: R. L. Polk and Co., 1967), when available, or from any other municipal listing of residents (e.g., voting lists). Outside the core ghetto, however, the procedure involved using persons at the randomly sampled addresses as informants about the location of nearby black families. The interviews were quite detailed and took between two and four hours, covering many features of the respondent's life situation along with more specific information about his migration history. The present report is preliminary and includes 452 cases from the core ghetto area and 50 from the larger metropolitan area.

areas, and by 1960 this proportion had grown to fully 95 percent.[4]

Although the prevailing trend of black migration throughout the past seven decades has been toward the North and West and from rural to more urban areas, there have been a number of changes in the patterns of movement over time. Thus during the decade 1870–79, the largest single migration stream out of the South was directed toward Kansas.

The rate of migration into Massachusetts has been one of the most variable of all. As a seat of abolitionist sentiment, the state had traditionally been an important destination of black migration prior to the turn of the century and received a disproportionately large number of black in-migrants compared to its total population size. During succeeding decades the numbers of in-migrants fell off in comparison with the continually expanding migration to other

TABLE 1. RECENCY OF ARRIVAL OF IN-MIGRANTS IN BOSTON ($n=360$)

Recency of Arrival	Number	Percentage
Within the last 2 years	45	12
3–5 years ago	56	16
6–10 years ago	105	29
11–15 years ago	60	16
16–20 years ago	36	10
21–25 years ago	34	10
26 or more years ago	24	7
Total	360	100

urban industrial areas like New York, New Jersey, and Pennsylvania in the East; Ohio, Michigan, Illinois, and Missouri in the Midwest; and Washington and California in the Far West.[5] However, in the period after the Second World War the rate of migration to Massachusetts, and especially to Boston, increased again. In fact, data for the period 1960–65 suggest that the recent in-migration of blacks to Boston was one of the largest proportionate increases in the United States.[6] The data also indicate that a larger number of black in-migrants came during 1960–65 period than in any other five-year period (see Table 1).

The Boston data answer different questions from those asked in the census. Nonetheless some confirmation is found of trends reported elsewhere and greater specificity is given to the results of large-scale demographic analysis. The most striking finding of all, for which there are no comparable demographic data, is the huge proportion of migrants among the population of the black ghetto, an area that contains approximately 85 percent of the black population of metropolitan Boston.[7] Fully 73 percent

---

[4] For some of the demographic facts of black migration, *see* Marc Fried, "Deprivation and Migration: Dilemmas of Causal Interpretation," in Daniel P. Moynihan, ed., *On Understanding Poverty* (New York: Basic Books, 1969); Joseph A. Hill, "Recent Northward Migration of the Negro," *Monthly Labor Review*, Vol. 18 (1924), pp. 1–14; Simon Kuznets et al., *Population Distribution and Economic Growth: United States, 1870–1950* (Philadelphia: American Philosophical Society, 1964); Dorothy K. Newman, "The Negro's Journey to the City—Part II," *Monthly Labor Review*, Vol. 88, No. 5 (May 1965), pp. 644–649; Henry S. Shryock, Jr., *Population Mobility Within the United States* (Chicago: Community & Family Study Center, 1964); Conrad Taeuber and Irene B. Taeuber, *The Changing Population of the United States* (New York: John Wiley & Sons, 1958); Karl E. Taeuber and Alma F. Taeuber, "The Changing Character of Negro Migration," *American Journal of Sociology*, Vol. 70, No. 4 (January 1964), pp. 429–441; Karl E. Taeuber and Alma F. Taeuber, *Negroes in Cities: Residential Segregation and Neighborhood Change* (Chicago: Aldine Publishing Co., 1965); Rupert Vance, *Research Memorandum on Population Redistribution Within the United States* (New York: Social Science Research Council, 1938); Thomas Jackson Woofter, *Negro Migration: Change in Rural Organization and Population of the Cotton Belt* (New York: Gray, 1920).

[5] For the statistical data on intercensus migration estimates, *see The Statistical History of the United States From Colonial Times to the Present* (rev. ed.; Stamford, Conn.: Fairfield Publishers, 1965).

[6] David Heer, unpublished report to the Joint Center for Urban Studies, Massachusetts Institute of Technology and Harvard.

[7] This figure is based on updated census statistics.

of this ghetto subsample were migrants.[8] Hence it is evident that the social characteristics of the migrants—their origins and background, education, class, and family structure—dominate the distribution of these characteristics in the entire black population of metropolitan Boston.

Place of origin. Many of the background characteristics indicate clear trends. For instance, the states from which the migrants tend to come are located along or near the Atlantic seaboard: 47 percent are from Georgia, North Carolina, South Carolina, or Virginia, with North Carolina contributing the largest single group. Alabama donates an additional 11 percent and the remaining 42 percent derive from twenty-five other states and seven foreign countries. Fully half of these twenty-five states are in the Deep or Border South. This tendency for most of the migrants in the northeastern area to have come from further south on the eastern seaboard is not unique to Boston. Statistics from the Department of Agriculture and other studies indicate a similar directional trend elsewhere.[9] Those born in the Southeast move in general to the Northeast, while those born in the south-central states move to the north-central states.

The evidence that most of the Boston migrants (77 percent) originally came from southern or Border states is substantiated by other data. In terms of size of place of origin, 34 percent came originally from purely rural areas (defined as places

with a population of 499 or less) regardless of geographic location, and 57 percent came from a combination of rural areas and towns (defined as places with a population of 10,000 or less). Rural areas in the South and Border states are the single largest source of persons eventually migrating into the Boston ghetto (one-third of the migrants). Of the in-migrants, a majority came from Deep South, Border South, or Caribbean rural areas or towns.

Data concerning migration from places immediately prior to the move to Boston confirms the Taeubers' findings that inter-metropolitan flows represent a large part of the total.[10] However, their data are based on comparisons across five years and conceal the underlying fact that the large inter-metropolitan flow often reflects only the latter half of an individual's migratory history. In the present study over one-third of the migrants into Boston came originally from rural areas, a figure considerably higher than the Taeubers give for any of the ten cities they discuss. However, over one-half of these migrants had an intervening residence between their place of origin and Boston. Since most of the intervening communities were urban, if only a short span of the migrant's history were examined, this would give the impression of a large number of urban-to-urban movers.

It is not easy to arrive at any one simple description of migratory patterns because of the large number of variables involved and because of the qualitative nature of much of the information. Nevertheless, some of the broader results indicate rather clear lines of movement. There is a fairly uniform tendency for migrants to move continually further north. Commensurate with this is a tendency always to move toward more urban environments. The continuous attrition rate from the rural areas, towns, and southern and Border regions is

---

[8] This figure is high compared to that of other studies (*see* Karl E. Taeuber and Alma F. Taeuber, *Negroes in Cities: Residential Segregation and Neighborhood Change*), but this is an artifact of the differences in the samples; the present study included only adults between the ages of 25 and 45, whereas in others the percentage of in-migrants is calculated as a proportion of the total population including children.

[9] *See*, for example, Otis Dudley Duncan and Beverly Duncan, *The Negro Population of Chicago: A Study of Racial Succession* (Chicago: University of Chicago Press, 1957); and Shryock, op. cit.

[10] Karl E. Taeuber and Alma F. Taeuber, *Negroes in Cities: Residential Segregation and Neighborhood Change.*

especially noticeable. Moreover, few migrants reverse this trend. When migrants do return to a more rural or southerly area, they rarely remain there for more than a few years, and the return is usually in connection with family ties in that area (e.g., being sent to grandparents as a child or returning to see parents as an adult).

Age. The tendency for the migrant population to consist mainly of young adults fits more thoroughly with the prevailing data on black migration. Sixty percent of the migrants arrived in Boston between the ages of 16 and 25, with an average age of 22. Although the youth of those involved is characteristic of all mass migrations, the average age of the black migrants is apparently lower than that of other migrating populations in the past. Hence it would seem that the migratory experience is associated in the main with late adolescence and early adulthood.

Certain other aspects of the migration process fit with the youth of the migrants. Thus a relatively small proportion migrate as intact families, and a rather high proportion (36 percent) move alone. While the high proportion who migrate alone is not a unique phenomenon—in fact, it characterized the Italian immigration of 1880–1910—fewer families were involved in migration to Boston than in most other migratory streams.

Multiple migration. It is also apparent from the data that few migrants move more than once after passing their eighteenth year. The conjunction of a small average number of moves and the tendency to move further north and to more urban areas is explained by the fact that most of the migrants (55 percent) came directly to Boston from their place of origin and another large proportion (23 percent) stopped only once between their original location and Boston.

The minority who stopped at other places before arriving is large enough to make consideration of these intervening places

TABLE 2. TEN MOST FREQUENTLY CITED INTERVENING LOCATIONS BETWEEN PLACE OF ORIGIN AND BOSTON

Location	Number of Migrants
New York City	30
Armed services	19
Philadelphia	10
Washington, D.C.	10
Chicago	10
Baltimore	7
Detroit	4
Atlanta	4
Richmond	4
Birmingham	4

TABLE 3. RESIDENTIAL PATTERNS OF SAMPLE LIVING OUTSIDE CORE GHETTO ($n=200$)

Residential History	Number	Percentage
Current residence		
Inside city (not in core)	78	39
Outside city	122	61
Total	200	100
City residents		
Ever lived in core	58	74
Never lived in core	20	26
Total	78	100
Suburban residents		
Ever lived in core	32	26
Never lived in core	90	74
Total	122	100

important. Intermediate moves are made more often by those from southern or rural areas than by those from northern or more urban areas; hence the role of the intervening place as a possible source of modernizing and urbanizing experiences is significant. The extent to which these intermediate residences provide modernizing, as opposed to urbanizing, opportunities for rural southern migrants is an open question. Migrants who come directly from their place of origin to Boston show no marked differences in modern-premodern background measures from those who stopped at one or more intervening places. The main differences are between migrants and nonmigrants rather than between migrants differentiated by the number of moves made.

Twenty-four percent of all the migrants or 54 percent of those migrants who stopped at intervening places originally came from rural areas or towns in the Deep South or Border South regions. In general most of the intervening places were large northern cities with populations of more than 100,000. However, those people who remained within the Deep South after first leaving home more often moved to rural areas or small towns before turning toward more urbanized and northern destinations. Thus the overall trend is urban and northern, and the further north, the larger the city to which the migrant initially moved.

A breakdown of the intervening locations by frequency of use indicates that one of the singular features of the intermediate stopping places is that they are not merely large cities, but some of the largest metropolitan areas in the United States (see Table 2). New York City is the most frequently utilized stopping place. There appears to be a marked trend, as in other mass migrations, for those cities that are most directly accessible to absorb the largest numbers of first-time migrants. On the one hand, Washington, Philadelphia, and New York are on the major railway and bus lines and precede Boston on these lines. On the other, their very size suggests that they will have more opportunities for the kinds of low-status jobs to which rural migrants (black and white both) are so often limited.

Recency of migration. In trying to understand the impact of in-migration on the black population of Boston, it is worth emphasizing that while migrants represent the large majority of the black population, they are not a long-established group.[11] As in other parts of the country, black migra-

tion to Boston has increased enormously since the Second World War, reaching its peak in the early 1960s and showing a slight tendency to drop off since then (see Table 1). Since most of the ghetto population between the ages of 25 and 45 is composed of migrants, this means that a majority of the adult population of the core black community—approximately 60 percent—arrived within the last fifteen years.

Several possible results may follow from this. On the one hand, as previously indicated, the characteristics of the Boston black population are, to a large extent, the characteristics introduced by in-migrants, if only because of their sheer numbers. Differences in social characteristics between migrants and nonmigrants will be examined. Clearly, however, the old, highly urban Boston black population is only a small part of the present black population of the area. On the other hand, the massive scale of population growth over a relatively short period of time, a growth that has been largely concentrated within a bounded geographic area of the city, is likely to present problems of absorption for the resident black community.

Like cities throughout the country, Boston has experienced extensive community organization in the black ghetto during the past decade. How much this widespread effort has affected the recent migrants of the lowest status and with the most inadequate preparation for urban life is entirely unknown, but as we shall subsequently show their need is perhaps greatest of all. Although Boston and other cities beyond the primary stopping places on the South-North axis frequently receive many migrants who have already had prior urban experiences, the number of black migrants who arrive directly from the South and from rural areas is great enough to suggest a major population that will require assistance in adjusting to an environment that superimposes the problems of social transition on a preexisting structure of inequality,

---

[11] Heer, op. cit. The large-scale in-migration of blacks to Boston appears to be more recent than similar movements to other large metropolitan areas.

discrimination, and ghettoization. In turning to comparisons of migrants and non-migrants in Boston and to some of the resources that migrants bring with them or have available to them, we must bear in mind these potential sources of strain both to the migrants themselves and to the stability of the community.

Some preliminary findings from the suburban sample are available for comparison with those for the black ghetto population.[12] The suburban sample indicates that the pattern of migration to areas outside the core black area of Boston is somewhat different from the pattern of movement into the core. This sample also allows us to make some estimates of the amount of movement from the central city to the suburbs.

Movement outside the core ghetto. Among the black population living outside the core ghetto area, the proportion of migrants is lower than within the core (61 and 72 percent respectively). However, the proportion of migrants remains substantial even in the larger metropolitan area. Black suburban dwellers who are migrants more often come from northern states than do migrants living in the core. About 30 percent of the black migrants now living outside the Roxbury–Dorchester–South End ghetto area were born in places north of the Mason-Dixon Line. However, while a greater number of in-migrant suburban residents come from the North than is the

case for the core ghetto in-migrants, almost half of the former are from southern or Border areas. Thus it would appear that migrants in the suburbs represent, to a greater extent than migrants in the ghetto, a redistribution of northern blacks.

One other demographic difference appears. Among those cities that function as intervening places in the process of migration to Boston, New York City, Philadelphia, and Washington, D.C., are the most common for both suburban and ghetto residents. Los Angeles follows in fourth place for suburban migrants, but does not appear among the top fifteen cities for migrants living in the core. This alone suggests that black in-migrants to the metropolitan Boston area who are living outside the core ghetto may represent a different migrant stream from ghetto-dwellers and, consequently, exhibit different characteristics.

In considering the movement of blacks from the core ghetto areas of Boston to other places in the metropolitan area (much of the movement within the city was the product of forced relocation rather than choice), it is useful to make a distinction among three areas: the core ghetto sections of the city itself, areas outside this core but within the city of Boston, and urban areas outside Boston proper (technically suburbs of metropolitan Boston). Among the total sample of blacks living outside the core ghetto area ($n=200$), a rather large proportion (39 percent) live within the city, presumably in integrated sections or in small black enclaves.[13] A majority of these people (74 percent) originally lived in the core, either having been born there or having migrated there initially. A dif-

---

[12] Although as stated earlier only 50 cases in the present report are from outside the core ghetto area, in this discussion preliminary findings from the full suburban sample of 200 cases have been used. This suburban sample consists of respondents drawn from the towns around the city of Boston and from within the city but outside the central ghetto area. Many of the towns around the city are more urban in character than suburban, but because of the administrative structure of the Boston area they retain their autonomous standing and are not part of the central city. This means that many of the "suburban" respondents do not come from areas that are normally thought of as suburban.

[13] While the distribution of these cases is not "representative" as a result of random sampling from the entire metropolitan area, subsamples were apportioned to different regions of the metropolitan area on the basis of estimates of their true distributions. Nonetheless the gross distributional data can only be viewed as approximate, a fact that places no serious limitation on derivative statements about the characteristics of the subsamples living in different locations.

ferent pattern of residence holds for those who live in the suburbs proper. Only a small proportion (26 percent) of that group came from the core ghetto area. The majority have never lived in the core and either were born in the greater Boston metropolitan area or migrated directly to the suburbs. (See Table 3.)

Social Characteristics

Mass migrations are rarely, in any true sense of the word, voluntary. Migrants are generally impelled by unrewarding circumstances and lack of opportunities in their place of origin. However, at any one point in time only a small proportion of the potential migrant population actually makes the decision to move. In view of the many social, psychological, and economic costs of migration, some of which the migrant can partially anticipate, the decision is based on a judgment—whether rational or irrational—that the difficulties are worth the chance. But much of the data on migrating populations indicates that, compared to the population in the area of destination, migrants arrive with numerous deficits and debilities that further exacerbate the problems of adjustment. Moreover, discrimination and inequality of opportunity are likely to make even these adjustments more tenuous. With respect to the black migration to Boston, however, we want to find out about the resources the migrant possessed on arrival, how well these resources equipped him for life in an urban industrial environment, and how well they served him in adaptation.

Although only provisional answers can be offered to some of these questions, we can begin to delineate some major factors that necessarily influence the course of transitional adaptation. There is little information about the financial status of arriving migrants, but there are many reasons for believing that they were generally quite poor. Substantial data exist, however, concerning many of their nonfinancial

resources: education, farm or nonfarm background, urban experience, and other educational and modernizing attainments. Since the impact of most of these experiences is greatest during childhood and migrants who arrived at an early age might have compensated for former deficits, a distinction will be made between those migrants who arrived in Boston up to the age of 18 and those who arrived after age 18. A finer breakdown of age of arrival in Boston indicates that this rough distinction masks the true strength, although not the direction or relative magnitude, of some relationships reported in this section. Occasionally reference will be made to these finer distinctions. The nonmigrant black Boston population will serve as the unit of comparative measurement.

Education. The entire in-migrant black population in the ghetto, whether they arrived before or after the age of 18, has substantially lower educational attainment and attended schools of a lower quality than is true for the nonmigrants. More than 20 percent of the migrants, compared to only 6 percent of the nonmigrants, did not go beyond elementary school (see Table 4). At the other end of the scale, 45 percent of the migrants who arrived as adults and 47 percent of those who arrived during childhood or adolescence achieved twelve years of education or more, while 63 percent of those born in Boston had gone this far in school. Moreover, the majority of migrants who had this high an education had come from other urban areas, while a majority of the migrants who arrived in Boston after the age of 18 and had meager or modest educations came from rural areas (the more rural the area, the lower the education).

While migrants are clearly at an educational disadvantage compared with nonmigrants, the relative difference between the two groups narrows somewhat at the upper end of the scale; thus 9 percent of migrants who arrived as adults and 13

TABLE 4.   EDUCATIONAL ATTAINMENT, BY MIGRATORY STATUS

| | Grade Completed | | | | | | | |
| | 1–8 | | 9–11 | | 12 and over | | Total | |
Migratory Status	Number	Per-centage	Number	Per-centage	Number	Per-centage	Number	Per-centage
Boston-born	9	7	43	30	89	63	141	100
Arrived age 18 and under	17	17	36	36	46	47	99	100
Arrived age 19 and over	55	21	86	33	118	45	259	100

percent of those who arrived during childhood or adolescence achieved more than twelve years of education; 16 percent of those born in Boston had gone this far in school. A further analysis of educational attainment based on finer age subdivisions indicates that nearly a quarter of the migrants who arrived in Boston before the age of 15 had not completed more than eight years of school, while only 11 percent of those who were between 15 and 18 on arrival had so little education.

There are many reasons to believe that for a significant migrant subgroup migration at an early age is associated with disruption of education. The present data neither confirm nor deny this but do lend some support to this view. In any event, migrants are clearly disadvantaged with respect to educational attainment. We should note, however, that other data indicate that this disadvantage is relative to the population in the place of destination and migrants tend to be of higher education than the population in the place from which they originated.

Education is an invaluable resource and there is much evidence to indicate that the more severe the level of discrimination in the environment, the more critical is the role of education in permitting even modest occupational achievement and other rewards of social mobility. While it is possible that migrants might have compensated for low education by greater experience in urban areas and by more widespread contact with modern environments and resources, rarely does this seem to be

the case. Although approximately one-third of the migrants have had considerable experience in urban environments, most of those coming to Boston had lived primarily in quite rural areas. In fact, a large proportion of those who came to Boston after the age of 18 (38 percent) had lived on farms; even among those who came to Boston at a younger age a substantial proportion (26 percent) had some farm experience. The effect of farm experience on the individual is somewhat ambiguous: On the one hand the organization and conception of work roles and relationships on the farm contrasts sharply with that of urban industrial occupations and one would expect farming to provide little preparation for the latter. On the other hand there is some evidence in the data that some farm migrants may have a rather sophisticated modern orientation and understanding, not unlike that of the idealized image of the "independent and self-determined" American farmer, and manage to achieve surprisingly high occupational levels despite rural backgrounds.

Compensatory resources. Relatively little work has been done, especially in recent years in the United States, concerning the indicators of premodern or modern environments that help to demarcate the resources and experiences that are most likely to facilitate adaptation to the demands and opportunities of urban environments. In struggling with this problem, a number of measures of potentially modernizing opportunities have been developed,

TABLE 5. CULTURAL PARTICIPATION: MUSIC, BY MIGRATORY STATUS

| | Cultural Participation: Music | | | | | | | | | |
| | None | | Low | | Medium | | High | | Total | |
Migratory Status	Num-ber	Per-centage	Num-ber	Per-centage	Num-ber	Per-centage	Num-ber	Per-centage	Num-ber	Per-centage
Boston-born	76	54	11	8	13	9	40	29	140	100
Arrived age 18 and under	64	65	9	9	5	5	21	21	99	100
Arrived age 19 and over	187	72	18	7	14	5	41	16	260	100

TABLE 6. RESIDENTIAL FACILITIES, BY MIGRATORY STATUS

| | Residential Facilities | | | | | | | |
| | Low | | Medium | | High | | Total | |
Migratory Status	Number	Per-centage	Number	Per-centage	Number	Per-centage	Number	Per-centage
Boston-born	5	4	40	29	95	68	140	100
Arrived age 18 and under	30	31	29	30	39	40	98	100
Arrived age 19 and over	126	49	65	25	67	26	258	100

TABLE 7. MODERNIZING POSSESSIONS, BY MIGRATORY STATUS

| | Modernizing Possessions | | | | | | | |
| | Low | | Medium | | High | | Total | |
Migratory Status	Number	Per-centage	Number	Per-centage	Number	Per-centage	Number	Per-centage
Boston-born	11	8	62	44	68	48	141	100
Arrived age 18 and under	24	24	43	43	32	32	99	100
Arrived age 19 and over	92	35	103	40	65	25	260	100

although they have as yet to be translated into fully developed scales or to be clarified as to the contribution they make to urban adjustment. These variables are closely linked to differences in premodern-modern environments, as is evident from their empirical associations (see Tables 5–9). Nonetheless these data reveal discrepancies in such opportunities and experiences between migrants and those who were born in Boston. Moreover, these discrepancies follow a similar pattern.

One such index has been called Cultural Participation: Music, an index that is based on the level of musical training during childhood. A substantially larger proportion of blacks born in Boston (29 percent) received high scores on this measure than did migrants from other areas, and the later the age of arrival, the lower the cultural participation score. Another related index, which has been called Residential Facilities, is based on the existence of a telephone, radio, and indoor toilet in the home during childhood. The large majority of the nonmigrants (68 percent) had high scores on this index; migrants had considerably lower scores, the lowest

TABLE 8. MODERNIZING EXPERIENCES, BY MIGRATORY STATUS

| | Modernizing Experiences | | | | | | | |
| | Low | | Medium | | High | | Total | |
Migratory Status	Number	Per-centage	Number	Per-centage	Number	Per-centage	Number	Per-centage
Boston-born	8	6	61	43	73	51	142	100
Arrived age 18 and under	8	8	48	48	44	44	100	100
Arrived age 19 and over	25	10	119	46	116	45	260	100

of all being found among those who arrived after the age of 18. Another overlapping index, referred to as Modernizing Possessions, gives credit to those who were brought up on farms if the farm contained mechanized equipment and includes as well both the ownership and use of a car or truck. The results with this index reveal almost exactly the same pattern of deprivation among the migrants. Only one index, Modernizing Experiences—based on opportunities and participation in spectator sports, availability of books and extensiveness of reading, and frequency of going to the movies—shows little difference between migrants and nonmigrants. With this one exception, however, the relative paucity of modern resources and opportunities among the migrant population is quite striking.

The pattern of urban and modern background among migrants and nonmigrants is most often reinforced by a similar pattern in parental background: 70 percent of the migrants from rural areas as compared with 37 percent of the Boston-born respondents come from family backgrounds with a long rural experience. Moreover, a much larger proportion of the fathers of migrants had been farmers compared to fathers of those born in Boston. Similarly, the educational attainments of the parents of migrants are considerably below those of nonmigrant families.

Despite this general pattern of disadvantage among migrants, it is theoretically possible that they may have sustained other childhood advantages. There are some in-

dications that this might have been the case. First, although the parental social class position of migrants is considerably lower than that of nonmigrants, this is almost entirely a function of the differences in parental education. When farm fathers are classified according to their different statuses as farmers rather than being treated uniformly as the lowest status level, there are only slight differences between the occupational statuses of the fathers of migrants and nonmigrants.[14] Second, migrants who arrived after age 18 more often came from intact parental families, suggesting more stable childhood experiences than nonmigrants. On the other hand, those who arrived before age 18, and more particularly before age 16, were less likely than nonmigrants to come from intact families, suggesting that parental family disruption is one reason for migration.

In light of these few compensatory resources of black migrants as compared to nonmigrants, it is interesting to note that migrants more often report that their childhood experiences were happy and more often say that they received love and affec-

---

[14] Farm laborers were grouped with unskilled manual workers; tenant farmers, sharecroppers, and other farm workers with supervisory responsibilities were grouped with semiskilled workers; farm owners were grouped with skilled workers. It is striking that among those migrants who came to Boston by the age of 18, a larger proportion of the families engaged in farming were of higher status (farm owners compared to sharecroppers, tenants, or laborers) than were those of migrants who came to Boston at a later age.

TABLE 9. RURAL-URBAN RESIDENCE, AGE 0–18, BY MIGRATORY STATUS

| | Rural-Urban: Objective 0–18 | | | | | | | | | |
| | Rural | | Town | | Small city | | Large city | | Total | |
Migratory Status	Num-ber	Per-centage	Num-ber	Per-centage	Num-ber	Per-centage	Num-ber	Per-centage	Num-ber	Per-centage
Boston-born	..	..	2	1	2	1	137	97	141	100
Arrived age 18 and under	16	16	17	17	25	26	40	41	98	100
Arrived age 19 and over	76	30	72	28	58	23	51	20	257	100

tion within the parental family than do those who were born in Boston. However, while they indicate happier childhoods, they often appear to have lived under conditions of more severe economic hardship. At the present time it is difficult to explain these findings. If the assumption is made that childhood happiness is similarly distributed among black children in Boston and in other—especially rural—places, then one could easily conclude that a happy childhood is a selective factor leading to migration. This is not entirely unreasonable if we bear in mind the widespread evidence that migrants show higher achievement and greater potentiality than other persons in the sending area. However, the possibility remains that the experience of childhood in the Boston ghetto is, in fact, both more demanding and less rewarding in a personal sense despite the ostensible advantages of resources and facilities provided by the urban environment.

A Migrant Typology

While it may be premature to generalize widely from these findings—and certainly we must bear in mind that these data do not yet include many blacks living outside the central city ghetto—a few broad patterns seem to emerge. Based on a qualitative reading of the cases, migrants fall into three groups depending on the context in which the decision to migrate to Boston was made:

1. The first and largest group consists of those whose decision to migrate rested more heavily on the frustrating, boring, degrading, or disparaging conditions in the place from which they migrated than on any specific positive feature of Boston. The members of this group generally have low education, premodern rural backgrounds, and are least well prepared for life in an urban area. They usually come to Boston via the well-traveled Atlantic seaboard route.

2. The second group consists of those migrants who come directly from their area of origin, who made a conscious decision to move to Boston at some time before they left that area, and who are at least as attracted by some positive aspect of life in Boston as they are repelled by conditions in the sending area. They are better educated, better informed about Boston before arrival, oriented to hard work and success, and come from intact families whose social status is higher than other families in their place of origin. These migrants often come from the Deep South or areas other than the Atlantic seaboard states and do not necessarily follow the traditional migration route to Boston.

3. The third group consists of persons who first migrated from their area of origin to a place other than Boston and whose decision to move to Boston was based at least as much on some positive aspects of life in Boston as on poor conditions in the place from which they migrated most re-

cently. This group is usually older, and although they are not necessarily better educated than other types of migrants, they have previously been subjected to the process of adaption to a new environment and have usually already had a fair amount of urban experience.

While motivational context provides one basis on which migrants may be classified, the broad outlines of a second, more typological basis have also begun to emerge from the data. These two classifications are formed along somewhat different dimensions but may easily overlap one another. The second classification contains three major types of migrants among the Boston ghetto population:

1. The largest group consists of those people who arrive in Boston quite late and, indeed, do not initiate migratory movements until adulthood. Often they have had farm experience and almost invariably they come from rural backgrounds. Usually they are of quite low educational and occupational status. For the most part they grew up in intact families and migrate as a family group. One would suspect that this group represents people who had made quite stable adaptations to a premodern rural environment but had few resources to allow them to adjust to the urban industrial environment except at lower levels of achievement.

2. Another smaller group would appear to be young people whose migration to Boston eventuated from any of a number of disturbing features of their former environments: parental family difficulties, an unhappy sexual affair that eventuated in the birth of a child, a school environment that was disturbing or frustrating, or merely the lack of reasonable employment opportunities. This is the group that often migrates at an early age and generally comes alone or without any other adult. The migrants in this category often have some further opportunities to reestablish themselves in the new environment unless they are beset with barriers to achievement in the form of low education or several children.

3. Finally, there is a small group of migrants who appear to derive from slightly higher statuses, whose parents had often been farm owners but appear to have migrated to more urbanized areas, and who often migrate to Boston with their parents or with other relatives. This group is probably best able to cope with the problems and challenges of the new environment, although, like the other migrant and nonmigrant groups, they still must deal with the inescapable problem of inequality and discrimination.

Transitional Processes

Some of the most poorly understood features of migration concern the early impact of transition on the migrant and its effect on the host community. We know that migrants are in a rather precarious situation and are especially vulnerable to the restrictions, impediments, and threats of the society or community they enter. But we know little about the range of conditions that affect the experience of initial adjustment for the migrants or about the resources on which they can draw. On the basis of the authors' examination of some origins and characteristics of the black migration to Boston and its impact on the resident black population, we can now consider some of the conditions that impose themselves on the newcomer.

The phenomenon of chain migration has been extensively observed and recorded. The term covers a wide variety of phenomena that are not always clearly distinguished: payment for passage by relatives who have already settled in a host society, encouragement and other forms of facilitation of the move itself directing the choice of location, and the simple availability of kin or friends in a given location, whether this determines the location of the in-migrant or involves more extensive material and psychological assistance. Al-

though all these different features of interpersonal and network participation in the
process of adjustment to migration cannot
be entirely separated, the self-conscious explanations migrants give for moving to a
given place can be isolated from some of
the objective circumstances that meet them
on arrival.

The analysis of motivation and stimulation in the migration process presents many
difficult problems, not only because of the
retrospective nature of such inquiries and
the difficulty of separating reasons for
leaving and/or choosing a place from
generalized dissatisfactions or yearnings,
but because the processes of subjective
formulation generally take place over some
period of time and are only partly conscious. At best, therefore, we can put
together pieces of information and try to
construct an image of process from a set
of rather static facts. The authors' preliminary results permit a few interesting
observations.

Kinship and Friendship Networks

Although there is a widespread view that
kinship and friendship networks dominate
the direction of migration, there is also
ample evidence that the search for employment is a major factor in the decision to
migrate.[15] The authors' data indicate that

the search for employment—whether to get
a job, a better job, or a wider choice of
jobs—is the primary reason given for migrating. By far the largest proportion of
migrants (37 percent) give such work-
related reasons and an additional 11 percent name other motives of specific betterment, while only a substantial minority
(21 percent) cite friends or relatives in
the area as their reason, and an even
smaller number (14 percent) report bore-
dom, uncertainty, or a vague search for
something "better" as a main stimulus.
It is notable, moreover, that if the specific
move to Boston is ignored and black migrants are asked only about their reasons
for leaving the last place in which they
lived before the age of 18 and their reasons
for going to the first place to which they
moved after that age (which in the largest
proportion of cases proves to have been
Boston), it is found that the lack of employment opportunities was the compelling
force in the decision to move. Indeed, lack
of employment is more often given as a
reason for leaving a place than is the search
for employment as a reason for selecting
a specific destination.

Tilly and Brown emphasized the importance of kin or friends in the migration
process, hypothesizing that blacks would
more often cite kin as "auspices" for migration since because of discrimination
blacks have to depend to a greater degree
than whites on kinship relationships.[16]

---

[15] *See* John S. MacDonald and Leatrice D.
MacDonald, "Chain Migration, Ethnic Neighbor-
hood Formation, and Social Networks," *Milbank
Memorial Fund Quarterly*, Vol. 42, No. 1 (January
1964), pp. 82–97; Charles Tilly and C. Harold
Brown, "On Uprooting, Kinship, and the Auspices
of Migration," *International Journal of Com-
parative Sociology*, Vol. 8, No. 2 (September
1967), pp. 139–164. *See also* Morton Rubin,
"Migration Patterns of Negroes from a Rural
Northeast Mississippi Community," *Social Forces*,
Vol. 39, No. 1 (October 1960), pp. 59–66; U.S.
Department of Commerce, Area Redevelopment
Administration, *The Geographic Mobility of
Labor* (Washington, D.C.: U.S. Government
Printing Office, September 1964) ; and Kuznets
and Thomas, op. cit.

[16] Tilly and Brown, op. cit., use the term
auspices to define the social structures that
establish relationships between the migrant and
the receiving community before he moves. Thus
an individual migrates under the auspices of
kinship when his principal connections with
the destination are through kinsmen, and under
the auspices of work when the labor market
provides the main organized relationship to the
new community. Their analysis of auspices,
however, is made largely through the reasons
reported for coming to a given place and sources
of information and help on arrival.

Contrary to their expectations they found in their sample of migrants to Wilmington that blacks give work-related auspices more often than do whites. The differences are not great, however, and their data also show that blacks tend to give specific auspices (either work or kin), whereas a higher proportion of whites in the sample said they came under no auspices at all.

In the authors' own sample, the reasons explicitly given for migration to Boston also are more likely to be work related. But while kin or friends are emphasized relatively infrequently, the fact is that three-quarters of the migrants did have kin or friends (most often kin) living in the Boston area before they moved there. Thus it may well be that premigration networks did not influence the decision to migrate, but that the more specific selection of destination was determined to a greater extent than the migrant recognized by the availability of personal contacts.

In view of the importance in recent black migrations of escaping conditions of unemployment or wholly inadequate employment opportunities and considering the young average age of the migrants, it is hardly surprising that so many came alone (36 percent). Although a substantial proportion came with a spouse (23 percent) or with other relatives or friends (11 percent), and a fair number came with their parents (16 percent), the largest proportion came unaccompanied by any other adult (45 percent). There are some sex differences in these patterns: men came alone more often than women and much more often with friends or relatives other than immediate family members. Women, on the other hand, came with a spouse more often than did men. Coming alone does not seem to have been affected by the existence of kin already in the Boston area. Equal proportions of those with and without kin or friends in the Boston area migrated without other adults.

But these are not isolated facts. Clearly a large proportion of those who migrated alone represent an exodus from areas and conditions that are severely deprived. Whether rural-urban origins, parental social class, employment status of the main breadwinner in the parental household, or the educational or occupational attainments of the migrant is considered, verification is found for the sad fact that those who were least prepared by background for the transition most often migrated under the most solitary conditions. Thus 58 percent of the migrants from the lowest status families came alone, but only 31 percent of the migrants from higher status backgrounds came without other adults. Those with the most urban backgrounds, whether because they were more confident in their abilities to cope with the move or because they were preparing the way for others, were more likely than those with less urban backgrounds to make the trip alone and without kin or friends already available in Boston.

But for many the existence of kin and friends who were already living in Boston before they arrived did serve to ease the transition. Not only did a small majority of the sample have close relationships with persons in the area before they came, but most of them later received some help in the adjustment process. More than half of those receiving help were assisted by relatives or friends, with kin or members of the immediate family as the most important contributors of aid. Yet a relatively large number (49 percent) received no help at all. But among those who did receive assistance during the course of migration, the majority found the help to be extremely valuable.

On the other hand, although those in greater need of assistance in making a transition across a large cultural gulf might have been expected to have required more help, they did not necessarily receive more. The amount or kind of help differed little with different migrant origins, status, or position, in effect exacerbating the situation for those lower-status rural migrants who came least prepared to adjust to the demands of an urban industrial environment.

Finding Employment

The single most urgent adjustment the migrant must ordinarily make, merely to sustain himself and his family, is to find and maintain a job. In fact, the majority were employed shortly after arrival.[17] A great many (40 percent) had jobs arranged before coming to Boston. In addition to those with prior job arrangements, 24 percent found jobs within two weeks and another 15 percent found jobs within two months. But approximately 14 percent remained without work four months after arrival. Of course some of these migrants were not in the labor force—e.g., housewives—thus reducing the actual proportion who did not have work. This appears to be a strikingly successful performance until, however, it is realized that at the end of four months the unemployment rate among the migrants remained more than twice as high as the 4 percent rate accepted by government economists as a reasonable unemployment level. Nonetheless, in the face of discrimination in the system and the deficiencies of education, training, and background of many of the migrants, it is lower than might have been anticipated.[18]

---

[17] These and some of the authors' other findings on employment history correspond with the early reports of results from the study undertaken by the Bureau of Social Science Research in 1967 and 1968 of "Southern Migrants to Cleveland" (Washington, D.C.: Bureau of Social Science Research, 1969). (Mimeographed.)

[18] The study of "Southern Migrants to Cleveland" (ibid.) indicates clearly that while both black and white migrants enter the labor force rapidly, white males do so more quickly than black males, and both do so more quickly than either white or black females (who take the longest to get jobs). Data from this study also suggest that many people entered the labor force after migrating, although they had no intention of doing so when they left home.

To what extent this low rate of unemployment was maintained because many migrants were willing to accept the most meager and unrewarding jobs in the absence of choice is, of course, not known. That this might well have been the case, however, is suggested by the interesting finding that the higher the occupational status of the migrant, the longer the period before he found a job. Among people from rural backgrounds these differences by occupational status were relatively small, but among people of moderately urbanized backgrounds, 6 percent of those at the lowest occupational levels had difficulty in finding jobs, but 23 percent of the migrants of higher occupational status had similar difficulties (see Table 10). The same effect occurs with education: the greatest relative difficulty in finding a job occurred among those with moderately high education from urbanized backgrounds.

Neighborhood Integration

Once the actual transition had been accomplished and the immediate demands for income and housing had been met, the migrant to Boston became a part of his local neighborhood in much the same way as those who had lived in the area for a long time. People who have been migrants are almost indistinguishable from those who have lived in Boston all their lives in the degree to which they are acquainted with their neighbors, help each other out, and interact in a more casual way on the streets and in the stores of their neighborhood. However, it does take quite some time before the migrant ventures beyond the immediate area in which he lives. Familiarity and experience with the Boston metropolitan area grow markedly with increasing number of years in the area. Thus 52 percent of those who came to Boston within the past two years know only the locality in which they live or the nearby area, whereas by the time a migrant has lived in the city for between eleven and

TABLE 10. EASE OF EMPLOYMENT OF MIGRANTS, BY OCCUPATIONAL STATUS AND DEGREE
OF URBANIZATION OF BACKGROUND

Background and Occupational Status	Ease of Employment							
	Hard		Moderate		Easy		Total	
	Number	Percentage	Number	Percentage	Number	Percentage	Number	Percentage
Rural								
Very low	10	25	2	5	28	70	40	100
Low	16	18	12	14	60	68	88	100
Moderate[a]	2	12	3	18	11	70	17	100
Medium								
Very low	1	6	4	25	9	56	14	100
Low	7	17	9	20	26	58	42	100
Moderate[a]	3	23	..	..	9	69	12	100
Urban								
Very low	2	17	1	8	9	75	12	100
Low	9	22	5	12	27	66	41	100
Moderate[a]	6	29	3	14	12	58	21	100

[a] Moderate occupational level includes skilled manual labor and above.

fifteen years only 25 percent remain so limited in territorial range.

While it is clear that it takes time for newcomers to familiarize themselves with specific new places, the ease and speed with which this is done is markedly affected by prior urban exposure. If a migrant has recently come from a rural area it takes much longer to move beyond the local neighborhood. Among those who first arrived in an urban area only two years ago, 67 percent are familiar with only the local area, and fully 40 percent of those who have lived in urban areas for eleven to fifteen years are still locally bound. The same effect shows up with respect to the activities in which people engage. On an overall local-metropolitan activity scale, the shorter the urban experience the more likely is shopping, church-going, entertainment-seeking, and other behavior to be limited to the immediate locality or to adjacent neighborhoods.

Membership in Voluntary Organizations

One final measure of integration into the larger urban environment—the extent of membership in voluntary organizations—indicates most sharply the differences between migrants and nonmigrants. The proportion of blacks living in Boston who belong to *any* organization is not high (33 percent). But recent entrants into urban areas are even less likely to have any affiliations with organizations of any kind. Thus only 8 percent of those who have arrived in an urban area within the past two years belong to any organizations, and even after ten years in an urban area, only 22 percent maintain any organizational membership.

To the degree that membership in organizations (such as community groups and the parent-teacher association) reflects the individual's effort to control and shape his environment to meet his needs, it is those with the greatest needs, the recent migrants to an urban area, who are least likely to do so. While this can be appreciated as a consequence either of lack of knowledge, lack of opportunity, or concentration of efforts on more pressing needs ranging from employment and housing to psychological adjustments to a new and unfamiliar environment, it perpetuates the situation of the in-migrant as a stranger in the urban environment.

TABLE 11. EDUCATION, BY URBAN AND REGIONAL BACKGROUND

Urban and Regional Background	Grade Completed									
	0–8		9–11		12		College		Total	
	Number	Percentage	Number	Percentage	Number	Percentage	Number	Percentage	Number	Percentage
Rural South	42	25	61	36	52	31	13	8	168	100
Mixed	30	19	54	34	57	36	17	11	158	100
Urban North	9	5	48	28	78	46	35	20	170	100

Effects of Migration on Adaptation

When black migrants and nonmigrants living in the Boston metropolitan area are compared, a number of important features of the migratory stream and of the processes of transition and adjustment emerge. Many of these features of migration and transition are quite typical of historical mass migratory movements, while a few distinctive characteristics also are evident. Ever since the work of Ravenstein, who sought to account for the dramatic shift in the English population during the nineteenth century, it has been widely acknowledged that many large-scale internal shifts in population distribution represent the accumulation of more numerous small-scale shifts.

While a full picture of these small-scale shifts cannot fully emerge from an examination of data at only one destination, the findings suggest a gradual process of movement for many migrants along the two dominant gradients: rural to urban and South to North. These data also document the fact that a large proportion of black migrants to Boston come from the Atlantic seaboard region. As with other migrant populations, a large proportion of the in-migrants are young adults, most of whom come alone or with relatives or friends rather than as members of conjugal families.

For reasons that are not entirely known, despite the attractiveness of Boston for black migrants from the South during the nineteenth century, the black population of Boston had remained relatively small at a time when most of the large cities in the eastern part of the United States began to incorporate large proportions of blacks. During the 1960s, however, when migration from the South diminished somewhat, the movement of blacks to Boston appears to have increased. By the time of the present study, the vast majority of the black population in metropolitan Boston, both within the black ghetto area and beyond it, were in-migrants. Indeed, approximately 60 percent of the adult black population of Boston are relatively recent arrivals and a substantial proportion come from southern, relatively rural backgrounds. Thus the educational and occupational structure of the Boston black population is influenced by the educational and occupational histories of recent migrations to the city.

Educational Attainments

As has already been indicated, black migrants to Boston had generally lower educational attainments than the native black population. That the lower educational level of in-migrants is largely a function of lower levels of urban experience is quite evident (see Table 11). If account is taken both of level of urbanization and of North/South residence in a combined measure of rural-urban background and regional modernization, it is found that there is a steep gradient of increasing education with increasing urban and northern residence. Moreover, quite apart from the

TABLE 12. OCCUPATIONAL STATUS OF HEAD OF HOUSEHOLD, BY EDUCATION

Grade Completed	Occupational Status							
	Low		Moderate		Moderately high		Total	
	Number	Percentage	Number	Percentage	Number	Percentage	Number	Percentage
0–8	47	69	20	29	1	2	68	100
9–11	94	69	34	25	9	6	137	100
12	67	37	85	47	28	16	180	100
College	12	18	16	25	37	57	65	100

effects on occupational status of rural or southern origins in their own right, the lower education of in-migrants is bound to affect their occupational achievement, since education and occupational status are quite strongly related (see Table 12). In contrast to some findings on the effect of different levels of education on occupation, when a combined occupational status measure that takes account of supervisory position as well as occupational level is used, each increase in education results in marked increases in occupational status and the most dramatic increase occurs between completion of high school and education beyond high school.[19]

These data show quite strikingly that while discriminatory treatment undoubtedly continues to result in unequal occupational rewards for educational achievements by blacks, education is a major avenue of access to better jobs—as it has always been for minorities. Moreover, there is reason to hope from these data that some of the most recent gains may yet bear fuller rewards. For example, it is clear that even within the narrow age range of 25–45 covered in this study, the younger people have received considerably more education than those just five or ten years older. Thus comparing the proportions of different age groups who have completed high school or have gone beyond high school reveals the following:

Respondent's Current Age	Completed Twelfth Grade or More (percentage)
40–45	39
35–39	40
30–34	44
25–29	65

Since levels of educational attainment have increased throughout the country, as abundant evidence reveals, higher levels of education are characteristic for younger in-migrants as well as for younger natives of Boston. Moreover, young migrants who arrived more recently tend to have slightly higher levels of education than migrants of the same current age who arrived at an earlier period, a fact that corresponds with the conclusions the Taeubers draw about the changing character of the Negro migration in the United States.[20]

Occupational Status

Apart from the intervening effects of education that account for some of the occupational differences between in-migrants and natives, Boston-born blacks have considerably higher occupational achievements than migrants to Boston, and those who migrate at a younger age show some occupational advantage over those who migrate when older (see Table 13). Indeed, there is suggestive evidence in

[19] *See,* for example, several of the articles in the Negro-American issue of *Daedalus,* Vol. 94, No. 4 (Fall 1965).

[20] Karl E. Taeuber and Alma F. Taeuber, "The Changing Character of Negro Migration."

TABLE 13. EDUCATION, BY MIGRATORY STATUS

| | Grade Completed | | | | | | | | | |
| | 0–8 | | 9–11 | | 12 | | College | | Total | |
Migratory Status	Number	Percentage	Number	Percentage	Number	Percentage	Number	Percentage	Number	Percentage
Arrived age 19 and over	55	21	86	33	85	33	33	13	259	100
Arrived age 18 and under	17	17	36	36	37	38	9	9	99	100
Boston-born	9	6	43	30	66	47	23	16	141	100

TABLE 14. HEADS OF HOUSEHOLDS IN HIGHEST OCCUPATIONAL CATEGORY, BY MIGRATORY STATUS AND EDUCATION (Percentage)

| | Grade Completed | | | |
Migratory Status	0–8	9–11	12	College
Arrived age 19 and over	2.1	5.6	17.1	42.4
Arrived age 18 and under	...	5.9	16.7	55.6
Boston-born	...	9.7	12.9	78.3

these data that within the limits of unequal opportunities for all blacks, motivation or ability among migrants to Boston is more likely to be realized in the form of more responsible positions within job categories than to result in mobility into higher occupational levels. In view of the strong relationship between education and occupation and the educational advantage of nonmigrants over migrants, some of the apparent occupational superiority of native blacks is due to greater educational opportunity and achievement.

But while these findings on differences between in-migrants and natives are influenced by the educational superiority of the native black population, the most striking finding is that those blacks born in Boston have an occupational advantage over in-migrants even when educational attainments are the same (see Table 14). This advantage is especially marked among those who have had at least some college.

There is an interesting reversal among those with only eight years of schooling or less. For this subgroup a larger pro-portion of native blacks than of in-migrants are in the lowest occupational categories. The explanation for this peculiarity seems to lie in the fact that so low a level of education for those living in areas with few resources and facilities implies no special deficits, but for those in this relatively young age group who were born in Boston, eight years of schooling or less almost certainly indicates severe limitations in either ability or motivation.

The more general pattern of marked occupational advantages among native-born blacks with similar educational attainments does not appear to be a peculiarity of Boston itself. If the data are examined from the vantage point of age at initial migration to an urban area (including but not limited to Boston) in contrast to birth in an urban area (including but not limited to Boston), the findings are even stronger.[21]

[21] In an effort to distinguish the specific effects of Boston birth or in-migration and more general consequences of urban experiences, two variables both categorized in exactly the same fashion are compared. In one case the variable uses any

TABLE 15. INTERGENERATIONAL EDUCATIONAL MOBILITY, BY MIGRATORY STATUS

Migratory Status	Integenerational Educational Mobility											
	Much down		Little down		No change		Little up		Much up		Total	
	Number	Percentage	Number	Percentage	Number	Percentage	Number	Percentage	Number	Percentage	Number	Percentage
Arrived age 19 and over	1	1	33	14	52	22	140	58	11	5	237	100
Arrived age 18 and under	..	..	18	19	19	21	54	59	1	1	92	100
Boston-born	1	1	29	23	36	28	59	46	2	2	127	100

TABLE 16. INTERGENERATIONAL OCCUPATIONAL STATUS MOBILITY, BY MIGRATORY STATUS

Migratory Status	Intergenerational Occupational Status Mobility											
	Much down		Little down		No change		Little up		Much up		Total	
	Number	Percentage	Number	Percentage	Number	Percentage	Number	Percentage	Number	Percentage	Number	Percentage
Arrived age 19 and over	1	1	32	33	22	23	39	41	2	2	96	100
Arrived 18 and under	1	1	16	19	24	28	39	46	5	6	85	100
Boston-born	3	1	38	15	46	19	127	52	31	13	245	100

Thus it is the level of urbanization of the childhood residential area that is a primary determinant of occupational status, initially through its differential consequences for education (and thus for occupation) and at a later stage through its direct effects on occupational achievement even for people with equivalent educational attainments.

Certainly one may wonder whether, given equivalence in grades completed, the education of black children and adolescents in northern urban areas and in southern rural areas is truly equal. In fact, we know from Coleman's data as well as from the measures we have used that quality of

area with a population of more than 10,000 as the urban reference point; in the other case the Boston area is the specific reference point. In both variables the categories are identical and, for present purposes, they are subdivided as natives to the area, arrived in the area by the age of 18, and arrived in the area at age 19 or older.

education is considerably poorer in the South and in rural areas than in the North and in urban areas.[22] And this, along with the lower levels of modernizing experiences and resources previously reported, may well be a major reason for the disadvantages of migrants. But that rural background remains, for several reasons, a disadvantage to achievement is quite evident.

With respect to the processes of transition and adjustment, the data revealed that even when in-migrants had a higher degree of local resources than blacks born in Boston, these were rarely sufficient to compensate for other deficits. And indeed, this is a more general observation that applies even to educational and occupational achievement. One of the important functions migration serves is to make available opportunities in new geographic areas for

[22] James S. Coleman et al., *Equality of Educational Opportunity* (Washington, D.C.: U.S. Government Printing Office, 1966).

TABLE 17. OCCUPATIONAL STATUS OF HEAD OF HOUSEHOLD, BY EDUCATIONAL LEVEL AND MIGRATORY STATUS

Grade Completed and Migratory Status	Occupational Status							
	Low		Medium		High		Total	
	Number	Percentage	Number	Percentage	Number	Percentage	Number	Percentage
Grade 0–8								
Age 19 and over	38	79	9	19	1	2	48	100
Age 18 and under	10	83	2	17	..	..	12	100
Boston-born	8	100	..	..	..	..	8	100
Grade 9–11								
Age 19 and over	59	82	13	18	..	..	72	100
Age 18 and under	26	77	8	23	..	..	34	100
Born in Boston	21	68	8	26	2	6	31	100
Boston-born								
Age 19 and over	44	54	35	42	3	4	82	100
Age 18 and under	15	42	19	53	2	5	36	100
Boston-born	25	40	32	52	5	8	62	100
College								
Age 19 and over	10	30	12	37	11	33	33	100
Age 18 and under	1	11	5	56	3	33	9	100
Boston-born	4	17	8	35	11	48	23	100

those who are dissatisfied with the opportunities in their regions of origin. In this light it is hardly surprising, although clearly noteworthy, that in-migrants show higher levels of intergenerational educational mobility than does the native black population (see Table 15). Nonetheless, they do not experience commensurate levels of intergenerational occupational mobility (see Table 16).

It is again quite evident that this disadvantage in occupational mobility is not mainly a function of migration as such but rather of differences in level of urbanization of childhood and adolescent background. On the other hand, although the frequency of upward occupational mobility from parental statuses among in-migrants to Boston is lower than that of the native black population and lower than their own educational mobility would warrant in a completely equitable situation, the differences between in-migrants and natives in levels of upward occupational mobility are not large. Thus while selective factors undoubtedly modify the strength of these relationships and, in particular, weaken the differences between migrants and nonmigrants because of the large number of migrants who have high educational levels and who have prepared for—possibly even prearranged—high occupational status positions, there is a persisting effect of migration on occupational status for people with equivalent education (see Table 17).[23] And as in previous instances, it is quite clear that the apparent migrant-nonmigrant differences in occupational status for those with equivalent educational attainments are largely due to the differences in urban background of migrants and nonmigrants.

---

[23] To the extent that mass migrations of people from deprived backgrounds are distinguished from the selective migratory movements of high-status people that have become extremely widespread (but remain individualized) during recent decades, our data confound the two types because of their common identity as blacks. It is clear, however, that were we to omit from the data the high-status selective movers, whose migratory patterns are exactly the same as those of the high-status white mover, the effect of rural-urban background on occupational achievement would be even more dramatic.

Major Influences

Most of these formulations are based on examining the relationships between two or three variables at a time and linking them to provide a sense of process. Through the use of multivariate statistical techniques, especially with multiple regression analysis, we can link the variables representing different life stages more directly and thus present a sequential analysis. In presenting the results of multiple regression analysis on occupational achievement, most of the previous observations and interpretations are confirmed although they are also specified and clarified: [24]

1. Modern-Premodern Background=.495 [.045] Rural/Urban Background+.207 [.038] Parental Family Social Class+.037 [.035] Parental Family Intactness+.042 [.047] North/South Background (R^2= .38).
2. Education (years completed)=.363 [.041] Modern-Premodern Background+ .248 [.041] Parental Family Social Class +.085 [.038] Parental Family Intactness (R^2=.27).
3. IQ=.270 [.048] Modern-Premodern Background+.242 [.041] Parental Family Social Class+.165 [.047] Rural-Urban Background (R^2=.28).
4. Head of Household Occupation=.310 [.046] Education+.131 [.047] IQ+.111 [.042] North/South+.099 [.039] Spirits of Self+.089 [.045] Parental Family Social Class+.083 [.039] Mastery—.054 [.038] Ease of Employment on Arrival (R^2=.29).

Many factors enter into the different equations that result in occupational achievement. But an overview of the

sequences and the major stages of influence of subsequent occupational functioning provides an impressively clear picture of the causal pattern. In the first place, it is evident that the two underlying factors that most powerfully influence the subsequent occupational history of urban black residents are the level of urbanization during childhood and adolescence and the parental social class position. These account directly for a considerable effect on the level of modern-premodern experience during childhood and adolescence. The level of modern-premodern experience is a true intervening force, however, in the sense that it encapsulates the effects of prior urbanization and parental status and becomes the major single determinant of educational attainment.

In similar fashion, once the array of prior forces influences the level of education an individual attains, his education becomes the major force in subsequent influences on occupational achievement. And indeed, while much of the variation in occupational achievement remains unexplained, a fact that is almost certainly accounted for mainly by the relatively arbitrary operation of discrimination against blacks, education is one of the major factors that does make a difference in occupational achievement.[25] At each stage the prior forces—level of urbanization, parental family social class, level of modern-premodern experience, and a number of closely related variables—continue to function as direct influences on educational attainment and occupational achievement.[26] But their major determinant

---

[24] The regressions were run on a sample of 502 cases. The weights presented are beta-weights on standardized variables. The numbers in brackets next to the weights are the standard errors of estimate of their respective weights. R^2 is the proportion of variance in the dependent variable accounted for by the independent variables.

[25] The data presented by Blau and Duncan reveal the difference between the empirical explanation of occupational achievement for whites and blacks even more sharply and also interpret the low level of explanation obtained for occupational achievement among blacks as a product of the operation of discrimination that distorts the ordinary sequences of cause and effect. Peter M. Blau and Otis Dudley Duncan, *The American Occupational Structure* (New York: John Wiley & Sons, 1967).

[26] Several variables other than the major ones discussed here warrant at least a brief word.

effect occurs at earlier phases that in turn determine subsequent developments. And it is through this somewhat intricate, but quite comprehensible, path that differences in rural and urban background and between migrants and nonmigrants eventuate in rather marked differences in their occupational histories.

From a practical point of view, while it is possible to influence the fate of migrants through intervention immediately prior to or following migration, it is evident that a more general form of intervention would more dramatically affect both migrants and nonmigrants from deprived regions. Edu-

---

Along with level of urbanization, which accounts for much of the difference among southern, Border, and northern regions, the regional differences along the North-South axis have a persisting, although relatively small, effect in many of the equations. It is also useful to observe that, although the number of grades completed and the IQ measure are determined by the same factors, some aspect of functioning that results in differential test performance that is referred to as IQ makes a contribution to occupational functioning in addition to educational attainment. Finally, the variable of parental family intactness shows up in several equations but is clearly contributing relatively little to the major outcome variables.

cation is certainly, as these data would indicate, one possible point at which intervention might occur. Improving educational opportunities and, in particular, ensuring equality of educational opportunity would almost inevitably affect subsequent occupational careers. But these findings indicate that earlier conditions may be even more potent influences and lend themselves equally well to modification.

Although it may be difficult to conceive of directly altering either levels of urbanization or even the parental social class positions of blacks in rural southern areas, improving the level of modern resources and facilities for deprived black populations would be neither too costly, too intricate, nor even too dangerous politically to be quite feasible. Providing assistance at later stages, after much of the influence of earlier forces has created serious limits to potential effectiveness, may be all our service resources allow, but this must not mask the need for broader, more massive, and earlier intervention in order to create reasonable levels of occupational opportunity for the stream of black migrants who continue to seek the rewards that the urban environment might, but often does not, provide.

Black Migration

JAMES A. GOODMAN

The United States has recently experienced four gigantic population movements: the European immigration, which up to 1920 must have brought 30 million or more persons into the country; the westward movement, in which from 1900 to the present close to 10 million persons have participated; the movement from the farms to the cities, which since 1900 has attracted some 30 million persons; and the migration of blacks to the North and West, which has involved, since World War I, about 5 million persons, including some 3 million between 1940 and 1960 alone.[1]

The European Immigration

Many of the European immigrants came from farm and rural village backgrounds.

They came in successive waves, each wave providing some minimal basis for upward mobility for the successive groups. Although a limited number went to farm areas, the majority settled in eastern cities. With this combination of two transitions—immigration and urbanization—a clashing of divergent cultures occurred.

This circumstance was not peculiar to the United States. Urbanization is a worldwide phenomenon associated with the Industrial Revolution. Schlesinger suggests the following:

All over the civilized globe the rural regions lay under a cloud—in Great Britain, France, Germany, Russia, Italy, Belgium. The introduction of farm machinery and the opening up of virgin fields in the Argentine and Australia, added to those of the new American West, rendered unprofitable much of the agricultural labor of the Old World, stirred rural conservatism into fierce discontent, and enhanced the attraction of the nearby city for the peasant toilers.[2]

---

[1] See U.S. Bureau of the Census, *United States Census of Population, 1960*, Vol. 1, chap. C, "General Social and Economic Characteristics," and Vol. 2, "Subject reports: Non-white Population by Race" (Washington, D.C.: U.S. Government Printing Office, 1963).

[2] Arthur M. Schlesinger, *The Rise of the City: 1878–1898* (New York: Macmillan Co., 1933), p. 58.

The story of internal migration in the U.S.A. is closely related to the nation's industrial and technological development. In the mid-1800s America was still a predominantly agricultural country. Even before the turn of the century there was clear evidence of vast economic and social changes taking place on the American scene. By 1900 America had become one of the leading industrial and manufacturing nations in the world. This tremendous socioeconomic growth was partly reflective of immense improvements in transportation, especially the railroad and the steamship, the development of power-driven machinery, the organization of business into large corporate structures, and the construction of giant factories and other industrial plants. This growth was also reflective of the human contributions made by a diverse people to the building of a nation. As the Taeubers put it:

Both Blacks and Whites originally came to North America as immigrants, and the history of their settlement is only a few hundred years old. Most of the White immigrants came in search of an increased measure of freedom and enlarged opportunity. Most of the Negro immigrants came after losing their freedom, in the bondage of others. As the years went by, both groups expanded in number, and participated in the settling of a continent and the creation of a gigantic urban and industrial nation out of a small number of agricultural colonies.[3]

This population expansion created social forces that served as the crucible in which much of contemporary black and white relationships were forged. In a larger sense these mobile Americans created a test for the effectiveness of the welfare system in dealing with the social problems generated by population mobility. In this paper patterns of geographic mobility and upward social mobility will be discussed as

prime factors related to the development of institutional arrangements designed to meet the needs of those involved in the population movements of the late nineteenth and twentieth centuries.

Problems of Urbanization

Between 1900 and 1960 the population of urban areas grew twice as fast as the total population. For example, Chicago, which in 1850 was a frontier town of 30,000 people, doubled its population each decade to become America's third largest metropolis. New York became the second largest city in the world. The day dreaded by Thomas Jefferson, when Americans would abandon farming and be piled high upon one another in cities, was clearly on the way.[4]

Although the modern urban center offers opportunities to many people for a standard of living higher than they could have known in a rural economy, it also confronts them with an unattractive environment. Large cities must deal with many technical and human problems of crowding. New sources of water have to be found to replace brooks and wells. Better means of transportation are demanded. The demand for space for specialized activities mushrooms. To some the new environment conveys a prison quality, cutting men off from sun, air, and the beauty of nature.

Even in the last century there was probably no more poverty in the great industrial cities than in agricultural areas. Indeed, there may have been less. But in the concentration of urban life poverty is highly visible. Poor people tend to live clustered together in certain districts, so crowded that they rapidly become slums. Industrial growth also brought with it recurring depressions that threw millions of people out of work through no fault of their own.

---

[3] Karl E. Taeuber and Alma Taeuber, "The Negro Population in the United States," in J. P. Davis, ed., *The American Negro Reference Book* (Englewood Cliffs, N.J.: Prentice-Hall, 1966), p. 96.

[4] Henry W. Bragdon and Samuel P. McCutchen, *History of a Free People* (New York: Macmillan Co., 1969), pp. 396–400.

Zorbaugh describes the nature and quality of life in the slums of that era:

The slum is an area of freedom and individualism. Over large stretches of the slum men neither know nor trust their neighbors. Aside from a few marooned families, a large part of the native population is transient: prostitutes, criminals, outlaws, hobos. Foreigners who came to make a fortune, as we used to go west, and expect to return to the Old Country as soon as they make their "stake," who are not really a part of American life, and who wish to live in the city as cheaply as possible, live in the lodging houses of the slum. Here, too, are the areas of immigrant first settlement, the foreign colonies. And here are congregated the "undesirable" alien groups, such as the Chinese and the Negro.[5]

These individuals, obviously unprepared for urban living, could have used a range of professional services. Historically such assistance and services were given only spasmodically. The limited services available tended to focus on the migrant's "adjustment" problems to the exclusion of an assessment of the social context in which his adjustment must take place.

Increased Black Mobility

Part of the American solution to problems of unrest and fear of foreign influence that accompanied the influx of immigrants was the passage of restrictive legislation. This legislation was instrumental in reducing immigration, but it did not do away with the economic pressures for new workers. A substitute had to be found. This substitute was black migration from the South.

Thomas hypothesizes that when there is a lull in immigration the rate of internal mobility increases, and vice versa.[6] As a case in point he examined the movement of the black population in relation to the corresponding fluctuations in immigration of aliens. Based on these comparisons he found for the period between 1870 and 1930

that when the rate of immigration slackened the number of Negroes moving to the Northern States increased and that when immigration was in full spate the tide of Negro internal migrants was at a low ebb. Comparing the nineties with the first decade of the century we find the rate of increase in the total foreign-born population of the United States rising sharply from 12 to 31%, whereas the net loss by migration of the native colored population in the South-East fell from 2 to 1% and the rate of increase of Negroes enumerated in the North from 26 to 17%. In the period 1910–30 when the inflow of aliens was much diminished, first by the World War, and then by the Immigration Restriction Act of 1924, an extraordinary increase took place in the mobility of Negroes.[7]

During World War I blacks migrated North in response to the wider economic opportunities available there. Black leaders and the black press, however, stressed the theory that migration was primarily a movement away from racism. Regardless of the motivating force, the black population began its journey into the predominantly urban status it holds today. Franklin points out:

In the search for better economic opportunities Negroes, like their white neighbors, continued to move into urban areas of both North and South. Negroes, compelled by the objections which rural poor whites registered to their presence, divorced themselves from the soil, as life became almost intolerable under dishonest merchants and cruel unscrupulous landlords. . . .[8]

These factors do not fully explain the continued passage of blacks into an urban environment where there were fewer opportunities than they imagined. Franklin makes it clear that

---

[5] Harvey W. Zorbaugh, *The Gold Coast and the Slum* (Chicago: University of Chicago Press, 1929), p. 128.

[6] Brinley Thomas, *Migration and Economic Growth* (London, England: Cambridge University Press, 1954), p. 130.

[7] Ibid., pp. 130–131.

[8] John Hope Franklin, *From Slavery to Freedom* (New York: Random House, Vintage Books, 1969), p. 435.

employment opportunities were fewer than the number of people coming to urban areas and Negroes found great difficulty in securing anything except the more onerous and less attractive jobs. They continued to exist around the "ragged edge of industry" with organized labor evincing a pronounced feeling of hostility. . . .[9]

It is likely that many complex and inter-related motives lie behind the decision of an individual or a family to leave one area to reside in another. History shows the impact of such factors as the threat of starvation, eviction, political oppression, a sense of adventure, racial persecution, a de-sire to see the world, and a host of other forces on the movement of people.

Impact of Migration

It is not by making a catalog of the various reasons people give for moving that one can hope to understand the relationship of patterns of migration to the provision of needed services. It would be relatively easy to compile a list of factors labeled "push" and "pull" and then suggest an account of the interaction between migrants and social institutions in terms of these two sets of forces. Such an approach, however, is of limited value in explaining the impact of migration on black people. As Simons points out:

Although mobility affects all income levels, the highest rates and adverse effects are asso-ciated with low income, unemployment, and underemployment, including workers and their families from depressed areas and those dis-placed by automation.[10]

Many of the individuals in these categories are black farm workers. Other recent re-search shed light on this phenomenon:

Postwar advances in technology have helped to bring about an era of economic opportunity

for American workers, but the benefits of change have not been shared equitably by all groups within the labor force. The most outstanding example of this employment in-equality is provided by America's Negroes, whose economic progress has been frustrated by discrimination, undereducation, and the lack of marketable skills.

Despite the general prosperity enjoyed to-day, Negroes continue to lag far behind white persons in both income and rate of employ-ment. In addition, this racial group has lately demonstrated an increasingly low pro-pensity to move geographically—a tendency that is further weakening its already dis-advantaged position in the labor force.

Many of the moves Negroes do make are misdirected, at least from an economic stand-point. In many respects the Negro who re-locates resembles the typical European emi-grant of the last century: he usually gravitates to the ghetto of a large central city, fre-quently because relatives already live there; quite often he seeks not a better job but merely the means of making a livelihood; and the job he obtains is usually a low-paying one for which the competition is nevertheless keen, thus making him a prime candidate for periodic unemployment.[11]

Changing one's position in space does not change one's identity; it is the nature and extent of racial involvement in the oppor-tunity structure that determines the ulti-mate outcome of the change in location.

A Search for Utopia

The forces that have operated on the black population during the past three cen-turies have been such as to create a dis-tinctly separate black world within the country. At the start there was the system of slavery with its basic assumption of an inherent difference between the white and black populations that gave rise to the rigid separation of the races.[12] Since the southern spokesmen were unable to recon-cile this caste system with their democratic

---

9 Ibid., p. 436.
10 Savilla M. Simons, "Migrants, Transients, and Nonresidents," *Encyclopedia of Social Work* (New York: National Association of Social Work-ers, 1965), pp. 512–517.

11 Robert E. Marsh, "Negro-White Differences in Geographic Mobility," *Social Security Bulletin,* Vol. 30, No. 5 (May 1967), p. 8.
12 Franklin, op. cit., p. 559.

or Christian ideals of the brotherhood of man, they developed a pseudo-scientific biological rationale to justify the superordinate-subordinate relationship between the races.

This effort to develop a permanent legal and social caste system was inconsistent not only with the American ideals of equality but also with the aims of other areas to keep society open for free labor and investment. The North won, with its belief in free labor and the open-class system, yet in the South the bitterness of defeat and the postwar urge to keep freed slaves in subjection served to expand the racist doctrine.[13]

The consequences of this doctrine were not limited to the South. Even in the somewhat more open West, which had joined the antislavery cause, movements developed after the Civil War to exclude Chinese immigration, again on grounds of their presumed racial inferiority to whites. The need for manpower was not a vital issue during this period. Not only did caste thinking develop along color lines, but America in effect declared officially that the stocks of eastern Europe, the Mediterranean countries, and Asia were less welcome as permanent residents than the supposedly "Aryan" stock of northern Europe and the British Isles.[14] As the Sherifs pointed out:

With some variations from region to region and from class to class . . . the rank order of various groups is remarkably similar throughout the country and has been substantially the same through decades that have witnessed both rapid changes and earth-shaking events. At the top are "native" white Americans followed by the Canadians, the British and the other north European groups. Next, in rough order, come the Slavic people, south Europeans, Jews and American Indians. At the bottom of the ladder are Oriental peoples, Mexicans, Near Eastern groups and Negroes.[15]

[13] Max Lerner, *America as a Civilization* (New York: Simon & Schuster, 1957), pp. 503–505.

[14] Ibid., pp. 504–506.

[15] Muzafer Sherif and Carolyn Sherif, "Psychological Harmony and Conflict in Minority Group

Minorities in general and blacks in particular have not witnessed the vanishing of the class inequities and ethnic discrimination of earlier periods. If the class, status, and power systems are to become meaningful in American life, social welfare policy must be directed toward dealing directly with problems of institutional racism. Franklin provides historical perspective:

Within a few years after the beginning of the Great Depression millions of American citizens were regarded as incapable of self support in any occupation. By 1934, for example, 17 percent of the Whites and 38 percent of the Negroes were placed in this category. Everywhere the relief rolls soared. In October, 1933, between 25 percent and 40 percent of the Negroes of several large urban centers were on relief, a figure three or four times the number of Whites on relief at the time. Approximately one-fourth of the one and one-half million Negro domestic workers were on relief in 1935. In some Southern cities the size of Negro relief rolls was appalling. In Atlanta, in 1935, 65 percent of the Negro employables were in need of public assistance, while in Norfolk no less than 80 percent of the group was on relief. Small wonder that there was utter distress and pessimism among Negroes generally. Added to the denials of freedom and democracy was the specter of starvation.[16]

In few places was relief administered on the basis of equality, even in the face of starvation. Some religious and charitable organizations, in the North as well as the South, excluded blacks from the soup kitchens that they operated to relieve misery. In many of the communities where relief work was offered, blacks were discriminated against, while in the early public assistance programs there was in some places as much as a six-dollar differential in the monthly aid given to white and black families.

Today's welfare policies do not officially endorse such blatant inequities. But public welfare services still reflect residence re-

Ties," *American Catholic Sociological Review,* Vol. 22, No. 3 (Fall 1961), pp. 213–214.

[16] Op. cit., p. 496.

quirements carried over from the settlement laws of Elizabethan England that affect migrants—increasingly black—more severely than settled persons. Even the reformist Social Security Act permits states to impose residence requirements in federally assisted programs.

If workable programs of assistance are to evolve, the social service professions must be able to deal with the implications of the nature of society. Methods must be devised to predict the migratory patterns of high-risk groups and to determine better the nature of the push-and-pull factors involved in internal migration.

Blacks cannot be considered to be as responsive as other groups in the country to the push-and-pull factors that operate to induce geographic mobility. According to the usual theory, a person moves from one place to another in order to satisfy a goal that was unrealizable in his first place of residence. In this context the push movement of blacks out of the South is significant, less because of the number of persons involved than because it reflects the move away from bigotry imposed by public policy. The pre-Civil War distribution of the black population shifted from 92 percent in the South, 4 percent in the Northeast, not quite 4 percent in the North-Central states, and none in the West to a distribution in mid-1900—a century later—of 68 percent in the South, over 13 percent in the Northeast, and nearly 15 percent in the West.[17]

Even though there were many objective push factors operating on blacks prior to 1915, the primary pull factor was World War I. The war provided more freedom of movement for them, along with hitherto unknown economic opportunities. But the gains blacks made during World War I were only a shadow of the gains made in the entire economy and lagged behind those of other population groups.

What is suggested here is that migration, economic development, and social mobility are closely related facets of the same phenomenon. Moreover, in the formulation of welfare policy consideration must be given to the impact of racial factors on access to opportunity for mobility in society. For example, one of the ways blacks compensate for their inferior position in the racial hierarchy is by maintaining a close attachment to relatives and friends in their immediate surroundings. Marsh found that despite the mass movements of the black population from South to North and from rural to urban areas within the South during the first half of the twentieth century, blacks on the whole seemed to have somewhat stronger emotional and family ties to their current place of residence than was true for the white population.[18]

Myrdal, in his classic study, observed the tendency of blacks to congregate in a few centers of the North. He noted:

There is enough industrial activity, and there could be opportunity for anonymity, as well as a low level of race prejudice, in many of the smaller centers of the North to permit a significant immigration of Negroes. That Negroes have not migrated to these places is as much of a mystery as the relative absence of migration to the West . . . much in the Great Migration after 1915 is left unexplained if we do not assume that there was before 1915 an existing and widening difference in living conditions between South and North which did not express itself in a mass migration simply because the latter did not get a start and become a pattern.[19]

The New Self-help Movement

After World War I there was a revival of interest in African life and black history. Much of this was stimulated by Marcus Garvey's "Back to Africa" movement, which had as its goal the establishment of a new

---

[17] Conrad Taeuber and Irene B. Taeuber, *The Changing Population of the United States* (New York: John Wiley & Sons, 1958), p. 72.

[18] Op. cit., p. 15.

[19] Gunnar Myrdal, *An American Dilemma: The Negro Problem and Modern Democracy* (New York: Harper & Bros., 1944), pp. 189–193.

black state in Africa. Although Garvey was eventually deported and interest in his plan dwindled, it is estimated that at one time he had as many as 2 million followers. What is highly significant about this as well as subsequent black protest movements is that they are products of the urban environment. Moreover, the largest single age group in the current black migratory pattern is people in their teens and 20s.

These young people provide the leadership for current protest movements in the black community. The central theme of black protest in the urban community is Black Power, with its implications for communal self-help. However, in migrating, black families and individuals have had to give up old patterns of behavior that would prove dysfunctional in the new urban environment. Problems had to be faced in breaking through limited and marginal employment, upgrading low educational levels, and overcoming various forms of personal and social maladjustment.[20] The self-help thrust on the part of black youths would therefore seem likely to generate more frustration than improvement in the status of a rural people in an urban setting. This is not to suggest that the potential for psychological liberation that is inherent in the Black Power concept should not be encouraged.

The retarded rate of progress associated with blacks in urban society is due in large part to the same factors that pushed them off the farms: the special stigma of race and an advance in agricultural technology that rendered many of their skills obsolete. Young blacks know that traditionally the cities have provided the loci for integrating immigrants into the American culture. Each incoming group successively climbed the social, economic, and political ladder, reflecting what is possible when the system is open. A comparable rise along these dimensions has, however, not yet been

achieved by the majority of blacks. Brimmer has observed that the dual problems of racism and technology must be resolved if appropriate means for providing upward mobility of black migrants are to be devised. As Taeuber says:

Some of the problems of the transplanted migrants are inevitable, for movement across centuries of experience can not occur painlessly within a few years. Some are associated directly with conditions of living in the initial areas of settlement, and some are associated with the barriers to mobility that lead to increasing density and more intense personal and social problems in areas of concentrated Negro settlement.[21]

With these considerations in mind, black youths are suggesting that politically—not economically—responsible activity is the better strategy for changing the system. Hamilton and Carmichael say:

The adoption of the concept of Black Power is one of the most legitimate and healthy developments in American politics and race relations in our time . . . It is a call for Black people in this country to unite, to recognize their own heritage, to build a sense of community . . . to begin to define their own goals, to lead their own organizations and to support those organizations.[22]

The political and cultural implications of this thrust are further clarified:

The concept of Black Power rests on a fundamental premise: before a group can enter the open society, it must first close ranks. By this we mean that group solidarity is necessary before a group can operate effectively from a bargaining position of strength in a pluralistic society.[23]

With the well-documented increase of blacks in the nation's ghetto areas, this

---

[20] Douglass Joseph II, "The Urban Negro Family," in Davis, ed., op. cit., p. 351.

[21] Irene B. Taeuber, "Migration, Mobility, and the Assimilation of the Negro," *Population Bulletin*, Vol. 14, No. 7 (November 1958), pp. 127–151.
[22] Stokely Carmichael and Charles B. Hamilton, *Black Power: The Politics of Liberation in America* (New York: Random House, Vintage Books, 1967), p. 44.
[23] Ibid., p. 45.

conceptualization of the nature of the problems generated by black migration in power terms will serve further to exacerbate tensions between blacks and whites. It is a matter of some urgency to develop strategies that reduce the sense of powerlessness felt by these individuals in the central cities.

More use must be made of social legislation to correct the conditions leading to poverty. Simple solutions will not do. The problems of poverty and racism are two sides of the same coin. Most important, all adaptations of social institutions should be made in the context of a changing society that seeks to give greater meaning to the democratic ideals and to fit some of those ideals to an emerging social system.

To determine what form and direction social institutions should assume and follow is a task of great proportion. There is, however, considerable social work knowledge and practice experience regarding the transactions of individuals and families with social institutions. Systematic investigation is indicated to answer with greater precision a number of questions in the area of mobility and migration. For instance, what determines when an opportunity is present for a given group? Since there are strong indications that individuals from low socioeconomic levels may be at high risk with regard to nonparticipation in opportunity for change, what combination of factors is contributory?

Nathan Glazer caught the essence of the indicated direction for social policy in his foreword to Frazier's *The Negro Family in the United States*:

There are parts of the society that are more legitimately subject to government intervention than the family—the economy, the educational system, the system of police and courts and prisons—and we may hope to influence the family through these institutions . . . We cannot interfere in the intimate spheres of life: we do not have the knowledge, and if we did, we should use it with restraint. We know that the family makes the social conditions. We know too that social conditions make the family. But it is the latter knowledge that is the basis of social policy.[24]

Historically migration has provided the opportunity for many individuals and groups of individuals to achieve this control. One of the prime outcomes was the development of large cities and subsequent changes in people's ways of life. Some areas experienced an increase in population density, especially in the inner city. Ethnic enclaves developed that provided socialization opportunities for newly arrived migrants. These ghettos afforded an opportunity for the newcomers to try new roles within a sheltered island of ethnic support. They also often helped ease the transition from old to new social patterns. Unlike the European immigrant of another century, the black person has no ethnic organizations to aid him in the transition from country to city. He is even more disadvantaged than are other minority groups.

People have migrated for many reasons. In nearly all cases movement aimed at improving their sense of control over significant aspects of their environment. For black migrants the incentives are identical, but only recently have blacks begun to receive a moderate degree of attention for their special requirements when on the move. Social policy, to be useful, must facilitate an optimum degree of access for all citizens to the opportunities that abound in this country.

[24] E. Franklin Frazier, *The Negro Family in the United States* (Chicago: University of Chicago Press, 1939), pp. xvii–xviii.

Discussion

MAURICE B. HAMOVITCH: In our study in California of a community of the elderly, the aged were interviewed *before* they moved into this planned "ghetto" and then again *after* they moved there to determine the effect on them. All the subjects were wealthy. Most married couples were intact and in excellent health. They moved to better their condition. The new location was less noisy, they wanted more security, readily available health care, and a home base from which they could travel. They wanted to be near relatives, but not *with* them. In other words, they wanted a ghetto.

These communities of the aged have done an excellent job of *acceptance* planning. The community is ready for the migrants because it was built for them. It also provides for maintenance of linkages with the family and the larger community.

Ghettos in the more accepted sense of the term have been rejected because originally they were places from which people were *not* allowed to move. There was an absence of freedom. But another aspect of the ghetto was highly prized. Many people prefer to live in homogeneous neighborhoods where there are mutual aid, common values, and a readiness to help new

people gain acceptance. This is why today so many people voluntarily move into what are in effect ghettos. They get support from people with whom they feel comfortable.

DEMITRI B. SHIMKIN: Inhibition of movement by black people and the degree to which the city can become a destructive place are of significance not only for the situation of the blacks but also for American society as a whole. In this sense the failure to assimilate black migrants throws light on the slowness of certain aspects of social progress.

A second point, more narrow although also important, is that the overcrowding of cities in the North and West is going to result in heavy pressure for out-migration. Some of this migration will be interurban and some will be back to the South. In general the old model of the southern origin of migration has become virtually obsolete. Intercity migration will become infinitely more important, requiring new research approaches.

Motives for Moving

RUBY B. PERNELL: One incentive for moving is fear. For example, people fear what will happen to their neighborhood when different groups—in particular blacks—move in. Some people move to escape negative surroundings. They are now stressing their own sense of identity rather than trying to "fit into" already well-established neighborhood patterns.

JAMES A. GOODMAN: Many blacks move to acquire increased control over their environment. Their attitudes toward migration are affected by their political stance. I can see blacks divided into the following categories in terms of their political view of social change: (1) universalists, (2) nationalists, (3) coalitionists, who want to form coalitions with radicals, (4) integrationists, and (5) separatists.

More on Holmes County

DEMITRI B. SHIMKIN: With respect to migration from Holmes County, Mississippi, the community of origin has changed substantially in the direction of what might be called a modernized community. Therefore, the transition to receiving areas has become easier for migrants in the past decade than in previous years.

Holmes County was transformed radically, especially during the period from the mid-fifties to the mid-sixties, from a primarily agricultural to a nonagricultural community. It has shifted from primary dependence on white people, in the sense of plantation or domestic employment, to more impersonal relationships and governmental and industrial employment. Education levels have risen; only 5 percent of the adults had a high school education in 1960, while today about 50 percent of the teenagers complete high school.

How did this change occur, and what are its implications? In essence the processes involved internal developments that rested on broadly accepted values arising from antecedents within the community itself. In part this stemmed from the absence of large or even medium-sized cities within close range of the community. In Holmes County the basis of socioeconomic strength is still the independent farmer, who is capa-ble and desirous of educational improvement. Thus modernization can take place as an internal change within traditional social units such as extended families and local communities.

The civil rights workers who went south in 1964 also had an accelerating effect on the local communities. Young people came in large numbers, and they were in such great physical danger that almost every black family was involved in protecting them. In turn each black family knew that their own involvement with the movement meant risking their homes, their jobs and resources, and their lives. This interdependence created a certain acceptance of change.

In contrast, in Alabama—where I have also done some work—there is a tremendous gap between urban communities such as Selma and the hinterland because the middle-class blacks—teachers, preachers, and others—tend to live in town and commute to the rural areas where they work rather than being organic members of the total society. Thus, the absence or presence of class divisions in an area has been a significant variable.

Even in areas of extensive out-migration, there is considerable in-migration to complicate the situation. Holmes County has received considerable in-migration from surrounding counties at the same time that it is an out-migration area. The resulting statistics are fantastically complicated.

Substantively, I think one of the important results of the Holmes County investigation is evidence of a new kind of community. This is a community of multiple residence but of single psychological focus, which I have called a spatially dispersed community. The community is maintained by a number of coordinated institutions: kinship, church affiliation, landownership, and land equity. The fundamental attitude is an emotional and ideological complex closely related to the land and landownership. Its most significant manifestation is in the wish of the people to be buried in their home soil. Once this attitude changes (generally in the second generation, especially if the parents are elderly), then the relationship with the community of origin disappears. Essentially, the bonds of kinship and of returning home for funerals are the most important ties.

Lack of Service to Migrants

LEON H. GINSBERG: We have reason to conclude that migration is one of the most significant factors affecting black Americans in the twentieth century. Much of what passes for information on the black ethnic group or community in graduate social work education reports on only one phase of migration—the urban experience. Dr. Shimkin's material sheds light on the migration process itself.

One is taken with a number of elements in Dr. Shimkin's enumeration of the strengths of Holmes County black families. For a variety of reasons this is a major contribution to current inquiries into human behavior. So much analysis of black community life focuses on deviance and pathology, with an implicit notion that blacks are inferior. A balance is provided here on the supportive aspects of black family life, for the individual at home and the migrants who want to return.

Dr. Shimkin's findings also lend credence to the ideas that services to migrants during the premigration phase are as important as their reception in urban areas. Social welfare professionals could, it would seem, be more effective in helping institutions such as churches, community political action groups, and extended families prepare potential migrants for their transition from rural to urban settings.

It is strange that the United States is willing to invest millions in the care and treatment of the mentally ill with limited knowledge of mental illness and limited evidence of the results of treatment. Similarly, services such as social casework have been provided aggressively or passively on a large scale and with large investments of resources throughout the United States

without especially impressive results and without any great amount of data supporting the value of using such a service. Yet so little has been done in the service professions to deal with the problems of migration. With the exception of a few small efforts, many of them privately funded, this critical social phenomenon has been ignored.

CATHERINE C. HIATT: Few people on welfare migrate in order to receive increased assistance. When people move, they often end up on welfare because the move is insufficiently planned. Many who migrate first use up all their resources and then ask for help. We need to plan with them before this happens.

Support Networks and Power Bases

HENRY P. DAVID: Dr. Fried has shown that a network of friends and relatives is important in migration. Fully two-thirds of migrants to Boston had friends or relatives awaiting their arrival; 40 percent had jobs prearranged for them. Even if the seeking of economic opportunity was the manifest reason for their coming to Boston, clearly there are strong latent factors that played a role. There seems to be considerable strength in this network of kinship and friendship. I am not saying that migrants are not exploited along the way. What I am saying is that there are resources on which many migrants can rely to a degree in their search for adjustment to their new environment.

HYLAN G. LEWIS: When migrants leave an area where they have power, they cannot normally take it along. They come into a new area where they have few social ties. Primary groups or kinship groups help in the adjustment. Some ethnic groups have latent power because they have a territorial base, such as the Mexicans who moved into California. They still enjoy some degree of protection from the Mexican government.

MAURICE B. HAMOVITCH: The history of social welfare shows that immigrants often formed self-help groups soon after arrival in this country. It was possible in this way, and perhaps more possible in those days with an expanding economy and expanding frontiers, to develop economic power and then parlay it into political power. Our more recent migrant groups— the black population, Mexican-Americans, and Puerto Ricans—are just beginning to develop a similar awareness of the value of organization. They have as yet few self-help groups. These groups are beginning to form agencies to deliver welfare services, but almost entirely with governmental funds. This accounts in part for the emphasis in these groups on politics. Political pathways also are related to reinforcement of positive ethnic identification.

Many of the earlier immigrant groups came with existing positive concepts of themselves. They hadn't had a sense of inferiority dunned into them before they arrived. When this happened after they arrived, they resented it and fought against it. The blacks are now beginning to see this; Mexican-Americans for the first time are beginning to identify their culture and to criticize some of the anthropological studies about them that stress unfavorable aspects of their way of life.

Migrant groups—at least *new* ethnic migrant groups—need to organize themselves. A sense of identity and self-pride facilitate this. It can result in political power, as shown in the organization of Mexican-American laborers in the California grape strike. As was found in earlier decades in the large urban slums, lower-class people who withdraw their labor or threaten to withdraw it have an impact.

SIMON SLAVIN: A few years ago a plan was drawn up to redistribute the population of Harlem, breaking up the ghetto. One important black leader said: "What do you want to do, kill off our political power?" Redistricting policies and patterns and extension of city borders to incorporate more white areas are sometimes advocated to contain the political influence of the black concentrations in the inner city.

ELEANOR B. SHELDON: I'm not sure what political power is. If we could operationalize what is meant by political power this would at least be a start, not necessarily toward planning power policy strategies, but perhaps toward research.

Part III

Toward a National Migration Policy

Federal Migration Policy: Present Reality and Future Alternatives

WILLIAM J. REID

The government of the United States has traditionally followed a laissez-faire policy toward internal migration. Federal restrictions on migration have been constrained by the general conviction that freedom to move about the country is, as Justice Stewart recently put it, "a virtually unconditional personal right." [1] It is true that at various times in this country's history certain groups have been deprived of the right to choose their place of abode: Under the Fugitive Slave Law Negro slaves were forcibly returned to their masters, at federal gunpoint if necessary; large numbers of American Indians were forced to leave their ancestral homelands under federal removal programs; Japanese-Americans were confined to federal internment camps for the duration of World War II. But with these significant exceptions, there has been little federal interference with freedom of movement.

In fact, more has been done to en-

[1] *Shapiro* vs. *Thompson*, 394 U.S. 618, 643 (1969). Stewart, J., concurring, citing *United States* vs. *Guest*, 383 U.S. 745 (1966).

courage mobility than to force or suppress it. The federal government facilitated migration to the West through the Homestead Act and other legislation. The Revenue Act of 1964 permitted income tax deductions for expenses incurred in job-related moves. Relocation assistance, often with supporting social welfare services, has been provided to special groups such as American Indians, Cuban refugees, and workers displaced as a result of tariff adjustments. Since 1965 assistance of this kind has been extended to unemployed workers on an experimental basis. Such isolated acts and programs do not add up, however, to a comprehensive migration policy.

While an overall policy does not exist, there has been no lack of isolated federal actions in other domains, each with consequences for internal migration, both unintended and intended. For instance, any federal program that affects the relative attractiveness of a specific region will influence patterns of migration. Federal housing policies supporting homeownership have stimulated the movement of the middle class to suburban areas. Federally sponsored enterprises in atomic energy and aerospace have created new meccas for migrants in various parts of the country. Defense procurement policies have stepped up migration to industrial centers on the West Coast. Urban renewal programs such as Model Cities might serve, if successful, to retain populations in the inner cities.

While none of these policies and programs has been pursued with migration control as a major objective, a part of the scheme may in certain cases be to influence migration. Federal efforts to improve opportunities for the southern black may be a case in point. More specifically, President Nixon's proposed family assistance plan, one effect of which would be to reduce current discrepancies in public assistance grants between southern and northern states, would probably serve to reduce out-migration from the South. Federal programs to aid depressed areas offer another example of a quasi migration-control effort. One openly stated purpose of the assistance is to curb the flow of out-migration from these areas by increasing employment opportunities within them.

While all these efforts may affect migration, they bring us no closer to a comprehensive migration policy. In most instances the consequences for migration are fortuitous. In programs with secondary or implicit migration control objectives, the intended influence on migration may be overshadowed by unforeseen developments. Thus the farm subsidy program was aimed in part at checking the flow of rural out-migration, but, driven by other logic, it has often worked to put small farmers at a competitive disadvantage and hence may have promoted the exodus it sought to prevent. Finally, none of these programs is related to a set of national migration objectives and none is controlled by a governmental structure primarily concerned with migration. Nevertheless, any consideration of migration policy must take into account all governmental programs that affect migration, re-

gardless of their objectives. They may affect efforts specifically concerned with migration or may themselves be redesigned to affect migration patterns in a more purposeful way.

Need for a Comprehensive Migration Policy

An overall federal migration policy would have as its core a system of efforts designed to influence the course of internal migration in a carefully planned way. Is such a policy needed? Advocates of planned migration base their case essentially on two assumptions: (1) that uncontrolled internal migration contributes to a number of serious social problems and (2) that well-planned federal intervention in migration can alleviate these problems.

There is little doubt that internal migration is a contributing factor to a host of social problems. The increasing concentration of the poor in central cities is perhaps the most salient of these current problems. That many of these poor persons also happen to be black, trapped in ghettos, and welfare recipients adds to its severity. As Cloward and Piven argue, rural-to-urban and South-to-North migration of black people may be the main cause of the steep rise in public assistance rates in northern and western cities.[2] It is certainly a major factor. According to their figures, almost half of the national increase of 1.6 million persons on the Aid to Families with Dependent Children rolls that occurred between 1960 and 1968 took place in two urbanized states, New York and California. It is doubtful that this rate of increase could be accounted for by factors other than in-migration.

Excessive migration to cities and insufficient migration from them have been offered as explanations of the complementary problems of growing congestion of urban

---

[2] Richard A. Cloward and Frances Fox Piven, "Migration, Politics, and Welfare," *Saturday Review* (November 16, 1966), pp. 31–32.

centers and growing underpopulation of rural areas. According to one forecast, by the year 2000 about two-thirds of this country's population will be concentrated in large cities occupying about 3 percent of the land.[3] One does not have to be an advocate of rural life to conclude that such a massing of the population in a few urban complexes is to be avoided if possible. Rural-to-urban migration certainly is one of the major forces pushing toward this imbalance.

Socioeconomic ills fostered by depressed areas have been attributed, somewhat contradictorily, to both excessive and insufficient out-migration, depending on whether out-migration is viewed as sapping the strength of an area that might be capable of rehabilitation or as an escape route from a region beyond redemption. But it is true that certain locales have suffered an erosion of their economic foundations, with resulting high levels of unemployment and high out-migration rates for youthful workers. Migration seems to be one of the keys to the problem despite uncertainties about its desired direction.

Problems to which migration may contribute are not necessarily confined to mismatches between populations and resources in given regions. Decisions to migrate may frequently lack a rational basis. People may move on the basis of incomplete or erroneous information about the employment opportunities and the facilities to be found at their destinations, or they may not move because they lack accurate information about conditions elsewhere. The result is a waste of human potential that may pass unnoticed in the statistics of population maldistribution.

Migration may be viewed as a cause of these problems in somewhat the same way as a bullet may be seen as the cause of a wound—as an immediate, visible, but only partial explanation in a complex explanatory chain. But altering proximate and partial causes may be one way of mitigating the problems to which they contribute.

This consideration leads us to the second of the two assumptions mentioned—that the contribution of migration to these problems can be lessened through governmental intervention. This is the critical assumption underlying a number of recent proposals. As a means of helping blacks escape from both northern ghettos and southern Black Belts, Schuchter calls for a program of "guided inter-regional and interurban . . . migration of 3 million Negroes during the coming decade."[4] Ylvisaker proposes a "national migration policy" directed toward the deghettoization of the inner-city poor.[5] To increase the percentage of migrants who "actually benefit from migration," Bishop recommends a "mobility policy" aimed at "rationalizing the migration process."[6]

These proposals raise a series of questions: Can federal intervention affect the course of internal migration toward socially constructive ends? If so, what kinds of intervention may best accomplish what ends? What achievement may realistically be expected?

The seriousness and scope of the problems seem to invite some kind of massive national effort to influence migration. But contemplation of the obstacles to such an effort tempts one to retreat to a more conservative stance: that problems resulting from internal migration are more or less inevitable, and that we must learn to live in our overcrowded cities or be prepared to leave our ghost towns without the expectation of imminent federal rescue. The author's position is somewhere in the

---

[3] Orville L. Freeman, "Their Gain is Your Loss," *Banking*, Vol. 40 (November 1967), p. 82.

[4] Arnold Schuchter, *White Power/Black Freedom: Planning the Future of Urban America* (Boston: Beacon Press, 1968), p. 374.

[5] Paul Ylvisaker, quoted in the *Washington Bulletin*, Vol. 32 (January 22, 1968), p. 155.

[6] C. E. Bishop, "The Need for Improved Mobility Policy," U.S., Congress, Joint Economic Committee, Subcommittee on Economic Progress, *Federal Program for the Development of Human Resources*, Vol. I (Washington, D.C.: U.S. Government Printing Office, 1968), pp. 215–223.

murky middle. An attempt will be made to explicate it by first setting down a possible domain for efforts to guide migration, then by examining foreign and domestic experience with programs operating within this domain, and finally by considering possible directions for migration policy and the difficulties to be faced in its pursuit.

A Domain for Intervention

A government wishing to influence migration may use both incentives and penalties to manipulate the flow of its population. In a nation such as the United States, which prides itself on the freedom of movement of its citizens, a general migration policy based on penalties would be unthinkable, even though penalties have been used to constrain the movement of the minority groups cited earlier and even though the government has supported de facto penalties against certain kinds of migration. For example, federal acceptance of state residence requirements in public assistance programs in effect sanctioned penalties against the mobile indigent. On the other hand a migration policy based on incentives would be consonant with our democratic values—could in fact be said to enhance these values if the incentives served to increase freedom of movement. Thus consideration of policy alternatives will be limited to incentive-based approaches.

Job-Related Incentives

There is considerable evidence to suggest that the most general incentives affecting decisions to migrate are related to job opportunities, both existing and prospective. According to one national survey, approximately half of the respondents (men aged 18–64) who migrated during the twelve months sampled (1962–63) gave primarily job-related reasons for moving.[7] Most of this group moved "to take a job"

[7] U.S., President, *Manpower Report of the President, 1965* (Washington, D.C.: U.S. Government Printing Office, 1965), Table J-2, p. 271.

or "to look for work." The remaining half gave reasons ranging from housing to health. When analysis was restricted to unemployed migrants, it was found that 69 percent moved chiefly for job-related reasons, the majority "to look for work." Since an unemployed worker is more likely to present migration problems, his motivations would be of special concern in a guided migration program.

The dominance of work incentives in migration decisions also emerged in a study by Marsh, who reported that "most people in the labor force who had crossed county lines gave job-related reasons for moving."[8] Thomlinson has put it well: "Factors inciting migration are complex and intertwined. Nonetheless the possibility of earning more money is generally preeminent among the several operating motives."[9] If the foregoing is correct, then attempts to control migration would logically be centered on influencing employment incentives, for example, to assist workers in locating and moving to jobs in other areas and to create job opportunities to attract workers to specific regions or to hold them there.

Other Incentives

But as Thomlinson has reminded us, migration decisions are not based on a single incentive. While job-related incentives may be paramount, they are more properly seen as the core of a system of incentives and disincentives. These would certainly include distance to be moved, the cost and stress of relocation, and the attractiveness of the potential destination area, which may in turn be affected by housing and living conditions in the area and whether friends or relatives live there. Moreover, for certain classes of migrants other kinds of in-

[8] Robert E. Marsh, "Geographic Labor Mobility in the United States, Recent Findings," *Social Security Bulletin*, Vol. 30, No. 3 (March 1967), p. 16.

[9] Ralph Thomlinson, *Population Dynamics* (New York: Random House, 1965), p. 225.

centives may be important. Actual or potential public assistance recipients, for example, may be influenced by grant levels and eligibility requirements in their own and other areas.[10]

Guiding Migration: Moving Workers to Jobs

Manipulation of socioeconomic incentives could then provide government with the means of guiding internal migration. Presumably these means would serve the ends of remedying the kinds of social problems associated with unguided migration: the massing of the poor in the inner city, urban congestion in general, the underpopulation of rural areas, the ills of depressed locales, and individual misfortune resulting from the wrong move to the wrong place for the wrong reasons. A planned and comprehensive migration policy addressed to such problems would need to be guided by clear objectives and carefully determined priorities.

The specific nature of such goals and priorities, or how they might be established, will not be considered in this paper. Rather, the writer will concentrate on the instrumentalities of guided migration. Emphasis will be placed on use of work-related incentives, broadly defined to include incentives arising from availability of job information, from financial assistance and social services provided for the mobile worker, and from expansion of job opportunities in specific regions. Consideration will then be given to how these instrumentalities might be shaped into possible programs of guided migration. Finally, some observations will be made on the difficulties

to be expected in implementing a comprehensive migration policy.

Job Information

A national job information system would be one of the essential tools of a comprehensive migration policy. In addition to serving as an adjunct to other programs (as will be shown), such a system would have an independent effect on mobility. Its greatest impact would be on working-class migrants who would move if they had knowledge of jobs available elsewhere. With the exception of private services for professional and technical occupations, there exists no structure through which a worker may readily learn of job possibilities in other regions.

The possible effect of inadequate or incorrect labor market information on migration decisions emerged quite clearly in one national study of migration into and out of depressed (redevelopment) areas.[11] Paradoxically enough, "purely economic reasons," including perception of available jobs, were given by almost half the family heads who moved *into* depressed areas, and economic reasons were mentioned by at least three-fourths of recent migrants to these areas. (It should also be noted that migration into depressed areas was by no means rare; for example, of all family heads who lived in chronically depressed areas, 14 percent had moved in during the previous five years.) Moreover, almost half the respondents living in these areas of persistent high unemployment perceived job opportunities to be as plentiful as or more plentiful than elsewhere. As the authors concluded:

Given job openings, any improvement in the plan of information about employment conditions in other places could serve two ends:

---

[10] Although there is no strong evidence that the migration decisions of the indigent are primarily shaped by welfare system incentives, these may still be taken into account, especially by migrants moving from low- to high-grant states. *See* Cloward and Piven, op. cit., and Margaret K. Rosenheim, "Shapiro versus Thompson, the Beggars are Coming to Town," *Supreme Court Review* (1969), pp. 303–346.

[11] U.S. Department of Commerce, Area Redevelopment Administration, *Migration Into and Out of Depressed Areas*, by the Survey Research Center of the University of Michigan (Washington, D.C.: U.S. Government Printing Office, 1964), p. 11.

(1) to step up migration out of depressed areas, and (2) to direct migrants to places of expanding economic opportunity (rather than places where they happen to have relatives).[12]

In the past few years there have been a number of proposals to establish a national job information system. One of the more recent and comprehensive was outlined by President Nixon in his 1969 congressional message on manpower training. He proposed that the Congress enact legislation "to establish a national computerized job bank to match job seekers and job vacancies. It would operate in each state with regional and national activities undertaken by the Secretary of Labor who would also set technical standards."[13]

The U.S. Department of Labor has already given financial support to job bank projects in a number of states with the apparent intent of developing the technology for a national system through trial and error at the state level. Results thus far from projects carried out by State Employment Services in California, Maryland, Utah, and Wisconsin suggest that a national system would be technically and economically feasible.[14] Wisconsin, for example, is developing an "on-line" placement system that automatically screens each applicant against all job openings for which he may be qualified. In Utah a computerized matching system brings together job and applicant data from fourteen regional offices of the state employment service. In most projects increases in job placement rates have followed the establishment of computerized information systems, although one does not know how much the systems themselves have contributed to the higher rates. It seems likely, however, that job banks are especially helpful to disadvantaged workers, a group whose access

to job information is especially limited. Thus in Maryland placements of such workers rose from 17 percent of total placements to 36 percent following the establishment of a partially computerized information system.[15] If developed to its logical limits, a national computerized system for matching workers with jobs would serve to facilitate migration from areas of labor surplus to areas of labor scarcity, to the benefit not only of individual migrants but of the economy as a whole. And it could accomplish such adjustments with a great deal of precision. Theoretically, an unemployed machine operator in Kansas could be informed of all job openings in his specialty anywhere in the country. The same facilities, of course, could be utilized by employers in search of workers.

A system of this kind is still a long way from realization. It would require not only sophisticated methods of computer processing of known job and applicant information, but also the administrative creation of a nationwide system for the exchange of this information. Development of the first is in the preliminary stages; little has been done with respect to the second. In fact the current federal strategy of subsidizing state endeavors could, if carried too far, retard the development of a national system. If each state were to perfect its own idiosyncratic system, one can readily imagine the difficulties of welding the resulting heterogeneous mass together.

Assisted Relocation

In addition to informing potential migrants of occupational opportunities in other regions, it is possible to offer them financial and other forms of assistance in carrying out their moves. Assisted relocation programs may be the government's most direct and best controlled means of affecting migration. Major disincentives to mobility, especially its monetary costs,

[12] Ibid., p. 28.

[13] Richard M. Nixon, quoted by Paul Delaney, "Job Training Plan is Given by Nixon," *New York Times*, August 15, 1969, p. 16.

[14] Ledford Day, "Computers Tested for Matchmaking Skills," *Manpower*, Vol. 1 (July 1969), pp. 7–8.

[15] Ibid.

can be reduced. Moreover, programs of this type can be specifically tailored to meet the special needs of given groups and individuals. In view of these considerations, it is important to learn what we can from foreign and domestic experiences with such programs.

Most major Western European nations, as well as Canada, have some form of government-assisted mobility program. Perhaps the most elaborate and most thriving is Sweden's.[16] Under the Swedish system relocation allowances cover a wide range of migration expenses, partially or completely, including travel costs for the worker and his family, the costs of moving household effects, and outlays for maintaining two households if it is not practical for the worker's family to join him immediately. In addition a worker can be given a grant to look a position over without having to make a commitment to accept it. Special bonuses (settlement grants) are awarded to workers moving out of designated low-employment areas. Although the program is directed mainly at unemployed workers, any worker judged likely to become unemployed is also eligible. A worker cannot qualify, however, if he intends to take a position in an area where labor surpluses exist for positions of that type. Although only a small minority of workers who migrate receive relocation assistance, most who do receive it come from designated labor surplus areas. Thus the program seems to be achieving desired effects on migration, even though these effects appear rather limited.

Canada's experience with financially assisted migration is of special interest because of the cultural, economic, and geographic similarities between that country

and the U.S.A.[17] In 1965 Canada began a Manpower Mobility Program designed to assist the migration of unemployed and underemployed workers. It is administered through Canada's Manpower Centers —a federal system of employment service facilities. The program awards only relocation grants, which are provided by federal sources and authorized by a special mobility counselor in the Manpower Center. Relocation grants of as much as $1,000 may be paid an unemployed worker and his dependents. In addition a homeowner's allowance of $500 is given if a home is sold or purchased in conjunction with the move. Workers may also receive exploratory grants to search for work. During fiscal year 1967, 4,436 exploratory grants and 5,745 relocation grants were awarded. Reluctance to move to or remain in receiving areas appears to be a major obstacle to further development of the program. It is significant, however, that the number of migrants receiving assistance doubled almost immediately after grants, instead of loans, became the primary form of assistance.

In the United States certain moving expenses have recently become more liberally deductible for income tax purposes. Public funds have been used for some time to provide indirect relocation assistance to key personnel in a large number of concerns engaged in contract work for the federal government. Defense and aerospace industries in particular have used funds from federal contracts to underwrite moving expenses of white-collar and skilled workers. Such indirect assistance has usually not been extended, however, to semiskilled and unskilled workers.

Direct relocation assistance to workers has been a fairly recent development and has thus far been confined to demonstration project status. Under provisions of the

---

[16] *See* especially Margaret S. Gordon, *Retraining and Labor Market Adjustment in Western Europe*, Manpower Automation Research Monograph No. 4. (Washington, D.C.: U.S. Department of Labor, August 1965), pp. 155–170; and Sol Swerdoff, "Sweden's Manpower Program," *Monthly Labor Review*, Vol. 89 (January 1966), pp. 1–6.

[17] U.S. Department of Labor, "Canada's Manpower Policy and Programs," *Manpower Research Bulletin* (Washington, D.C.: U.S. Government Printing Office, 1968).

Manpower Development and Training Act of 1962, the U.S. Department of Labor was authorized to conduct a series of labor mobility demonstrations in which relocation allowances were to be given to unemployed workers willing to move to obtain jobs. Assistance was to be restricted to unemployed workers who could not reasonably expect to find jobs in their own community and who had definite job offers elsewhere. In the first series of projects (1965–66), individuals meeting these criteria could be granted relocation allowances of up to 50 percent of actual expenses or loans covering all expenses. These provisions were subsequently liberalized in later projects (1967–68). Emphasis was shifted from loans to grants; lump-sum living allowances and compensation for dual-residence expenses were also included in later projects.

The results of the first series of projects reported suggest that relocation assistance is a feasible way of promoting certain kinds of geographic mobility. The majority of the 1,200 workers who received relocation assistance in the sixteen projects begun in 1965 were young heads of families who were helped to move relatively short distances (more than two-thirds of the moves were intrastate) at relatively low cost to obtain jobs that probably represented a step up the occupational ladder. Forty percent of those receiving relocation assistance were under 25; only 12 percent were over 45. Over 70 percent of those moving were accompanied by dependents. The average government expenditure per move, in the form of a loan or grant, fell between $300 and $400.[18]

Not surprisingly, a large proportion of these workers had skills that were surplus

in their own communities but were in demand elsewhere. Many would probably have moved on their own. There is no way of determining the proportion of relocated workers for whom assistance made the critical difference between moving and not moving. While it may be assumed that most workers receiving loans or grants found the money useful, the current rationale for relocation allowances requires the money to result in moves that otherwise would not have taken place.

By 1967, according to Mangum, some 6,500 workers had been relocated through forty projects conducted in twenty-nine states.[19] The great majority of these workers (about 80 percent) remained in the areas to which they relocated, although follow-up periods on which this finding was based were quite short (from two to four months). There is some evidence that the proportion of workers returning home has been lower in the later projects than the earlier ones. The average cost per move in the 1967 projects has been estimated at $750, but this figure apparently includes operating costs of the projects in addition to financial assistance given the workers.[20] Although the findings from the later projects have not been fully reported, it appears that they are generally consistent with earlier results.

Job Training

On the whole the projects have demonstrated the importance of job training and social service components in relocation programs. Several projects provided job training in addition to relocation assistance, with apparently good results. In fact, one of the most successful of the labor mobility

[18] *Report of the Secretary of Labor on Manpower Research and Training Under the Manpower Redevelopment and Training Act of 1962* (Washington, D.C.: U.S. Department of Labor, 1966); *see also* John L. Fulmer and James W. Robins, "Worker Mobility and Government Aid," *Business and Government Review*, Vol. 7 (September–October 1966), pp. 14–22.

[19] Garth L. Mangum, "Moving Workers to Jobs: An Evaluation of the Labor Mobility Demonstration Program," *Poverty and Human Resources Abstract* (Ann Arbor: University of Michigan Institute of Labor and Industrial Relations, 1968).

[20] *Manpower Report of the President, 1969* (Washington, D.C.: U.S. Government Printing Office, 1969), p. 207.

demonstrations reported thus far was a combined training and relocation effort.[21] In this project, which was carried out in Texas, 688 unemployed Mexican-American farm laborers from the Rio Grande Valley were trained as sheet-metal workers and assisted in relocating to Dallas, 450 miles away, to take jobs paying $3.00–$4.00 an hour. At the time the project began the unemployment rate was close to 20 percent in the Rio Grande Valley but only 2 percent in Dallas. An eight-week training course was conducted in the sending area by personnel of the hiring concern, an aerospace plant whose cooperation had been obtained at the outset. Relocation expenses averaged $551 per family. Assistance in locating housing and enrolling children in school was provided in cooperation with local offices of the Office of Economic Opportunity and the U.S. Department of Housing and Urban Development. The great majority of trainees were still employed a year after relocation. By this time the recipients had figuratively more than repaid the U.S. Treasury for the relocation allowance through income taxes. The project points up the possible advantages that may accrue not only from combining relocation with training but also from provision of supportive services and coordination with employers.

Counseling Services

The potential role that counseling services might play in a relocation program has been more fully demonstrated in one of the few mobility projects that made use of professional social workers. In this project, as described by Abrams, intensive group counseling was used prior to relocation "to ease the client's fears of city life and provide an orientation to the new community." [22] Through the group sessions

information was provided on housing and services in the receiving community (Minneapolis–St. Paul) and participants' apprehensions about their moves and their new jobs were discussed. Following relocation, participants were assisted through casework services centered chiefly on problems of housing, finances, job retention, and assimilation into the new community. It was found that this service was used most heavily by clients during the first two months following relocation.

Other relocation projects have made use of professional casework services provided by the Travelers Aid Society, a useful resource for two reasons: its expertise in the problems of migrants, who normally constitute a large share of its caseload, and its capacity to provide coordinated services in both sending and receiving areas through a nationwide network of local offices.[23] In relocations involving temporary separations of family members this kind of service system seems especially needed.

Problems Encountered

Certain problems were encountered in initiating and maintaining relocations. A substantial proportion of those approached were unwilling to move, among them low-income workers subsidized by welfare payments. These workers would have perhaps little to gain, and even something to lose, through relocation. Many who did not move returned to their place of origin rather quickly—overall about 20 percent within the first two months.[24] Difficulties in obtaining suitable housing seemed to be one reason for returns. Problems of assimilation into urban areas appeared to be a factor in relocation failures among low-income migrants from rural settings.

---

[21] Charles B. Rainett, "Beanpickers from Rio Grande Valley Now Make Jets in Dallas," *Employment Service Review*, Vol. 5 (December 1968), pp. 22–25.

[22] Harvey A. Abrams, "The Role of Social Work in Relocation for Employment," *Social*

Casework, Vol. 44, No. 8 (October 1968), pp. 475–480.

[23] *See* Savilla Millis Simons, "Social Services for the Mobile Poor in Urban Areas," *Social Work Practice 1965* (New York: Columbia University Press, 1965), pp. 162–173.

[24] Mangum, op. cit.

Finally, some of the projects invite the thought that the success of relocation programs may be diminished by unexpected developments or by unanticipated consequences of the programs themselves. In one apparently successful project reviewed by Somers, workers from depressed areas in northern Michigan and Wisconsin were assisted in moves to Milwaukee, where labor shortages existed.[25] At the time the project began, unemployment rates in the sending areas varied from 15 to 20 percent, while the rate in Milwaukee was less than 2 percent. The moves evidently resulted in increased incomes for the workers, but it so happened that employment conditions in the sending areas improved considerably after the workers moved—to the point at which they were no longer classified as depressed. Perhaps in due course these workers would have gotten jobs in their home areas.

At the same time one must not forget that the 2 percent unemployment rate in Milwaukee, the receiving area, represented several thousand workers who were searching for jobs. Many of these workers were chronically unemployed and unskilled blacks living in ghettos. In their search for labor, Milwaukee employers would normally have had some incentive to help train these persons, but the relocation programs gave them an alternative—perhaps a preferred one—of hiring white in-migrants who most certainly had more skills to offer and better work histories. As this project well illustrates, the evaluation of relocation programs cannot be limited to the programs themselves.

It should be noted that such relocation projects provide to marginal, usually blue-collar, workers benefits that many white-collar workers take for granted. Managerial, technical, and professional personnel are routinely reimbursed for moving ex-

penses incurred in intraorganizational transfers; frequently such expenses are paid by the hiring organization when a change of job involves a change of residence.

The mobile white-collar worker often can also count on equivalents to the concrete services and counseling components of governmental relocation efforts. At times his support system may include company purchase of his home in the sending area and financing for the purchase of a new home in the receiving area, the services of nationwide real estate concerns that specialize in intersuburban moves, information about his new community from his new organization, and a readymade social network provided by his new co-workers and local chapters of national organizations to which he may belong. It should be further noted that he may receive such benefits without being designated a "case" in need of special assistance. Perhaps the point of this comparison is already clear: while recent federal relocation programs have provided much-needed help to the marginal worker, they still fall short of providing the kind of support that large numbers of migrant white-collar workers expect and receive as part of the economic benefit scheme built into their career development.

Regional Job Development: Moving Jobs to Workers

The preceding section was concerned with efforts to move workers to existing jobs. Let us now consider a complementary strategy: job development programs designed to hold workers within a region and to attract others to it. As noted earlier, migration control constitutes only one aspect of these undertakings, which usually have as their major immediate objective the relief of unemployment in depressed areas.

Foreign Programs

Again some consideration of foreign experience may be instructive. All major

25 Gerald G. Somers, "Evaluation of Manpower Development Programs," in Edward J. Jakubauskas and C. Phillip Baumel, eds., *Human Resources Development* (Ames, Iowa: Iowa State University Press, 1967), pp. 143–152.

European countries and Canada have regional economic development schemes in which creation of jobs is a central aim. Typically, various forms of assistance, including grants, loans, interest subsidies, and tax incentives, are offered by regional economic planning bodies to industries willing to locate in designated redevelopment areas. In Great Britain, for example, a considerable array of governmental supports has been developed to facilitate industrial relocation in depressed areas. In addition to receiving loans and grants, a firm moving to a redevelopment area may also be able to lease at low cost a government-built factory, may be reimbursed for moving expenses, and may be assisted in locating and importing key manpower; government funds may also be allocated to improve environmental facilities such as transportation, power, and sanitation.[26] The Canadian program, established by the Department of Industry Act of 1963, relies mainly on cash grants to induce firms to locate in designated areas. One-third of the capital cost of building new plants and one-half of the cost of equipping them can be assumed by the national government.[27]

The more advanced of the Western European programs are now stressing "growthpoint" policies under which depressed areas or subareas with the greatest potential for growth are selected for intensive development. Growth points may be developed through building up a concentration of new industry by special incentives with concomitant efforts to improve housing and community facilities. As Gordon writes, the trend "has been away from policies which treat all depressed or underdeveloped areas alike."[28] There has been an increasing realization in these countries that some

areas do not lend themselves to economic development and that, without some selectivity, limited resources may be dissipated.

Redevelopment Programs

In the United States certain programs have been developed to increase employment and other opportunities in depressed areas. The legislative framework has been built through the Area Redevelopment Act (1961), the Appalachian Redevelopment Act (1965) and the Public Works and Economic Development Act (1965).

The most intensive of these efforts, the Appalachian redevelopment program, has been directed in part at reducing the high rate of migration from Appalachia, which has been sending large numbers of its poorly educated and unskilled inhabitants to the mountaineer ghettos of midwestern cities. This goal has been one of many in an ambitious attempt to "realize the potential inherent in the region's underdeveloped resources." [29]

The building of a modern highway system to serve the region has been the major thrust thus far. Almost three-fifths of the $600 million appropriated for Appalachian redevelopment through fiscal year 1968 has been allocated for highway construction. This emphasis has been justified on the grounds that a highway system is needed to attract industry to this isolated area and to permit its residents to commute to jobs. In recognition of the need to develop the human resources of Appalachia so that its inhabitants can take advantage of employment opportunities when they become available, efforts are under way to improve its primary education system and to establish vocational and technical training programs.

A regional redevelopment program of national scope is being carried out by the Economic Development Administration (EDA). A locality may seek federal assistance if it can pass what is essentially a

---

[26] *Manpower Policy and Programs in Five Western European Countries* (Washington, D.C.: U.S. Department of Labor, Manpower Administration, Office of Manpower Policy, Evaluation, and Research, 1966), pp. 27–34.

[27] U.S. Department of Labor, "Canada's Manpower Policy and Programs."

[28] Op. cit., p. 173.

[29] *Manpower Report of the President, 1968* (Washington, D.C.: U.S. Government Printing Office, 1968), p. 152.

means test requiring demonstration of a relatively low family income level and relatively high rates of unemployment and out-migration. The locality is also required to submit an acceptable plan for its projected economic development. As of 1968 some nine hundred areas, mainly cities or counties, had demonstrated eligibility for assistance. Most of these redevelopment areas were located in Appalachia or in one of five designated regions: Upper Great Lakes, Ozarks, New England, Four Corners (parts of Utah, Colorado, Arizona, and New Mexico) and Coastal Plains (the Carolinas and Georgia). Redevelopment efforts within each of these five regions are coordinated by regional commissions consisting of governors of the affected states and a federal representative. Federal assistance, which is given directly to local areas, consists largely of subsidies for public works and facilities and of business loans. In 1968 over 1,400 public work projects, with a total funding of $700 million, were in operation; there were 188 active business loan projects with a total funding of $158 million.[30]

There has been little systematic study of the extent to which area redevelopment programs have achieved their objectives. As a result one would be hard put to say whether these efforts have had the intended effect—curbing out-migration. It is true that out-migration from Appalachia has declined since the inauguration of redevelopment programs for that region, but it is not known if the decline is due to the program's effects or to other factors. While the EDA estimated that during 1966 and 1967 15,000 new jobs were developed through its business loan program alone, this estimate probably includes jobs that were created by economic expansion during this period.[31] Moreover, there is no way of determining the impact of the program on migration.

One finding from the labor mobility projects is relevant here, however. Participants in these projects were reluctant to move if prospects for getting jobs in their home areas were brightening. It is possible that redevelopment efforts in specific locales create expectations of better times and that such expectations may cause potential migrants to stay, at least a little longer. If it is true that redevelopment programs create an atmosphere of hope that inhibits out-migration, it would also be true that this atmosphere would dissipate unless the programs delivered.

Given their present structure, these programs would probably be of rather limited use as instruments of a comprehensive migration policy. The EDA programs in particular are heavily dependent on local initiative, a condition certainly not conducive to national migration planning. Localities in less need of help to stem out-migration may be just those localities with the necessary leadership to draft plans qualifying them for assistance. Spreading resources over too many locales—the kind of problem that European countries have tried to circumvent through use of growth-point policies—seems to be a defect of both the EDA and the Appalachian programs.

The job development strategies used thus far have some definite shortcomings. The lopsided emphasis on highway construction in Appalachia does not promise to produce the balanced economic development and diversity of jobs that may be needed to reverse the outward flow of its population. The incentives available to the EDA to promote industrial growth in redevelopment areas are limited to loans, a relatively weak stimulant. Moreover, the loans have been used in a fragmented way to support isolated and often marginal concerns rather than to build agglomerative industrial complexes capable of self-sustaining growth.

Finally, no solutions have yet been found

---

[30] *Directory of Approved Projects as of December 30, 1968* (Washington, D.C.: U.S. Department of Commerce, Economic Development Administration, 1969), p. vi.

[31] *Manpower Report of the President, 1968,* p. 154.

for the conflict between redevelopment programs and assisted mobility programs—the former attempt to check out-migration from depressed areas while the latter attempt to encourage it. For a concrete example, it may be recalled that earlier reference was made to a successful relocation project in which unemployed workers were helped to move from northern Michigan and Wisconsin to Milwaukee. The sending areas, as it turns out, are part of the Upper Great Lakes redevelopment region, which has received EDA funds for "education and training to upgrade the skills of a work force depleted by migration." [32] At least some of this migration has been deliberately brought about by another federal program. Other examples of lack of congruity between relocation and redevelopment efforts could readily be offered.

Possible Policy Directions

A comprehensive migration policy based on manpower programs could assume a variety of forms. Two possible policy directions, somewhat different in purpose and scope, will be considered.

Facilitating Mobility

One kind of policy that could be pursued would be aimed at facilitating the mobility of workers whose moves would serve the public interest. A policy of this sort could be shaped primarily through implementation of job information and assisted relocation programs. It would be directed primarily at helping unemployed and underemployed workers to learn of and move to jobs in other areas, thereby augmenting and rationalizing labor market forces that normally guide such workers to areas of expanding employment opportunities.

Development of the relocation component could be guided by the lessons of experience thus far:

32 Ibid.

1. Allowances, preferably in the form of grants, would need to be liberal and comprehensive enough to compensate the migrant for the major portion of both direct and indirect relocation costs. The allowances should provide funds for exploratory trips, for moving the worker and his family and their household possessions to the receiving area, and for maintaining dual residences when necessary. In addition a lump sum resettlement grant could be paid to cover miscellaneous and unanticipated costs incurred during moving.

2. Provision should be made for incentive payments for migration from or to specific areas—for example, from areas that cannot be rehabilitated and that are populated by persons it would be difficult to move.

3. The relocation program should include adequate supportive services, including counseling and housing assistance.

4. Job training given either in the sending or receiving community should be an integral part of relocation efforts. Through this means assisted migration might be brought to the service of unemployed, unskilled workers (often black) in central cities and rural areas. Without concomitant job training, relocation programs would tend to pass over this group.

5. Finally, a relocation program should be carried out with continued feedback from other systems. Information on changing labor market conditions is especially important. The possible effects of assisted migration on other manpower programs or on employment conditions needs to be taken carefully into account.

Means of avoiding or minimizing conflict between relocation and development programs would need to be provided. For example, the programs can be directed at different target groups. The prime recruits for a relocation program may be workers with skills that are not needed in a certain area but are in demand in another. A redevelopment program might be concerned with another kind of population, for example, workers without special skills who might be trained to fill jobs being created in the area. This kind of meshing would require careful coordination of the kind that can be best achieved by a single planning agency. The immediate target of policy at this level would be potential migrants likely to make socially dysfunctional migration decisions. It would not be directed, however, at altering basic migration patterns in order to alleviate major population imbalances.

Altering Migration Patterns

Intervention to alter these patterns would obviously need to be more vigorous, more comprehensive, and structured differently. A possible strategy for this more ambitious effort will be outlined briefly. Although it is offered essentially for illustrative purposes, it incorporates what may be the essential characteristics of comprehensive migration planning—that is, the meshing of employment information, assisted relocation, and job development components.

Under this strategy migration would be guided to designated growth centers. Job opportunities and supporting infrastructures would be developed in centers where further growth would be deemed both desirable and feasible. These centers would serve in effect as "magnets" for workers from other areas who could receive both training for employment in the centers and assistance in moving to them. Given national scope, a program of this kind could be used to reduce migration to already overburdened metropolitan areas, to stimulate out-migration from these areas, and to constrain out-migration from locales that would benefit from population retention and growth.

The growth centers could be communities of moderate size. Although most might be selected from redevelopment areas, they would need to have sufficient infrastructures to support fairly intensive and rapid industrial growth. A mix of incentives, including low-interest loans, relocation sub-

sidies, tax write-offs, and cash grants, would be used to attract industries. An attempt would be made to build up industrial complexes with self-generating growth capacities. Special incentives could be granted to those industries that could provide employment (after job training) to certain classes of potential migrants, such as poorly educated and relatively inexperienced workers.

Although employable and trainable workers living in and near the growth centers might be the immediate beneficiaries of expanded job opportunities, the long-range emphasis would be on in-migration. Through a computerized job information system, employment placement and training centers in potential sending areas would be informed of forthcoming and actual job vacancies. At the same time information about potential employees would be transmitted from the potential sending areas to the growth centers. Publicity and active recruitment procedures could be used in the sending areas to increase the input of applicants. A full complement of relocation allowances would be available to assist workers willing to move to the growth centers.

Job training, if needed, could be provided in either the sending or receiving areas, depending on the type of training needed and the type of worker to be trained. Whichever the site, workers would be trained for actual or forthcoming jobs, with potential employers participating in the planning and conduct of the training.

All facets of the program would be related to migration objectives, especially to the stimulation and guidance of certain kinds of migration. Stimulating migration of the unemployed or underemployed from large, labor-surplus urban areas to the growth centers would be one priority objective. Another would be the diversion to the growth centers of migration that would normally flow to these areas. Of specific concern here would be rural migrants with poor prospects of finding stable employment in such areas. Designated sending areas could be given preferential treatment with respect to job vacancy data, training facilities, and funds for relocation. For the growth centers to remain viable, however, professional and skilled workers, probably already employed elsewhere, would also need to be recruited, in some cases through special incentives. Housing, social services, and other facilities would be planned and developed in relation to the community's anticipated rate of growth.

Obstacles to These Programs

Before the programs described could operate with any degree of effectiveness, some major obstacles would need to be overcome. Indeed, any national undertaking to influence internal migration would have to face these obstacles.

To begin with, an awesome planning effort would be required to develop and synchronize the essential programs, especially those envisioned under the growth center plan. The latter, for example, would require close coordination on the part of several large federal bureaucracies, notably the U.S. Departments of Labor, HEW, Commerce, and HUD and the OEO.

A planning structure bringing these agencies together does exist in the form of the "Cooperative Area Manpower System" (CAMPS). Under CAMPS, regional and metropolitan offices of these agencies and other related organizations attempt to develop coordinated manpower programs at local levels. As Schuchter has noted, the CAMPS experience has amply demonstrated the difficulties in achieving coordination among these agencies, even around limited manpower programs.[33] But a program involving migration to growth centers would demand even more extensive coordination involving far more complex decisions. The pan-regional nature of this kind of migration control program requires

coordination among these agencies at a national level as well as the cooperation of local governments in different parts of the country. Lodging of the program in one existing agency, perhaps the Department of Labor, or the creation of a new super-agency (an Office of Internal Migration?) might be advisable but would not in itself solve problems of interagency and intergovernmental coordination.

Moreover, sound planning decisions must be based on adequate data. At this point the kind of informational system required by a large-scale guided migration program really does not exist. A portion of this information base, such as a national job bank, can be built through application and extension of recent technological advances. But much of it must be built from research addressed to a broad range of critical questions, most of which cannot be cast directly into researchable form. By what indicators can centers of potential growth be identified? What mix of incentives can most effectively induce industries to relocate? By what criteria can potential sending areas be determined? What kinds of incentives and supportive services are most effective in facilitating the relocation of migrants? What kinds of migrants prove to be successful (or unsuccessful)?

Perhaps even more formidable are political obstacles that would act to constrain or even to transmogrify a national undertaking to influence internal migration. Strong political counterforces have been generated thus far against both federal labor mobility and economic redevelopment programs. The labor mobility demonstration projects have been opposed by congressmen from depressed and rural areas on grounds that they would abet further out-migration from these areas. This opposition has been instrumental in limiting federally assisted mobility to demonstration projects and in withholding further appropriations for such projects. And as the Koziaras point out, those very congressmen are apt to have the greatest investment

---

[33] Op. cit., p. 430.

in manpower problems—and consequently substantial influence over manpower legislation, simply *because* they represent labor-surplus areas.[34]

Federal redevelopment programs have faced similar opposition. In his analysis of the operations of the Area Redevelopment Administration, Levitan cites the "ample sympathy in Congress for businessmen who complained about ARA loans to potential competitors." [35] In testifying before Congress against the Public Works and Economic Development Act, William C. Heyn (National Association of Manufacturers) spoke perhaps for many businessmen and conservative congressmen when he commented that "it is unfair to existing industry to use their tax money to subsidize new industry which will compete for their markets." [36]

Attempts to expand such programs would doubtless bring forth even more intense protests from their traditional opponents and might well invite opposition from new sources. Thus relocation efforts that might serve to break up concentrations of minority groups in central cities might be opposed by those with a stake in the political power that such concentrations generate. It is easy to see how the shape of a complex migration control effort could become badly mangled in the ensuing struggles and accommodations among diverse interest groups representing rural areas, the cities,

the business community, leaders of minority groups, and, in general, groups standing to gain or lose from the migration plan.

The writer does not wish to convey the impression that planning toward an ambitious migration policy is fruitless because of the enormity of the political obstacles to be faced. The planner may assume that such obstacles are surmountable—and indeed they may be—but certainly they must be taken into account if the planning is to have any basis in reality.

Conclusion

The architects of a comprehensive migration policy would be confronted, then, with refractory planning problems and with a number of unsympathetic publics. Given these hurdles, not to mention the constraints of costs and competing priorities, one cannot be sanguine about prospects for extensive programs aimed at altering major migration patterns. But neither can we dismiss the possibility that such programs may ultimately provide workable solutions to some of the problems resulting from unguided migration. The pressure of these problems will force us to give increasing thought and study to proposals similar to the growth center plan.

In the meantime, less ambitious undertakings utilizing job banks and assisted relocation to facilitate individual mobility may be both immediately useful and feasible. A cohesive program incorporating these ingredients would not only serve the national interest by bringing about a better match between populations and resources, but would also enable individual migrants and their families to make more effective use of mobility as a means of self-betterment. Standing to gain in particular would be the less affluent and less well-educated members of society—those without the information and wherewithal to move to the place of greatest advantage at the most appropriate time.

---

[34] Edward and Karen Koziara, "Development of Relocation Allowances as Manpower Policy," *Industrial and Labor Relations Review*, Vol. 20 (October 1966), pp. 66–75.

[35] Sar A. Levitan, *Federal Aid to Depressed Areas* (Baltimore: Johns Hopkins Press, 1964), p. 125.

[36] U.S., Congress, Senate, Committee on Banking and Currency, Subcommittee on Production and Stabilization, *Hearings on Titles II and IV of S. 1648*, 89th Cong., 1st Sess., May 7, 1965 (statement of William C. Heyn), reported in *Public Works and Economic Development* (Washington, D.C.: U.S. Government Printing Office, 1965), p. 196.

A National Internal Migration Policy: Suggestions from a Demographer

ALBERT J. MAYER

The population of the United States now numbers more than 200 million persons. By the year 2000 another 100 million people will be added to this total. This not only sounds like a lot of people—it *is* a lot of people. More than 70 percent of these people live on only 2 percent of the total land available. In this sense the country's population is too concentrated, too packed in. Life is thereby rendered unnecessarily complicated and burdensome in many ways.

At the same time anyone who is familiar with the face of America has seen villages and small towns dying in every part of this country. In the South, in New England, in the West, places that were functional in their time have ceased to exist or have shriveled and become stagnant. The young people leave to seek opportunities in larger cities, often settling in suburbs. This is the pattern this nation has spawned in its pursuit of technological development.

This clustering of the nation's population is of even greater magnitude than first appears, for the Atlantic and Pacific coasts contain undue concentrations of people. Forecasts of population growth indicate increased concentration in these areas in the years ahead. Two super-megalopolises, one stretching from San Francisco to San Diego and the other from Boston to Washington, are forming rapidly. The remainder of the country is not nearly so densely populated, except for parts of the Midwest.

Industry believes it is gaining an economic advantage by locating in densely populated areas near markets and large labor pools. Labor unions are well organized, which creates higher wages in unionized trades, which in turn makes urban job opportunities more attractive. This in turn attracts more migrants to these highly populated areas, and the cycle begins again: Larger population concentrations lead to greater specialization of occupations and services, and the urbanization process leads to an even greater concentration of people and diversity of opportunity.

These circular processes are self-stimulating and self-sustaining. They are so powerful and pervasive that one wonders why the entire population of the United States has not been drawn into the existing coastal industrial centers.

But there are countervailing forces. The nation's military and defense establishment, which has been increasing in size and scope since 1940, has operated to develop population concentrations in quite different geographic locations. Politics, climate, and proximity to vast open spaces are important factors in locating military and military-industrial complexes. Military-industrial expansion has been the principal source of growth for many large cities in both the South and West. Whether one approves or disapproves of this it has at least served as a balance to the vast civilian-industrial concentration in the Northeast. Only in southern California has an area been the locus of both the civilian-industrial and military-industrial force. As a result, within relatively few years California has become the most populous state in America. Population diffusion has never been a conscious aim of the government-inspired military-industrial growth. To the contrary, its growth has been notoriously underplanned, but it nevertheless has served an important distributive function.

It will be noted that this is just another example of how society operates primarily in behalf of "things" rather than people. Whether it is the individual business or corporation choosing a new industrial site in terms of water, sewers, transportation, and land values, or the government-inspired industrial or military facility doing the same thing, human values are often considered only as an afterthought. Mass job opportunities are created with little regard to environmental and human effects. We jump headlong into new technologies without researching the probable human consequences with anything equal to the thoroughness with which the technical aspects are investigated.

This has certainly been the case with the concentration of huge numbers of people in cities as well as the subsequent suburbanization process that now has much of the American population caught in a permanent traffic jam between two unpleasant environments, their place of work and their area of residence. A subsystem with especially virulent consequences has been the growth of urban ghettos in large industrialized cities. After the flood of immigration was deliberately halted in the mid-1920s, large employers went into the South and consciously sought black people as a source of new labor. After a respite during the Depression of the 1930s, large-scale internal migration again took place during and after World War II. Although migration itself has slowed down recently, high birthrates have further crowded the ghettos and served to increase the population concentration in large cities.

Thus there are the general problems of undue concentrations of people in large industrial centers and the more focused, more vexing problem of the immense concentrations of poor black people in these same cities. While some black families have attained secure economic status and acquired middle-class attitudes and some have been able to move to the suburbs and outer rings of the city, the mass of blacks seem trapped in poverty and in the ghetto.

The two problems are interrelated. It is hard to say which begs for attention first. A possible solution for both lies in a redistribution of people to ease the tensions created by high population densities. The United States has no official or even unofficial stance toward internal migration, except after a crisis such as the movement out of the Dust Bowl during the Depression and similar mass movements in response to traumatic events. The ordinary movements of people are not considered within the province of government. At this point in our history this may be a mistake.

In view of this, consideration needs to be given to a national internal migration policy aimed at relieving the population pressure in the large cities. This proposed policy has two aspects, one directed toward the creation of entirely new cities and one directed toward deconcentrating over-crowded urban centers where the quality of life is below what we have learned to expect and accept.

Creating New Cities

The first part of a national internal migration policy would be aimed at redistribution of people and jobs to areas where the environment can sustain them at a better level of "quality." New markets will come into existence as a consequence of such a population redistribution. The choice confronting us is as follows: If the United States grows by 50 percent it can either grow by further consolidation and concentration of existing centers, or by dispersion to new localities. The present method of locating a new industrial facility is to examine existing markets for the product absorptive capacity, the presence or absence of a suitable labor force, the transportation costs of materials, and the number of specific site location variables such as water, taxes, land costs, and the like. Often these factors favor continued concentration of people and of industry in existing metropolitan clusters.

Such a system perpetuates itself. Consider the case of a manufacturer or business that might consider breaking out of this circular system. Entrepreneurial risks must be taken in going into a new area far from markets, subcontractors, and labor resources. However, if huge corporate enterprises were to combine in a jointly planned effort they could build a new base of moderate-sized urban concentrations, each with an ultimate population of perhaps half a million persons and distributed in well-planned locations throughout the country. This is quite different from the present-day "new towns," which often have an inadequate economic base or only a single industry. Columbia, Maryland, might be considered an example

of the former; Huntsville, Alabama, an example of the latter. Huntsville, in the beginning totally dependent on the space program, is currently scurrying around to add new industry just in case the space program becomes defunct. Why must we scurry?

During the last twenty years the technology of systems analysis has come into existence; this country has the capability to build various models of its economic system and to test these models. Large corporations do this today in terms of their own operations. Why, then, can they not combine in a nationwide analysis and formulation of a plan for the relocation and planned expansion of industrial and financial resources and—hence—population? Probably they could and would if it had any relation to their immediate and long-range profit.

If some economist could demonstrate that such a plan would indeed be more profitable, and if the financial powers believed him, then the face of America might be changed. New cities could be created in new places, and the present tendency to superconcentrate population could be halted, or at least slowed. Perhaps a modest governmental subsidy to a presently existing or newly founded economic research institute might provide the necessary impetus. Most important would be the recognition that nationwide economic and social planning is imperative if society is to progress.

Once it could be demonstrated that by following such a plan profits could not only be maintained but enhanced, systematically planned cities would become the "in" thing. Millions of job opportunities, some new, but others representing relocations, would arise. Is there any doubt that these jobs would be filled by a stream of applicants in a rush reminiscent of the California Gold Rush of 1849? A manufacturing job nucleus is all that is needed to create service jobs, professional jobs, and all of the secondary forms of employment. The usual city with a population of about 500,000 persons has between ten and fifteen large manufacturing establishments, or about 90,000 industrial jobs. This is all that is necessary to make a sustaining economic base for a city of this size. It is not necessary to begin with raw farmland or pastures; there are many existing urban areas of from 10,000 to 200–300,000 that could be augmented by strategic location of expanded industrial facilities.

Implementation of this industrial relocation policy would be left to private enterprise, but it would take much more foresight than the private sector has yet shown. More likely the federal government will have to take the initiative and provide the direction, knowledge, and leadership. It is suggested that it create a Bureau of Internal Migration. One purpose of such a bureau would be to organize the separate elements of the nation's industrial structure to bring about a more rational order of industrial growth and redistribution of facilities and population. A second purpose would be to develop a plan to assist people in finding jobs and programs to aid their relocation, such as planning of housing, schools, and recreational space.

If this is so easy, why has it not been done well and systematically? It has not been done well because in the past society was simpler, and individual efforts and decision-making had consequences only for those immediately involved. (At least it appeared that way superficially.) However, as the twentieth century progresses it is quite clear that we all, by our very presence, concentration, and numbers, are stepping on each other's toes, blowing automobile exhaust over our neighbor's flowers and into his lungs, and bathing in each other's drinking water. We long for the freedom of the past; but we cannot go back to the old frontier. When this frustration is added to the accumulated anger built up by past discrimination and the slow pace of present change, explosive ghettos

result. However, we can exercise some initiative, use our scientific know-how to cure societal ills, and in general take the necessary steps truly to plan our future urban population growth so that all people will benefit thereby.

Redistributing Population

Wealth generates wealth and poverty generates poverty, both on an individual and societal basis. Wealthy persons, with the exception of those who are inept or unlucky, can use their money to make more money. Conversely, poor persons often cannot afford the clothes or carfare that will enable them even to begin to seek employment. Much of the slum ghetto population is caught in this circular trap. It is true that some escape, but they are more than replaced by the large number of babies who are the product of the high fertility rates characteristic of the slum. Some of the proposals for a negative income tax are based on this assumption.

Certainly on the societal level the same is true. An underdeveloped nonindustrialized country cannot pull itself up without outside investment and know-how. The struggle of sheer day-to-day survival, near-starvation, and exhausting labor prevent the accumulation of resources and capital necessary to trigger an upward spiral. The ghetto cannot repair itself any more than an underdeveloped nation can. Many resources now channeled into the ghetto yield poor dividends because they attempt to alleviate specific conditions that do not really exist in isolation but are only part of a whole disadvantaged social pattern. This has also been the experience with much of this country's foreign aid, and this is and will continue to be the experience in the helpless inner cities.

Ghetto schools can be staffed with the best and most experienced teachers, and still most high school graduates will be little more than functional illiterates. The now numerous studies of urban schools bear out this fact. The motivation and the atmosphere of learning are not there.

Ghetto housing can be renewed and rebuilt. But without far more complex changes in neighborhood cohesion, incentives of homeownership, and self-pride, the rehabilitated areas will in a few years once again be battered, littered, crawling with vermin. Testimony to the validity of this can be found by examination of existing public housing in many parts of the country.

We do offer ghetto residents jobs as busboys, car washers, laundry employees, porters, janitors, and in other menial positions. Most will not stick to these jobs because they are aware that they lead nowhere and the compensation is little more than public assistance affords. In the 1930s college graduates were, if not glad, at least relieved to obtain jobs that are today spat upon by high school dropouts. Our Calvinistic society looks on this with dismay. It is still a social fact and we will have to live with it.

The question is: How can we relieve at least some of this ghetto superheat? A partial solution might be in another aspect of a national internal migration policy. This program would be aimed at systematically helping people to leave the large ghettos, through incentives to move to other parts of the country where economic opportunities are better and living conditions are more relaxed. This is not a panacea or a dramatic cure. The problems exist because poverty exists. But resettlement in suburbs, new towns, and underpopulated regions is one way of improving the quality of American life.

The principal purposes of this aspect of a national internal migration policy would be to decrease the concentration of lower-class persons, including blacks, in the dilapidated city ghettos and to distribute them more equally throughout the country, especially to the new cities suggested previously. Along with the disruption that comes with migration is the hidden hope

that life will be better in the new location. This hope, if fulfilled, might be the best thing for the black person who has lived too long on a diet of crushed hope.

This would be an additional weapon in the struggle to reduce segregation, discrimination, and poverty—not a substitute and certainly not a cure. But the proposal rests on an assumption that has become politically controversial in an unexpected way. It takes the view that racial problems can be solved best by integration rather than separatism. Yet diluting the residential concentrations of black and poor persons will diminish their potential for exercising local political and economic power. Would this not mean that the black man as a black will become less strong? In short, it appears to be just another white man's trick to defeat development of black identity through dispersion.

It must be remembered that today's Black Power movement is not a long-time response but a recent, necessary, last-ditch, desperate movement based on the correct and realistic diagnosis that white society does not intend to introduce honest, sincere programs to correct the injustices of several hundred years. The black American had no adjectival status in the first place; the white man gave it to him. At this late date one wonders whether any rapprochement at all is possible, but it is highly probable that there are many black persons who would respond to a concrete and sincere effort on the part of the general society to restore a large measure of equity.

Characteristics of the Program

The relevant characteristics of a national migration policy would be as follows: The program would be created either by Congress or by the executive branch of the government. Each community would report to the state employment services any job openings at all skill levels, from laborer to professional. This is done to some extent already, but coverage is not complete. Additional governmental funds would be needed to encourage private employment agencies to report job sources to the state. The various state employment services would then list these sources with a national clearinghouse. This step is new and would be made feasible by a computerized system. (It would be clearly understood that any job position listed in this system would be free from discrimination.)

The entire program would be accompanied by extensive publicity. Surely it is as worthwhile to sell this type of program as it is to sell the space program. The federal government would see that the job positions were listed in appropriate places, publicized through the newspapers of all large cities, as well as on radio and television, regardless of where the openings existed. Publicization of job opportunities would not be confined to black persons, but would be focused on them, for their need is greatest.

The program, presumably under the management of the proposed Bureau of Internal Migration, would essentially be one of communication of employment opportunities. However, for persons of marginal skills the possibility of incentives and moving subsidies or loans needs to be considered. This is done all the time. Corporations move professionals and executives; the air force moves mechanics. We have the experience and the know-how. Why can we not simply extend this?

The policy is not coercive, but incentive. No one is pushed to go anyplace. The policy simply provides a needed means of communication between blacks, walled into segregated areas, and the remainder of the United States. Not all blacks will want to leave their present surroundings. Many lack the skills needed in any market, but there should be considerable numbers who would welcome a change, a release from the pressures of a ghettoized existence.

It can be argued that this suggested program ignores the principal problem of ghettoized blacks who have never had an opportunity to acquire skills salable in today's market and who, no matter where a job was located, could not meet the qualifications for it. However, it should be recognized that a national internal migration policy is not a cure-all, but only an additional tool. It must be placed in the context of job-training, job-upgrading, better schools, and so on.

The function of this program would be to move some persons out of the crowded urban centers. Every black person of any skill level who leaves Detroit or Chicago or New York creates a vacancy for another person. Those without marketable skills cannot fill this vacancy, but it is also true that impetus to train further persons is provided if real vacancies or shortages exist. For example, if a black man employed in an office job at General Motors in Detroit leaves for a job in Portland, Oregon, GM will search widely to find a suitable replacement. Thus additional opportunities are created.

Several important questions might be asked as to whether the intended place of migration, presumably a smaller city with a smaller black population or a smaller percentage of blacks in the population, would represent an upward step for the black migrant. Is it not true that these cities have had their share of unrest? Is it not also true that incomes of and opportunities for blacks are less in the relatively smaller, relatively isolated communities? Both are correct, yet this does not negate the major proposition that the principal obstruction to black progress is the tremendous concentration of poverty in large cities.

An Illustrative Case

An actual case illustrating this is that of Phoenix, Arizona. The Phoenix metropolitan area contains over 900,000 persons, of whom 30,000, or 3.5 percent, are black.[1]

---

[1] *Inside Phoenix*, a yearly in-depth field study (Phoenix: *Phoenix Republic and Gazette*, 1968), p. 9.

In addition, 60,000, or 6.5 percent, are Mexican-Americans. The latter are somewhat better off, but there is no question that they are also an economically deprived minority group. Most of the members of these two groups live in the innermost areas of the central city, which has a population of nearly 600,000.

In 1967 the income of black families in Phoenix was only 40 percent of that of white families, substantially less than the U.S. average for blacks, which was 58 percent of the income of whites. Black persons are less well off in the strict economic sense. Part of the reason for this income differential is that young people, especially educated young people, move to areas of greater economic opportunity such as Los Angeles. This is precisely the wrong direction. If economic opportunities were created in Phoenix, then the native and inmigrant blacks could constitute a strong nucleus of economically sufficient leaders, who could cope with the problem of the then relatively small numbers of poor black persons. Phoenix has the standard set of racial problems, but in greatly reduced quantity. This is the key to this aspect of the national internal migration policy.

For example, let us consider the Phoenix school system. In the high school system 80 percent of the students are majority group members; the minority group students are divided into 12 percent Mexican-American, 6 percent black, and 2 percent other races.[2] Of all minority group members, 46 percent, or almost half, are in one of the ten city high schools and 22 percent are in a second high school, with 32 percent distributed among the other eight. Thus one high school contains a concentration of almost half the minority group student population.

If schools need to be augmented and enriched, concentrating the effort in one high and a dozen elementary schools is a

[2] Yearly survey, Phoenix Union High School System, 1968.

task within the realm of possibility—at least its scope can be grasped. However, if a city contains ten to thirty all-poor, all-black or Puerto Rican high schools, as New York, Chicago, and Detroit do, then the solution defies the mind. Sheer size becomes a crucial variable.

At this point if the employers in the area could be galvanized into constructive aggressive action to make sure that of the many thousands of migrants who pour into the Phoenix area each year at least some are blacks with salable skills, the existing black community could acquire leadership, economic strength, and hope. To do this employers would have to go out of their way. They would have to advertise in newspapers—especially black newspapers in large cities—to communicate with the New York, Michigan, California, and Illinois state employment services.

Would they really do this? This cannot be answered, because it has never been tried. However, if an agency or commission created by executive order of the President of the United States were promoting this and providing leadership, technique, and persuasion, they might comply.

If it worked, would it not create another superghetto? The answer is no, because the newcomers would be economically viable. This would not be like the past, when the unskilled farm migrant was cast adrift in the city. In the present case urbanites would be exchanging cities. The skilled would be coming to use their skills, as many whites do when they migrate.

It is in this spirit that encouraging migration from urban ghettos is offered. If the new towns program and the ghetto outmigration program could be implemented simultaneously, they would strengthen one another. At the risk of seeming repetitious, it is pointed out again that the internal migration program is just one phase of a total program to enhance the quality of life in this country. Migrants from the ghetto would also be encouraged to move to the new cities. This could be especially useful as an outlet for persons of lesser skill, who could be helped and encouraged by a move. Obviously such a move on the part of currently economically defenseless persons and families is not possible without economic subsidy as well. The government subsidizes other things, why not the movement of human beings to a new environment?

Summary

Two interrelated internal migration programs have been proposed. The nation can subsidize the movement of human beings to new environments or it can subsidize the movement of industry into areas with underemployed populations. It is certainly necessary to work on all types of solutions to the general urban problem of overconcentrated populations in presently existing cities. This paper is focused on the strategy that through a process of national economic planning a number of new cities will be created that are located in areas of the lowest population density. From our knowledge of past behavior with respect to migration, we can be fairly sure that new cities with real opportunities will attract migrants from existing blighted cities and allow us to tear down slums, sometimes even to create new parks.

The second aspect of the proposed national internal migration policy would be focused on the minority group ghetto resident who at present is caught in a difficult situation. He would be encouraged through better communication of job opportunities on a national scale to seek opportunities not only in the new cities but in the many existing cities where no massive ghettos have yet developed. While this proposal does not solve the problem of mass poverty and discrimination, hopefully it would reduce some of the existing pressure in the largest cities.

Critics of these suggestions have suggested that they have more logical holes than the proverbial Swiss cheese. However, if we will keep in mind the endless suburbs and decaying centers of present-day cities, if we will further envision the ghetto high school, the ghetto apartment, and the ghetto street, we are likely to agree that somebody had better do something. This paper is presented in this spirit.

Comments

LEON H. GINSBERG

Serious questions can be raised about the assumptions that underlie the policy suggestions presented in the preceding paper by Albert J. Mayer. In addition, because the elements of Dr. Mayer's policy suggestions are based on these assumptions, one must also question his proposals. His apparent assumptions will first be identified and the discussion that follows will be organized around these points.

Underlying Assumptions

The assumptions underlying Dr. Mayer's paper appear to be these:

1. There is something inherently wrong with packing people into small land areas. Yet this is the trend in the United States today and it is a trend that will accelerate for the next thirty years, during which time there will be a 50 percent increase in the population.

2. Lack of information about employment opportunities outside metropolitan areas is a principal factor encouraging migration from rural areas and small communities to metropolitan areas and discouraging migration from those metropolitan areas to less populous regions.

3. Lack of opportunity in areas outside the major cities encourages concentration of people in these cities.

4. Large concentrations of minority group members in the ghettos of major American cities is in itself a problem that should be addressed by a national migration policy.

Projected Population Increase

In his first assumption Dr. Mayer has neglected to account for the effects of technology during the next three decades. Does anyone really know what the population of the United States will be in the year 2000? Perhaps what Dr. Mayer means is that there will be a 50 percent population increase by 2000 if present birth and mortality trends continue. But can anyone assume that these trends will continue in the face of the almost certain perfection of an effective technology for contraception that is likely to revolutionize not only population control but definitions of conventional morality, family life, and relations between the sexes? A national campaign is being conducted to inform low-income people,

181

especially public assistance recipients, about contraception. Is that not likely to affect population trends? Other factors such as disease, war, and some that may as yet be unknown may also modify Dr. Mayer's projections.

Similarly, technological developments may invalidate the notion that high population density is inherently problem-causing. It is not the concentration of many people on little land that is a problem. Rather, it is inadequate public transportation, inadequate housing, inadequate handling of solid wastes, and other technical inadequacies that make central-city living difficult. If the United States would commit the resources needed to overcome these inadequacies (the technology for dealing with them is already available), the location of most of the population in a few densely populated areas might not be a problem. In other words there may be no such thing as "undue concentrations of people," a term Dr. Mayer uses but does not define, except in terms of the physical aspects of the areas in relation to the size of their populations.

Reasons for the Rural-Urban Shift

But perhaps the most serious gap in Dr. Mayer's presentation is his failure to identify some of the reasons for the shift in the American population from rural and small communities to megalopolises. It would seem to the writer, based on inquiries conducted into the nature of rural and small community life and also on some of the other papers prepared for this institute, that there is good reason for the urbanization of the American population.

First, as Dr. Mayer implies, the American population has become urbanized because the greatest opportunities for economic security exist in metropolitan areas. Wages are higher there than in rural areas. There is a diversity of work and—more basically—there *is* work, even if it is the kind that is, to quote Dr. Mayer, ". . . spat

upon by high school dropouts." There are places in the United States where there is no work of any kind to be spat upon.

Parenthetically it should be mentioned that many rural people move to cities because of technological displacement. The man who is no longer employed because of automation of the coal industry or mechanization of agriculture is as technologically displaced as New York elevator operators. One may argue, in fact, that automation has contributed to unemployment in rural areas more dramatically than it has in the cities, a fact seldom mentioned in discussions of the effects of automation.

Second, public services are likely to be better in the cities, especially in the large cities of the East and West coasts. Certainly there are inadequacies in the health and welfare programs of metropolitan areas, and it is doubtful that one could find large numbers of people who have moved to cities primarily to receive those services. However, America's rural and small communities frequently offer no services whatever to the poor or the sick. People are simply less likely to starve and less likely to go without medical attention in the cities than they are in the rural South, the isolated communities of Appalachia, or the unprofitable farming areas of the plains. Thus the cities attract people because of their seeming higher degree of humanity.

Third, in line with the last statement, people have learned that the cities are generally more humane than rural areas, especially toward minority group members. The frequent charges of brutality made against large-city police forces cannot be questioned, but in comparison to law enforcement in many rural areas, metropolitan police behavior is genteel. Continuing discrimination in rural law enforcement, employment, housing, and education is oppressive to minority group members who refuse to remain in a subservient position. Therefore they move.

Rural and small-community nonminority

and nonpoor people also move to the cities. The cities are exciting. There are new people to meet, different kinds of work, escape from relatives and a locked-in social structure, cultural and social activities— all the things that make city life attractive. The brightest young men and women in rural and small communities frequently express their postcollege ambitions in terms of moving to a city—Washington, New York, San Francisco, Dallas—any place that is not home. American cities are perceived as superior to the countryside by both the rich and the poor. In many ways their perceptions are correct.

As some of the other papers prepared for this institute make clear, there are many reasons for rural-urban migration. While some have emotional overtones, few of the causes of migration are nonrational. Thus any national policy for dealing with migration would have to deal with the inadequacies of the rural areas too, a point that will be reexamined later and a point that is partially handled by Dr. Mayer's suggestions for the creation of new cities.

The Problem of Ghettos

But it is Dr. Mayer's assumptions about ghettos that cause the greatest concern. He seems to imply that large concentrations of minority group members—he mentions blacks—cause the problems of the ghettos. He says that enriching the staffs of ghetto schools does not change the fact that ghetto high school graduates will be functionally illiterate, that ". . . now numerous studies of urban schools bear out this fact." He says that ghetto housing, even when rebuilt and renewed is ". . . in a few years . . . battered, littered, crawling with vermin."

Dr. Mayer's diagnosis seems to be that too many blacks in one place is in itself a problem. His solution is to ". . . decrease the concentration of lower-class persons, including blacks, in the dilapidated city ghettos and distribute them more equally throughout the country. . . ." He assumes

that redistributing blacks into a number of areas, thereby ending their majority status in the ghettos, would alleviate racial problems, which he tends to define in terms of black unrest and disturbances. He says that although many blacks would want to stay where they are, " . . . there should be considerable numbers who would welcome a change, a release from the pressures of a ghettoized existence."

The essence of Dr. Mayer's comments seems to be that blacks function more adequately and with less turmoil when they are a small segment of a population of whites rather than the major or total population of a ghetto. That is the kind of argument that some would call racist. It assumes (without examining other factors) that large aggregates of blacks create problems. It proposes a kind of voluntary relocation plan that some would call a program of "black removal" and that sounds like Phase One in the popularly rumored plans for black internment camps throughout the United States.

One would have to ask Dr. Mayer if he views as problematic large concentrations of white people. Or if he assumes that the smaller ghettos of Phoenix, Arizona, and Eugene, Oregon, are qualitatively different from the larger ghettos of Harlem and Watts. Or if he has a plan to ensure the integration into the general population of the black migrants to his new cities or older small cities. Or if he has really examined the causes of ghettos.

The writer would suggest that the causes of ghettos and the reasons for their status as social problems are rooted in a number of factors, but that the major cause is discrimination against minorities. Discrimination in housing, in education (before moves to cities and within cities themselves), in public transportation patterns (making access to adequate jobs from the ghettos impossible), and in employment all make discrimination against blacks and other minorities the central domestic problem of the United States today. And even when overt discrimination is alleviated, the unwillingness of the American people to provide sufficient funds to overcome the results of past discrimination perpetuates the problems into the foreseeable future. Discrimination leads, among other things, to poverty. And poverty leads to discrimination.

The writer suggests that there is nothing wrong with large concentrations of blacks —if those concentrations are created by choice. As for living conditions in the ghettos, it ought to be clear to everyone that most people in the United States have economic aspirations that are middle class, at least. Few people choose to live in squalor or in danger of violence or with inadequate educational opportunities for their children.

A much larger and more important problem than the distribution of minority group members throughout the United States is the further humanization of the nation so that minority groups will no longer face the economic, educational, social, and housing discrimination they now face almost everywhere. In fact it may be the existence of larger groups of minority people, especially blacks, functioning as political blocs in the major cities that may force an end to discrimination. At this point, however, the ghettos of Harlem and Watts are no more severe in their conditions than the smaller ghettos of Phoenix, Charleston, West Virginia, or Austin, Texas. They are simply more visible. In many cases they are probably less destructive of the human spirit than minority group life in the smaller cities and rural areas. In general the large city ghettos represent an improvement for minority group migrants.

Proposals

Dr. Mayer has two basic proposals intended to solve the nation's problems as he views them: (1) the creation of new cities and (2) a national job clearinghouse.

Creation of New Cities

Essentially Dr. Mayer proposes that private industry and government combine to develop a series of cities with populations of about half a million that would alleviate overcrowding in metropolitan areas, use the lands of the United States more efficiently, and generally help overcome the intense problems facing the major cities. He suggests the development of a Bureau of Internal Migration that would do some of the basic planning and organizing of these new cities. Although Dr. Mayer is not terribly clear on this point, he seems to imply that it is unnecessary to start from scratch with these cities. He visualizes helping existing small areas of population grow.

All of his proposals in this context seem reasonable and desirable. Some agencies, among them the Appalachian Regional Commission, are already dealing with the concept of "growth center." It is likely that the technical skills needed for planning such a program are already available. There may even already be plans in the offices of dozens of professors of city planning and architecture, who regularly give such assignments to their students.

However, two questions should be raised. The first need only relate back to an earlier comment in this discussion. That is, are there inherent problems in large cities or has the United States simply been unwilling to commit the resources necessary for resolving those that exist? Is the value of low population density more important than the cultural values of a metropolitan area such as New York City that cannot be duplicated in any city of half a million population?

The second question can be channeled into a crucial research proposal. How can one do what is proposed? How can Congress be sold on the idea? How can the designated growth centers be encouraged to commit themselves to the orderly planning inherent in such a proposal? How can industry be motivated to locate plants and factories in line with the development of new cities?

Presuming that the new cities idea is viable, the difficult questions, for which few have answers, are related to implementation. It is not so much a question of what the policy ought to be as of how it can come to be. The knowledge gaps are not in designing ideal models. They are in effecting public policy so that those models can be implemented. The political questions, more than any others, require careful research. Until social science knows how to get things done, society is likely to continue facing its familiar problems surrounded by cabinets full of utopian plans that are never even publicly debated, much less implemented.

National Job Clearinghouse

Dr. Mayer's second proposal is that a national clearinghouse on employment opportunities be established. Again the proposal seems quite satisfactory.

The writer, however, would raise two questions. First, the proposal, as stated by Dr. Mayer, implies that the problem of the cities is the ghetto and that the problem of the ghetto is the black. The main purpose of the clearinghouse seems to be to redistribute the black population. The objections to that have already been noted.

Second, is the plan responsive to the real problems? Any Sunday *New York Times* help wanted section seems to confirm the existence of a labor shortage in New York City. Anyone living in a large city who is a teacher, mechanic, or carpenter ought to be able to find work in that city.

The manpower problem is not one of redistributing skilled people of any ethnic group. The problem is a lack of skilled manpower in all areas. And that problem has several dimensions such as the discrimination of some labor unions against minority group members who want to enter

apprenticeship programs, inadequate trade schools that fail to prepare students for employment, and the arbitrary imposition of educational standards such as high school graduation for jobs that need no such standards. People with skills that are salable in Eugene, Oregon, probably do not have to leave their homes to find work.

Dr. Mayer says ". . . if a black man employed in an office job at General Motors in Detroit leaves for a job in Portland, Oregon, GM will search widely to find a suitable replacement. Thus additional opportunities are created." He may be right, but why would he not be just as right if the situation were reversed? Would not the Portland employer have been searching widely for an employee too? Or if a man left Portland for the job in Detroit, would not an opportunity have been created in Portland? Shuffling employed people around does not seem to be a solution. People who are in demand in both Detroit and Portland are not the problem.

Issues for Consideration

It would seem that the essential dimensions of the problem are not covered in Dr. Mayer's paper and therefore that his policy proposals are not responsive to the issues. The issues that the writer would suggest for more productive consideration are these:

1. How may life in rural and small communities be modified in a way that will make it possible for those who prefer to stay where they are to do so without facing poverty and discrimination?

2. How can the larger problem of discrimination against minority groups be overcome in the cities as well as the rural areas so that all people will have access to adequate housing, a quality education, and a meaningful job?

3. How can society be convinced to provide extensive programs of job training so that the person without marketable skills

can have an adequate job wherever he chooses to live?

4. How can American society be convinced that an adequate national program of income maintenance is required?

It would seem to the writer that these are the crucial issues that must be addressed in any national migration policy. All areas of the country must be humanized—discrimination must be alleviated, the victims of discrimination must be helped to catch up, and there must be strict enforcement of the laws that forbid discrimination. And, further, there must be an adequate income maintenance program for those who are not employable. The suggestions offered by Dr. Mayer do not deal with these concerns.

Rejoinder

ALBERT J. MAYER

The two coasts of the United States are piling up populations at an enormous rate. The estimated U.S. population of 300 million by the year 2000 is a Bureau of the Census estimate, based on current birthrates. Unless zero population growth is achieved immediately, this projection will be realized.

The present distribution of population in the United States is still much a function of factors no longer relevant and of local resources. For instance the largest cities are located on the coasts or on rivers because the oceans and waterways were the principal means of transportation at the time they were established. We now live in a different world.

Some cities are nearly inoperable even now and may shortly pass over the line of viability. The fact that our cities are in desperate shape can be illustrated all too easily. A determined move toward redistributing the population and thereby relieving some of this crowding must be considered.

Many inner-city students, whether white or black, are receiving insufficient education to enable them to function well in our culture, to get a job that will pay a good wage. They may be able to make a living when they graduate, but events of the last ten years have shown that this is not sufficient. People have been protesting the situation.

This problem is exacerbated with respect to the black population; it is not just the black population that is in trouble. And the situation will get worse. We need more than new towns like Columbia or Reston. We need new cities of perhaps half a million people with a growth expectation of a million or more people.

It has been said that if the concentrations of blacks are reduced some of their political power base is destroyed. But I would argue that most of the black people in this country at the present time are not disaffected from the system. Probably they should be, and if we continue on our present course, the great majority will be— along with a large proportion of younger people of all groups. I don't think I'm a racist. I don't see the black problem as being a black problem—the problem is with the whites, not the blacks. Nevertheless, it has resulted in certain realities.

If the overcrowding of cities continues there will be a revolution in this country. In terms of physical violence, the blacks and the "third-world" people are going to lose, because they are vastly outnumbered. But this is not what we want to see happen in the United States.

Therefore I gave particular attention to the idea that there would be more opportunities for black persons in the new cities. I based this idea on such experiences as that of Phoenix, which has a small black population and is a relative improvement over cities like New York and Chicago, despite the fact that the income of blacks in relation to the white population is not as high as it might be in those cities. Yet the life of the average black person in Phoenix is better. The schooling is better and so are opportunities. Not nearly good enough, perhaps, but better.

I was not arguing, as Dr. Ginsberg seems to think, for a sort of ruralization of the United States. With high-speed air and ground transportation there need be no isolation consequent to a more equitable distribution of the population in smaller cities. And I do not feel that cities as such are all bad. They have given us much. But I would like to see the quality of life improved.

As far as the physical frontiers of the nation are concerned, they have been closed for a long time. As far as our economic frontier is concerned, it has been devoted largely to increasing consumerization. To me these proposed new cities represent new frontiers, something we desperately need to recover our national spirit.

Blacks were not given much consideration in the early days of this nation. In the creation of the proposed new frontier they will have their share.

Migration, Residential Mobility, and Community Health Policy

SIMON SLAVIN

This paper is concerned with the ways in which migration and mobility may affect the allocation and delivery of health services in American communities.[1] While the economic consequences of population movement have been subjected to considerable study, little attention has been given to parallel health consequences. The association of spatial movement and mental health has been examined at great length. Similar study must be made of the hazards to physical health that accompany resettlement and that result from ignorance about or lack of skill in locating health services, local insurance and residence requirements, the drain on the economic resources of a family attendant to displacement, and people's greater vulnerability owing to changed environmental conditions and stress.

Health policy needs to be based on a consideration of the essential characteristics of population movement and the hu-

man response it engenders. What follows are a review of certain salient aspects of the problem and an attempt to draw inferences for action from the data thus identified.

The American Situation

It has long been recognized that the United States is a nation of migrants, former migrants, and descendants of migrants. The consequences for public social policy, while frequently noted, have been little studied.[2] This is nowhere more true than in the health field. The National Committee on Vital and Health Statistics of the U.S. Public Health Service recently noted "the diverse but little explored relations between vital processes, the movements of people, and health."[3] The cumu-

---

[1] The U.S. Bureau of the Census classifies changes of residence within counties as short-distance mobility and those from one county to another as migration.

[2] Russell H. Kurtz, "Foreword," in Philip E. Ryan, *Migration and Social Welfare* (New York: Russell Sage Foundation, 1940), p. vii.

[3] *Migration, Vital and Health Statistics* (Washington, D.C.: U.S. Department of Health, Education & Welfare, Public Health Service, November 1968), p. 1.

lative impact of migration and, more recently, the abolition of residence requirements for public welfare assistance have highlighted the issues implicit in the widespread movement of people from one part of the country to another and from one residential area to another in local communities.[4]

While one American in five changes residence annually, the bulk of these are short-distance moves and take place within the same county. Only one move in six is across state lines, although by 1950 all the states had received at least ten percent of their population from other states.[5] According to the 1960 census, of the entire population over 5 years of age about one-third were no longer living in the state of their birth. A roughly similar proportion of all heads of families were born in the area where they were currently living, although a quarter of these lived elsewhere at some time.[6] Some indication of residential instability is suggested by the fact that about one-third of all moves made between 1950 and 1962 were by people who had lived one year or less in the places they were leaving. About one-fourth of all moves since 1950 were returns to areas of former residence. Some three-quarters of all urban citizens lived in different places in 1950 as compared to 1940.[7]

Two facts seem thus inevitably to intrude in discussions of spatial mobility: its widespread character and the predominance of short-distance movement. As shall be seen, given the social character of those who participate in the latter, important conclusions affecting health policy will have to be drawn.

In recent decades there have been major movements of southern blacks and Puerto Ricans to central cities, especially those located in the North. Yet in spite of this massive geographic shift, there were nearly 700,000 more black residents in southern states in 1960 than in 1940.[8] There seem to be more blacks in the South each decade. Thus the reservoir for continued movement of blacks to urban areas seems well filled, suggesting that similar movements might well be expected in subsequent years. Such migration involves population segments that are highly vulnerable with respect to health conditions. These persons tend to be poor, relatively unskilled, and to have many health deficits. Their prior inability to purchase health care, its lack of availability, or their inadequate use of established resources, together with widespread nutritional deficits have resulted in physical conditions that have frequently gone long unattended.

Paralleling this regional redistribution of population are the shift of whites to outer areas of cities and, more recently, migrations between metropolitan areas. The historic movement from rural to urban areas seems now to have been replaced as a central process largely by intermetropolitan population exchanges.[9] Increasingly the farm-born are moving to nonmetropolitan areas, while those born in large cities are relocating to other parts of metropolitan areas.[10] Some significance should be attached to the finding in Chicago

---

[4] It should be pointed out that mobility rates for persons on public assistance for a year or less are close to that of the population as a whole. Long-term public welfare cases are generally unlikely to move. See *The Geographical Mobility of Labor* (Washington, D.C.: U.S. Department of Commerce, Area Development Administration, September 1964), p. 27.

[5] Henry S. Shryock, Jr., *Population Mobility Within the United States* (Chicago: University of Chicago Press, 1964), p. 411.

[6] *The Geographical Mobility of Labor*, p. 7.

[7] Peter Rossi, *Why Families Move* (Glencoe, Ill.: Free Press, 1955), p. 1.

[8] William F. Ogburn and Meyer F. Nimkoff, *Sociology* (4th ed.; Boston: Houghton Mifflin Co., 1964), p. 357.

[9] *Migration, Vital and Health Statistics*, p. 10.

[10] Karl E. Taeuber, "Cohort Population Redistribution and the Urban Hierarchy," in *Millbank Memorial Fund Quarterly*, Vol. 43, No. 4, Part I (October 1965), p. 458.

that, with respect to given characteristics, native urbanites resemble rural farm migrants more closely than they do migrants from other cities.[11]

Significant Variables

While it is clear that the extent, character, and cumulative impact of mobility and migration require a response with respect to social and health policy, the general phenomenon provides few clues for specific action. Far from constituting a homogeneous population, migration involves a complex of categories requiring specific diagnostic study and differentiation for the effective planning of health service delivery.[12] It is necessary to disaggregate the data, selecting the most significant variables for special study and concentrating on the most sensitive aspects of the social and psychological correlates of social movement. By itself migration of individuals and families may represent no special social or health problem. Those who have ample personal and financial resources and who move quite willingly from one area to another may require relatively little specialized community provision.

Even a cursory review of the data suggests that migrants differ from one another, that differences abound from one part of the country to another, and that in different decades migrants represent social phenomena that are similar in some respects yet markedly different in others. The task of analysis, then, is to make distinctions and to specify social, psychological, and physical conditions that are most useful for the planning task. Such diagnostic insight is further complicated by a little-explored aspect of the problem: When do social effects

of migration become dissipated? In a word, when does migrant status end and normal residence begin? Finally, analysis is complicated by the fact that neighborhoods in urban areas are themselves mobile. Areas that receive those who are mobile shift and there are accompanying changes in the loci of basic institutions. This latter fact, of course, has an important bearing on health service and its delivery.

The following are some of the more salient elements that bear on the social definition of migration:

1. Young families—that is, couples with young children—are the most mobile of all households in areas where migrants settle. Mobility tends to be greatest when families experience their greatest growth and especially when they have just increased in size.[13] Migration generally, and especially from rural areas and small cities to large cities, is a phenomenon of the young.

2. There is a strong ethnic imprint on mobility, especially in urban areas. Not only have blacks and Puerto Ricans replaced substantial numbers of out-migrant whites in recent decades—a process likely to continue for some time to come—but movement of families within a city is much more marked among nonwhites than among the white population. Thus Lavell found that between 1955 and 1960, 45 percent of nonwhites had moved at least once within the city of Philadelphia, as compared to 28 percent of the whites.[14]

3. The place of migrants in the social class structure has a marked bearing on the social effects of changed residence. Inner urban areas provide points of entry for large numbers of low-status in-migrants and are the scene for intracity movement largely stimulated by urban redevelopment

---

[11] Ronald Freedman, *Recent Migration to Chicago* (Chicago: University of Chicago Press, 1950), p. 209.

[12] *See* Martin H. Keeler and Mintauts M. Vitols, "Migration and Schizophrenia in North Carolina Negroes," *American Journal of Orthopsychiatry,* Vol. 33, No. 3 (April 1963), p. 556.

[13] Rossi, op. cit., pp. 122, 180.

[14] Martha Lavell, *Philadelphia's Non-White Population* (Philadelphia: Commission on Human Relations, December 1962). *See also* Shryock, op. cit., p. 423.

programs. Much in-migration is a consequence of unemployment or the threat to continued employment. According to a Department of Commerce study this explains about one move in five.[15] The mobility rate for employed males over 14 years of age is about half that of the unemployed. In addition to location in the social structure, upward, downward, or horizontal social mobility accompanying residential mobility helps determine the social consequences of change in physical location.

4. Ethnic and socioeconomic variables have a strong relationship among migrant populations. Thus Struening et al., in their study of two boroughs of New York City, found that "migrants tend to move into health areas with a relatively large number of persons belonging to ethnic minority groups, and with low educational levels, low family incomes and high welfare rates." They conclude that "it appears likely that a very large proportion of migrants are drawn from minority groups with low economic status."[16]

5. Migrants differ in their perception and experience of the permanence of their settlement. Some remain only briefly, hoping to better their living conditions, others plan to move on but remain, and still others hope to sink permanent roots in their new neighborhoods. Short- versus long-term residence is an important factor in assessing the consequences of mobility.

6. The personal and social consequences of voluntary as opposed to involuntary mobility are vastly different. The readiness of people to move or relocate is a significant determinant of their subsequent capacity to adapt to the demands of their new environment.[17] Much intra-area movement is coerced and creates patterns of disruption that inevitably demand a social response. Motivational distinctions are an important aspect of social diagnosis.

7. Whether people on the move settle in areas populated by friends or strangers similarly determines to a large degree their capacity to adjust to their new communities; the absence of cultural, interpersonal, or family ties makes this task vastly more difficult. The institution of the *landsmanschaften*, or groups of people from the same hometown, absorbs much of the shock of change. The absence of such mechanisms or their analogues creates distinctive social problems.

8. Migrants with high or low employment potential present special issues to the communities that receive them.

9. Areas of origin and of destination place a distinctive mark on the social definition of migration. Migrants from different parts of the country differ in significant ways, as do migrants from similar areas but who are located differentially on the rural-urban continuum.[18]

10. A certain degree of transiency grows out of the phenomenon of the migratory counterstream: "Large migration streams tend to have large counterstreams."[19] Thus some understanding of net and gross migration in specific areas would appear to be important.

11. While the bulk of migration has economic roots, most frequently being motivated by an attempt to improve family income, many people change residence for health-related reasons. They may be seeking better medical services, want more

---

[15] *The Geographical Mobility of Labor*, p. 13.
[16] Elmer L. Struening, Judith G. Rabkin, and Harris B. Peck, "Migration and Ethnic Membership in Relation to Social Problems," p. 23. Paper presented at the Research Institute on the Social Welfare Consequences of Migration and Residential Movement, November 4–7, 1968, San Juan, Puerto Rico. (Mimeographed.)

[17] Mark Fried, "Transitional Functions of Working Class Communities: Implications for Forced Relocation," in Mildred B. Kantor, ed., *Mobility and Mental Health* (Springfield, Ill.: Charles C Thomas, 1965), p. 159.
[18] *See* Leonard Blumberg, *Migration as a Program Area for Urban Social Work* (Philadelphia: Urban League of Philadelphia, July 1958), p. 11.
[19] Shryock, op. cit., p. 282.

congenial weather conditions, or wish to settle in areas more suited to specific health problems, such as asthma.

12. Finally, two patterns of migration are so distinctive as to call forth quite specialized social and health responses. Retirement migration, which seems to have increased markedly in recent years, and the migratory farmwork system present quite distinctive social phenomena, especially with respect to health needs.

These aspects of migration—that is, young families, low economic status, and so on—suggest some specialized approaches to health planning based on similar characteristics in the general population. For example, since so large a part of the migrant population comes from and goes to poverty areas, many of the same health problems and policies are applicable to them as to the poor. The factor of residential instability compounds these problems and calls for some special emphases in addition to the same general provisions as for the category as a whole.

The association of poverty, especially among minority ethnic groups, with negative health indexes is too well known to warrant elaboration here.[20] A similar association between selected health indicators and ethnic mobility populations will be pointed out later.

Individual and Social Effects

While there seems to be general agreement that migration and mobility have social and personal consequences of substantial significance, there is considerable question as to their character and extent. It is difficult to make unqualified judgments since so much of the empirical evidence is contradictory. Yet some patterns

of migration and mobility seem to exact a marked human toll, whereas others may be either neutral or positive in their effects.

A Crisis of Transition

Evidence of a crisis of transition growing out of the disruption of viable social networks does seem to be available in abundance.[21] Fried found that dislocation from Boston's West End led to intense personal suffering for the greatest number even in spite of moderately successful adaptation to the total situation.[22] Gans similarly found that disruption of the same neighborhood through the destruction of a functioning social system exacted social and psychological losses, especially for the aged, among whom a number of deaths were recorded.[23] In their study of migration characteristics of two boroughs of New York City, Struening and his co-workers found that the number of migrants as compared with the number of relatively permanent residents played an important role in predicting the extent of physical illness, mental illness, family disruption, poor socioeconomic conditions, deviant behavior, and reproductive casualty (e.g., premature birth, infant mortality, and the like).[24]

The conclusion that migration from the South and from Puerto Rico was strongly related to divorce and separation confirmed early findings in Philadelphia.[25] As for other aspects of social disorganization, evi-

---

[20] *See*, for example, Monroe Lerner, "Social Differences in Physical Health," in John Kosa, Aaron Antonovsky, and Irving K. Zola, *Poverty and Health* (Cambridge, Mass.: Harvard University Press, 1969).

[21] Robert J. Kleiner and Keith Lovald, "An Overview of Research on the 'Inner City.'" Unpublished paper, undated. (Mimeographed.)

[22] Marc Fried, "Grieving for a Lost Home," in Leonard J. Duhl, ed., *The Urban Condition* (New York: Basic Books, 1963), p. 167.

[23] Herbert J. Gans, *The Urban Villagers* (New York: Free Press of Glencoe, 1962), p. 320.

[24] Op. cit, p. 37.

[25] Leonard Blumberg found that 11 percent of women who left their husbands migrated. Op. cit., p. 6.

dence on the association of migration with
drug addiction and suicide is inconclu-
sive.[26] Different studies come to divergent
conclusions. The same is apparently true
of studies of its relation to juvenile delinquency.[27]

Mobility and Mental Illness

The social problem that seems to have
received the most study in relation to
mobility and migration is mental illness.
It is also an area of research with the
most bewildering array of contradictory
findings. Early studies, like those of Malzberg and Lee, Faris and Dunham, and
Tietze, Lemkau, and Cooper, suggested a
marked association between migration and
high mobility rates.[28] Others failed to find
such an association.[29] Leighton and her
colleagues reported no observable relation
between migration and mental health, except for individuals who had moved three
or more times before they were 21 years
of age.[30]

----

[26] John C. Ball and William M. Bates, "Mi-
gration and Residential Mobility of Narcotic
Drug Addicts," *Social Problems*, Vol. 14, No. 1
(Summer 1966), pp. 56–69; Ronald W. Maris,
Social Forces in Urban Suicide (Homewood, Ill.:
Dorsey Press, 1969), pp. 142–144.

[27] *See* Leonard Savitz, *Delinquency and Migration* (Philadelphia: Commission on Human
Relations, 1960); and Bernard Lander, *Towards
an Understanding of Juvenile Delinquency* (New
York: Columbia University Press, 1954), p. 38.
A high delinquency rate is apparently associated
with high horizontal mobility unaccompanied by
vertical mobility.

[28] Benjamin Malzberg and Everett S. Lee, *Mi-
gration and Mental Disease* (New York: Social
Science Research Council, 1956); Robert E. Faris
and H. Warren Dunham, *Mental Disorders in
Urban Areas* (Chicago: University of Chicago
Press, 1939); Christopher Tietze, Paul Lemkau,
and Marcia Cooper, "Personality Disorder and
Spatial Mobility," *American Journal of Sociology*,
Vol. 48, No. 1 (July 1942), pp. 29–39.

[29] *See*, for example, Seymour Parker and Robert
J. Kleiner, *Mental Illness in the Urban Negro
Community* (New York: Free Press, 1966).

[30] Dorothea C. Leighton, John S. Harding,
David B. Macklin, Allister M. Macmillan, and

The situation seems much clearer when
selected aspects of mobility are examined
in relation to mental health. The following
conclusions seem especially relevant to the
development of approaches and strategies
intended to deal with the negative impact
of migration and mobility:

1. The early findings in Baltimore that
high rates of mental disturbance are associated with intracity mobility [31] were recently confirmed in Philadelphia by Parker
and Kleiner, who found that the mentally
ill showed more intracity mobility than
their non-mentally ill community counterparts.[32] While one is inclined to think
that the negative effects of residential movement must be positively correlated with distance, it is clear that some of the most
hazardous circumstances flow out of relatively short-distance mobility. This is
understandable in light of the strong orientation to localism among low-income populations. Moves of even relatively short
distances disrupt social and familial networks and tend to break institutional bonds,
leading to a sense of isolation and social
withdrawal.

2. It is easy to underestimate the negative impact of interurban mobility. The
Philadelphia study found that among
blacks moving to the city, rates of mental
illness were generally higher for northern
migrants than for southern migrants.[33]
Given the recent trend toward intercity mobility, this observation is especially significant.

3. The effects of mobility on mental
health seem to vary according to location
and movement on the status ladder. The
occupationally downwardly mobile represent the highest risks and the upwardly
mobile the lowest. However, with increas-

Alexander H. Leighton, *The Character of Danger*
(New York: Basic Books, 1963), p. 301.

[31] Tietze et al., op. cit., p. 39.

[32] Op. cit., p. 235.

[33] Ibid., p. 333.

ing position on the status hierarchy, illness rates tend to increase for the upwardly mobile and to decrease for the downwardly mobile.[34] Fried similarly found a marked relationship between class status and depth of grief following forced displacement as a result of urban renewal: the higher the status, the smaller the proportion of severe grief.[35]

4. Rates of mental illness of migrants as indicated by hospitalization seem to be largely affected by the cultural character of the communities in which they settle. Rates are high when the cultural differences are great and migrants are unable to become attached to groups and institutions similar to those they left behind. An example is found in a recent study of Chinese migrants in Canada. The minority group with the lowest hospitalization rate of all minorities in British Columbia was the Chinese, who had settled there in large numbers. In Ontario, where the Chinese population was sparse, they had the highest hospitalization rate of all ethnic groups.[36] Settling among strangers apparently creates substantial emotional and psychological strains.

5. While considerable evidence suggests that movement from a rural to an urban environment creates individual and social difficulties in adjustment, the same is true of rural-rural and urban-urban migration. Other social and cultural variables play a part in determining whether the mental health consequences of such movement will be benign or malign.

6. The age of the person moving and the frequency of moves seem strongly associated with the prevalence of psychiatric disorder. Psychiatric risks increase positively with the number of moves made by persons under 20 years of age.[37] Since migration tends to involve the young disproportionately, the deleterious effect of migration during childhood and adolescence on an individual's subsequent mental health suggests that concentration should be on the problems of children and youths in mobility-prone areas.

7. There is some evidence that sex differences play a role in precipitating psychiatric difficulties among migrants. Parker and Kleiner found that southern male migrants tend to be hospitalized more frequently than native males.[38]

8. The most hazardous time in a migrant's residence in a new area is during the first year. Wilson and his colleagues found a negative correlation between migrants' length of stay and the rates of hospitalization for mental illness, with most hospitalizations occurring within a year of the move.[39] The early stages of new residence obviously require the greatest amount of social provision.

Other Health Circumstances

There is some evidence to suggest that the relationship that obtains between mental health and mobility also characterizes other health circumstances. While little appears in the literature on the association between mobility and physical health, the study by Struening and his colleagues referred to earlier provides some relevant data.[40] They examined infant deaths and premature births in two boroughs of New York City, finding both indexes strongly linked to the number of migrants from the South (largely black) and Puerto Rico. If one accepts Lerner's judgment that the most sensitive index of health conditions

[34] Ibid., p. 335.

[35] "Grieving for a Lost Home," p. 157.

[36] H. B. M. Murphy, "Migration and the Major Mental Disorders," in Kantor, ed., op. cit., p. 25.

[37] Leighton et al., op. cit., p. 485.

[38] Op. cit., p. 225.

[39] Arnold Wilson, Gordon Saver, and Peter A. Lachenbruch, "Residential Mobility and Psychiatric Help-Seeking," *American Journal of Psychiatry*, Vol. 121 (May 1965), p. 1109.

[40] Op. cit., pp. 29–31.

within a community is the infant mortality rate, then clearly migratory status and health hazards bear strongly on one another.[41]

Planning and Policy Implications

Several patterns of residential movement and some salient characteristics of mobility and of the mobile have been identified, and some especially vulnerable segments of this population have been pointed to. What follows is an effort to suggest some directions that seem indicated in planning effective health services that are responsive to the needs of people on the move.

General Considerations

What is discernible currently with respect to population mobility is only a prelude to what should be anticipated in the decades ahead, just as present circumstances are heir to the cumulative trends of the recent and remote past. The fluidity of settlement has, through accretion, dramatically transformed the ethnic and cultural profile of American urban areas, creating a social situation that is unique among the developed countries of the world. The descendants of four million slaves brought to the South continue to move northward and westward. A careful student of mobility patterns leads to the inevitable conclusion that because of both social and economic factors, it is likely that the prevailing stream of black migration will long continue to be out of the South. Figuratively, the large cities of the North and West still represent a New World for the southern black.[42]

Given the relatively stable mobility rates in recent decades, it is reasonable to anticipate continued population changes in directions similar to those now observable.[43]

Certain areas of a city are likely to be sought out as points of entry for people leaving the South and Puerto Rico, as well as for those who leave one urban area to settle in another. Redevelopment programs that respond to urban obsolescence will continue to scatter people from one section to another in given cities, with all the consequences that follow disruption of social and institutional networks. New sections of cities can be expected to become areas of new settlement, thus compounding personal mobility with area mobility. These areas will continue to be populated by low-income segments of definable ethnic groups—precisely those persons who are likely to require a maximum of social and health services—and yet will provide a minimum of resources to make such services effectively available. These observations are especially significant since much that is problematic in migration with respect to health considerations affects segments of the urban low-income, poorly educated, unskilled minority group population.

In a word, in the light of the negative impact of mobility on mental and physical health, the planning and policy issues that are currently troublesome are likely to become even more pronounced and difficult with the accumulated trends in the years ahead. Some clues to the institutional response potential of communities are found in Rossi's study of the movement of families in one major city.[44] He identified four major modes of adjustment made by organizations in attempting to cushion the impact of mobility: (1) modification of organizational structure, (2) changes in location and geographic orientation, (3) changes in approaches to population segments, and (4) initiation of special activities designed to meet specific problems in dealing with a population influx. Each of these strategies will need to be adapted in health planning, as well as other considerations that are peculiarly related to the na-

---

[41] Op. cit., p. 91.
[42] Shryock, op. cit., p. 420.
[43] Ibid., p. 411.

[44] Op. cit., pp. 60–63.

ture of health problems. The following are suggested areas for planning and policy development intended to respond to the challenges posed by a mobile society.

Universal Provision of Health Care

Perhaps the first order of priority for a fluid population is the establishment of a system of universal health provision as a matter of right. The widespread character of mobility and migration makes local administration of health care obsolete. The skewed distribution of health resources, including medical personnel, tends to an undersupply of health services in areas where migrants tend most to settle, as it does in poverty sectors as a whole. A universal payment and delivery mechanism that gives people in these areas the resources with which to purchase health services would create its own supply and thus deal with a first essential—the availability of appropriate services. Voluntary insurance plans tend to differ from state to state. Such variations can succumb only to universal provision of resources.

The recent past has been witness to considerable discussion concerning universal health insurance plans. It will be important for such plans to include provisions for federal financing of coverage for those who cannot afford insurance and to provide for adequate publicity so that people who are transient or irregularly employed both know about the available health care system and make practical use of it.

Whatever forms a compulsory health insurance system assumes, it will be important, in the words of Wilbur Cohen, to see them as "public utilities that are oriented toward the consumer, rather than doctors and hospitals." [45] While continuity and comprehensiveness of care are not easily achieved by migrants, the worst pitfalls of discontinuity can be alleviated

---

[45] Quoted in the *New York Times*, September 28, 1969.

through a national comprehensive and compulsory health service system.

Problems of Delivery

The vast amount of movement between contiguous counties, especially from the central city to the suburbs, puts the planning spotlight on the metropolitan area. The shift from white to nonwhite neighborhoods as the white suburban exodus results in black and Puerto Rican population concentration has dramatically changed central cities. The peripheries of cities seem much more stable than the inner cores, yet the latter are where past generations placed major hospital facilities as well as highly specialized services. These hospitals are now largely dilapidated and often in chronic crisis. The highly specialized services are used more frequently by those on the periphery than by the inner-city resident.

The changed relationship of the local neighborhoods to the metropolitan area as a whole needs to be translated into planning terms, and the transiency of geographic areas to be related to a similar transiency of services. With relatively little capital outlay neighborhood health centers may be able to serve migrant populations more readily than huge agglomerations of outmoded facilities and be more readily shifted to accommodate changes in character and concentration of inner-urban populations. They can be located more closely to centers of migrant settlement, more readily reflect specific needs and cultural continuity, involve affected people in planning and generating service goals, provide comprehensive rather than fragmented care for a person-and-family-centered service, and be moved, discontinued, or changed as the social environment changes its character. The significance of contiguity of service resources can hardly be exaggerated in the light of the strong localistic orientation of the migrant poor once they reach an area of settlement.

The closeness of the relationship between decentralized local units and major centers of health care is, of course, central to their effectiveness. Complex laboratory, radiological, and other diagnostic services available in central institutions need to be linked to the neighborhood centers, perhaps through a network of health stations. More experience in evaluating existing programs and in establishing utilization ratios (such as between centralized and local resources) will suggest ways in which optimum use of limited means can be adapted to specific migrant needs. What seems hardly in question is the advisability of looking at the system of health services in its metropolitan context and of viewing the relationship of urban periphery to urban center and of diverse elements of the urban core to one another.

Mobile communities and mobile populations will best be served if a *community* emphasis provides a central organizing principle underlying health planning. The current health care system is often implicitly based on the needs of the producers rather than those of the consumers. The demands of medical schools and hospitals, as defined by those in control of specialty study and treatment, become practical levers for the distribution of health resources, frequently to the detriment of treatment of the more common, if less interesting, health problems of people living in adjacent communities. In the words of White: "The medical care establishment tends to distribute its skills and knowledge more in accordance with selective individual utilization of services than with the collectively perceived needs and expressed demands of the community." [46] Organizational priorities should follow community priorities, not vice versa.

One value flowing from community-based facilities is their potential for monitoring and feedback. Institutions that are close to the people make it possible to establish organizational mechanisms for collecting responses concerning the adequacy of services as perceived by those using the services. The current demand for local community control of service institutions is a movement in this direction. One means of relating people to services is to give them and their representatives an organizational stake in the planning and administration of the services. The changing realities of health needs among mobile populations will best be reflected in a community rather than an institutional focus.

An important aid in spotlighting mobile neighborhoods as targets for health services lies in the ways in which community data are gathered and processed. The Committee on Vital and Health Statistics strongly recommended that health questions be included in population surveys and, similarly, that mobility questions be included in health surveys.[47] Continuous monitoring of data relating the two will facilitate the adaptation of services to needs of an ever changing population group. With respect to individual families on the move, some centralization of data processing will assist the continuity of service, at least for the short-distance mobiles who represent a substantial proportion of the total mobile segment.

A community orientation for health planning should lead to the identification of specific neighborhoods for specially directed health service delivery programs, based on diagnosed changes in neighborhood health profiles that follow shifting patterns of neighborhood in-migration.

When substantial population segments and neighborhoods are mobile, it follows that services and service centers should be similarly mobile. Facilities that are relatively small and that require relatively modest capital investments can be moved with relative ease and follow population

---

[46] Kerr L. White, "Organization and Delivery of Personal Health Services," *Millbank Memorial Fund Quarterly*, Vol. 46, No. 1 (January 1968), Part 2, p. 226.

[47] *Migration, Vital and Health Statistics*, p. 3.

flow with minimal disruption and discontinuity. The important point to remember is the advisability of keeping medical centers close to residential areas. This suggests the use of branch ambulatory care clinics and the upgrading and redirection of services in the emergency rooms and clinics of large urban hospitals. The latter, in the words of Brown, "will continue to be an important element in the care of the poor, the clinic being the caring source for the chronically ill, and the emergency room for the acute episodes of the healthy poor." [48] The significance of public hospitals or clinics is suggested in Blumberg's finding that 45 percent of migrants received their medical care through those sources.[49]

An example of the development of decentralized satellite services is found in the Ross-Loos Medical Group in Los Angeles, California, which established a dozen such units.[50] Similar approaches have been developed in both community mental health programs and in the comprehensive health centers financed by the Office of Economic Opportunity.

When feasible, providing health services for adults near work areas and near or in schools for children may be the most effective way of making them available to people. In some communities proximity to churches, shopping areas, or frequently used commercial establishments such as laundromats or beauty parlors may be similarly effective.

Since the schools, both public and private, are perhaps the most universal of community institutions, linking them to

hospitals, medical schools, and health centers may provide the quickest material for community diagnosis. Teachers may be the best source of information on movements and social characteristics of families. Since mobile populations are so heavily constituted by young families, school–health agency cooperation, coordination, and planning are of primary importance.

Mobile personnel are an important aspect of adaptability to changing health needs. This calls for movement from the health center or hospital to the home of nurses, nutritionists, social workers, and health educators. The main point is to keep health provision flexible and responsive to the specific characteristics and problems of mobile people and shifting areas.

Personnel

A shifting population characterized by strong cultural and ethnic identity requires a new type of manpower. The scarcity of qualified physicians in areas inhabited by low-income migrants underscores the suggestion of Dr. George Silver that "we need to train and develop new cadres of medical service personnel and reform our existing role concepts for traditional medical service personnel." [51]

There is a great deal of experimental work now under way in various community-based health and mental health programs in which a wide range of medical auxiliaries are extending scarce medical care. There are some who think professionals will increasingly shift roles in the direction of preparing and supervising such personnel. Miller, for example, suggests:

The future task of the well trained will be to make it possible for less trained people to perform adequately. . . . The professional will not be primarily performing direct client services but making it possible for less

---

[48] Howard J. Brown, "Delivery of Personal Health Services and Medical Services for the Poor," *Millbank Memorial Fund Quarterly,* Vol. 46, No. 1 (January 1968), Part 2, p. 214.

[49] Op. cit., pp. 9–10.

[50] Milton I. Roemer, "New Patterns of Organization for Providing Health Services," in *New Directions in Public Policy for Health Care* (New York: New York Academy of Medicine, 1966), p. 1230.

[51] "New Types of Personnel and Changing Roles of Health Professionals," in *New Directions in Public Policy for Health Care,* p. 1220.

trained people to perform such services. A distinctly secondary task of the professional will be to deal with acute difficult cases that cannot be dealt with by the less trained person.[52]

During a recent interview Dr. Roger O. Egeberg, Assistant Secretary for Health and Scientific Affairs, U.S. Department of Health, Education, and Welfare, suggested that the problem of improving health care delivery topped his list of priorities in health, and that more manpower and new types of manpower, together with new arrangements for medical care financing and new concepts of the kind of care people need, would enable the country to deal effectively with that problem.[53]

In their recent study, a federal group—the Program Analysis Group on the Delivery of Health Services to the Poor—pointed to the need to train neighborhood health aides, technical assistants, and physicians' assistants.[54] The following "three major categories of new health personnel" were specified: (1) persons whose major role involves communicatory, facilitative, and advisory functions such as family health advisor-neighborhood health aide, (2) persons whose major role involves the application of narrowly defined, wholly technical skills, such as urologist's assistant or emergency room technician, and (3) persons, usually those with previous training—trained, generally for a considerable period, for a combination of technical and advisory functions that require a greater degree of judgment and independent action (e.g., pediatric assistant).[55] While these suggestions are intended to deal effectively

with health service delivery for poor people, they have an even more cogent rationale for the mobile poor, who are least likely to have resources or know-how in utilizing existing facilities.

As far as trained medical personnel are concerned, encouragement needs to be given to the recruitment of doctors without a high degree of specialization who can assume new professional roles, including the training of adjunctive personnel. The essential professional medical skill can in this way have a multiplier effect, from the point of view of the availability and accessibility of service personnel prepared to render specific medical help.

While the importance of developing indigenous personnel for health-related services is widely recognized, there is a built-in ideological dilemma that should be noted. Too wide a use of health personnel with relatively modest training and skill is likely to engender hostility on the part of recipients and lead to the charge of second-class health service. This is especially to be anticipated when families literally face questions of life or death and insist on obtaining access to highly trained medical personnel.

In the short run, however, health needs of the poor and the mobile will best be served with such procedures. The alternative is a critical lack of manpower and an absence of meaningful attention to even the most obvious health demands. In the long run, a different pattern of health service delivery, including universally available prepaid group practice, will meet the inevitable political test as well as consumer demand. When differentiated use of medical manpower is widely accepted in nonpoor and stable areas of the community, the same can more readily be expected in unfavored areas.

There is considerable discussion in the literature of the ways in which group practice patterns can assist in health outreach. The Program Analysis Group on the Delivery of Health Services to the Poor,

---

[52] S. M. Miller, "Solving the Urban Dilemma in Health Care," in *New Directions in Public Policy for Health Care*, p. 1155.

[53] Interview with Harold M. Schmeck, Jr., *New York Times*, September 21, 1969, p. 62.

[54] *Human Investment Programs—Delivery of Health Services for the Poor* (Washington, D.C.: U.S. Department of Health, Education, and Welfare, December 1967), p. 5.

[55] Ibid., p. 8.

referred to earlier, urged that support and encouragement be given

the development, expansion, and involvement of group practices in the care of the poor by providing salaries for physician's assistants, family health advisors, and social work assistants. . . . The physicians would have to be in full time practice and have appointments in hospitals certified to participate in Medicare.[56]

In addition to personnel directly involved in health service delivery, other staff functions can play an important part in connecting people and services. Community organization and health education workers, health visitors, and nutrition aides can play bridging roles as they move from the service center to neighborhood associations, community action agencies, and local institutions. As patient advocates they are strategically placed to ensure feedback, assist in the mutual engagement of service and client personnel, and participate in the process of assuring quality control.

Implicit in this discussion is the suggestion that there be a change in priorities affecting the application of resources in the health care system. Widespread use of mobile facilities and the utilization of more and different personnel implies a shift from a high rate of investment in capital to a high rate of investment in services. A shifting population requires flexibility in planning and provision and a relative abundance of human skill that can move with the changing human tides. Manpower is more elastic than fixed capital. Mobile health care requires a national manpower policy and program, one that classifies and differentiates technical skill and that invests heavily in training, recruitment, and supervision of all levels of health service personnel.

Additional Considerations

A series of considerations for health planning grow out of some especially salient characteristics of mobile populations that bear negatively on their health.

1. There is evidence to suggest that the period immediately following migration is the most hazardous and that the more mobile a neighborhood, the less likely its residents are to form personal ties with their neighbors.[57] With fewer informal associations, less information about service facilities passes from neighbor to neighbor. This suggests the need for a network of information and referral services that can readily provide new residents with knowledge about resources. Locating them near local indigenous institutions like churches, lodges, and schools would maximize their utility. Something on the pattern of the British Citizens' Advice Bureaus could be adapted for use in this connection.[58] Adequate information, combined with decentralized diagnostic services that are easily available, and more thorough health data collection should provide an effective early warning system for spotting individual health care need as well as the collective indication of such need.

2. Because so much of the trauma that accompanies residential mobility is found in low-income areas to which minority groups move, cultural and socioeconomic considerations seem imperative in fashioning health service programs. However one views the current debate on the so-called culture of poverty, there is sufficient reason to believe that there is need for a different kind of medical practice from that found in white middle-income neighborhoods. Urban areas are more and more becoming the locus of settlement of diverse cultural and racial groups—black and Puerto Rican in the Northeast, Mexican-American in the West, and native whites from Appalachia and the Ozarks in the Midwest. Their dis-

---

[56] Ibid., p. 74.

[57] Rossi, op. cit., p. 39.

[58] *See* Alfred J. Kahn et al., *Neighborhood Information Centers* (New York: Columbia University School of Social Work, 1966), for a review of this experience and a series of suggestions for its application to the American environment.

tinctive patterns of cultural adaptation and their patterns of use of community facilities are an important source of data for health service personnel. Health aides drawn from members of in-migrant groups and from among local residents and social scientists and social workers attuned to the nature of cultural impact have important contributions to make in this connection. Migration and mobility change the social class structure and ethnic character of communities and neighborhoods, hence requiring changes in patterns of service organizations, service delivery, and service personnel.

3. Since mobility is so largely a phenomenon affecting young families, high priority is indicated for an emphasis on maternal care and on infants, children, and youths. The risks in connection with premature births and infant mortality are vastly greater for poor nonwhite families. Mobile prenatal clinics that deal with informational, nutritional, and medical intervention oriented to prevention and early symptom detection are clearly indicated. Concentration on maternal and infant care programs is similarly suggested. These early periods in the family cycle are generally times of stress and risk. For the mobile, especially when poorly educated and having an uncertain income, these are especially critical and hazardous.

Relationships between health service agencies and the public schools are of central significance in this connection. The reciprocal influences of nutrition, health, and learning disabilities are increasingly recognized. Efforts to develop comprehensive programs for children and youths are under way and will yield clues that health planners will want to pursue in the years ahead. Some instances of creative cooperation among medical schools, hospitals, and public schools are similarly in evidence.

4. There is considerable evidence that low-income migrants present to a substan-

tial degree a problem in crisis medicine. Past and present neglect, ignorance of health services or of how to use them, fatalistic orientations to ill health, lack of health resources, and lack of financial capacity all predispose this population segment to chronicity of illness. Upgrading emergency and clinic services seems clearly indicated. Maintaining day and evening services—if necessary on an around-the-clock basis, but surely through day and evening hours—will fill a significant void in service delivery at crucial points. The provision of crisis clinics in community mental health programs is one illustration that this element has been given recognition in community health practice. Relegation of those least trained for practice to hospital emergency rooms and clinics defies this aspect of health care and serves to multiply rather than reduce community health problems.

5. A word should be said about the meaning of this discussion for medical education. A focus on education for community health service coordinated with that for private health service will produce increasing numbers of physicians prepared to work in environments now largely eschewed by medical graduates. The broad health needs of the nation will never be met adequately by an entrepreneurial orientation to private health care. Too many disadvantaged groups in the population, of which the mobile are one, are overlooked in this way, largely because the obvious rewards for service under current arrangements are relatively meager.

The community is increasingly recognized as an essential locus for medical practice and this will inevitably affect the ways in which medical schools organize their curricular and clinical experiences. As suggested by Bamberger, "There are those who say that a community laboratory for the provision of primary medical care to a defined population may soon be as crucial to the medical school as the basic science laboratory is today." [59] What is also indicated is a greater concentration on culturally based studies, attuning physicians to sociocultural variables that have an important bearing on the receptivity and use of health services. Finally, interest in problems of health service delivery and on the organizational and community context in which they develop, coordinated with an interest in medical technology, will lead to training more in line with the health needs of the future.

Conclusion

Two things have been attempted in this discussion: (1) identification of some significant characteristics of people in movement from one place to another as these bear on problems of health and (2) suggestion of some directions that health planning should take if it is to be responsive to these matters. It seems clear that migration and residential mobility are widespread and are likely to remain so for the foreseeable future. Not all movement from place to place is harmful. Indeed, many people leave their accustomed residences and thereby enhance their capacity for effective living. But many others find

---

[59] Lisbeth Bamberger, "Health Care and Poverty—from the Community Point of View," in *New Directions in Public Policy for Health Care*, p. 1141.

the impact of change stressful and disruptive. These persons present a real challenge to the providers of social and health services and to the nation as a whole.

National growth has been stimulated in substantial part by migration from abroad and geographic movement within. The cumulative impact of migration and mobility is transforming the urban social environment. Many who come to the cities now do so under the press of home circumstances beyond their control. Displacement continues even in the new centers of settlement. Withal, cities have changed their ethnic and social class character, probably irreversibly. Urban health faces a new challenge and health services, like all social services, face new tasks and opportunities.

Urban slums serve as reception centers for many on the move. In time the migrants become settlers in and residents of neighborhoods that are either friendly or hostile to new migrants. In effect, then, a good migrant service is a good slum service, or—to put it more happily—a good migrant service is a good human service. Special recognition of the most wearing and disabling aspects of residential instability is essential, and numerous leads in that direction have been suggested. But in the last analysis we will deal satisfactorily with the health problems of migrants only when we have developed a national health policy that is inclusive of the entire nation, as a matter of right.

Comments

ALFRED H. KATZ

The preceding paper by Simon Slavin consisted of two parts: (1) an analysis of some of the evidence linking the migration experience to susceptibility to health problems and (2) an outline of policies for improving health care for the poor and disadvantaged, including the migrant poor. The writer's comments on this paper will be in the form of a series of propositions, addenda, or dissents, presented, because of space limitations, with little documentation.

1. There can be no question of the massive, accumulating evidence regarding health care and health status deficits of the poor, of their heightened vulnerability to disease, or of the high incidence of unidentified and uncorrected defects among them.

2. There is strong evidence for an association between stressful life circumstances and heightened susceptibility to disease. While Dr. Slavin adduces data from mental health studies, impressive evidence along similar lines for infectious and other physical disease is also available—one example being the work of Holmes and his associates, who showed a positive relationship between vulnerability to tuberculosis and life-stress, including the specific stresses of mobility and migration.[1] In fact, such associations have been demonstrated historically in the health experience of migrant groups in the United States and other countries.

3. Methods are available for measuring such psychosocial stress factors for an individual, which can lead to ultimate prediction and control through the identification of high-risk persons in migrating groups and the design of appropriate services for these.

4. In such an undertaking the threefold public health approach to prevention is useful: (a) *primary* prevention—when specific causal relationships are known, removal of the noxious or stress-inducing agent, as in antismoking campaigns, (b) *secondary* prevention—early case-finding through mass screening and surveillance programs that can identify and correct pathological tendencies before they develop, (c) *tertiary* prevention—disability limitation through prompt comprehensive

_____

[1] Thomas H. Holmes et al., in P. J. Sparer, ed., *Personality, Stress, and Tuberculosis* (New York: International Universities Press, 1956).

treatment. Implications of the threefold approach in this field would include provisions for premigration evaluation, counseling, and treatment in the sending community and special reception centers and a social support system in the receiving community.

Dr. Slavin's recommendations for policy are generally unexceptionable, but the following comments are pertinent. The health and medical care services of the United States are one of the most important of the country's growth industries, accounting for a steadily increasing portion of the Gross National Product and manpower resources.

It seems inevitable that some form of national system of health care, based on universalistic coverage, will be legislated within the next decade to complete social insurance coverage for all residents against the customary hazards of life. Such a system will require a major redistribution of medical manpower and resources so that differences in quality and accessibility of care among different parts of the country will diminish. Such redistribution will require more careful training and creation of placement opportunities for all manner of paramedical, subprofessional health and mental health workers.

As Dr. Slavin points out, health care should be localistic in its orientation, based in communities and neighborhoods and taking into account cultural, behavioral, and organizational particularities of the population under care. A massive effort of rethinking and evaluating appropriate structures for delivery of health services is needed. For example, the present separation among categorical health programs (e.g., for crippled children and disabled adults) and between community mental health centers and neighborhood health centers, must be thought through and assessed.

Despite Dr. Slavin's optimism, there seems little chance that the public schools will be used more effectively in health screening and health service, because of major differences in outlook and administration between the educational and health service establishments. On the other hand, much closer co-operation among local, state, and national health and welfare services is immediately feasible and necessary.

Discussion

WILLIAM J. REID: I considered three components of a national migration action program from the point of view of foreign and domestic experience:

1. A job information data bank that could match workers to jobs, thus helping an individual to make a rational decision about migration.

2. A federally assisted relocation effort. In a series of demonstration projects that took place between 1965 and 1967, the federal government provided relocation aid to at least 6,500 workers and their families. There may have been more; it is hard to say with the data we have.

3. Bringing jobs to people through public works and redevelopment of overpopulated areas by attracting industry to them by means of loans, subsidies, and other grants.

The first idea is moderately feasible, the second ambitious but probably unrealizable, and the third is being tried in many localities. At a modest level the federal government could attempt to facilitate the movement of workers to serve their own and public interests. This could be done with the creation of a national job information and assistance relocation program.

The policy could be directed mainly at assisting unemployed and underemployed workers to move to jobs in other areas. But such a policy would not be directed at altering basic migration patterns in order to alleviate major population imbalances. In order to accomplish this objective, a more ambitious and comprehensive undertaking would be needed. There are several possibilities, but the one I finally settled on is a plan whereby migration could be guided to designated growth centers. These centers or growth points would be developed by attracting industries to the area. Various incentives, including subsidies—federal, state, and local—would be used.

Supreme Court Role in Policy-Making

BERNARD M. SHIFFMAN: The U.S. Supreme Court, in a six–three decision, ruled that any residency requirement is unconstitutional. Three months after this ruling, an Associated Press survey found that state welfare administrations barely experienced a change in their caseloads as a result of this decision. It appears that the fears of mass migration as a consequence of the elimination of such requirements were groundless, in spite of the existence of a wide range in the size of grants between such states as Mississippi, where a family of four receives only $38.75 per month, and New Jersey, where a family of four receives $263.

What the Supreme Court decision did demonstrate was that the judicial system can be an instrument of social justice even for the poorest of our citizens. In fact, there is some evidence that the court reversed the intent and desire of the elected representatives of the "welfare-lashing" majority. But the *New York Times,* in an April 22, 1961, editorial, hailed the decision, which it said restored to the poor the same flexibility and mobility that all other citizens already enjoy. While this sentiment is noble, it was always doubtful that welfare residency requirements alone keep the poor "down on the farm."

America is a nation of immigrants. Yet here, as in most societies, the earliest arrivals have often tried to discriminate against late-comers. Formal residency requirements were only one of these controls. While the issue of residency requirement for welfare assistance seems to be settled unless the Nixon Supreme Court overrules the Warren Supreme Court, there is no question that the social problems of the city and their supporting catch-basin—public welfare—are compounded by in-migration and out-migration. If we have settled anything in the sixties, it is that public welfare is "the bag" into which the immigrants are driven as a consequence of the failure of our conventional employment, education, training, and housing systems and of the supportive human services.

Are the Policy-Planners Scientific?

ELEANOR B. SHELDON: Dr. Mayer presents the reader with two interrelated problems that have presumably emerged from unplanned internal migration: (1) "undue concentrations of people in large industrial centers," and (2) "superconcentrations of poor black men in these same centers." For the solution of these two interrelated problems he recommends a Bureau of Internal Migration that will create new cities or expand existing small cities and that will serve to deconcentrate the population. I have a suspicion that if these two problems had been treated as separate—even though they might be related in many aspects—a wide variety of different solutions would have resulted.

Dr. Mayer's solution, "to urge the private sector to establish new centers of employment and to publicize job openings in these new centers," is quite similar to what Dr. Reid said with respect to a job data bank and growth centers. Dr. Mayer also calls for systems analysis that would plan scientifically for the relocation and expansion of industrial and financial resources and hence, population. Dr. Reid has tried to provide similar kinds of plans. He has faced up to not only the political problem, but some of the logical holes in it.

All systems models require one of two alternative approaches: one either aggregates data or disaggregates them. We can't rely on systems analysis or construction of models to solve our problems. They're not going to do it.

The two policy papers certainly do a good piece of work. One of the next steps in refining the relocation notions would be to look into systems analysis and see whether we have the requisite knowledge—not attitudinal assertions—for the relocation of industry.

DEMITRI B. SHIMKIN: I personally take no position except that people should be free to make a decision. Whether we wish to maximize jobs locally or in the proposed new cities, it involves a whole new set of issues that this institute is really not equipped to handle.

FRANK MONTALVO: The army made a cost-benefit analysis of personnel movement, which found that one of the main reasons people were leaving the service was their unwillingness to move frequently. As a result the army adopted a program of relocation assistance that included the following: (1) each person moved has a job waiting for him, (2) payment of an allowance, (3) income tax deduction for moving costs, and (4) the army "community," their status, and many social relationships are taken with them.

Nevertheless they are still problems. The noneconomic incentive has not been adequately considered.

ROBERT MORRIS: Do the theories that have thus far been mentioned emerge from observations of natural phenomena? Do the facts we know help us formulate these theories?

I'm conscious of what Eleanor Sheldon said in a previous discussion, that we may be asking too much of the social sciences—after all, they are relatively new. We also may be asking the wrong questions, but we are forced to act on policy choices because we are asked to do so by society.

Supportive Programs

RUBY B. PERNELL: A public welfare system with a national income floor for the working and nonworking poor is one of our priority requirements for the future. Also needed is a guaranteed minimum income to tide migrants over the initial transitional period. An adequate minimum income plan plus a good job training program could facilitate movement of workers with their migratory decisions being based primarily on economic considerations.

Such policies would greatly benefit another group of migrants who have barely been touched on at this institute: our nomadic tribes, the agricultural workers. Would this sort of economic underwriting enable migrant rural families to be less dependent on child labor? And coupled with this kind of relief, could imaginative new programs for the education of migrant children be developed? A host of concerns for this group have to be considered, aside from the ways in which they may give each other mutual support. More attention

must be given to federal programs that can be developed, such as a minimum wage in agriculture.

The local receiving community is often hostile to migrants, who cannot easily shield themselves from hostility and rejection. Their employment status is likely to be tenuous, their wage levels are low, and they are given little or no job training. The migrant's family becomes subject to all the disorganizing and defeating forces a community can muster. And then we blame them for not making it!

BERNARD SHIFFMAN: The people who are on the move are unique, with an infinite variety of motivations and needs. The sheer numbers involved defy an individualistic, psychosocial, or casework approach. The task requires a national contract between the federal government and the local communities involved. Such a contract would make it possible for the federal government to provide the resources and technical assistance to the local community so that it could design and operate the unique services to meet its unique problem. The range of local services is infinite and could run the gamut from kibbutzim in Wyoming to individual rent subsidies for people who must live in high rental areas that are near developing suburban job opportunities.

DEMITRI B. SHIMKIN: We should not try too hard to protect migrants or anyone else from unpleasant experiences. Life involves the making of mistakes and the opportunity to test oneself. If all the dissonance is removed from life, we also take away its challenge.

JOSEPH W. EATON: The suggestion has been made a number of times that when we make policy recommendations we must be practical because you can't sell utopias to politicians. This kind of pessimism has been too pervasive in social work and may explain why the professional organizations have so limited an impact on policy.

Actually many innovative social service ideas do gain acceptance. For instance, if you emigrate or leave the United States even temporarily some precise health questions are asked upon your return. Measures are taken to make sure that the health of the community is not threatened.

Considering the numbers of internal migrants, a health program could be conceived that would be quite salable. This would be assumption by the public of responsibility for a thorough preventive medical examination for any child moving into a new school—not the superficial screening that is now done in most schools—unless he has had one recently.

This is not utopian. The public might be willing to pay for such a program.

BERNARD SHIFFMAN: The alternative to the present laissez-faire migration policy is a nationally planned and guided mobility policy. This poses the American dilemma: without planning, we are headed for disaster, but in America there exists a universal resistance to planning *if* it includes the authority to implement. We are tolerant only of planning without such authority. In addition, serious planning would result in a demand for a major investment of national resources in people. As a nation we have found this much more difficult than investment in rockets or other technological developments.

One exception should be noted. New York City made a radical innovation. For the first time a city took capital funds and invested it in people—$30 million of capital funds were used to develop a comprehensive manpower program.

The impact of migration on the size and composition of welfare applicants and welfare expenditures is all but unknown. Guesses have been made to justify restrictive social policies that were designed to discourage the migration of poor people. The absence of systematic research or analysis of the mountains of statistics produced by the welfare system led New York City Commissioner Mitchell I. Ginsberg to observe: "Our welfare system which is a billion dollar enterprise in New York City is run like a neighborhood candy store."

ALFRED H. KATZ: In planning for migration there is a need to prevent the residual casualties. Most people who migrate do so because they hope to benefit thereby. But others who are involved may suffer. For instance the husband may migrate to take a better job but the wife will have to part from her friends and associates. The children must make the transition to a new school and will miss their friends. They are "residual casualties," which could be reduced through the work of migration expediters, social workers or persons with other professional backgrounds.

Unplanned Migration

RUBY B. PERNELL: I was struck by the mention of "flight" as a basis for migration. I have recently been watching a small community changing rapidly as a result of the in-migration of blacks with a certain amount of economic power—enough to be able to consider private homeownership. The flight response of white residents in the area occurred in an extremely short period of time. Now the community has changed almost wholly.

In terms of the multiplier social overhead aspect, panic migration puts a great strain on various services for the community into which the movers are coming. What we don't know is what kind of strain it puts on the communities to which the out-migrants are going. We also don't know what kind of stress this puts in turn on the individual mover, that is, the person who has reached an economic level that enables him to better his circumstances.

BERNARD H. SHIFFMAN: The combination of in- and out-migrations now threatens the viability of large cities. The in-migrants are often poor and have few skills; the out-migrants more often have the skills and take their earning capacity elsewhere. Unplanned migration is a disaster for the city, and often migrants are punished for coming. Even when officials in the receiving area want to help, they don't have the tax resources.

In New York City, for one, some attempts have been made such as job training programs. But if there were a comprehensive plan would the people vote for it? I fear they would not in the numbers required to pass such a bill.

Public welfare, which is crucial to so many people, is forced to operate with virtually no investment in research or evaluation. One result of this situation is that the phenomenal growth of a welfare program occurs without analysis of the factors that have contributed to dependency. In New York City, for example, 59.6 percent of those receiving public assistance are children under 21 years old; 19.1 percent are adults caring for these children. Four out of five welfare clients are, therefore, unemployable. With an increase in divorce and family separations and the rising rate of children born out of wedlock, we can account for a large part of the phenomenal welfare increase even if we do not know how to apply the brakes.

While we know the characteristics of the welfare population, we continue in a system of nonanalytic bookkeeping. We simply add up the spiralling costs of welfare, but seem scared to ask why. *Why* did the New York City caseload move from 300,000 persons in 1960 to 600,000 in 1966? Why did it increase to more than 1 million in 1969? This increase is especially difficult to explain when economists claim that we have had unparalleled and uninterrupted prosperity during the same period of time.

RAUL A. MUNOZ: Research does not guarantee implementation. Even though Puerto Rico has a much longer tradition of planning than the United States, we have been able to put across and imple-

ment all sorts of planning processes with more success and frequency in Puerto Rico than any of the democratic and capitalistic countries. But the time has come when planners are being challenged in Puerto Rico, especially by the deprived population sectors.

Lessons from Overseas

HENRY P. DAVID: It seems to me it's high time to admit that we have something to learn from other countries, both the developed and the developing—and, I might add, especially from the advanced social security programs of Scandinavia and Israel and the public health policies of the socialist countries of Central and Eastern Europe. In Hungary and the Soviet Union, for example, abortion is available on demand to any woman who wants it, with no questions asked.

I think it's high time also to learn from the enlightened abortion legislation in the United Kingdom and to go beyond the ideological differences that scare so many of us. Something can be learned from other countries regardless of political or ideological differences. Let us do so and let us adapt what has been successful elsewhere to our specific circumstances.

As far as migration and family planning are concerned, there is a distinct relationship. A realistic population policy is an important component of any plan to ease the pressures that give rise to migration. It cannot be ignored.

In this regard as well as in other areas of social innovation, I suggest that we look beyond our own shores and bring into the mainstream of social welfare practice the pertinent experience from other lands.

Postscript

ALVIN L. SCHORR

The conference illustrates the difficulty of moving directly from pieces of research and knowledge to social policies. People tend to feed into a discussion assumptions and hopes that reach far beyond the specific policy at issue. Only the weakest limits are placed on this tendency by research when, as so often, it appears fragmentary. Moreover, migration policy can be discussed sensibly only in a framework of other national policies. But specifying the framework is a large-scale, not to say speculative enterprise. Still, we arrived at some agreement.

In the first place, we see mobility as various. The conference has focused on low-income migrants, but middle-income people are also highly mobile. Many move as individuals or families, but others move in a loosely organized migratory stream. Much movement is oriented to finding work or better work, but many move for family reasons, for education, for adventure, or in search of an easier way of life. Mobility has effects on the individual who makes the decision, but also on the members of his family and on the communities that he leaves and enters. So we take care when we generalize that we are not preoccupied with one type of client or situation and doing damage or missing the point regarding others.

On the whole, we seek policies in regard to migration that enhance individual and family choice. Therefore, we are uneasy even about the concept of a national migration policy. Such a policy might be formulated in terms of choice, to be sure, but conversation about grand policy seems quickly to take a prescriptive turn. We have not faced that some kinds of policies open up some choices and close others. For example, the ways in which we distribute medical care facilities and social services make it possible or desirable to live in some places and not in others. At some level of provision or lack of provision, people are forced to move. In general, the tone of discussion suggests that the conferees favor societal choice but not in forms that are experienced as coercion. Societal choice is reflected in the planned distribution of resources and services; that, we seem to favor. Coercion is experienced when individuals or families identified as being specific types or living in particular places are thought of as needing to stay or go and by policy we press them to take that course; that, we seem to oppose.

We are also for other reasons strongly

in favor of large-scale planning. We feel that the nation is proceeding chaotically and we have a sense of impending doom. The planning that we favor would take into account that mobility is various and that individuals should make their own choices, which naturally makes planning more complicated. If planning leads to large-scale expenditures, it would show a reasonable sense of proportion and we shall not be surprised. The conferees are all New Deal liberals, including even the economists among us.

We think social workers and social scientists should have a role in such planning, but they have so far failed to integrate available knowledge and say what it means in policy terms. We think we are not powerful enough as a group for the role we should play, but power is different from and no doubt harder to attain than relevance.

In talking of planning, we are troubled by a sense that important events proceed unplanned. It is not exactly that they are unplanned, but that they are planned for private profit or for the wrong objectives, without including social costs in the weighing-up of what should be done. A simple example is the desperate plight of cities that has resulted from drawing people to cities by concentrating jobs in them. In part, this is a function of government failing to be given or to accept responsibility in vast areas of public policy.

There is a dilemma in these views. The conferees recoiled from the type of large-scale policy proposed in Albert Mayer's paper, possibly, as he conceded, because he had not time to make his case well. But there is also a sensation of manipulation that troubles us. We resolve this dilemma by facilitating the choice we wish to encourage, without requiring it. For example, we recommend investing large resources in enriching life in rural areas. That makes it practical for families to stay in rural areas, although they need not do so. This stance of facilitating but not requiring staying or going is complicated— it makes it hard to put forth a monolithic

program—but it is probably a practical stance and anyway it is sounder.

In planning, we think information about individuals and people important. That is, data somehow have to be collected and stated in terms that reflect what real people do. Studies of the sort presented by Myrtle Reul and Demitri Shimkin are examples. The importance of visualizing individuals is not only an article of faith; policy proceeds better when such material is available. For example, the knowledge that people move back and forth between Mississippi and Chicago helps in formulating a program of information for rural people who are likely to move.

We are clearest in our view about social services: we want them provided. We have had some difficulty with two problems, however. In general, we think that mobile people are not a distinguishable part of the population. Migratory labor is distinguishable, of course, but most mobile families are like you and me last year or two years from now. For that reason, and because we have some concern for rational organization, we look to sound and plentiful services for *all* the population—health services, family planning, manpower, housing, income maintenance, providing business opportunities, and so forth. The difficulty is that such a position is so general that it has little effect.

A second difficulty, which was not discussed, is that we do not know how to organize large-scale social services in the United States. We are in a handicraft stage in the organization of social services, tailoring what we do in each city and county to the resources and skills at hand. Extensive discussion of guided mobility programs such as William Reid proposes would illustrate how little we know. When we talk about the organization of services in rural areas, we seem to know even less. Possibly income maintenance gets mentioned so often in these discussions because we do at any rate know how to deliver a uniform product across the country.

Although we do not in general think of creating special services for mobile families, at certain points we identify special needs. One point is the reception areas in our cities—the ghetto, downtown. Apart from thinking that services in these areas ought to be adequate, there should be special forms of organization—outreach, acculturation, and the use of indigenous personnel. The same might be said for migratory farm labor. There ought to be special services, too, that reach back to the sending community, where paths of flow are well established. This reaching back can be used to support migrants in new communities and to begin acculturation before families actually move.

We also want to reach mobile people, as individuals or families, to prepare them for special difficulties or to identify them when they may suffer too acutely. The need in this respect ranges all the way from educational material to halfway houses for people for whom the transition is too difficult. We are so far perhaps better able to prepare movers with information than to advise them on the best adjustive mechanisms. We do not know what to advise, but perhaps we can know soon if we follow the lead of some of the work that has been presented to us (e.g., Marc Fried et al.).

We do want the gatekeepers of various social services and other institutions freed of prejudice. We know how to proceed at one level—using educational measures and defining acceptable behavior. At another level, the problem is one of how we define strangers in our society and how we treat them. We seem to be able to draw together only by excluding some classes of people; the newcomer is the classic example. This problem cuts across our society, and we have not really taken it on.

Although social and health services are the solution on which we have readiest agreement, political power is the solution that most grabs us in this winter of 1971. We have said that political power is how minorities historically have solved their problem. Still, reservations have been expressed. Eugene Brody suggests that, half-hidden, the political power solution moves us to a depersonalized view of our clients.

That is, political moves become the important thing and justify using people for political purposes without a full degree of attention to their individual plights. I have wondered whether we—government and social agencies—abdicate our responsibility when we join poor people or other client groups in the view—which is sound on their part—that they will improve matters only by becoming strong enough. Government and agencies are supposed to be improving services; that is *their* responsibility. But the group as a whole favors Black Power, poor people's power, and so forth as a solution and doubts that, in its absence, other solutions will even be developed. Fostering that seems for some to imply a degree of separation between these groups and others is a troublesome point. We did not talk about the means to a political solution but seem to intend such devices as community action, legal services, and of course independent political action.

Two themes run through the papers and the discussion of them. First, social services and planning are seen as surface expressions of political power. Minority groups such as migratory laborers will better their positions only as they gain power. But underneath that, mobile people are likely to be treated well only when we learn to regard strangers and aliens of all sorts in our midst in a more friendly way. This observation is not meant to diffuse the issue so that it leaves nothing to do, but to highlight the urgency of developing a more tolerant society.

And second, the individual and family dominate the discussion—whether considering how to formulate research or what the policy objectives of migration policy might be. The importance of the individual reaches even to our image of the professional who is working on the problem. Unless the professions—social work, the social sciences, research—include a strong strain of people for whom the work is an individual vocation, the professions will become unresponsive. As long as dedicated individuals find themselves driven to service, we have hope for progress.

Appendix

Appendix

Annotated Bibliography

OXANNA S. KAUFMAN

Literature in the field of migration, internal and international, is extensive in English and in other languages. A monumental work, *Human Migration: A Guide to Migration Literature in English, 1955–1962*, compiled by J. J. Mangalam with the assistance of Cornelia Morgan (Lexington: University of Kentucky Press, 1968), has brought together those references for one decade. Much has appeared since, published and retrievable as well as unpublished research not easily available.

International Migration Review covers the field with contributions to theory and research. Of special importance is the coverage of research in progress. Journals in the fields of demography, economics, population study, and sociology are other sources of references in the area of migration study. Even popular periodicals have on occasion published significant material. Professional publications in social work have published accounts of services to migrant groups. These are all too few and are concerned most often with one group— the poor migrant laborer.

The references in this bibliography are those the compiler feels are most relevant within the framework of the institute's goals. All have appeared since 1960, are in English, and refer to migration in the United States. Included also are the bibliographic references pertinent to migration cited by the authors of the papers presented at the institute. These are indicated by an asterisk (*).

The bibliography is classified. It is hoped that this arrangement will facilitate the user in locating items of interest in a specific area.

General

Hartman, Edward C. *A History of American Migration.* Chicago: Rand McNally Co., 1967.

Jackson, J. H. (ed.). *Migration.* Cambridge, England: Cambridge University Press, 1969.

A collection of specially commissioned papers that develop the theories of long- and short-distance migration.

Jansen, Clifford J. (ed.). *Readings in the Sociology of Migration.* New York: Pergamon Press, 1970.

This compilation affords an excellent overview. The articles are carefully selected and balanced and international in scope. Material on migration in the

United States includes the following: "Participation of Migrants in Urban Structures" by B. G. Zimmer, "Distance of Migration and Socio-economic Status of Migrants" by A. M. Rose, and "Kentucky Mountain Migration and the Stem-Family" by James S. Brown, Harry K. Schwarzweller, and J. J. Mangalam.

Statistics

The United States government regularly publishes various statistical data on migration and mobility. The Bureau of the Census in its *Current Population Reports* series makes available such data as the following:

Series P-20:

No. 134. Mobility of the Population of the U.S., March 1962–63.
No. 150. Mobility of the Population of the U.S., March 1964–65.
No. 154. Reasons for Moving, March 1962–63.
No. 171. Mobility of the Population of the U.S., March 1966–67.
No. 175. Negro Population: March 1967.
No. 181. Population of the U.S. by Metropolitan-Nonmetropolitan Residence: 1968 and 1960.
No. 182. Lifetime and Recent Migration, 1969.

Series P-23:

No. 24. Social and Economic Conditions of Negroes in the U.S., 1967.
No. 27. Trends in Social and Economic Conditions in Metropolitan Areas, 1969.

The U.S. Public Health Service publishes material such as *Migration, Vital and Health Statistics: A Report* (1968).

Lee, Everett S. "A Theory of Migration," *Demography*, Vol. 3, No. 1 (1966), pp. 47–57.

Factors that enter into the decision to migrate are discussed. The author hy-

pothesizes that in regard to volume of migration, the significant variables are the establishment of stream and counterstream and the characteristics of migrants.

MacDonald, John S. and Leatrice D. MacDonald. "Chain Migration, Ethnic Neighborhood Formation, and Social Networks," *Milbank Memorial Fund Quarterly*, Vol. 42 (January 1964), pp. 82–97.

Chain migration is defined as "movement in which prospective migrants learn of opportunities, are provided with transportation, and have initial accommodation and employment arranged by means of primary social relationships with previous migrants." This is a survey of American secondary sources on Italian migration, pointing out some of the consequences of this social situation.

Morrill, Richard L., and Forrest R. Pitts. "Marriage, Migration, and the Mean Information Field: A Study in Uniqueness and Generality," *Annals of the Association of American Geographers*, Vol. 57 (June 1967), pp. 401–422.

The authors suggest that recently available experimental data on the spatial behavior of mobile individuals as they shop, go to work, marry, and migrate permit the study of individual fields of information (measures of the tendency to communicate over distance). The aggregation of such fields into a community mean information field has proved useful in the computer simulation of how information is spread over populated areas and how innovations are adopted.

Rogers, T. W. "Differential Net Migration Patterns in the AMSA's of the Southern U.S., 1950–1960," *International Migration*, Vol. 6 (1968), pp. 22–32.

The research discussed here was concerned with identifying some of the demographic, economic, and social factors responsible for differential net migration rates among the eighty areas studied.

Senior, Clarence. "Migration As a Process, and Migrant As a Person," *Population Review*, Vol. 6 (January 1962), pp. 30–41.

Taeuber, Carl E., Leonard Chiazze, Jr., and William Haenszel. *Migration in the U.S.: An Analysis of Residence History*. Public Health Monograph No. 77. Washington, D.C.: U.S. Government Printing Office, 1968.

This study is based on the fact that migration is an unplanned experiment. It provides an opportunity to compare the morbidity and mortality experience of natives and migrants residing in the same area. This facilitates assessment of the relative contribution of environmental variables to specific diseases.

Wilbur, George L. "Migration Expectancy in the United States," *American Statistical Association Journal*, Vol. 58 (June 1963), pp. 444–453.

A migration expectancy table is developed and its use for estimating future movement is discussed.

Adaptation

Under the umbrella of adaptation the problems of assimilation as well as mental health are included. This area is one of deep interest to professionals delivering services to migrant groups.

The September–October 1969 issue of the *American Behavioral Scientist* is devoted to "Migration and Adaptation." In his overview Dr. Eugene B. Brody, the editor, defines "the nature of the problem." The articles included are adapted from conference working papers. These papers have been expanded and papers by other leading anthropologists, psychiatrists, and sociologists added to form the volume, also edited by Dr. Brody, *Behavior in New Environments: Adaptation of Migrant Population* (New York: Russell Sage Foundation, 1970).

Ball, John C., and William M. Bates. "Migration and Residential Mobility of Narcotic Drug Addicts," *Social Problems*, Vol. 14, No. 2 (Summer 1966), pp. 56–69.

This study indicates that the assumed relationship between mobility and crime and deviant behavior "has been oversimplified and ambiguously presented." Drug addiction is suggested as being an "urban phenomenon."

Berardo, Felix M. "Internal Migrants and Extended Family Relations: A Study of Newcomer Adaptation in the Cape Kennedy Region," *Research Reports in Social Science*, Vol. 10 (August 1967), pp. 23–50.

An examination of the relation of kinship groupings to migration and the functions each grouping performed in the adjustment phase of the migration process. The full study appears in *Journal of Marriage and the Family*, Vol. 29, No. 3 (August 1967), pp. 541–554, under the title "Kinship, Interaction and Communication Among Space-Age Migrants." The conclusions are that extended family identification can be maintained despite geographic mobility, especially with modern communications networks, and that women are the primary maintainers of contact and communication with the extended family.

David, Henry P. (ed.). *Migration, Mental Health and Community Services*. New York: American Joint Distribution Committee, undated. Proceedings of a conference convened by the American Joint Distribution Committee, cosponsored by the World Federation for Mental Health, Geneva, November 28–30, 1966.

A selection of reports on the mental health consequences of persecution and concentration camp experiences. Along with primarily Jewish data on the absorption of immigrants in Israel and other countries the reports deal with the pathological potential of uprooting.

There is less emphasis on environmental therapy—the reorganizing potential of moving from one area to another, from little to greater opportunity, freedom, and environmental support.

Dollot, Louis. *Race and Human Migration.* New York: Walker, 1964.

The book's theme stresses the importance of conceptualizing in ecological terms the assimilation process with respect to minority groups.

Family Mobility in Our Dynamic Society. Ames: Iowa State University, Center for Agriculture and Economic Development, 1965.

Papers focus on "Societal Setting," "Changing Family Roles," "Problems and Adjustments of Families Who Stay," "Problems and Adjustment of Families Who Move."

Fitzpatrick, Joseph P., S.J. "The Importance of 'Community' in the Process of Immigrant Assimilation," *International Migration Review,* Vol. 1 (Fall 1966), pp. 5–17.

Gordon, Milton Myron. *Assimilation in American Life: The Role of Race, Religion and National Origins.* New York: Oxford University Press, 1964.

Kantor, Mildred B. (ed.). *Mobility and Mental Health.* Springfield, Ill.: Charles C Thomas, 1965.

The essays range widely over the effects of mobility on mental health.

Keeler, Martin H., and Mintauts M. Vitols. "Migration and Schizophrenia in North Carolina Negroes," *American Journal of Orthopsychiatry,* Vol. 33, No. 2 (April 1963), pp. 554–557.

Data for this study are based on patients diagnosed as schizophrenics at time of admission to a hospital serving a black population. Forty percent had a history of migration preceding admission. The authors conclude that the data indicate the "necessity of thinking of migration as well as any other changes in an indi-

vidual's circumstances as the result of the interplay of intrapsychic and social forces as well as a dynamic factor that will influence subsequent adjustment."

Landis, Judgson R., and Louis Stoetzer. "An Exploratory Study of Middle-Class Migrant Families," *Journal of Marriage and the Family,* Vol. 28, No. 1 (February 1966), pp. 51–53.

Questionnaires were sent to a sample of one hundred recent migrants to a California urban area. All had a history of frequent moves on short notice. The respondents reported that they settled into new communities quickly and without apparent difficulty. Implications for further research are suggested.

McKain, Jerry L. "Alienation, Geographical Mobility and Army Family Problems: An Extension of Theory." Unpublished paper based on the author's doctoral dissertation, Catholic University, 1969.

This was an exploratory field study to assess the relationships among mobility, family problems, and the feelings of alienation of the army wife. It hoped to extend the boundaries of behavioral science theory.

Malzberg, Benjamin. *Migration in Relation to Mental Illness.* New York: Research Foundation for Mental Hygiene, 1968.

Pedersen, Frank A., and Eugene J. Sullivan. "Effects of Geographical Mobility and Parent Personality Factors on Emotional Disorders in Children," *American Journal of Orthopsychiatry,* Vol. 34, No. 2 (April 1964), pp. 575–580.

The authors found that the mothers of normal children were more likely to be satisfied with military life as expressed in their positive identification with the military community and their acceptance of moving than mothers of disturbed children.

Pfister, Maria. "Community Mental Health Work for Migrants," *Migration News*, Vol. 16 (September–October 1967), pp. 1–5.

A conference paper describing the use of migrants as paraprofessionals.

Piore, Michael J. "Negro Workers in the Mississippi Delta: Problems of Displacement and Adjustment." Paper presented at the Annual Winter Meeting, Industrial Relations Research Association, Madison, Wisc., 1968.

Richardson, Allan. "A Theory and a Method for the Psychological Study of Assimilation," *International Migration Review*, Vol. 2 (Fall 1967), pp. 3–30.

The author contends that sociopsychological analysis is a necessary step before any study of structural assimilation can be undertaken. The problems of immigrants must be approached from their individual perspective as well as from the perspective of the two societies: the sending and the receiving.

Shannon, Lyle W. "The Assimilation and Acculturation of Migrants to Urban Areas." Madison, Wisc.: Urban Program, 1961.

The author presents an overview of the literature and proposes a theory of cultural integration—value assimilation—under certain conditions of interaction.

Switzer, Robert E., et al. "The Effects of Family Moves on Children," *Mental Hygiene*, Vol. 45 (October 1961), pp. 528–536.

Known research on changes in a child's life is reviewed. Ways to help children cope with the anxiety attached to moving are suggested—preventive interventions relative to family moves.

Tilly, Charles, and C. Harold Brown. "On Uprooting, Kinship, and the Auspices of Migration," *International Journal of Comparative Sociology*, Vol. 8 (September 1967), pp. 139–164.

The role of kinship groups in migration to cities is discussed. A study of Wilmington seems to show that the conclusion that genuine uprooting is widespread in cities or that its occurrence eventually brings on individual malaise and social disintegration is not justified.

Wilson, Arnold, et al. "Residential Mobility and Psychiatric Help-seeking," *American Journal of Psychiatry*, Vol. 121 (May 1965), pp. 1108–1109.

This is an abstract of a study of 322 patients who sought help at two psychiatric facilities. There is indication that the incidence of migrants in such a sample is at least 2½ times higher than their incidence in the general population. The study found no significant correlations between frequent childhood moves and adult diagnostic categories or between frequent childhood moves and incidence of adult illness.

Wolpert, Julian. "Migration As an Adjustment to an Environmental Stress," *Journal of Social Issues*, Vol. 22 (October 1966), pp. 91–102.

Labor Mobility

Unplanned labor mobility is not an answer to underemployment or unemployment. All too frequently a move to where the jobs are is not feasible economically either for the worker or the areas in question. Only recently has the government begun to look at planned relocation as a means of redistributing the labor force. Retraining programs have been funded and many, together with relocation, have been demonstrated as feasible.

The amendments to the Manpower Development and Training Act of 1962 authorized demonstration projects in labor mobility, which are now being reported. Some are these:

Georgia. Final Report of the Georgia labor mobility demonstration project, December 1, 1967–December 31, 1968. Atlanta: Georgia Department of Labor, March 1969.

Illinois. *Relocation in Illinois,* a final report. Chicago: Illinois State Employment Service, January 1969.

Texas. *Texas Labor Mobility Project,* final report. Texas Employment Commission, April 1969.

West Virginia. *West Virginia Labor Mobility Demonstration Project,* No. 6613, final report, and No. 7891. Charleston: West Virginia Department of Employment Security, October 1967 and March 1969, respectively.

Abrams, Harvey A. "The Role of Social Work in Relocation and Employment," *Social Casework,* Vol. 49, No. 8 (October 1968), pp. 475–480.

A high percentage of families relocated through state employment services experience much stress in the areas to which they move. Often they leave their new home in a few months to return to their old community. A program involving the participation of social workers in preparing clients for relocation is described.

American Economic Review, Vol. 50, No. 2 (May 1960).

Three papers are devoted to "Facilitating Movements of Labor Out of Agriculture": Dale E. Hathaway, "Migration From Agriculture: The Historical Record and Its Meaning" (pp. 379–391), James G. Maddox, "Private and Social Costs of the Movement of People Out of Agriculture" (pp. 392–402), and D. Gale Johnson, "Policies To Improve the Labor Transfer Process" (pp. 403–412). Discussion of the three papers by economists follows the section.

Bahr, Howard M., and Theodore Caplow. "Homelessness, Affiliation and Occupational Mobility," *Social Forces,* Vol. 47, No. 3 (September 1968), pp. 28–33.

Bishop, C. E. "The Need for Improved Mobility Policy," in Joint Economic Committee, 90th Cong., 2d Sess., *Federal Programs for the Development of Human Resources.* Washington, D.C.: U.S. Government Printing Office, 1968.

A summary of some of the findings of recent research on the occupational and geographic mobility of labor. Suggestions are offered concerning programs needed to improve mobility. Since there is a high rate of movement back to rural areas, there is a need for reception centers, guidance counselors, and improved housing, especially in areas receiving large numbers of migrants.

Bodenhofer, Hans-Joachim. "The Mobility of Labor and the Theory of Human Capital," *Journal of Human Resources,* Vol. 2, No. 3 (Fall 1967), pp. 431–448.

An Exploration Analysis of a New Community and Regional Development Relocation System and *A New Community and Regional Development Relocation System.* Louisville, Ky.: University of Louisville. Urban Studies Center, 1968 and 1969, respectively.

Ferman, Louis A., and Michael Aiken. "Mobility and Situational Factors in the Adjustment of Older Workers to Job Displacement," *Human Organization,* Vol. 26, No. 4 (Winter, 1967), pp. 235–241.

Fishman, Betty G. "Economic Effects of Internal Migration: An Exploratory Study," *Business and Economic Studies* (West Virginia University), Vol. 10 (June 1968), pp. 3–9.

The author's hypothesis is that migration may distribute the labor force more efficiently. This study investigates the relationship between migration and the level and pattern of expenditures of urban families.

Freedman, Audrey. "Labor Mobility Projects for the Unemployed," *Monthly Labor Review,* Vol. 91, No. 6 (June 1968), pp. 56–62.

Described are the results of a pilot program in twenty-nine geographic areas to provide relocation assistance to unemployed workers, both experienced (often skilled) and unskilled.

Friedland, William H. "Migrant Labor as a Form of Intermittent Social Organization and as a Channel of Geographic Mobility," in Senate Subcommittee on Migratory Labor, 90th Cong., 2d Sess. *Hearings on Migratory Labor Legislation.* Washington, D.C.: U.S. Government Printing Office, 1968. Part 4, Appendix II.

Fulmer, John L. "Worker Mobility and Government Aid," *Business and Government Review* (University of Missouri), Vol. 7 (September–October 1966), pp. 14–22.

A successful project facilitating relocation of unemployed workers with marketable skills is described.

* Galloway, Lowell E. "Geographical Labor Mobility in the U.S., 1957–1960," Research Report No. 28. Washington, D.C.: U.S. Social Security Administration, Office of Research and Statistics, 1969.

This report is based on data collected by SSA. "In general, the geographic mobility patterns of the male workers studied appear to bear out the hypothesis that . . . earnings differentials are a significant factor in influencing the allocation of labor within the U.S." Also, "geographic mobility on the part of Negro men is characterized by involuntary movements brought about by job displacements rather than by movements that represent a voluntary decision to change the region of major job."

Gannon, James P. "U.S. Looks for Snags in a Negro Relocation Plan and Finds Plenty," *Wall Street Journal,* February 17, 1967, p. ix.

Discussion of a government experiment in moving unemployed young blacks out of the Chicago slums to jobs and homes in the suburbs.

Hammerman, Herbert. *Case Studies of Displaced Workers: Experiences of Workers After Layoff,* U.S. Department of Labor Bulletin 1408. Washington, D.C.: U.S. Government Printing Office, 1964.

Five case studies reporting on the effects of employees of shutdown or large-scale layoff related to technological change. Services provided to assist the workers to find new positions are described. Other variables such as retirement, impact on union membership, and effects on earnings were also studied. Social or emotional aspects of this experience were not dealt with.

Haywood, Charles F. *The Unemployed Poor: Labor Mobility and Poverty.* Washington, D.C.: U.S. Chamber of Commerce, 1966.

An exploration of the question of the extent to which the existence of poverty in the United States can be attributed to the impediments of labor mobility. The author points out—offering supportive statistical data—that mobility in the American labor force is high. He concludes, however, that deficiencies in communication of labor market information is only one of many variables contributing to unemployment. For instance, union rules relating to apprenticeship, seniority, and other factors are also relevant. The author expresses the view that mobility of the labor force has been remarkably adequate from an economic point of view in spite of institutional impediments.

"The Impact of Involuntary Mobility on the Physical Well-being of Retired Couples in an Urban Renewal Area." Research project by Sister M. Frederick Just, Janet Lohr, and Gerhard Becker, Graduate School of Social Work, University of Pittsburgh, 1966.

Jakubauskus, Edward B., and Neil A.

Palomba. "Relocation of Farm Workers from Mississippi to Iowa." Paper presented at the annual spring meeting of the Industrial Relations Research Association, Des Moines, Iowa, 1969.

Report of a successful project of planned migration of Negro families that has offered hope of social and economic improvement to a small number of underemployed Mississippi Delta families.

Jenness, R. A. "Manpower Mobility Programs: A Benefit-Cost Approach." Paper presented at the North-American Conference on Cost-Benefit Analysis and Manpower Policies, Madison, Wisc., May 14–15, 1969.

The author's model for analysis centers on the family rather than on the individual worker.

Koziara, Edward C., and Karen S. Koziara. "Development of Relocation Allowances as Manpower Policy," *Industrial and Labor Relations Review*, Vol. 20, No. 4 (October 1966), pp. 66–75.

How the concept of federally provided relocation allowances has developed in the United States. The objectives and limitations of relocation allowances as a method of measuring labor mobility are pointed out.

Lansing, John B., and Eva Mueller. *The Geographic Mobility of Labor.* Ann Arbor: University of Michigan, Institute for Social Research, 1969.

This in-depth study covers geographic mobility and the poverty problem in terms of black-white differences in geographic mobility, depressed areas, and the impact on mobility of welfare, aid, and assistance.

Levitan, Sar A. "The Right Steps for Now," *New Generation*, Vol. 50, No. 2 (Summer 1968), pp. 15–17.

In an attack on rural poverty, reliance on mobility is necessary for a realistic program. Planning is needed so that migrants can be channeled into areas with job opportunities and relocation services.

————, and Garth L. Mangum. *Federal Training and Work Programs in the Sixties.* Ann Arbor, Mich.: Institute for Labor and Industrial Relations, 1969.

Lurie, Melvin, and Elton Rayack. "Racial Differences in Migration and Job Search: A Case Study," *Southern Economic Journal*, Vol. 23, No. 3 (July 1966), pp. 81–85.

Middletown, Conn., was used as the case study. The researchers found that the relatively poor employment record of blacks may be explained in part by the less adequate sources of job information available to them than to whites of comparable skill. Whites use "informal" methods of job search. To break out of the pattern blacks must turn to institutional intermediaries that are not now holding out much hope. The authors stress the need for a more vigorous policy position by the federal government.

McKechnie, Graeme H. "Retraining and Geographic Mobility: An Evaluation." Ph.D. thesis, University of Wisconsin, 1966.

Data showed that retrained men who relocated earned more per month after training and migration than others who were not retrained. Older workers did not have as much success after training and mobility in terms of earnings as did the younger workers. The less educated workers received lower earnings than those with more education. Both types of mobility were successful, however, from the standpoint of increased earnings. The need for more research to determine the strength of each of the effects retraining may exert on geographic movement is stressed.

Maddox, James G. "Private and Social Costs of the Movement of People Out of Agriculture," *American Economic Review*, Vol. 50 (May 1960), pp. 392–402.

The author focuses his attention on (1) the costs to the migrant, (2) the costs to the sending community, and (3) the costs to the receiving community. He attempts to draw conclusions about these costs and their relevance to policy formation. Appropriate public action such as capital and income transfers is suggested.

Nichols, Jack L., and Harvey A. Abrams. "The Relocation of the Hard Core Unemployed." Minneapolis: Minnesota Rehabilitation Center, 1968.

The report is based on a study made between June 1966 and June 1967 of eighty unemployed residents of small communities in northern Minnesota who were brought into the Minneapolis–St. Paul metropolitan area to live and work.

Okun, Bernard. "Interstate Population Migration and State Income Inequality: A Simultaneous Equation Approach," *Economic Development and Cultural Change*, Vol. 16, No. 1 (January 1968) Part 1, pp. 297–313.

The effect of interstate migration on the inequality of per capita income among the states is examined. Two econometric models are presented.

"Planning for Moving Non-settled People in a Tricounty Area." New York: National Study Service, 1962.

A 1960 study in Albany, Schenectady, and Troy, New York, of people to be relocated as a result of redevelopment.

Rainett, Charles B. "Beanpickers from Rio Grande Valley Now Make Jets in Dallas," *Employment Service Review*, Vol. 5, No. 12 (December 1968), pp. 22–25.

A report of successful combined training and relocation effort made as part of a labor mobility demonstration project.

Ruesink, David C., and Michael C. Kleibrink. "Mexican Americans from the Rio Grande to Ling-Temco-Vought."

Paper presented at the annual spring meeting of the Industrial Relations Research Association, Des Moines, Iowa, 1969.

Personal characteristics associated with positive relocation, which were investigated in a study of permanent relocation, are identified.

Schnitzer, Martin. "Programs for Relocating Workers Used by Governments of Selected Countries," *Economic Policies and Practices*. Washington, D.C.: U.S. Congress, Joint Economic Committee, 1966.

Existing policies in twelve countries are discussed and each country's programs are described in detail: family allowances to workers who cannot find housing for their families in the new areas, moving allowances for household effects, payment of travel expenses to the new place of employment, among others. These programs are in depressed areas, the key factor being the inability to find employment without governmental intervention. The article concludes with a discussion of the demonstration projects authorized in the United States under the 1963 amendments to the Manpower Development and Training Act.

———. "Relocation Allowances and Labor Mobility," *Federal Programs for the Development of Human Resources*. Washington, D.C.: U.S. Congress, Joint Economic Committee, 1968.

Programs of relocation allowances, their rationale, and so on are described and possible benefits are suggested. The author illustrates his remarks with the example of a West Virginia demonstration project which showed that unemployed people were interested in migrating to other areas if they were assisted in the move and in the subsequent adjustment period.

Shannon, Lyle W., and Elaine M. Krass. *The Economic Absorption and Cultural*

Integration of Immigrant Mexican-American and Negro Workers. Iowa City: University of Iowa Press, 1964.

Watts, Lewis, C., et al. *The Middle Income Family Faces Urban Renewal.* Waltham, Mass.: Florence Heller Graduate School for Advanced Studies in Social Welfare, Brandeis University, 1964.

A survey of 250 middle-income families in an area where urban renewal was just getting under way. Young black couples who were well educated, had small families, had lived for a relatively short time at their present address, or who were renting were most likely to be potential movers. The study found that readiness to move out of this neighborhood was less than had been anticipated. The number of families who moved into white parts of the inner city or into predominantly white suburbs was too small to enable generalization.

Zitter, Meyer, and E. Lagy. "Use of Social Security's Continuous Work History Sample for Measurement of Net Migration by Geographic Area." Paper presented at the annual meeting of the American Statistical Association, August 19–22, 1969.

Migrant Groups

"Who are today's migrants?" asked Elizabeth J. Harper in a paper presented at the National Conference on Social Welfare session on "The Changed Pattern of Current Immigration: Its Social Demand and Consequences," May 27, 1969. Miss Harper addressed herself to immigrants from other lands, both regular quota and refugee. Excluded were the rural-urban black American, Puerto Rican, and American Indian migrant. These groups as much as—if not more than—any other are in need of social services, so included in this section is background material on all of them. Other aspects of these groups as migrants are to be found in the appropriate sections.

American Indians

Ablon, Joan. "American Indian Relocation: Problems of Dependency and Management in the City," *Phylon*, Vol. 26, No. 4 (Winter 1965), pp. 362–371.

The special cultural and historical factors that have fostered dependency among the majority of Indians are pointed out. An agency must be aware of these factors before any meaningful services can be offered.

Price, John A. "Migration and Adaptation of American Indians to Los Angeles," *Human Organization*, Vol. 27, No. 2 (Summer 1968), pp. 168–275.

Urban cultural adaptation is analyzed in terms of assimilation, with data on marriage, formal association, and information association.

Appalachian Mountaineers

Brown, James S., George A. Hillery, Jr., and Gordon De Jong. "Migration Systems of the Southern Appalachians: Some Demographic Observation," *Rural Sociology*, Vol. 30 (March 1965), pp. 33–48.

Hirschberg, David A. "The Impact of Geographic Mobility on the Appalachian Region, 1957–63." Master's thesis, New York University, 1968.

The author concludes that "those who migrate increase their wages faster than those who do not . . . those who migrate longer distances . . . have wages increase faster than those who migrate shorter distances."

Martin, Richard. "City 'Hillbillies,'" *Wall Street Journal*, September 30, 1965, p. ix.

Appalachian migrants in slums fail to benefit from antipoverty drives—they tend to be overlooked.

Black Americans

Bagdikian, Ben H. "The Black Immigrants," *Saturday Evening Post,* July 15, 1967, pp. 25–29.

The plight of the southern black migrating to northern urban ghettos is illustrated by case after case. The disillusion and grief of finding oneself in a "foreign land" with no one and nothing available to help one adjust is compounded by the appalling conditions in the ghetto.

Bernard, William S. "Interrelationships Between Immigrants and Negroes," *International Migration Review,* Vol. 3, No. 2 (Summer 1969), pp. 47–57.

A summary of the proceedings of the ninth annual seminar on the integration of immigrants, Columbia University, 1969.

Fitzpatrick, Joseph P., S.J. "Preparing Today's Ethnic Groups for Their Role in the Current Scene." Paper presented at the National Conference on Social Welfare, New York, N.Y., May 1969.

The rise of the black community as an ethnic group and the implication for services today are discussed.

Fried, Marc. "Deprivation and Migration: Dilemmas of Causal Interpretation." Unpublished paper based on a report to U.S. Office of Economic Opportunity, June 1968.

An historical overview of deprivation factors in out-migration and in-migration, with emphasis on black migration within the United States.

Marsh, Robert E. "Negro-White Differences in Geographic Mobility," *Social Security Bulletin,* Vol. 30, No. 5 (May 1967), pp. 8–19.

The article is based on a study using sixty-six socioeconomic and social-psychological factors to explain the differences between blacks and whites.

Mobility in Negro Communities: Guidelines for Research and Economic Prog-
ress. Washington, D.C.: U.S. Commission on Civil Rights, 1968.

The Negroes in the U.S.: Their Economic and Social Situation, Bulletin No. 1511. Washington, D.C.: U.S. Department of Labor, 1966.

O'Kane, James M. "Ethnic Mobility and the Lower-Income Negro: A Sociohistorical Perspective," *Social Problems,* Vol. 16, No. 3 (Winter 1969).

The author contends that the problems the black faces in the city are ethnic rather than racial. His basic problem is therefore one of upward mobility, but unlike previous ethnic migrations into cities, the black's is more difficult because of present sociopolitical and economic developments.

Migratory Labor

A large number of reports from the various states describe the migrant labor situation within the state. Examples are the following:

California. *Annual Farm Labor Report.* Sacramento: Farm Labor Service, published annually. *Migrant Master Plan.* Sacramento: Farm Labor Service, 1967.

Michigan. *Report and Recommendations on the Status of Migratory Farm Labor in Michigan.* Lansing, Mich.: Civil Rights Commission, 1968.

New Jersey. *Dental Education of Migrants and Children in New Jersey* 1966. *Family Counseling Service Among Migrant Families,* 1966.

Migrant Health Program. Camden: Migrant Health Program.

New York. *Annual Report.* Albany: State Interdepartmental Committee on Migrant Labor, published annually.

Ohio. *Migratory Labor in Ohio.* Columbus: Governor's Committee on Migrant Labor, 1968.

Oregon. *Annual Migrant Health Seminars.* Portland, Oreg.: Migrant Health Project.

The 1960s produced numerous books and articles on migrant labor. Some of these are the following:

Allen, Steve, *The Ground Is Our Table.* New York: Doubleday, 1966.

Basta! Enough! The Tale of Our Struggle. Delano, Calif.: Farm Worker Press, 1966.

Dunne, John G. *Delano: The Story of the California Grape Strike.* New York: Farrar, Straus & Giroux, 1967.

Farm Labor Organizing, 1905–1967: A Brief History. New York: National Advisory Committee on Farm Labor, 1967.

Fogel, Walter. "Mexican-Americans and the Southwest Labor Markets." University of California at Los Angeles, Mexican-American Study Project, Advance Report No. 10, October 1967.

The author contends that there is clear evidence that the quality and quantity of education and training received by Mexican-Americans needs substantial upgrading and that increased education pays off in terms of concrete economic gains.

Galarza, Ernesto. *Merchants of Labor: Mexican Bracero History.* Santa Barbara, Calif.: McNally & Loftin, 1964.

Glass, Judith Chanin. "Organization in Salinas," *Monthly Labor Review,* Vol. 91, No. 6 (June 1968), pp. 24–27.

A brief account of unionization of the lettuce industry in the Salinas Valley. The impact of technological change on humanization is analyzed on the basis of data from a specific industry employing a large number of migrant workers.

Harward, Naomi. *Socio-economic and Other Variations Related to Rehabilitation of Mexican Americans in Arizona.* Tempe: Arizona State University Press, 1969.

"The major objective of this study [is] . . . to increase understanding of the Mexican-American and analyze the ef-

fectiveness of vocational rehabilitation services to this ethnic group."

Hill, Herbert. *No Harvest for the Reaper.* New York: Friendship Press, 1966.

Koch, William H., Jr. *Dignity of Their Own.* New York: Friendship Press, 1966.

———. *Next Move for the Migrants.* New York: Friendship Press, 1966.

McBride, John G. *Vanishing Bracero.* San Antonio, Tex.: Naylor Co., 1963.

Moore, Truman E. *The Slaves We Rent.* New York: Random House, 1965.

Nelson, Eugene. *Huelga: The First Hundred Days of the Great Delano Grape Strike.* Delano, Calif.: Farm Worker Press, 1966.

Piven, Richard L. "One Million Migrants: The Revolution Is Not Coming: It is Here," *Saturday Review,* August 17, 1968, pp. 12–15.

A review article on contemporary conditions among migratory laborers, including the activities of the labor union led by Cesar Chavez.

Reul, Myrtle R. *Where Hannibal Led Us.* New York: Vantage Press, 1965.

Scholes, William E. "The Migrant Worker," in Julian Samora, ed., *La Raza.* Notre Dame, Ind.: University of Notre Dame, 1966.

This is a historical account of what the author terms "forgotten Americans"— Mexican-Americans in Texas. It identifies the problems of several groups: wetbacks, braceros, green carders (resident aliens), and commuters (those with visitors' passes).

Shotwell, Louisa R. *The Harvesters: The Story of the Migrant People.* New York: Doubleday & Co., 1961.

U.S. Office of Economic Opportunity. First Conference on Antipoverty Programs for Migrant and Seasonal Farm Workers, 1966.

U.S. Select Committee on Western Hemisphere Immigration. *Hearings on the*

Impact of Commuter Aliens Along Mexican and Canadian Borders. Washington, D.C.: U.S. Government Printing Office, 1969.

Hearings were held in early 1968 in El Paso and Brownsville, Texas, San Diego, California, and Detroit, Michigan, on migrant workers holding green cards —those who live in Mexico or Canada but commute to work in the United States. The evidence of the hearings indicates that these workers would move to the United States if it were possible. Present policy as well as low wages acts to prevent this because of the fear that these workers might become public charges. The committee's recommendations included a statement to the effect that some policy of reasonable adjustment assistance should be initiated to permit these workers and their families to live in the United States.

U.S. Senate, Committee on Labor and Public Welfare, Subcommittee on Migratory Labor. *Migratory Labor Legislation: Hearings.* Washington, D.C.: U.S. Government Printing Office, 1968.

———. *The Migratory Farm Labor Problem in the United States.* Washington, D.C.: U.S. Government Printing Office, 1968.

The University of California at Los Angeles conducted a Mexican-American Study Project. The reports from this study deal with various facets of the Mexican-American's life. Data were collected from 1965 through 1967, primarily in the Southwest. One report, issued in 1966, was "Mexican Migration to the U.S." A 1967 report was "Mexican-Americans in a Midwest Metropolis: A Study of East Chicago."

Wright, Dale. *They Harvest Despair: The Migrant Farm Worker.* Boston: Beacon Press, 1965.

The federal government has held hearings on this problem area, and a conference on it was held by the Office of Economic Opportunity.

Professional Migrants

Adams, Walter (ed.). *The Brain Drain.* New York: Macmillan Co., 1968.

Included are papers presented at an international conference held in Lausanne, Switzerland, in August 1967. The volume is divided into sections on "Education and Migration," "Case Studies," and "Conclusions." The main conclusion is that both the receiving and sending countries need to rethink policy whereby the educated are drawn by large federal and/or publicly financed programs.

Aitken, N. D. "The International Flow of Human Capital: Comment and Reply," *American Economic Review,* Vol. 58 (June 1968), pp. 539–548.

A discussion of the emigration of highly skilled individuals.

Bayer, Alan E. "The Effect of International Interchange of High-Level Manpower in the United States," *Social Forces,* Vol. 46, No. 2 (June 1968), pp. 465–477.

———. "Interregional Migration and the Education of American Scientists," *Sociology of Education,* Vol. 41, No. 4 (Winter 1968), pp. 88–102.

An analysis indicating that the reputation of educational institutions within a region is a major attraction.

Brown, Louie A., and John L. Belcher. "Residential Mobility of Physicians in Georgia," *Rural Sociology,* Vol. 31 (December 1966), pp. 439–448.

This study, based on a questionnaire, attempted to discover the relationship between specific latent social roles and migration. The evidence indicates that the latent roles of physicians are much more important in determining their propensity to change location than are the variables traditionally discussed in migration studies.

Committee on International Migration Talent. *International Migration of High Level Manpower.* New York: Frederick A. Praeger, 1970.

Fleming, Donald, and Bernard Bailyn. *The Intellectual Migration: Europe and America, 1930–1960.* Cambridge, Mass.: Harvard University Press, 1969.

Ladinsky, Jack. "Sources of Geographic Mobility Among Professional Workers: A Multivariate Analysis, *Demography,* Vol. 4, No. 1 (1967), pp. 293–309.

This study reports investigation into three categories of determinants of geographic mobility among professional workers: family life cycle, life-style, and regional variation.

Levin, Melvin R. "Talent Migration: Distressed Area Dilemma," *Community Regional Planning.* New York: Praeger, 1969. Pp. 220–244.

The "brain drain" dilemma raises a number of fundamental questions involving national policies for redevelopment areas. The author advocates that such policy be designed, coordinated, and evaluated within a controlling national framework.

U.S. Immigration and Naturalization Service. *Annual Indicators of the Immigration into the United States of Aliens in Professional and Related Occupations.* Washington, D.C.: U.S. Government Printing Office, 1968.

Puerto Ricans

Alvarez, Jose Hernandez. *Return Migration to Puerto Rico.* Population Monograph Series No. 1. Berkeley: University of California Press, 1967.

An intensive study analyzing data relating to geographic mobility, family structure, and fertility. Conclusions concern resettlement and economic aspects of return migration.

International Migration Review, Vol. 2, No. 1 (Spring 1968), pp. 96–102.

This issue contains an annotated bibliography on Puerto Rico and Puerto Rican migration.

Refugees

Brody, Richard A., Richard Fegan, and Thomas O'Leary. *Cubans in Exile.* Stanford, Calif.: Stanford University Press, 1968.

Cohen, Allen. "New Patterns for Service: Chinatown and Chinese Immigration." Paper presented at the National Conference on Social Welfare, New York, N.Y., May 1969.

Northrup, Bowen. "Chinatown's Overflow, *Wall Street Journal,* September 13, 1966, p. ix.

As relaxed immigration laws permit more people in, more problems arise in the ethnic settlement, but the Chinese are reluctant to seek help.

Soskis, Philip. "Adjustment of Hungarian Refugee Families in New York City," *International Migration Review,* Vol. 1, No. 3 (Fall 1967), pp. 40–46.

This report of a survey of two hundred families by the New York Association for New Americans points out the self-sufficiency and vitality of Jewish Hungarian refugees. Covered are occupations, housing, general standard of living, and children's mobility.

Wenk, Michael G. "Adjustment and Assimilation: The Cuban Refugee Experience," *International Migration Review,* Vol. 3, No. 3 (Fall 1968), pp. 38–49.

Rural-Urban Migration

Today's urban area has within its boundaries two types of migrants: the rural migrant trying to find himself and the migrant who moves within the urban area. Rural to urban migration has been studied in depth. Mobility within the urban area is now an area for research. *Proceedings of the Association of American Geographers,* Vol. 1 (1969), includes two papers in this area: R. B. Adams, "U.S. Metropolitan Migration: Dimensions and Predictability," and W. A. U. Clark, "Information Flows and Intraurban Migration: An Empirical Analysis."

* Beardwood, Roger. "The Southern Roots of Urban Crisis," *Fortune,* Vol. 78 (August 1968), pp. 80–87.

Forced off the farms into destitution, thousands of blacks migrate to northern slums. Bigotry, misguided policy, and technology all have a hand in this tragic upheaval.

Brown, John A., and C. Bron Cleveland. "Ghettos in Your Town." Urban Planning Project Publication No. 3. Atlanta, Ga.: Southern Regional Council, 1968.

A pamphlet on the problem of rural migration to cities that discusses neighborhood stabilization and housing.

"City Riots Focus New Attention on Rural Problems," *Congressional Quarterly, Weekly Reports,* November 10, 1967, pp. 2285–2287.

The results of migration to cities and the existing aid programs available to rural Americans are discussed. Proposals for solving these problems in the future are offered.

Cloward, Richard A., and Frances Fox Piven. "Migration, Politics, and Welfare," *Saturday Review,* November 16, 1968, pp. 35–51.

The authors suggest that rural-to-urban and South-to-North migration of black people may be the "main cause" of the steep rise in public assistance rates in northern and western cities.

Coles, Robert. "The Lives of Migrant Farmers," *American Journal of Psychi-* *atry,* Vol. 122 (September 1965), pp. 271–285.

A brief psychiatric report of an interview survey of ten families, which notes a number of social similarities, such as the prevalence of feelings of inadequacy in children of migrants. Many of these youngsters move directly into adulthood, work, marriage, and parenthood in their early teens. The author notes an apparent tendency to avoid the very food they harvest, "often in a phobic manner," and urges study of why this occurs. He expresses the view that many psychiatric illnesses—such as mood swings, violence, heavy drinking, and a severe kind of apathy with loss of appetite, aimlessness, and indifference that may become a more severe clinical depression with suicidal preoccupations and paranoid thinking—seem to be related to migratory status.

* ———. "The Migrant Farmer." Atlanta, Ga.: Southern Regional Council, 1965.

The author relates his personal experiences with the eastern migrant stream: the migrant farmers' confusion about the bureaucratic procedures in urban areas.

Fairchild, Charles K. "Transfer of Population from Rural to Urban Areas: Rural Disadvantaged Mobility." Paper presented at the annual spring meeting of the Industrial Relations Research Association, Madison, Wisc., 1969.

A discussion of the North Carolina Mobility Project, which was designed to test the effectiveness of a subsidized relocation program for disadvantaged rural workers. The results demonstrate that the employment and earnings of the rural disadvantaged can be increased through migration even though the long-term effects on incomes and earnings are uncertain.

Graves, Theodore D. "Alternative Models for the Study of Urban Migration,"

Human Organization, Vol. 25, No. 4 (Winter 1966), pp. 295–299.

The Navaho Urban Relocation Research Project (Denver) is discussed in terms of the decision, assimilation, and economic adjustment models.

Hamilton, C. Horace. "The Negro Leaves the South," *Demography*, Vol. 1, No. 1 (1964), pp. 273–295.

This address focuses on the migration of the black population from southern rural communities into metropolitan centers of the North and West.

Hansen, Niles M. "Urban Alternatives to Rural Poverty." Paper presented at the annual spring meeting of the Industrial Relations Research Association, Des Moines, Iowa, 1969.

The author attempts to examine the interrelationships among lagging rural areas, large metropolitan areas, and intermediate cities, and to suggest policy measures that might be applied in view of the opportunity costs that face decision-makers responsible for both public and private investment.

Hanson, Robert C., and Ozzie G. Simmons. "Role Path: A Concept and Procedure for Studying Urban Communities," *Human Organization*, Vol. 27, No. 2 (Summer 1968), pp. 152–158.

The specific objective of this study was to "identify and explicate the social processes leading to successful or unsuccessful performance of urban roles by a rural migrant," using the concept of role path.

Lansing, John B., Eva Mueller, and Nancy Barth. *Residential Location and Urban Mobility*. Ann Arbor: University of Michigan, Institute for Social Research, 1966.

This study examines decisions relating to residential location, using data derived from interviews. A 1969 study by John

B. Lansing, Charles Wade Clifton, and James N. Morgan, *New Homes and Poor People*, continues examination of residential density, location preferences, factors influencing the choice of a home, and the journey-to-work variable.

Lewis, Hylan. "Syndromes of Contemporary Urban Poverty," *Psychiatric Research Report*, No. 21 (April 1967), pp. 1–11.

Lowry, Ira S. Migration and Metropolitan Growth: Two Analytical Models. San Francisco: Chandler Publishing Co., 1966.

The author attempts to clarify the interrelations between local or regional changes in labor market conditions and concurrent changes in population, especially as they bear on the problem of forecasting for such areas.

Maitland, Sheridan T., and Stanley M. Knebel. "Rural to Urban Transition," *Monthly Labor Review*, Vol. 91, No. 6 (June 1968), pp. 28–32.

Proposals are presented for assisting low-income rural-to-urban migrants in order to achieve a more systematic matching of workers and opportunities.

Morrill, Richard L. *Migration and the Spread and Growth of Urban Settlements*. Lund Studies in Geography, Series B, No. 26. Lund, Sweden: C. W. K. Gleerup Publishers, 1965.

An in-depth discussion of migration and urbanization in terms of a general critique of present knowledge and relevant migration theory. A general model and theory for further study are presented.

National Advisory Committee on Rural Poverty, *The People Left Behind*. Washington, D.C.: U.S. Government Printing Office, 1967.

This is the final report of the President's committee set up to make a comprehensive study and appraisal of the current economic situation and trends in American rural life. It deals with problems of low income, the status of rural labor including migratory labor, unemployment, and underemployment. The report also tries to evaluate proposals and programs to enhance the welfare of rural people. Recommendations for action are set forth.

————. *Rural Poverty in the U.S.* Washington, D.C.: U.S. Government Printing Office, 1968.

A comprehensive report including a major section on mobility and migration.

"Rural Poverty: Is Migration the Cure?" *New Generation*, Vol. 50, No. 2 (Summer 1968), entire issue.

A collection of articles arguing the pros and cons of the concept.

Schuchter, Arnold. *White Power/Black Freedom: Planning the Future of Urban America.* Boston: Beacon Press, 1968.

The author calls for a program of "guided inter-regional and inter urban . . . migration of three million Negroes during the coming decade as a means of helping Blacks escape from both the northern ghetto and the southern belts."

Schwarzweller, Harry K., and James S. Brown. "Social Class Origins, Rural-Urban Migration and Economic Life Chances: A Case Study, *Rural Sociology*, Vol. 32 (March 1967), pp. 5–19.

This article is based on data from a restudy of persons who had been living in three isolated mountain neighborhoods in eastern Kentucky.

Senior, Clarence. "Integration Problems of Recent Rural Migrants to United States Cities." Paper presented to the United Nations World Population Conference, Belgrade, Yugoslavia, 1965.

Simmons, James W. "Changing Residence in the City: A Review of Intraurban Mobility," *Geographical Review*, Vol. 58, No. 4 (October 1968), pp. 622–651.

Using census data, the author discusses who moves and why. Types of social change, economic and social status, and individual decisions are other variables influencing mobility. He concludes that the destination of an intercity move is determined by the interaction of a series of constraints: housing preferences and availability, relationship between job and residence, access to the rest of the city, and cultural restraints.

Suval, Elizabeth M., and Horace C. Hamilton, "Some New Evidence on Educational Selectivity in Migration to and from the South," *Social Forces*, Vol. 43, No. 2 (May 1965), pp. 536–547.

The authors report that the growing metropolitan areas of the South are net gainers of well-educated migrants from the rural South and the North.

Tilly, Charles. "Race and Migration to the American City," *The Metropolitan Enigma: Inquiries into the Nature and Dimensions of America's Urban Crisis.* Washington, D.C.: U.S. Chamber of Commerce, 1967. Pp. 124–146.

————, and C. Harold Brown. "On Uprooting, Kinship and the Auspices of Migration," *International Journal of Comparative Sociology*, Vol. 8 (September 1967), pp. 139–164.

This study of Wilmington, Delaware, attempts to define the role of kinship groups in migration to cities. The evidence seems to lead to the conclusion that although genuine uprooting is indeed widespread in urban areas, it does not inevitably bring on individual social disintegration.

Wolpert, Julian. "Distance and Directional Bias in Interurban Migratory Streams," *Annals of the Association of American Geographers*, Vol. 57 (September 1967), pp. 605–616.

234 | *Migration and Social Welfare*

Social Services

Historically the immigrant to the United States has had available various social services. The early literature is filled with accounts of these. Since the 1940s the literature has ranged from Philip E. Ryan's *Migration and Social Welfare* (New York: Russell Sage Foundation, 1940), Edith T. Bremer's "Development of Private Social Work with the Foreign Born," in 1949 *Annals,* to Loula Dunn's *The Newcomer: A Public Welfare Challenge* (Chicago: America Public Welfare Association, 1962). Savilla M. Simons, in her article for the *Encyclopedia of Social Work* (New York: National Association of Social Workers, 1965), "Migrants, Transients, and Nonresidents," covers the history of social services for this client group.

Bernard, William S. "Initial Integration: Programs and Concepts in the Resettlement of Immigrants and Refugees by American Voluntary Agencies." New York: American Immigration and Citizenship Conference, 1969.

An analysis of various agencies and the concepts and techniques they use in order to arrive at a common denominator in their programs, especially those programs that lead to successful integration.

"Caseworker Programs Report for Newcomer Youth." Washington, D.C.: Travelers Aid Society, Newcomer Program, 1965. Mimeographed.

A report on a joint project of Travelers Aid in cooperation with the Washington Urban League with youths aged 16–21 and families with school-age children. Counseling as well as practical assistance was provided to these newcomers to the city.

Changing Services for Changing Clients. New York: Columbia University Press for the National Association of Social Workers, 1969.

Papers by six social workers on various aspects of providing services in a chang-

ing society: John S. Morgan, "The Changing Demand for Social Service," George A. Brager, "Advocacy and Political Behavior," Maurice F. Connery, "Changing Services for Changing Clients," Duane W. Beck, "Changing Concepts of Social Work Treatment and Prevention of Problems on a Community Level," Myrtle R. Reul, "Deprivation Amid Abundance: Implications for Social Work Practice," and Norman A. Polansky, "Changing Concepts of Social Work Treatment of the Multiproblem Client."

Chaskel, Ruth. "Effect of Mobility on Family Life," *Social Work,* Vol. 9, No. 4 (October 1964), pp. 83–91.

Ways of preventing or lessening some of the problems that develop as a result of mobility are presented.

Fallers, Lloyd A. (ed.). *Immigrants and Association.* The Hague: Mouton, 1967.

These essays focus on internal organization of immigrant communities and on the institutions developed for the purpose of coping with the new environment.

Gathercole, Doreen J. "Mobility: Its Implications for Child Welfare and Social Casework," *Child Welfare,* Vol. 46, No. 1 (January 1967), pp. 16–23.

This study of an agency's highly mobile clients indicates that mobility is often an immature response to conflict and that "effective casework treatment requires holding on to the client and using the conflict situation to help him find a more positive way of coping."

Gilkeson, Connie Holmes, and Gisela M. Lamarsh. "Migrant Families and Their Use of Community Resources." Master's thesis, Jane Addams School of Social Work, University of Illinois, 1969.

This descriptive-diagnostic study of Spanish surname nuclear migrant families concludes that migrant social systems and the community social system

are separate. Reciprocal material benefits cause minimal overt conflict between
the two systems. Individual social controls maintain the separateness of the
two.

Having the Power, We Have the Duty.
Washington, D.C.: U.S. Advisory Council on Public Welfare, 1966.

This report reviews the administration
of public assistance and child welfare
programs and recommends the abolition
of residence requirements.

Hiatt, Catherine C., and Ruth E. Spurlock.
"Crisis-Flight: Clients in One Travelers
Aid Caseload." Washington, D.C.: Trav-
elers Aid Society, 1969. Mimeographed.

In the 1967 caseload of this agency, two
hundred cases of geographic flight were
related to emotional distress. The report
summarizes by case histories some of
these problems and their treatment.

Jacobs, Ethel W. "New Ways of Serving
Agricultural Migrants," *Social Work
Practice 1965.* New York: Columbia
University Press, 1966. Pp. 150–161.

A presentation of the New Jersey project
on migrants of the national Travelers
Aid Society.

Montelius, Marjorie. "Final Report on
Demonstration Project on Transient
Young Adults in San Francisco." San
Francisco: Travelers Aid Society of San
Francisco, 1968. Mimeographed.

This project experimented with the group
method in reaching and holding clients
in this category.

Reul, Myrtle R. "Communication with the
Migrant." Paper presented at the Na-
tional Association of Social Workers
Regional Institute, Norfolk, Va., 1968.

Schorr, Alvin L. "Mobile Family Living,"
Social Casework, Vol. 37, No. 4 (April
1956), pp. 175–180.

This is a description of an experimental
family agency set up to serve a tricounty
area that had planned for drastic expansion resulting from the construction of
an atomic plant. A professional staff of
two gave service to 122 mobile families
at one full-time office and two part-time
offices. Of the 122 families, 76 were
judged to have problems related to their
mobility.

Simons, Savilla M. "Services to Uprooted
and Unsettled Families," *Social Welfare
Forum, 1962.* New York: Columbia University Press, 1962.

The author argues that social services
are given as they were when people spent
most of their lives in a limited geographic area. She stresses the need to
recognize mobility as a problem area, to
change existing programs, and to do
more research.

————. "Social Services for the Mobile
Poor," *Social Work Practice, 1965.* New
York: Columbia University Press, 1965.

The author discusses the use of professional casework services as provided by
Travelers Aid. Fundamental changes
are advocated involving public policy
that should be made in order to give
needed services to those who cross state
lines.

Vulcan, Beatrice. "The Role of Social
Work in Immigration." Unpublished
paper, 1969.

An overview of immigration in the
United States, including a historical re-
cap of social work's role. The author
concludes that social workers have no
official part in the U.S. Immigration and
Naturalization Service because they have
not concerned themselves actively and
professionally with this phase of helping.

Winitt, Ben. "The Immigration Social
Service Agency—Its Unique Role in Law
and Social Work," *International Migration Review,* Vol. 3, No. 1 (Spring
1969), pp. 54–66.

A review article on work with the immigrant.

Agenda

---

*Research Institute on the Social Welfare Consequences
of Migration and Residential Movement*

November 2–5, 1969
San Jeronimo Hilton, San Juan, Puerto Rico

Alvin L. Schorr, Institute Chairman and Discussion Leader

The Focus: Examination of the phenomena of migration and residential movement
within the framework of existing and needed research from the specific
perspective of their consequences for social welfare planning, services,
policy, and action.

Sunday, November 2
7:45–8:45 P.M. Presentation of Conference Objectives—Joseph W. Eaton, Institute
Director

Monday, November 3
9:00 A.M.–12:00 NOON Area of Concentration: Migration As a Field of Research
"Movers, Migrants, and the National Interest," resource paper by Clarence Senior
Comments by Alfred H. Katz and Hylan G. Lewis
Response by Dr. Senior
General Discussion

"Economic Cost-Benefit Approaches to Migration," resource paper by George F.
Rohrlich
Comments by Catherine C. Hiatt and Stephen P. Simonds
Response by Dr. Rohrlich
General Discussion

4:00–7:00 P.M. Area of Concentration: Migration: Past, Present, and Future
"Black Migration: An Overview," resource paper by James A. Goodman
Comments by Oxanna S. Kaufman and Jane E. Lynch
Response by Dr. Goodman
General Discussion

"Federal Migration Policy: Present Reality and Future Alternatives," resource
paper by William J. Reid
Comments by Frank F. Montalvo and Jack Wiener
Response by Dr. Reid
General Discussion

237

Tuesday, November 4
    9:00 A.M.–12:00 NOON Area of Concentration: Migration: Patterns of Migration
"A National Internal Migration Policy: Suggestions from a Demographer," resource
paper by Albert J. Mayer
    Comments by Eleanor B. Sheldon and Leon H. Ginsberg
    Response by Dr. Mayer
                     General Discussion

"Migration: The Confrontation of Opportunity and Trauma," resource paper by
Myrtle R. Reul
    Comments by Henry P. David and Maurice B. Hamovitch
    Response by Mrs. Reul
                     General Discussion

    4:00–7:00 P.M Area of Concentration: Migration and Welfare Policy
"Migration, Residential Mobility, and Community Health Policy," resource paper
by Simon Slavin
    Comments by Eugene B. Brody and Alfred H. Katz
    Response by Dr. Slavin
                     General Discussion

"Migration, Residential Mobility, and Welfare Policy," resource paper by Bernard
M. Shiffman
    Comments by Ruby B. Pernell and Raul A. Muñoz
    Response by Mr. Shiffman
                     General Discussion

Wednesday, November 5
    8:45–11:45 A.M. Area of Concentration: Migration Theory and Patterns
"Patterns of Migration and Adjustment: A Comparative Analysis," resource paper
by Marc Fried et al.
    Comments by Henry P. David and Hylan G. Lewis
    Response by Dr. Fried
                     General Discussion

"Black Migration and the Struggle for Equity: A Hundred-Year Record," resource
paper by Demitri B. Shimkin
    Comments by Leon H. Ginsberg and Robert Morris
    Response by Dr. Shimkin
                     General Discussion

    12:00 NOON–12:30 P.M. Summary Session and Adjournment
    1:30–3:00 P.M. Post-conference "Bull Session"—*attendance optional, but encour-*
          aged

Participants

Eugene B. Brody, MD, Professor and Chairman, Department of Psychiatry, and Director, Psychiatric Institute, School of Medicine, University of Maryland, Baltimore, Maryland.

Henry P. David, Ph.D., Associate Director, International Research Institute, American Institutes for Research, Silver Spring, Maryland.

Joseph W. Eaton, Ph.D., Professor of Sociology in Public Health and Social Work Research, School of Public Health, University of Pittsburgh, Pittsburgh, Pennsylvania.

Marc Fried, Ph.D., Research Professor, Institute of Human Sciences, Boston College, Chestnut Hill, Massachusetts.

Leon H. Ginsberg, Ph.D., Professor and Director, Division of Social Work, College of Human Resources and Education, West Virginia University, Morgantown, West Virginia.

James A. Goodman, Ph.D., Associate Professor, Social Work and Sociology, and Vice-Provost, University of Washington, Seattle, Washington.

Maurice B. Hamovitch, Ph.D., Dean, School of Social Work, University of Southern California, Los Angeles, California.

Mrs. Marjorie J. Herzig, MSW, Director of Program, National Association of Social Workers, New York, New York.

Catherine C. Hiatt, MSS, Executive Director, Travelers Aid Society of Washington, D.C., Washington, D.C.

Alfred H. Katz, DSW, Professor of Public Health and Social Welfare, School of Public Health, University of California, Los Angeles, California.

Mrs. Oxanna S. Kaufman, MLS, Librarian and Assistant Professor in Social Work Bibliography, Graduate School of Social Work, University of Pittsburgh, Pittsburgh, Pennsylvania.

Hylan G. Lewis, Ph.D., Professor of Sociology, Brooklyn College of the City University of New York, Brooklyn, New York; and Vice President, MARC Corporation, New York, New York.

Jane E. Lynch, Ph.D., Executive Secretary, Social Problems Research Review Committee, National Institute of Mental Health, Chevy Chase, Maryland.

Albert J. Mayer, Ph.D., Professor of Sociology, Department of Sociology, Arizona State University, Tempe, Arizona.

Lt. Col. Frank F. Montalvo, DSW, Social Work Consultant, Army Community Service, Department of the Army, Deputy Chief of Staff for Personnel, Washington, D.C.

Robert Morris, DSW, Professor of Social Planning, Florence Heller Graduate School for Advanced Studies in Social

239

Welfare, Brandeis University, Waltham, Massachusetts.

Raul A. Muñoz, MSW, Undersecretary, Department of Social Services, Commonwealth of Puerto Rico, Santurce, Puerto Rico.

Ruby B. Pernell, Ph.D., Professor of Social Work, School of Applied Social Sciences, Case Western Reserve University, Cleveland, Ohio.

William J. Reid, DSW, Associate Professor and Director, Research Center, School of Social Service Administration, University of Chicago, Chicago, Illinois.

Mrs. Myrtle R. Reul, Ed.D., Professor, School of Social Work, University of Georgia, Athens, Georgia.

George F. Rohrlich, Ph.D., Professor of Political Economy and Social Insurance, Department of Economics, School of Business Administration, and Director, Institute for Social Economics, Temple University, Philadelphia, Pennsylvania.

Alvin L. Schorr, MSW, Professor, Brandeis University, and Director, Brandeis University Income Maintenance Project, Washington, D.C.

Clarence Senior, Ph.D., Director, Center for Migration Studies, and Professor of Sociology, Brooklyn College of the City University of New York, Brooklyn, New York.

Eleanor B. Sheldon, Ph.D., Sociologist and Executive Associate, Russell Sage Foundation, New York, New York.

Bernard M. Shiffman, MSW, Deputy Administrator, Human Resources Administration, New York, New York.

Demitri B. Shimkin, Ph.D., Professor of Anthropology and Geography, Department of Anthropology, University of Illinois, Urbana, Illinois.

Simon Slavin, Ed.D., Dean, School of Social Administration, Temple University, Philadelphia, Pennsylvania.

Jack Wiener, MA, Assistant Chief, Social Problems Center, National Institute of Mental Health, Chevy Chase, Maryland.

1½M/P&K/6-71